VOLUME FIVE

bake
FROM SCRATCH®

ARTISAN RECIPES
FOR THE HOME BAKER

Brian Hart Hoffman

83 PRESS®

83 Press
1900 International Park Drive, Suite 50
Birmingham, Alabama 35243
83press.com

ISBN: 978-1-940772-86-8
Printed in China

VOLUME FIVE

bake
FROM SCRATCH®

ARTISAN RECIPES
FOR THE HOME BAKER

Brian Hart Hoffman

THE FIFTH ANNIVERSARY COOKBOOK,

BAKE FROM SCRATCH: VOLUME FIVE

I remember the moment I first dreamed about creating *Bake from Scratch*. Like many inspired ideas, it began with a question: why isn't there a magazine just for bakers? A magazine that caters to people who don't bake just for the holidays or special events but who want to constantly up their baking game? I knew there had to be more people like me out there, craving this content. This idea would become *Bake from Scratch*, a magazine dedicated to tapping into the most incredible niche community of artisan bakers. From there came our next big leap: diving into the realm of cookbooks. Our cookbooks were created to give our audience a way to enjoy an entire year's worth of recipes inside one beautiful book and another way to bridge the gap between bakers who collect cookbooks and *Bake from Scratch*. Five years later, and the books keep getting bigger, better, and sweeter.

This cookbook, as always, opens with cakes, the baked good destined for celebrations of every kind. Whether layered, tubed, or in one delectable layer, these recipes cater to all cravings. For the Bundt enthusiasts, try our milk chocolate twist on the classic Tunnel of Fudge Cake, the recipe that kicked off the Bundt craze in 1966, or give my French-meets-Southern Basque Bundt Cake a whirl. If you're looking for the height of elegance, turn to our Layer Cakes chapter and find photography and technique for a masterclass in frosting decoration. Alternatively, you can land on our one-layer cakes, one of my favorite incarnations of cake, from the brunch-primed Blueberry Sour Cream Coffee Cake to the decadent Dark Chocolate Sheet Cake with Peanut Butter Frosting.

Moving from batter and into the realm of dough, our breads section features everything you've come to expect from our cookbooks: beautiful photography, step-by-step techniques,

and flawless recipes. For the busy baker, tackle one of our quick breads, from the addictive Cheddar-Pecan Loaf to the crunchy Hazelnut-Banana Sour Cream Muffins. In our Yeast Breads chapter, you can revisit classics like babka, deli breads, and pretzels. Or welcome some new worldly favorites into your home kitchen, from the French yuletide Le Gibassier to the everyday Irish Soda Bread.

The next collection of recipes is what I call "Everything's better with butter." These are your pastries, pies, and tarts, recipes that encase juicy fruit or creamy fillings in butter-rich pastry packages. From a Sparkling Wine Chocolate Ganache Tart to Mile-High Creamy Apple Pie, these recipes dive deep into the magical intersection of flaky crust and decadent fillings. Up next is a collection near and dear to my heart: cookies and bars. Taking you from summery Pecan Pinwheels to wintry Eggnog Sandwich Cookies, our Cookies chapter is stacked, packed, and crowding the cooling rack. In the Bars chapter, we've got every kind of brownie your heart could desire, with plenty of blondies, cheesecake bars, and crumb bars thrown in.

If you've picked up this book, welcome. Welcome to or welcome back to the wonderful world of artisan baking. This is just the beginning of another adventure in dough and batter, butter and flour. So, dust your surfaces with flour and preheat your ovens, bakers. Let the baking begin.

Brian

Brian Hart Hoffman
Editor-in-Chief

CAKES

LAYER CAKES

Stunningly tall and made for celebration, these cakes deserve to be put on a pedestal. Whether you opt for a decadent pudding-rich Brooklyn Blackout Cake or an elegant peaches and cream showstopper, these recipes will elevate any occasion.

BROOKLYN BLACKOUT CAKE

Makes 1 (8-inch) cake

Ebinger Baking Company made famous the Brooklyn Blackout Cake. It was a triple-layer feat of chocolate finery: a tender devil's food cake layered with satiny chocolate pudding, topped with a thick cocoa frosting, and coated in leftover cake crumbs. Sadly, in 1972, the bakery closed and the beloved original recipe was lost. However, you can try our espresso-laden version for a tasty introduction—or reintroduction—to this cherished cake. Our pudding-filled take on the blackout cake gets an aromatic boost from freshly brewed coffee in the batter and espresso in the fudgy Whipped Chocolate Frosting. Otherwise, it's a true-blue tribute to the dark, crumb-covered original that launched a thousand other sweet reproductions.

½   cup (113 grams) unsalted butter, softened
¾   cup (64 grams) Dutch process cocoa powder
1¾ cups (385 grams) firmly packed dark brown sugar
1   cup (240 grams) hot brewed coffee
¾   cup (180 grams) whole buttermilk
2   large eggs (100 grams), lightly beaten
2   teaspoons (8 grams) vanilla extract
1½ cups (188 grams) all-purpose flour
2   teaspoons (10 grams) baking powder
½   teaspoon (2.5 grams) baking soda
½   teaspoon (1.5 grams) kosher salt
Chocolate Pudding (recipe follows)
Whipped Chocolate Frosting (recipe follows)

1. Preheat oven to 325°F (170°C). Spray 3 (8-inch) round cake pans with baking spray with flour.
2. In a medium saucepan, melt butter over medium heat. Whisk in cocoa, and cook until fragrant, about 1 minute. Remove from heat, and whisk in brown sugar, coffee, and buttermilk until sugar dissolves. Whisk in eggs and vanilla.
3. In a medium bowl, stir together flour, baking powder, baking soda, and salt. Slowly add flour mixture to cocoa mixture, whisking just until combined. Divide batter among prepared pans.
4. Bake until a wooden pick inserted in center comes out with a few moist crumbs, 25 to 30 minutes. Let cool completely in pans.
5. Remove from pans, and cut top ¼ inch off each cooled cake layer; reserve cake tops for garnish. Place a cake layer on a serving platter. Whisk Chocolate Pudding until smooth; spread half of pudding onto cake layer. Top with second cake layer, and spread remaining pudding on top. Place remaining cake layer on top of pudding. Spread Whipped Chocolate Frosting on top

and sides of cake. Crumble reserved cake tops, and press into sides of cake, if desired. Cover and refrigerate until ready to serve.

CHOCOLATE PUDDING
Makes about 2 cups

⅔   cup (133 grams) granulated sugar
2½ tablespoons (20 grams) cornstarch
¼   teaspoon kosher salt
1   cup (240 grams) heavy whipping cream
½   cup (120 grams) whole milk
3   ounces (86 grams) 60% cacao bittersweet chocolate, chopped
1   teaspoon (4 grams) vanilla extract

1. In a medium saucepan, stir together sugar, cornstarch, and salt. Whisk in cream and milk. Whisk in chocolate. Bring to a boil over medium heat. Cook, whisking constantly, for 3 minutes. Remove from heat, and stir in vanilla. Transfer to a medium glass bowl, and cover with plastic wrap, pressing wrap directly onto surface of pudding to prevent a skin from forming. Refrigerate until completely chilled, 2 to 3 hours.

WHIPPED CHOCOLATE FROSTING
Makes 2½ cups

1¾ cups (298 grams) finely chopped 60% cacao bittersweet chocolate
1¼ cups (300 grams) heavy whipping cream
1   tablespoon (21 grams) light corn syrup
1   teaspoon (2 grams) instant espresso powder
2   tablespoons (28 grams) unsalted butter, softened
1   teaspoon (4 grams) vanilla extract

1. In a large heatproof bowl, place chocolate.
2. In a small saucepan, whisk together cream, corn syrup, and espresso powder. Cook over medium-low heat just until bubbles form around edges of pan. (Do not boil.) Pour cream mixture over chocolate, and let stand for 2 minutes. Starting in center of bowl and using a rubber spatula, slowly stir mixture until well combined. Add butter and vanilla, and stir until well combined. Place bowl in an ice water bath, and let stand, stirring occasionally, until firm.
3. In the bowl of a stand mixer fitted with the whisk attachment, beat chocolate mixture at medium speed until it starts to lighten in color. Use immediately.

SOUR CREAM ALMOND CAKE

Makes 1 (9-inch) cake

A stunning classic, this two-layer cake has a velvet crumb and subtle almond flavor. But the real star of the show? The generous swoops of supremely smooth Sour Cream Buttercream.

¾ cup (170 grams) unsalted butter, softened
1½ cups (300 grams) granulated sugar
5 large egg whites (150 grams), room temperature
¾ teaspoon (3 grams) vanilla extract
¾ teaspoon (3 grams) almond extract
2½ cups (312 grams) cake flour
2 teaspoons (10 grams) baking powder
½ teaspoon (1.5 grams) kosher salt
⅛ teaspoon baking soda
¾ cup (180 grams) sour cream
¾ cup (180 grams) whole milk
Sour Cream Buttercream (recipe follows)

1. Preheat oven to 350°F (180°C). Butter and flour 2 (9-inch) round cake pans.
2. In the bowl of a stand mixer fitted with the paddle attachment, beat butter and sugar at medium speed until fluffy, 3 to 4 minutes, stopping to scrape sides of bowl. Add egg whites, and beat until well combined, about 2 minutes. Beat in extracts.
3. In a medium bowl, whisk together flour, baking powder, salt, and baking soda. In a small bowl, whisk together sour cream and milk. With mixer on low speed, gradually add flour mixture to butter mixture alternately with sour cream mixture, beginning and ending with flour mixture, beating just until combined after each addition. Divide batter between prepared pans, and run a knife or wooden pick through batter to release any large air bubbles.
4. Bake until a wooden pick inserted in center comes out clean, 25 to 30 minutes. Let cool in pans for 10 minutes. Remove from pans, and let cool completely on wire racks.
5. Place a cooled cake layer on a cake plate. Spread about 2½ cups Sour Cream Buttercream on cake layer, and top with remaining cake layer; freeze for 2 hours.
6. Spread a thin layer of Sour Cream Buttercream on top and sides of cake to create a crumb coat; freeze for 30 minutes.

7. Spread remaining Sour Cream Buttercream on top and sides of cake, swirling as desired. Refrigerate in an airtight container.

SOUR CREAM BUTTERCREAM
Makes about 7½ cups

1 cup (227 grams) unsalted butter, softened
1 teaspoon (3 grams) kosher salt
3 pounds (1,362 grams) confectioners' sugar
1½ cups (360 grams) sour cream

1. In the bowl of a stand mixer fitted with the paddle attachment, beat butter and salt at low speed until smooth. Gradually add confectioners' sugar, about 1 cup (120 grams) at a time, alternately with sour cream, about 2 tablespoons (30 grams) at a time, beating just until combined after each addition. Increase mixer speed to medium, and beat until smooth and fluffy, about 2 minutes. Cover and refrigerate until slightly stiffened, about 30 minutes, stirring every 10 minutes.

CHOCOLATE GUINNESS CAKE WITH WHITE KNIGHT FROSTING

Makes 1 (8-inch) cake

Recipe by Zoë François

This is a sophisticated cake full of cheer, a celebration of Ireland's love of chocolate and spirits.

1½ cups (188 grams) all-purpose flour
1½ cups (300 grams) granulated sugar
½   cup (43 grams) Dutch process cocoa powder, sifted
1½ teaspoons (7.5 grams) baking soda
¾   teaspoon (2.25 grams) kosher salt
¾   cup (180 grams) whole buttermilk
⅓   cup (75 grams) vegetable oil
1   large egg (50 grams)
1   large egg yolk (19 grams)
1   teaspoon (4 grams) vanilla extract
¾   cup (180 grams) Guinness or stout
White Knight Frosting (recipe follows)
Whipped Cream Topping (recipe follows)
Garnish: Dutch process cocoa powder

1. Preheat oven to 350°F (180°C). Butter a tall-sided 8-inch round cake pan. Line bottom of pan with parchment paper.
2. In a large bowl, whisk together flour, sugar, cocoa, baking soda, and salt until combined.
3. In a medium bowl, whisk together buttermilk, oil, egg, egg yolk, and vanilla until well combined. Add buttermilk mixture to flour mixture, and whisk until smooth. Slowly add Guinness, whisking until smooth and fully combined. (Batter will be quite thin.) Pour into prepared pan.
4. Bake until a wooden pick inserted in center comes out clean, about 50 minutes. Let cool completely in pan.
5. Remove cake from pan, and place on a serving platter. Top with White Knight Frosting. Spread Whipped Cream Topping onto frosting in a smooth layer. Place a clover stencil on topping, and garnish with cocoa, if desired. Using a warm offset spatula, smooth sides of cake.

WHITE KNIGHT FROSTING

Makes 1⅔ cups

⅓   cup (57 grams) finely chopped 60% cacao bittersweet chocolate
¼   cup (60 grams) heavy whipping cream
2   tablespoons (30 grams) Irish whiskey
2   cups (240 grams) confectioners' sugar
½   cup (113 grams) unsalted butter, room temperature
1   tablespoon (5 grams) Dutch process cocoa powder

1. In the top of a double boiler, combine chocolate, cream, and whiskey. Cook over simmering water until chocolate is melted; whisk until smooth. Remove from heat, and let cool completely.
2. In the bowl of a stand mixer fitted with the paddle attachment, beat confectioners' sugar, butter, and cocoa at medium speed until smooth. Add cooled chocolate mixture, and beat until smooth and combined, stopping to scrapes sides of bowl. Use immediately.

WHIPPED CREAM TOPPING

Makes 2 cups

1   cup (240 grams) heavy whipping cream
2   tablespoons (30 grams) crème fraîche*
1   tablespoon (7 grams) confectioners' sugar
1   tablespoon (15 grams) Irish whiskey*

1. In the bowl of a stand mixer fitted with the whisk attachment, beat all ingredients at medium speed until medium-stiff peaks form.

If you don't have crème fraîche, the same amount of mascarpone cheese or sour cream can be substituted. Coffee liqueur, such as Kahlúa, can be substituted for whiskey.

Photo by Zoë François

TRIPLE-CHOCOLATE LAYER CAKE

Makes 1 (8-inch) cake

With dark and milk chocolate cake layers enrobed in a velvety White Chocolate Buttercream, this ombré layer cake is drop-dead decadent.

Milk chocolate layer:
½ cup (113 grams) unsalted butter, melted and cooled slightly
½ cup (100 grams) granulated sugar
½ cup (110 grams) firmly packed light brown sugar
2 large eggs (100 grams)
½ teaspoon (2 grams) vanilla extract
1¼ cups (156 grams) all-purpose flour
2 tablespoons (10 grams) unsweetened cocoa powder
½ teaspoon (2.5 grams) baking powder
¼ teaspoon (1.25 grams) baking soda
¼ teaspoon kosher salt
¾ cup (180 grams) whole buttermilk
3 ounces (85 grams) milk chocolate, melted and cooled slightly

Dark chocolate layer:
½ cup (113 grams) unsalted butter, melted and cooled slightly
½ cup (100 grams) granulated sugar
½ cup (110 grams) firmly packed light brown sugar
2 large eggs (100 grams)
½ teaspoon (2 grams) vanilla extract
1¼ cups (156 grams) all-purpose flour
3 tablespoons (15 grams) Dutch process cocoa powder
½ teaspoon (2.5 grams) baking powder
¼ teaspoon (1.25 grams) baking soda
¼ teaspoon kosher salt
¾ cup (180 grams) whole buttermilk
3 ounces (85 grams) 60% bittersweet chocolate, melted and cooled slightly

White Chocolate Buttercream (recipe follows)
Garnish: chopped milk chocolate, chopped bittersweet chocolate, chopped white chocolate

1. Preheat oven to 350°F (180°C). Spray 2 (3-inch-tall) 8-inch round cake pans (see Note) with baking spray with flour.
2. For milk chocolate layer: In a medium bowl, place melted butter. Whisk in sugars, eggs, and vanilla.
3. In another medium bowl, whisk together flour, unsweetened cocoa, baking powder, baking soda, and salt. Gradually add flour mixture to butter mixture alternately with buttermilk, beginning and ending with flour mixture, stirring just until combined after each addition. Stir in melted milk chocolate until combined. Pour into a prepared pan.
4. For dark chocolate layer: In a medium bowl, place melted butter. Whisk in sugars, eggs, and vanilla.
5. In another medium bowl, whisk together flour, Dutch process cocoa, baking powder, baking soda, and salt. Gradually add flour mixture to butter mixture alternately with buttermilk, beginning and ending with flour mixture, stirring just until combined after each addition. Stir in melted bittersweet chocolate until combined. Pour into remaining prepared pan.
6. Bake until a wooden pick inserted in center comes out clean, 40 to 45 minutes. Let cool in pans for 15 minutes. Remove from pans, and let cool completely on wire racks.
7. Place cooled dark chocolate layer on a cake stand. Spread 1½ cups White Chocolate Buttercream on layer. Top with milk chocolate layer. Spread remaining buttercream on top and sides of cake. Garnish with chopped chocolates, if desired.

Note: *You can also bake the cake layers in 2 (9-inch) round cake pans. Bake at 350°F (180°C) for about 40 minutes.*

PRO TIP
We used two different kinds of cocoa powder: plain unsweetened cocoa for the milk chocolate cake layer and Dutch process cocoa for the dark chocolate cake layer. This helped us create an ombré look for our cake layers, with the unsweetened cocoa powder imparting a lighter hue than the Dutch process cocoa powder.

WHITE CHOCOLATE BUTTERCREAM
Makes about 4 cups

1 cup (227 grams) unsalted butter, softened
⅛ teaspoon kosher salt
12 ounces (340 grams) white chocolate, melted and cooled slightly
3 cups (360 grams) confectioners' sugar
3 tablespoons (45 grams) whole milk

1. In the bowl of a stand mixer fitted with paddle attachment, beat butter and salt at medium speed until smooth, 1 to 2 minutes. Beat in melted white chocolate. With mixer on low speed, gradually add confectioners' sugar alternately with milk, beating until combined after each addition. Increase mixer speed to medium, and beat until light and fluffy, 2 to 3 minutes.

CHOCOLATE CHIP CAKE WITH CHOCOLATE AMERICAN BUTTERCREAM

Makes 1 (8-inch) cake

Recipe by Erin Clarkson

Chocolate and vanilla are lovely complements in this cake decorated with Chocolate American Buttercream, which is fudgy and luscious from the high ratio of heavy cream whipped into it. It pipes into the most perfect points on the outside of the cake.

1¼	cups (300 grams) whole milk
4	large eggs (200 grams), room temperature
½	cup (120 grams) whole Greek yogurt
2	large egg yolks (37 grams), room temperature
2	teaspoons (12 grams) vanilla bean paste
4¾	cups plus 1 tablespoon (602 grams) all-purpose flour
2¼	cups (450 grams) granulated sugar
3¼	teaspoons (16.25 grams) baking powder
½	teaspoon (1.5 grams) kosher salt
1½	cups (340 grams) unsalted butter, cubed and softened
1½	cups (255 grams) 60% cacao bittersweet chocolate chips (see Notes), roughly chopped
2	recipes Chocolate American Buttercream (recipe follows) (see Notes)

Garnish: sprinkles*

1. Preheat oven to 350°F (180°C). Butter and flour 3 (8-inch) round cake pans. Line bottom of pans with parchment paper.
2. In a medium bowl, whisk together milk, eggs, yogurt, egg yolks, and vanilla bean paste.
3. In the bowl of a stand mixer fitted with the paddle attachment, beat flour, sugar, baking powder, and salt at low speed just until combined. Add butter, 1 cube at a time, beating until well combined after each addition. (Mixture should resemble sand.) Add half of milk mixture, beating just until combined. Add remaining milk mixture, and beat at medium speed just until combined. Using a rubber spatula, fold batter to ensure that no dry ingredients remain. Fold in chocolate chips until combined. Divide batter among prepared pans.
4. Bake until cake springs back when touched in center and a wooden pick inserted in center comes out clean, 35 to 40 minutes. Let cool in pans for 15 minutes. Remove from pans, and let cool completely on wire racks.
5. Place a cooled cake layer on a cake turntable. (To help hold cake in place, smear about 1½ teaspoons [about 6 grams] Chocolate American Buttercream onto center of turntable before adding first cake layer.) Spread ¾ cup (153 grams) Chocolate American Buttercream on cake layer. Top with second cake layer, pressing very lightly to secure, and seal edge where cake layers meet with a thin layer of buttercream. Spread ¾ cup (153 grams) buttercream on second cake layer, and place remaining cake layer, upside down,

on top. Apply a thin layer of buttercream to top and sides of cake to create a crumb coat, smoothing with an offset spatula or icing scraper. Refrigerate until crumb coat is set, 20 to 30 minutes. Cover remaining buttercream.
6. Place buttercream in a pastry bag fitted with a French star piping tip (Ateco #866). (Do not fill pastry bag too full or it will be hard to pipe; keep remaining buttercream covered.) Pipe buttercream all over outside of cake, refilling pastry bag as needed. Garnish with sprinkles, if desired. Refrigerate until ready to serve. Let stand at room temperature for 1 hour before serving. Refrigerate in an airtight container for up to 1 week.

We used Layer Cake Shop Pastel Sequin Sprinkles, available at layercakeshop.com.

Notes: *Finely chopped chocolate will also work.*

Because this cake's frosting design requires a larger amount of buttercream, you'll make two batches—the first for the crumb coat and stacking, reserving the rest, and the second to add to the first batch for covering the outside of the cake.

CHOCOLATE AMERICAN BUTTERCREAM
Makes 5 cups

1½	cups (340 grams) unsalted butter, softened
1½	cups (128 grams) Dutch process cocoa powder
5¾	cups (690 grams) confectioners' sugar, sifted
¾	cup plus 2 tablespoons (210 grams) heavy whipping cream
1	teaspoon (3 grams) kosher salt
1	teaspoon (6 grams) vanilla bean paste

1. In the bowl of a stand mixer fitted with the paddle attachment, beat butter and cocoa at low speed until well combined. Add confectioners' sugar, 1 cup (120 grams) at a time, alternately with cream, 1 tablespoon (15 grams) at a time, beating just until combined after each addition. Add salt and vanilla bean paste. Increase mixer speed to medium-high, and beat until smooth, about 1 minute. Increase mixer speed to high, and beat until soft and spreadable. (See Note.) Reduce mixer speed to low, and beat for 1 to 2 minutes to release any air bubbles. Use immediately, or cover with a piece of plastic wrap, pressing wrap directly onto surface of buttercream, until ready to use.

Note: *You want the texture of this to be fluffy and easy to pipe. Add 1 to 2 teaspoons (5 to 10 grams) additional heavy whipping cream if needed to get it to the right consistency for piping.*

Photos by Hector Sanchez

MAKE YOUR POINT

Using a French star piping tip to do a finish such as this is one of my favorite ways to finish a cake. Starting at the top of the cake, begin adding little stars of frosting to cover the surface.

Hold the pastry bag directly above where you want to apply the buttercream, and squeeze gently to release it. Stop applying pressure to the bag once your star is almost finished, and pull away quickly so the frosting comes to a nice closed point at the top.

Move onto the sides of the cake. I find it less time-consuming to apply the stars ½ inch apart at first and then go back to fill in the smooth space with more until the entire cake is covered.

EARL GREY LAYER CAKE WITH VANILLA BEAN GERMAN BUTTERCREAM

Makes 1 (8-inch) cake

Recipe by Erin Clarkson

This cake is delicately flavored with Earl Grey tea and finished with a simple textured edge and some decorative piping on top.

2⅓   cups (560 grams) whole milk
½   cup plus 1 tablespoon (54 grams) loose-leaf Earl Grey tea
4   large eggs (200 grams), room temperature
½   cup (120 grams) whole Greek yogurt
2   large egg yolks (37 grams), room temperature
2   teaspoons (12 grams) vanilla bean paste
4¾   cups plus 1 tablespoon (602 grams) all-purpose flour
2¼   cups (450 grams) granulated sugar
3¼   teaspoons (16.25 grams) baking powder
½   teaspoon (1.5 grams) kosher salt
1½   cups (340 grams) unsalted butter, cubed and softened
Vanilla Bean German Buttercream (recipe follows)

1. In a small saucepan, heat milk over medium heat just until bubbles form around edges of pan. (Do not boil.) Remove from the heat, and add tea; cover and let stand for 20 minutes. Strain through a fine-mesh sieve into a small bowl, pressing down on tea leaves to extract as much liquid as possible; discard solids. Let cool to room temperature.
2. Preheat oven to 350°F (180°C). Butter and flour 3 (8-inch) round cake pans. Line bottom of pans with parchment paper.
3. In a medium bowl, whisk together 1¼ cups (330 grams) Earl Grey milk, eggs, yogurt, egg yolks, and vanilla bean paste.
4. In the bowl of a stand mixer fitted with the paddle attachment, beat flour, sugar, baking powder, and salt at low speed just until combined. Add butter, 1 cube at a time, beating until well combined after each addition. (Mixture should resemble sand.) Add half of milk mixture, beating just until combined. Add remaining milk mixture, and beat at medium speed just until combined. Using a rubber spatula, fold batter to ensure that no dry ingredients remain. Divide batter among prepared pans.
5. Bake until cake springs back when touched in center and a wooden pick inserted in center comes out clean, 35 to 40 minutes. Let cool in pans for 15 minutes. Remove from pans, and let cool completely on wire racks.
6. Place a cooled cake layer on a cake turntable. (To help hold cake in place, smear about 1½ teaspoons [about 7.5 grams] Vanilla Bean German Buttercream onto center of turntable before adding first cake layer.) Spread 1 cup (184 grams) Vanilla Bean German Buttercream on cake layer. Top with second cake layer, pressing very lightly to secure, and seal edge where cake layers meet with a thin layer of buttercream. Spread 1 cup (184 grams) buttercream on second cake layer, and place remaining cake layer, upside down, on top. Apply a thin layer of buttercream to top and sides of cake to

create a crumb coat, smoothing with an offset spatula or icing scraper. Refrigerate until crumb coat is set, 20 to 30 minutes.
7. Spread Vanilla Bean German Buttercream in a thick, smooth layer on top and sides of cake. Create a pattern by holding an offset spatula against sides of cake and rotating the turntable while slowly moving spatula up. Smooth top edge.
8. Place remaining buttercream in a pastry bag fitted with a French star piping tip (Ateco #866). Pipe a shell design or your desired design on top of cake. Refrigerate until ready to serve. Let stand at room temperature for 1 hour before serving. Refrigerate in an airtight container for up to 1 week.

VANILLA BEAN GERMAN BUTTERCREAM
Makes 10 cups

1⅔   cups (333 grams) granulated sugar
4   tablespoons plus 1 teaspoon (35 grams) cornstarch
3   large eggs (150 grams), room temperature
3   large egg yolks (56 grams), room temperature
1   teaspoon (3 grams) kosher salt
2¼   cups plus 2 tablespoons (570 grams) whole milk
1   tablespoon (18 grams) vanilla bean paste (see Note)
4½   cups (1,021 grams) unsalted butter, cubed and softened

1. In a medium bowl, whisk together sugar and cornstarch. Add eggs, egg yolks, and salt, whisking to combine.
2. In a medium saucepan, heat milk and vanilla bean paste over low heat just until bubbles form around edges of pan. (Do not boil.) Pour half of hot milk mixture into sugar mixture, whisking constantly; whisk until well combined. Pour sugar mixture into remaining hot milk mixture in pan, and heat over medium heat, whisking constantly, until it begins to bubble and is thickened; cook for 1 minute. Pour into a shallow container or the bowl of a stand mixer, and cover with a piece of plastic wrap, pressing wrap directly onto surface of pastry cream to prevent a skin from forming. Refrigerate for at least 4 hours or preferably overnight. (If you need to speed this process up, place pastry cream in a bowl, and place bowl in an ice water bath. Stir frequently.)
3. In the bowl of a stand mixer fitted with the whisk attachment, beat pastry cream at medium speed until creamy and smooth. Add butter, a few cubes at a time, beating until well combined after each addition. (Mixture may look curdled at this point, but it will come together.) Switch to the paddle attachment, and beat at low speed for 2 to 3 minutes to help release any air bubbles. Store in an airtight container until ready to use. If refrigerating, let stand at room temperature to warm slightly, and rewhip until smooth before using.

Note: *The vanilla flavor in this buttercream comes from vanilla bean paste, which also gives the buttercream little black flecks of vanilla bean seeds. Vanilla extract will work well, too.*

Photos by Hector Sanchez

RING AROUND THE LAYER CAKE

Start on the outermost edge of the cake and pipe a shell design. Hold piping tip at an angle, with the tip pointing toward the middle. Using even pressure on pastry bag, form a shell shape by making a smooth motion with your wrist to pipe buttercream toward outer edge and then back toward the center on itself as you release pressure.

Create a ring of smaller stars piped directly in front of each piped shell on the outer edge. Hold your pastry bag perpendicular to the cake, and gently apply pressure to pipe. Finish by releasing your grip and pulling up slightly.

Hold piping tip at an angle, with tip pointing down. Form a shell shape by piping the buttercream up and over onto itself and then giving it a little tail. Finish the shape by releasing your grip on the pastry bag. Pipe the following shell over the end of the previous one to give it a seamless finish.

VANILLA AND RASPBERRY CAKE WITH OMBRÉ RASPBERRY SWISS MERINGUE BUTTERCREAM

Makes 1 (8-inch) cake

Recipe by Erin Clarkson

This beautiful cake has raspberries baked into it and is finished with a Swiss meringue buttercream colored and flavored with freeze-dried raspberries.

- 1¼ cups (300 grams) whole milk
- 4 large eggs (200 grams), room temperature
- ½ cup (120 grams) whole Greek yogurt
- 2 large egg yolks (37 grams), room temperature
- 2 teaspoons (12 grams) vanilla bean paste
- 4¾ cups plus 1 tablespoon (602 grams) all-purpose flour
- 2¼ cups (450 grams) granulated sugar
- 3¼ teaspoons (16.25 grams) baking powder
- ½ teaspoon (1.5 grams) kosher salt
- 1½ cups (340 grams) unsalted butter, cubed and softened
- 3 cups (390 grams) fresh or frozen raspberries (see Note)

Raspberry Swiss Meringue Buttercream (recipe follows)

1. Preheat oven to 350°F (180°C). Butter and flour 3 (8-inch) round cake pans. Line bottom of pans with parchment paper.
2. In a medium bowl, whisk together milk, eggs, yogurt, egg yolks, and vanilla bean paste.
3. In the bowl of a stand mixer fitted with the paddle attachment, beat flour, sugar, baking powder, and salt at low speed just until combined. Add butter, 1 cube at a time, beating until well combined after each addition. (Mixture should resemble sand.) Add half of milk mixture, beating just until combined. Add remaining milk mixture, and beat at medium speed just until combined. Using a rubber spatula, fold batter to ensure that no dry ingredients remain. Divide batter among prepared pans. Arrange raspberries evenly on top of batter in each pan, pressing a few slightly into batter. (This will help to distribute them more evenly.)
4. Bake until cake springs back when touched in center and a wooden pick inserted in center comes out clean, 35 to 40 minutes. Let cool in pans for 15 minutes. Remove from pans, and let cool completely on wire racks. (Once cool, wrap tightly in plastic wrap if not using immediately.)
5. Place a cooled cake layer on a cake turntable. (To help hold cake in place, smear about 1½ teaspoons [about 6.5 grams] Raspberry Swiss Meringue Buttercream onto center of turntable before adding first cake layer.) Spread 1 cup (160 grams) light pink Raspberry Swiss Meringue Buttercream on cake layer. Top with second cake layer, pressing very lightly to secure, and seal edge where cake layers meet with a thin layer of light pink buttercream. Spread 1 cup (160 grams) light pink buttercream on second cake layer, and place remaining cake layer, upside down, on top. Apply a thin layer of light pink buttercream to top and sides of cake to create a crumb coat, smoothing with an offset spatula or icing scraper. Refrigerate until crumb coat is set, 20 to 30 minutes.
6. To create an ombré effect, spread dark pink Raspberry Swiss Meringue Buttercream on bottom one-third of cake, light pink buttercream on middle one-third of cake, and white buttercream on top one-third and top of cake. Using a cake scraper pressed lightly against buttercream, blend colors, adding more where needed to help blend and fill in any patches. Using an offset spatula, add swoops and swirls to sides of cake to give texture.
7. Place remaining buttercream (both pink and white—this will create a pretty swirl effect) in a pastry bag fitted with an open star piping tip (Wilton 1M). Pipe buttercream on top of cake as desired. Refrigerate until ready to serve. Let stand at room temperature for 1 hour before serving. Refrigerate in an airtight container for up to 1 week.

Note: *You can use either fresh or frozen raspberries in this recipe. If using frozen, let thaw on a paper towel to absorb extra moisture before using. Adding them to the batter at the end ensures they won't sink and burn at the edges of the pan. If you are using frozen, the berries may weep a little juice into the batter as they bake.*

RASPBERRY SWISS MERINGUE BUTTERCREAM
Makes about 9 cups

- 8 large egg whites (240 grams)
- 2 cups (400 grams) granulated sugar
- 1 teaspoon (3 grams) kosher salt
- 2 teaspoons (12 grams) vanilla bean paste
- 4 cups (908 grams) cold unsalted butter, cubed
- 14 tablespoons (70 grams) powdered freeze-dried raspberries (see Note), divided

Pink gel food coloring (optional)

1. In the heatproof bowl of a stand mixer, whisk together egg whites, sugar, and salt by hand. Place bowl over a saucepan of simmering water. Cook, whisking constantly, until sugar dissolves and an instant-read thermometer registers 160°F (71°C).
2. Carefully return bowl to stand mixer. Using the whisk attachment, beat at high speed until white and fluffy, 5 to 6 minutes. Add cold butter, 1 cube at a time, beating until combined after each addition. (Mixture may look curdled at this point, but it will come together.) Beat at high speed for 3 minutes. Beat in vanilla bean paste. Transfer 1¼ cups (200 grams) buttercream to a small bowl, and set aside. (This will be your white buttercream for the ombré effect.) Add 10 tablespoons (50 grams) raspberry powder to remaining buttercream, and beat until combined. Transfer 1¼ cups (200 grams) buttercream to another small bowl, and stir in remaining 4 tablespoons (20 grams) raspberry powder and a few drops of food coloring (if using). Use immediately.

Note: *To make powdered freeze-dried raspberries, place 3 ounces (85 grams) freeze-dried raspberries in the work bowl of a food processor, and process until they are a fine powder.*

Photos by Hector Sanchez

OMBRÉ ALL DAY

Use an offset spatula to create an ombré effect by spreading dark pink Raspberry Swiss Meringue Buttercream on the bottom one-third of the cake.

Coat the middle with the light pink Raspberry Swiss Meringue Buttercream and the top one-third and top of the cake with the reserved white buttercream.

Do a few passes with a cake scraper to blend the colors, adding more buttercream where needed to help blend and fill in any patches. Use a clean offset spatula to create swoops and swirls on the side of the cake to give texture.

PRO TIP
When you pipe frosting on the top of the cake, fill the pastry bag with the remaining pink and white frosting. This will create a pretty two-tone effect on each ruffle. Hold your pastry bag directly over the top of the cake, and pipe around the perimeter. No need to move your hand to create the swirl effect as you pipe—the star piping tip will create the ruffles for you.

VANILLA BEAN CAKE WITH LEMON CURD AND TORCHED SWISS MERINGUE

Makes 1 (8-inch) cake

Recipe by Erin Clarkson

Swiss meringue buttercream is used to assemble this cake, and the frosting around the perimeter acts as a seal to prevent the Lemon Curd from leaking out.

1¼ cups (300 grams) whole milk
4 large eggs (200 grams), room temperature
½ cup (120 grams) whole Greek yogurt
2 large egg yolks (37 grams), room temperature
2 teaspoons (12 grams) vanilla bean paste
4¾ cups plus 1 tablespoon (602 grams) all-purpose flour
2¼ cups (450 grams) granulated sugar
3¼ teaspoons (16.25 grams) baking powder
½ teaspoon (1.5 grams) kosher salt
1½ cups (340 grams) unsalted butter, cubed and softened
Vanilla Swiss Meringue Buttercream (recipe follows)
Lemon Curd (recipe follows)
Swiss Meringue (recipe follows)

1. Preheat oven to 350°F (180°C). Butter and flour 3 (8-inch) round cake pans. Line bottom of pans with parchment paper.
2. In a medium bowl, whisk together milk, eggs, yogurt, egg yolks, and vanilla bean paste.
3. In the bowl of a stand mixer fitted with the paddle attachment, beat flour, sugar, baking powder, and salt at low speed just until combined. Add butter, 1 cube at a time, beating until well combined after each addition. (Mixture should resemble sand.) Add half of milk mixture, beating just until combined. Add remaining milk mixture, and beat at medium speed just until combined. Using a rubber spatula, fold batter to ensure that no dry ingredients remain. Divide batter among prepared pans.
4. Bake until cake springs back when touched in center and a wooden pick inserted in center comes out clean, 35 to 40 minutes. Let cool in pans for 15 minutes. Remove from pans, and let cool completely on wire racks. (Once cool, wrap tightly in plastic wrap if not using immediately.)
5. Place ½ cup (80 grams) Vanilla Swiss Meringue Buttercream in a pastry bag fitted with a medium round piping tip (Ateco #805).
6. Place a cooled cake layer on a cake turntable. (To help hold cake in place, smear about 1½ teaspoons [about 6.5 grams] buttercream onto center of turntable before adding first cake layer.) Spread 1 cup (160 grams) Vanilla Swiss Meringue Buttercream on cake layer; pipe a ring of buttercream around outside edge of cake layer. Fill buttercream ring with ½ cup (140 grams) Lemon Curd. Top with second cake layer, pressing very lightly to secure, and seal edge where cake layers meet with a thin layer of buttercream.

Spread 1 cup (160 grams) buttercream on second cake layer; pipe a ring of buttercream around outside edge, and fill buttercream ring with ½ cup (140 grams) Lemon Curd. Place remaining cake layer, upside down, on top. Return buttercream in pastry bag to bowl with remaining buttercream. Apply a thin layer of buttercream to top and sides of cake to create a crumb coat, smoothing with an offset spatula or icing scraper. Refrigerate until crumb coat is set, 30 to 45 minutes.
7. Using an offset spatula, spread Swiss Meringue on top and sides of cake, adding swoops and texture as desired. (Make sure cake is cold before applying meringue.) Using a kitchen torch, carefully brown meringue. (See Note.) Refrigerate in an airtight container for up to 1 week.

Note: *The Swiss Meringue is best added and torched as close to serving as possible.*

VANILLA SWISS MERINGUE BUTTERCREAM
Makes about 4½ cups

4 large egg whites (120 grams)
1 cup (200 grams) granulated sugar
½ teaspoon (1.5 grams) kosher salt
2 cups (454 grams) cold unsalted butter, cubed
1 teaspoon (6 grams) vanilla bean paste

1. In the heatproof bowl of a stand mixer, whisk together egg whites, sugar, and salt by hand. Place bowl over a saucepan of simmering water. Cook, whisking constantly, until sugar dissolves and an instant-read thermometer registers 160°F (71°C).
2. Carefully return bowl to stand mixer. Using the whisk attachment, beat at high speed until white and fluffy, 5 to 6 minutes. Add cold butter, 1 cube at a time, beating until combined after each addition. (Mixture may look curdled at this point, but it will come together). Beat at high speed for 3 minutes. Beat in vanilla bean paste until combined and buttercream is smooth. Switch to the paddle attachment, and beat at low speed for 1 minute to release any air bubbles.

LEMON CURD
Makes about 1½ cups

8 large egg yolks (149 grams)
⅔ cup (133 grams) granulated sugar
3 tablespoons (9 grams) lemon zest (about 3 medium lemons)
⅔ cup (160 grams) fresh lemon juice
6 tablespoons (84 grams) unsalted butter, room temperature

1. In the top of a double boiler, whisk together all ingredients. Cook over simmering water, stirring frequently, until mixture is thick enough to coat the back of a spoon and a clear track is left when you can drag a finger through it. (Watch edges of mixture carefully to ensure it does not catch and go lumpy, using a flexible rubber spatula as needed to help clear sides of bowl.) Cook for 5 minutes. (It will thicken more as it cools.) Strain through a fine-mesh sieve into a medium heatproof bowl. Cover with a piece of plastic wrap, pressing wrap directly onto surface of curd to prevent a skin from forming. Refrigerate until completely cool. Refrigerate in an airtight container until ready to use.

Note: *The curd will cook much faster if you use a metal mixing bowl in your double boiler rather than a glass one.*

SWISS MERINGUE
Makes about 8½ cups

7   large egg whites (210 grams)
1½ cups (300 grams) granulated sugar
1   teaspoon (6 grams) vanilla bean paste
¼   teaspoon kosher salt

1. In the heatproof bowl of a stand mixer, whisk together all ingredients by hand. Place bowl over a saucepan of simmering water. Cook, whisking constantly, until sugar dissolves and an instant-read thermometer registers 160°F (71°C).
2. Carefully return bowl to stand mixer. Using the whisk attachment, beat at high speed until white and fluffy and stiff peaks form, 5 to 6 minutes. Use immediately.

Photos by Hector Sanchez

PEACHES & CREAM CAKE

Makes 1 (8-inch) cake

This three-tiered cake pairs one of summer's most beloved stone fruits with vanilla cake layers made fluffy by whipped cream folded into the batter. A vanilla frosting veil covers the peach-packed layers within.

½   cup (113 grams) unsalted butter, softened
2¾ cups (550 grams) granulated sugar, divided
½   cup (112 grams) vegetable oil
4   large eggs (200 grams)
1   tablespoon (13 grams) vanilla extract
3   cups (375 grams) cake flour
1   tablespoon (15 grams) baking powder
1   teaspoon (3 grams) kosher salt
1   cup (240 grams) cold heavy whipping cream, divided
6   cups (844 grams) sliced fresh peaches (about 6 peaches)
2   teaspoons (10 grams) lemon juice
Vanilla Buttercream (recipe follows)

1. Preheat oven to 350°F (180°C). Spray 3 (8-inch) round cake pans with baking spray with flour. Line bottom of pans with parchment paper.
2. In the bowl of a stand mixer fitted with the paddle attachment, beat butter and 2 cups (400 grams) sugar at medium speed until fluffy, 4 to 5 minutes, stopping to scrape sides of bowl. With mixer on medium-low speed, add oil in a slow, steady stream, beating until combined. Increase mixer speed to medium, and add eggs, one at a time, beating well after each addition. Beat in vanilla.
3. In a medium bowl, whisk together flour, baking powder, and salt. With mixer on low speed, gradually add flour mixture to butter mixture alternately with ½ cup (120 grams) cold cream, beginning and ending with flour mixture, beating just until combined after each addition.
4. In another medium bowl, whisk remaining ½ cup (120 grams) cold cream by hand until soft peaks form. Fold whipped cream into cake batter in two additions. Divide batter among prepared pans, smoothing tops. Run a wooden pick through batter to release any large air bubbles.

5. Bake until a wooden pick inserted in center comes out clean, 25 to 30 minutes. Let cool in pans for 10 minutes. Remove from pans, and let cool completely on wire racks.
6. In a large bowl, toss together peaches, lemon juice, and remaining ¾ cup (150 grams) sugar. Let stand until sugar dissolves, 15 to 20 minutes, stirring occasionally. Drain peaches, reserving liquid.
7. Place a cooled cake layer on a serving platter. Brush layer generously with reserved peach liquid. Place Vanilla Buttercream in a pastry bag fitted with a ½-inch round piping tip (Wilton No. 2A). Pipe a border of buttercream around outside edge of cake layer. Place 1½ cups (211 grams) peaches within border. Top with second cake layer; brush with reserved peach liquid, pipe a border of buttercream around outside edge of cake layer, and place 1½ cups (211 grams) peaches within border. Top with remaining cake layer, and brush with reserved peach liquid. Spread a thin layer of buttercream on sides of cake. Spread a layer of buttercream on top of cake, letting it hang over edge of cake slightly. Using an offset spatula or bench scraper, smooth sides of cake. (This will push up extra buttercream hanging over sides of cake to create an edge.) Refrigerate until ready to serve. Top with remaining peaches before serving.

VANILLA BUTTERCREAM
Makes about 3 cups

1   cup (227 grams) unsalted butter, softened
¼   teaspoon kosher salt
1   (1-pound) package (454 grams) confectioners' sugar
¼   cup (60 grams) heavy whipping cream
¼   teaspoon (1 gram) vanilla extract

1. In the bowl of a stand mixer fitted with the paddle attachment, beat butter and salt at low speed until smooth. Gradually add confectioners' sugar, about 1 cup (120 grams) at a time, alternately with cream, about 1 tablespoon (15 grams) at a time, beating until smooth and fully combined. Beat in vanilla. Increase mixer speed to medium, and beat until fluffy, about 1 minute.

ASSEMBLE & FROST YOUR CAKE

1. Place a cooled cake layer on a serving platter. Brush layer generously with reserved peach liquid.

2. Place Vanilla Buttercream in a pastry bag fitted with a ½-inch round piping tip (Wilton No. 2A). Pipe a border of buttercream around outside edge of cake layer.

3. Place 1½ cups (211 grams) peaches within border.

4. Top with second cake layer; brush with reserved peach liquid, pipe a border of buttercream around outside edge of cake layer, and place 1½ cups (211 grams) peaches within border.

5. Top with remaining cake layer, and brush with reserved peach liquid. Spread a thin layer of buttercream on sides of cake. Spread a layer of buttercream on top of cake, letting it hang over edge of cake slightly.

6. Using an offset spatula or bench scraper, smooth sides of cake. (This will push up extra buttercream hanging over sides of cake to create an edge.)

STRAWBERRY ICEBOX CAKE

Makes 1 (9-inch) cake

Our icebox cake is a like a delicious magic trick. Three thin cake layers are encased in a voluminous coat of Strawberry Cream Cheese Mousse, transforming two sweet pieces into a delicious strawberry-packed whole.

¼   cup (57 grams) unsalted butter, softened
½   cup (100 grams) granulated sugar
1   large egg (50 grams)
1   large egg yolk (19 grams)
½   teaspoon (2 grams) vanilla extract
¾   cup (94 grams) cake flour
½   teaspoon (2.5 grams) baking powder
¼   teaspoon kosher salt
⅛   teaspoon baking soda
2½   tablespoons (37.5 grams) whole buttermilk
¼   cup (28 grams) finely chopped pecans
¼   cup (80 grams) strawberry preserves
6 to 7 drops red liquid food coloring
12   medium fresh strawberries (168 grams), hulled and halved
2¼   cups (330 grams) thinly sliced hulled fresh strawberries (⅛ to ¼ inch thick)
Strawberry Cream Cheese Mousse (recipe follows)
Sweetened Whipped Cream (recipe follows)
Garnish: fresh strawberries

1. Preheat oven to 325°F (170°C). Line bottoms of 3 (8-inch) round cake pans with parchment paper; spray parchment and sides of pans with baking spray with flour.
2. In the bowl of a stand mixer fitted with the paddle attachment, beat butter and sugar at medium speed until fluffy, 3 to 4 minutes, stopping to scrape sides of bowl. Add egg and egg yolk, one at a time, beating well after each addition. Beat in vanilla.
3. In a medium bowl, whisk together flour, baking powder, salt, and baking soda. With mixer on low speed, gradually add flour mixture to butter mixture alternately with buttermilk, beginning and ending with flour mixture, beating just until combined after each addition. Add pecans, preserves, and food coloring, beating just until combined. Divide batter among prepared pans, smoothing tops.
4. Bake until a wooden pick inserted in center comes out clean, 12 to 15 minutes. Let cool completely in pans. Remove from pans; discard parchment paper.
5. Line bottom of a 9-inch springform pan with parchment paper. Cut 2 (3½-inch-wide) strips of parchment paper to line sides of pan. (You want parchment to extend about ¼ inch higher than sides of pan.)
6. Place a cooled cake layer in center of prepared pan. Place halved strawberries, cut side out, around cake layer and against sides of pan. Place ¾ cup (110 grams) sliced strawberries in a tight single layer on top of cake layer. Place 2⅓ cups (about 401 grams)

Strawberry Cream Cheese Mousse in a large pastry bag, and cut a ½-inch opening in tip. Pipe mousse between halved strawberries (this ensures there are no gaps); pipe mousse on top of sliced strawberries, and smooth top. Top with second cake layer. Place ¾ cup (110 grams) sliced strawberries in a tight single layer on top of second cake layer. Place 2⅓ cups (about 401 grams) Strawberry Cream Cheese Mousse in pastry bag. Pipe mousse in gap between cake and sides of pan; pipe mousse on top of sliced strawberries, and smooth top. Top with remaining cake layer, remaining ¾ cup (110 grams) sliced strawberries, and remaining 2⅓ cups (about 401 grams) mousse, smoothing top. Cover with plastic wrap, and refrigerate overnight. (Alternatively, refrigerate for at least 4 hours and then freeze for at least 1 hour before serving).
7. When ready to serve, remove sides of pan and parchment paper. Using a hot, dry metal offset spatula, smooth sides and top of cake. Place Sweetened Whipped Cream in a small pastry bag fitted with an open star piping tip (Wilton 4B). Pipe onto cake as desired. Garnish with fresh strawberries, if desired. Serve immediately, or refrigerate until ready to serve.

STRAWBERRY CREAM CHEESE MOUSSE

Makes about 7 cups

16   ounces (454 grams) cream cheese, softened
1   cup (200 grams) granulated sugar
⅓   cup (107 grams) strawberry preserves
1   teaspoon (6 grams) vanilla bean paste
2   cups (480 grams) cold heavy whipping cream
2 to 3 drops red liquid food coloring

1. In the bowl of a stand mixer fitted with the paddle attachment, beat cream cheese at medium-low speed until smooth, about 1 minute. Add sugar, and beat at medium speed until smooth. Beat in preserves and vanilla bean paste until combined. Transfer to a large bowl, and set aside.
2. Clean bowl of stand mixer. Using the whisk attachment, beat cold cream at medium speed until thickened. Slowly increase mixer speed to medium-high, and beat until stiff peaks form. Using a whisk, fold about one-third of whipped cream into cream cheese mixture until combined. Fold in food coloring and remaining whipped cream until no streaks remain. Use immediately.

SWEETENED WHIPPED CREAM

Makes 1 cup

½   cup (120 grams) cold heavy whipping cream
2   tablespoons (14 grams) confectioners' sugar

1. In a medium bowl, whisk together cold cream and confectioners' sugar by hand until medium peaks form. Use immediately, or refrigerate until ready to use.

BANANA CAKE WITH CHOCOLATE BUTTERCREAM

Makes 1 (8-inch) cake

The iconic flavors of banana and chocolate meet in our whimsical naked cake. Mashed banana adds a soft tenderness to the crumb of our stir-together buttermilk cake base while piped dollops of Chocolate Buttercream impart a boost of cocoa richness.

1   cup (220 grams) firmly packed dark brown sugar
1   cup (240 grams) whole buttermilk
1   cup (227 grams) mashed ripe banana
½   cup (100 grams) granulated sugar
½   cup (112 grams) vegetable oil
2   large eggs (100 grams)
1   tablespoon (13 grams) vanilla extract
3   cups (375 grams) cake flour
1   teaspoon (5 grams) baking soda
1   teaspoon (5 grams) baking powder
1   teaspoon (3 grams) kosher salt
Chocolate Buttercream (recipe follows)
Garnish: chopped chocolate

1. Preheat oven to 325°F (170°C). Spray 2 (8-inch) round cake pans with baking spray with flour. Line bottom of pans with parchment paper.
2. In a large bowl, whisk together brown sugar, buttermilk, banana, granulated sugar, oil, eggs, and vanilla.
3. In a medium bowl, whisk together flour, baking soda, baking powder, and salt. Slowly add flour mixture to sugar mixture, whisking just until combined. Divide batter between prepared pans.
4. Bake until a wooden pick inserted in center comes out clean, 35 to 40 minutes. Let cool in pans for 10 minutes. Remove from pans, and let cool completely on wire racks.
5. Level cooled cake layers, if desired. Place a cake layer on a serving platter. Place Chocolate Buttercream in a pastry bag fitted with a ⁹⁄₁₆-inch round piping tip (Ateco #807). Starting from edge and working toward center, pipe tall circles (about 1¾ inches at base of circle) on cake layer. Top with remaining cake layer. Pipe tall buttercream circles on cake layer. Use any remaining buttercream to fill in any holes and decorate top of cake. Garnish with chopped chocolate, if desired. Refrigerate in an airtight container for up to 5 days.

CHOCOLATE BUTTERCREAM
Makes about 5½ cups

2   cups (454 grams) unsalted butter, softened
½   teaspoon (1.5 grams) kosher salt
5   cups (600 grams) confectioners' sugar
1   cup (85 grams) Dutch process cocoa powder
5   tablespoons (75 grams) heavy whipping cream
½   teaspoon (2 grams) vanilla extract

1. In the bowl of a stand mixer fitted with the paddle attachment, beat butter and salt at low speed until smooth.
2. In a large bowl, sift together confectioners' sugar and cocoa. Add sugar mixture, about 1 cup at a time, to butter mixture alternately with cream, about 1 tablespoon (15 grams) at a time, beating until smooth after each addition. Beat in vanilla. Increase mixer speed to medium, and beat until fluffy, 2 to 3 minutes. Use immediately.

GLUTEN-FREE HUMMINGBIRD CAKE

Makes 1 (8-inch) cake

One of our most popular recipes of all time, our Hummingbird Cake is a classic Southern layer cake, packing pineapple, banana, and pecans under a dreamy Cream Cheese Frosting. This gluten-free version boasts the same iconic tropical flavor, tender texture, and creamy frosting. The best part? The only change to the original recipe is a simple swap of gluten-free flour for all-purpose flour.

3   cups (444 grams) gluten-free baking flour*
1½ cups (300 grams) granulated sugar
1   teaspoon (2 grams) ground cinnamon
¾   teaspoon (3.75 grams) baking soda
½   teaspoon (1.5 grams) kosher salt
¼   teaspoon ground nutmeg
½   cup (57 grams) chopped toasted pecans
1   cup (224 grams) canola oil
¾   cup (170 grams) mashed ripe banana (about 2 medium bananas)
3   large eggs (150 grams), room temperature
1   teaspoon (4 grams) vanilla extract
1   cup (200 grams) chopped fresh pineapple

4   cups (1,000 grams) Cream Cheese Frosting (recipe follows)
Pineapple-Pecan Filling (recipe follows)

1. Preheat oven to 350°F (180°C). Butter 3 (8-inch) round cake pans. Line bottom of pans with parchment paper.
2. In a large bowl, sift together flour, sugar, cinnamon, baking soda, salt, and nutmeg; stir in pecans.
3. In a small bowl, stir together oil, banana, eggs, and vanilla. Add oil mixture to flour mixture, stirring just until moistened. Fold in pineapple. Divide batter among prepared pans.
4. Bake until a wooden pick inserted in center comes out clean, 20 to 25 minutes. Let cool in pans for 10 minutes. Remove from pans, and let cool completely on wire racks.
5. Place a cooled cake layer on a cake plate. Place 1 cup (250 grams) Cream Cheese Frosting in a pastry bag fitted with a ½-inch round piping tip. (Alternatively, cut a ½-inch opening in tip of pastry bag.) Pipe around edge of cake layer. Spread half of Pineapple-Pecan Filling (about 300 grams) on layer inside piped border. Top with second cake layer, and pipe border around edge. Spread remaining Pineapple-Pecan Filling inside piped border. Top

with remaining cake layer. Spread a thin layer of Cream Cheese Frosting on top and sides of cake to create a crumb coat. Refrigerate until filling is set, 30 to 45 minutes. Cover and refrigerate remaining frosting.
6. Using a spatula, fold remaining frosting until smooth and workable. Spread frosting on top and lightly on sides of cake. Using a bench scraper, smooth sides until desired amount of frosting is left. Cover and refrigerate for at least 2 hours or up to overnight before serving.

We used Bob's Red Mill Gluten Free 1-to-1 Baking Flour.

CREAM CHEESE FROSTING
Makes about 6 cups

16 ounces (454 grams) cream cheese, softened
½   cup (113 grams) unsalted butter, softened
1   teaspoon (4 grams) vanilla extract
1   (2-pound) package (907 grams) confectioners' sugar

1. In the bowl of a stand mixer fitted with the paddle attachment, beat cream cheese and butter at medium-low speed until smooth and creamy, about 1 minute. Add vanilla, beating until combined. With mixer on low speed, gradually add confectioners' sugar, beating until combined. Increase mixer speed to medium, and beat until fluffy, about 1 minute.

PINEAPPLE-PECAN FILLING
Makes 2½ cups

2   cups (500 grams) Cream Cheese Frosting (recipe precedes)
½   cup (57 grams) finely chopped toasted pecans
⅓   cup (67 grams) finely chopped fresh pineapple, patted dry

1. In a medium bowl, gently stir together Cream Cheese Frosting, pecans, and pineapple until combined.

FROSTING 411

1. Place a cooled cake layer on a cake plate. Place 1 cup (250 grams) Cream Cheese Frosting in a pastry bag fitted with a ½-inch round piping tip. (Alternatively, cut a ½-inch opening in tip of pastry bag.) Pipe a border around edge of cake layer. Think of this piped border as a sweet dam. This border will keep your filling from spilling out and seeping into the frosting on the outside of the cake.

2. Spread half of Pineapple-Pecan Filling on layer inside piped border. You want to smooth down the filling slightly so your cake layers will stack evenly. Our tools of choice? An offset spatula or a straight-sided icing spatula.

3. Top with second cake layer, and pipe a border around edge. Spread remaining Pineapple-Pecan Filling inside piped border. Top with remaining cake layer. As you place your second cake layer on top of the first, press it down lightly on top to make sure everything is even and level.

4. Spread a thin layer of Cream Cheese Frosting on top and sides of cake to create a crumb coat. A crumb coat is the baker's term for a thin coat of frosting spread over a cake that is then refrigerated before being frosted with the final, thicker layer of frosting. The crumb coat helps keep any crumbs from getting into the final coat and fills any gaps where the border missed.

5. Refrigerate until filling is set, 30 to 45 minutes. Cover and refrigerate remaining frosting. Chilling your cake allows the filling to set and helps firm up the crumb coat, making it easier to frost. You also need to refrigerate your frosting, as it will get too soft at room temperature while the cake chills.

6. Using a spatula, fold remaining frosting until smooth and workable. This just ensures that the frosting is an even consistency and smooth before working with it on the cake.

7. Spread frosting on top and lightly on sides of cake. Using a bench scraper, smooth edges until desired amount of frosting is left. Use an offset spatula or straight-sided icing spatula to apply the frosting in generous swaths. Then switch to a bench scraper to smooth and scrape down the sides. The bench scraper will leave the frosting in an even layer all the way around, as well as make the sides straight.

8. Cover and refrigerate for at least 2 hours or up to overnight before serving. A last chill in the refrigerator will further set up your smooth frosting and pineapple-rich filling.

BANANA-BLUEBERRY OAT CAKE

Makes 1 (9-inch) cake

Oats in cake? Prepare to have your mind blown. Quick-cooking oats bring a revolutionary delicate crumb to this banana- and blueberry-packed layer cake. For a bright, tangy finish, we blanketed our cake with a smooth Buttermilk Frosting.

1	cup (227 grams) unsalted butter, softened
2½	cups (500 grams) granulated sugar
4	large eggs (200 grams), room temperature
1	tablespoon (13 grams) vanilla extract
2¾	cups (344 grams) plus 1½ tablespoons (12 grams) all-purpose flour, divided
¾	cup (68 grams) oat flour
⅓	cup (27 grams) quick-cooking oats
2	teaspoons (10 grams) baking powder
2	teaspoons (10 grams) baking soda
1¼	teaspoons (3.75 grams) kosher salt
½	teaspoon (1 gram) ground cinnamon
¼	teaspoon ground ginger
2	cups (472 grams) mashed ripe banana
1	cup (240 grams) whole buttermilk, room temperature
1½	cups (246 grams) fresh blueberries

Buttermilk Frosting (recipe follows)
Garnish: fresh blueberries, banana slices, toasted
    quick-cooking oats (see Note)

1. Preheat oven to 350°F (180°C). Spray 2 (9-inch) round cake pans with baking spray with flour. Line bottom of pans with parchment paper.

2. In the bowl of a stand mixer fitted with the paddle attachment, beat butter and sugar at medium speed until fluffy, 3 to 4 minutes, stopping to scrape sides of bowl. Add eggs, one at a time, beating well after each addition. Beat in vanilla.

3. In a large bowl, whisk together 2¾ cups (344 grams) all-purpose flour, oat flour, oats, baking powder, baking soda, salt, cinnamon, and ginger. In a medium bowl, whisk together mashed banana and buttermilk. With mixer on low speed, gradually add flour mixture to butter mixture alternately with banana mixture, beginning and ending with flour mixture, beating just until combined after each addition.

4. In another medium bowl, toss together blueberries and remaining 1½ tablespoons (12 grams) all-purpose flour; fold blueberry mixture into batter until well combined. Divide batter between prepared pans. Tap pans on a kitchen towel-lined counter several times to settle batter and release any air bubbles.

5. Bake until a wooden pick inserted in center comes out clean, about 50 minutes, rotating pans halfway through baking and loosely covering with foil to prevent excess browning, if necessary. Let cool in pans for 10 minutes. Remove from pans, and let cool completely on wire racks.

6. Level cooled cake layers, if desired; discard parchment. Place a cake layer on a serving plate. Spoon 2½ cups (about 430 grams) Buttermilk Frosting into a large pastry bag fitted with a ½-inch round piping tip (Wilton 1A). Pipe frosting evenly on top of cake layer; smooth with a small offset spatula. Top with remaining cake layer. Spoon 2½ cups (about 430 grams) frosting into pastry bag, and pipe evenly on top of cake; smooth into an even layer.

7. Spoon remaining frosting into pastry bag, and pipe all over sides of cake; holding a bench scraper or a large offset spatula flush against sides of cake, scrape off excess frosting until sides are smooth and layers are somewhat exposed. Pile excess frosting on top of cake; using the back of a spoon or a large offset spatula, spread and swirl frosting as desired. Using a bench scraper or a large offset spatula held flush against cake layers, scrape frosting again to give sides a smooth, finished look. Garnish with blueberries, banana slices, and toasted oats, if desired.

Note: *For toasted quick-cooking oats, preheat oven to 350°F (180°C). Place oats on a parchment-lined baking sheet. Bake until lightly toasted, about 10 minutes, stirring occasionally. Let cool completely on pan on a wire rack.*

BUTTERMILK FROSTING
Makes about 7 cups

2	cups (454 grams) unsalted butter, softened
½	teaspoon (1.5 grams) kosher salt
1	(2-pound) package (907 grams) confectioners' sugar
½	cup (120 grams) whole buttermilk
2	teaspoons (8 grams) vanilla extract

1. In the bowl of a stand mixer fitted with the paddle attachment, beat butter and salt at medium speed until creamy, about 1 minute, stopping to scrape sides of bowl. With mixer on low speed, gradually add confectioners' sugar alternately with buttermilk, beginning and ending with confectioners' sugar, beating just until combined after each addition. Beat in vanilla. Increase mixer speed to medium, and beat until light and fluffy, about 2 minutes, stopping to scrape sides of bowl. Use immediately.

GLUTEN-FREE CHOCOLATE CAKE

Makes 1 (8-inch) cake

Behold the perfect chocolate cake that just happens to be gluten-free! Sporting a groundbreaking gluten-free flour blend, this cake has all the tenderness of a traditional one and still packs rich chocolate flavor. The cake offers decadence and dynamic texture for the ultimate gluten-free experience.

1	cup (200 grams) granulated sugar	
1	cup (227 grams) unsalted butter, melted	
1	cup (240 grams) unsweetened applesauce	
½	cup (170 grams) maple syrup	
5	large eggs (250 grams), room temperature and lightly beaten	
2	teaspoons (8 grams) vanilla extract	
1¼	cups (185 grams) gluten-free baking flour*	
¾	cup (72 grams) super-fine almond flour*	
¾	cup (64 grams) Dutch process cocoa powder	
½	cup (30 grams) gluten-free oat flour*	
¼	cup (28 grams) coconut flour*	
1	teaspoon (5 grams) baking powder	
1	teaspoon (5 grams) baking soda	
1	teaspoon (3 grams) kosher salt	
1	cup (240 grams) whole buttermilk	

Swiss Buttercream (recipe follows)

1. Preheat oven to 350°F (180°C). Line bottoms of 2 (8-inch) round cake pans with parchment paper; spray parchment and sides of pan with cooking spray.

2. In a large bowl, whisk together sugar, melted butter, applesauce, and maple syrup. Whisk in eggs and vanilla.

3. In a medium bowl, whisk together baking flour, almond flour, cocoa, oat flour, coconut flour, baking powder, baking soda, and salt. Sift flour mixture once. Gradually add flour mixture to sugar mixture alternately with buttermilk, whisking just until combined after each addition. Divide batter between prepared pans.

4. Bake until a wooden pick inserted in center comes out clean, 40 to 45 minutes. Let cool in pans for 15 minutes. Remove from pans, and let cool completely on wire racks.

5. Level cooled cake layers, reserving tops. Place a cake layer on a cake stand. Spread 1¾ cups (315 grams) Swiss Buttercream on cake layer, smoothing with an offset spatula. Top with remaining cake layer. Spread remaining buttercream on top and sides of cake. Crumble reserved cake tops; sprinkle onto buttercream as desired. Cover and refrigerate until ready to serve. Let stand at room temperature for 30 minutes before serving.

We used Bob's Red Mill Gluten Free 1-to-1 Baking Flour, Bob's Red Mill Super-Fine Almond Flour, Bob's Red Mill Gluten Free Oat Flour, and Bob's Red Mill Organic Coconut Flour.

SWISS BUTTERCREAM
Makes about 5 cups

1¾	cups (350 grams) granulated sugar	
¾	cup (180 grams) egg whites (about 6 large egg whites)	
2	cups (454 grams) unsalted butter, softened	
1	teaspoon (4 grams) vanilla extract	
¼	teaspoon kosher salt	

1. In the top of a double boiler, combine sugar and egg whites. Cook over simmering water, whisking occasionally, until an instant-read thermometer registers 120°F (49°C) to 130°F (54°C).

2. Carefully transfer sugar mixture to the bowl of a stand mixer fitted with the whisk attachment. Beat at high speed until stiff peaks form and bowl is cool to the touch, 7 to 8 minutes. Add butter, 2 tablespoons (28 grams) at a time, beating until combined after each addition. (If buttercream breaks, beat for 2 to 3 minutes, and emulsion will come back together.) Beat in vanilla and salt. Use immediately, or refrigerate in an airtight container for up to 3 days. If refrigerating, let come to room temperature and rewhip before using.

SWEET POTATO CAKE WITH MASCARPONE BUTTERCREAM

Makes 1 (9-inch) cake

Richly spiced and packing a helping of walnuts and cranberries, this layer cake has moist texture due to the grated sweet potato folded into the batter. A silky Mascarpone Buttercream wraps the cake up in a smooth coat that complements the nut- and fruit-laden cake.

3½ cups (376 grams) grated peeled sweet potato (about 3 medium sweet potatoes)
1¾ cups (350 grams) granulated sugar
1 cup (214 grams) vegetable oil
4 large eggs (200 grams), room temperature
2 teaspoons (8 grams) vanilla extract
2 cups (250 grams) plus 1 tablespoon (8 grams) all-purpose flour, divided
2 teaspoons (10 grams) baking powder
2 teaspoons (4 grams) ground cinnamon
1½ teaspoons (3 grams) ground ginger
1 teaspoon (5 grams) baking soda
1 teaspoon (3 grams) kosher salt
½ teaspoon (1 gram) ground allspice
⅔ cup (102 grams) lightly packed dried sweetened cranberries, plumped (see Note), drained, and chopped
⅔ cup (75 grams) finely chopped toasted walnuts
½ cup (88 grams) finely chopped candied ginger
Mascarpone Buttercream (recipe follows)
Garnish: chopped candied ginger, chopped dried sweetened cranberries, fresh thyme sprigs

1. Preheat oven to 325°F (170°C). Spray 2 (9-inch) round cake pans with baking spray with flour. Line bottom of pans with parchment paper.
2. In the bowl of a stand mixer fitted with the paddle attachment, beat sweet potato, sugar, oil, eggs, and vanilla at medium-low speed until well combined, about 2 minutes, stopping to scrape sides of bowl.
3. In a medium bowl, whisk together 2 cups (250 grams) flour, baking powder, cinnamon, ground ginger, baking soda, salt, and allspice until well combined. With mixer on low speed, gradually add flour mixture to sweet potato mixture, beating until combined and stopping to scrape sides of bowl.
4. In a small bowl, stir together cranberries, walnuts, candied ginger, and remaining 1 tablespoon (8 grams) flour. Fold cranberry mixture into batter. Divide batter between prepared pans. Tap pans on a kitchen towel-lined counter 3 to 4 times to settle batter.
5. Bake until a wooden pick inserted in center comes out clean, 35 to 40 minutes. Let cool in pans for 10 minutes. Run a knife around edges of cakes to loosen; remove from pans, and let cool completely, parchment side down, on a wire rack.
6. Level cooled cake layers; discard parchment. Place a cake layer on a cake stand or serving plate on a turntable; spoon 2 cups (about 378 grams) Mascarpone Buttercream onto cake layer, smoothing with a large offset spatula. Top with remaining cake layer, cut side down. Spread remaining Mascarpone Buttercream on top and sides of cake. Garnish with candied ginger, cranberries, and thyme, if desired. Refrigerate for 30 minutes to 1 hour before serving.

Note: *To plump dried sweetened cranberries, place them in a small heatproof bowl, and add enough hot water to completely submerge. Let stand until slightly softened and plumped, 15 to 20 minutes. Drain thoroughly before using.*

MASCARPONE BUTTERCREAM
Makes about 7 cups

2 cups (454 grams) unsalted butter, softened (see Notes)
4 cups (480 grams) confectioners' sugar
4 teaspoons (20 grams) heavy whipping cream
2 teaspoons (8 grams) vanilla extract
¼ teaspoon kosher salt
16 ounces (454 grams) mascarpone cheese, softened (see Notes)

1. In the bowl of a stand mixer fitted with the paddle attachment, beat butter at medium speed until creamy, about 1 minute, stopping to scrape sides of bowl. With mixer on low speed, gradually add confectioners' sugar, beating just until combined. Beat in cream, vanilla, and salt; increase mixer speed to medium, and beat until fluffy, 2 to 4 minutes, stopping to scrape sides of bowl. Fold in mascarpone by hand just until combined. (Do not overmix; mascarpone will start to break down.) Use immediately.

Notes: *For best results, it's important that the butter and mascarpone are both softened and at about the same temperature. An instant-read thermometer inserted into the center of each is an easy way to gauge when they're ready to go. Our butter and mascarpone were at about 65°F (18°C).*

Try to handle the buttercream as little as possible; overworking it on your cake could cause the mascarpone to start breaking down.

PEANUT BUTTER-CHOCOLATE MARBLE CAKE

Makes 1 (8-inch) cake

This peanut butter layer cake looks worthy of the bakery case, and the stir-together layers come together so easily.

1½ cups (330 grams) firmly packed light brown sugar
⅔ cup (150 grams) unsalted butter, melted
½ cup (128 grams) creamy peanut butter
3 large eggs (150 grams), room temperature
1½ teaspoons (6 grams) vanilla extract
2¼ cups (281 grams) all-purpose flour
2½ teaspoons (12.5 grams) baking powder
1 teaspoon (3 grams) kosher salt
½ teaspoon (2.5 grams) baking soda
1½ cups (360 grams) whole buttermilk, room temperature
⅔ cup (113 grams) chopped 66% cacao dark chocolate, melted and cooled slightly
Chocolate Cream Cheese Frosting (recipe follows)

1. Preheat oven to 350°F (180°C). Spray 2 (8-inch) round cake pans with baking spray with flour. Line bottom of pans with parchment paper.
2. In a large bowl, whisk together brown sugar, melted butter, and peanut butter until combined and creamy. Add eggs and vanilla, whisking just until combined.
3. In a medium bowl, whisk together flour, baking powder, salt, and baking soda. Gradually add flour mixture to sugar mixture alternately with buttermilk, beginning and ending with flour mixture, whisking just until combined after each addition. Transfer one-third of batter (about 2 cups [454 grams]) to a medium bowl; gently fold in melted chocolate until combined. Using 2 (2-tablespoon) spring-loaded scoops, alternately scoop peanut butter and chocolate batters into prepared pans. (Each pan will get about 2 cups [about 453 grams] peanut butter batter and about 1 cup [about 283 grams] chocolate batter). Using a wooden pick, swirl batters together. Gently tap pans on a kitchen towel-lined counter 2 to 3 times.
4. Bake until a wooden pick inserted in center comes out clean, 35 to 40 minutes. Let cool in pans for 10 minutes. Remove from pans, and let cool completely on wire racks.
5. Place a cooled cake layer on a cake stand. Spread 1½ cups (about 375 grams) Chocolate Cream Cheese Frosting on cake layer. Top with remaining cake layer. Spread remaining frosting on top and sides of cake. Cover and refrigerate until ready to serve.

CHOCOLATE CREAM CHEESE FROSTING
Makes about 5 cups

16 ounces (454 grams) cream cheese, softened
1 cup (227 grams) unsalted butter, softened
1 teaspoon (4 grams) vanilla extract
½ teaspoon (1.5 grams) kosher salt
4½ cups (540 grams) confectioners' sugar
1 cup (85 grams) Dutch process cocoa powder

1. In the bowl of a stand mixer fitted with the paddle attachment, beat cream cheese and butter at medium-low speed until smooth and creamy, about 1 minute. Beat in vanilla and salt until combined.
2. Sift together confectioners' sugar and cocoa. With mixer on low speed, slowly add sugar mixture, about ¾ cup (about 90 grams) at a time, to cream cheese mixture, beating until combined after each addition and stopping to scrape sides of bowl. Increase mixer speed to medium, and beat until light in color and fluffy, 2 to 3 minutes, stopping to scrape sides of bowl.

IRISH SPONGE CAKE WITH STRAWBERRY PRESERVES AND CREAM

Makes 1 (8-inch) cake

The Irish have elevated the base recipe of Victoria sponge cake—in prominent circulation since Queen Victoria's reign—with their classic Irish ingredients of excellent butter from County Kerry and the sweet strawberry preserves of County Wexford.

1¾   cups (219 grams) self-rising flour
4   large eggs (200 grams), room temperature
1   cup (200 grams) plus 2 tablespoons (24 grams) castor sugar, divided
1   cup (227 grams) unsalted butter, room temperature (see Note)
1   cup (240 grams) cold heavy whipping cream
1   teaspoon (6 grams) vanilla bean paste
1   cup (320 grams) strawberry preserves
Confectioners' sugar, for dusting
Garnish: halved fresh strawberries

1. Preheat oven to 350°F (180°C). Butter 2 (8-inch) round cake pans. Line bottom of pans with parchment paper.
2. In the bowl of a stand mixer fitted with the paddle attachment, beat flour, eggs, 1 cup (200 grams) castor sugar, and butter at low speed just until combined. Increase mixer speed to medium, and beat until well combined, about 1 minute, stopping to scrape sides of bowl. Divide batter between prepared pans, smoothing tops with a small offset spatula. Tap pans on a kitchen towel-lined counter several times to release any air bubbles, smoothing tops again, if necessary.
3. Bake until golden brown and a wooden pick inserted in center comes out clean, about 20 minutes. Let cool in pans for 10 minutes. Remove from pans, and let cool completely, parchment side down, on wire racks.
4. In a large chilled bowl, whisk together cold cream, vanilla bean paste, and remaining 2 tablespoons (24 grams) castor sugar by hand until stiff peaks form.
5. Level cooled cake layers, if desired; discard parchment. Place a cake layer on a cake plate. Tuck strips of parchment paper under layer.
6. In a small bowl, whisk preserves until mostly smooth. Using a small offset spatula, spread ½ cup (160 grams) preserves on top of cake layer. Carefully spoon whipped cream onto preserves, spreading into an even layer.
7. Spread remaining ½ cup (160 grams) preserves on bottom of remaining cake layer; place, preserves side down, on top of whipped cream.
8. Using a small fine-mesh sieve, dust confectioners' sugar on top of cake in an even layer; carefully remove parchment paper strips. Dust with confectioners' sugar and garnish with strawberries, if desired.

Note: *Unlike softened butter, room temperature butter should provide no resistance when pressed with a finger. At this point, the butter is softened enough to easily incorporate into your cake batter.*

ALMOND-CRANBERRY CAKE

Makes 1 (9-inch) cake

Tart cranberries and nutty almond extract give the simple 1-2-3-4 cake a boost of bright holiday flavor. The Sugared Cranberries garnish serves a dual purpose, creating a beautiful holiday topping as well as a simple syrup that you'll brush onto your cake layers to make them extra-tender.

1	cup (227 grams) unsalted butter, softened
2	cups (400 grams) granulated sugar
4	large eggs (200 grams), room temperature
2	teaspoons (10 grams) tightly packed orange zest
¾	teaspoon (3 grams) vanilla extract
¾	teaspoon (3 grams) almond extract
3	cups (375 grams) cake flour
1	tablespoon (15 grams) baking powder
½	teaspoon (1.5 grams) kosher salt
1	cup (240 grams) whole milk, room temperature
1½	cups (165 grams) fresh or frozen cranberries
½	cup (140 grams) simple syrup, reserved from Sugared Cranberries (recipe follows)

Almond Buttercream (recipe follows)
Garnish: sliced lightly toasted almonds, Sugared Cranberries (recipe follows)

1. Preheat oven to 350°F (180°C). Spray 2 (9-inch) round cake pans with baking spray with flour.
2. In the bowl of a stand mixer fitted with the paddle attachment, beat butter and sugar at medium speed until fluffy, 3 to 4 minutes, stopping to scrape sides of bowl. Add eggs, one at a time, beating well after each addition. Beat in orange zest and extracts.
3. In a medium bowl, whisk together flour, baking powder, and salt. With mixer on low speed, gradually add flour mixture to butter mixture alternately with milk, beginning and ending with flour mixture, beating just until combined after each addition. Transfer half of batter (about 323 grams) to a large bowl; fold in half of fresh or frozen cranberries. Fold remaining fresh or frozen cranberries into remaining batter in mixer bowl. Pour into prepared pans, smoothing tops with an offset spatula.
4. Bake until a wooden pick inserted in center comes out clean, 35 to 40 minutes. Let cool in pans for 10 minutes. Remove from pans, and let cool completely on wire racks.
5. Trim cooled cake layers flat, and brush each with simple syrup. Spread 2 cups (490 grams) Almond Buttercream between layers. Spread remaining buttercream on top and sides of cake. Garnish with almonds and Sugared Cranberries, if desired.

SUGARED CRANBERRIES
Makes 1 cup

1	cup (200 grams) granulated sugar, divided
½	cup (120 grams) water
1	cup (110 grams) fresh cranberries

1. In a medium saucepan, heat ½ cup (100 grams) sugar and ½ cup (120 grams) water over medium heat, stirring occasionally, just until sugar dissolves. Let cool slightly.
2. Stir cranberries into syrup. Remove cranberries using a slotted spoon, and let excess drip off. Place on a sheet of parchment paper, and let dry for 1 hour. Reserve ½ cup (140 grams) simple syrup for Almond-Cranberry Cake.
3. Toss together cranberries and remaining ½ cup (100 grams) sugar.

ALMOND BUTTERCREAM
Makes about 6 cups

2	cups (454 grams) unsalted butter, softened
½	teaspoon (1.5 grams) kosher salt
1	(2-pound) package (907 grams) confectioners' sugar
½	cup (120 grams) cold heavy whipping cream
¼	teaspoon (1 gram) almond extract

1. In the bowl of a stand mixer fitted with the paddle attachment, beat butter and salt at medium-low speed until smooth. With mixer on low speed, add confectioners' sugar, about 1 cup (120 grams) at a time, alternately with cold cream, about 1 tablespoon (15 grams) at a time, beating until smooth after each addition. Increase mixer speed to medium, and beat until smooth and fluffy, 1 to 2 minutes. Add almond extract, and beat until combined.

CHOCOLATE-COFFEE MAYO CAKE

Makes 1 (9-inch) cake

Mayonnaise gives this coffee-boosted chocolate cake a luxurious crumb unlike any other while a dreamy chocolate frosting doubles down on the decadence.

1⅓ cups (320 grams) hot strong brewed coffee
¾ cup (64 grams) unsweetened cocoa powder
1⅔ cups (367 grams) firmly packed light brown sugar
3 large eggs (150 grams), room temperature
1 cup (206 grams) mayonnaise*, room temperature
2½ cups (250 grams) sifted cake flour*
1¼ teaspoons (6.25 grams) baking soda
½ teaspoon (1.5 grams) kosher salt
¼ teaspoon (1.25 grams) baking powder
Creamy Chocolate Frosting (recipe follows)

1. Preheat oven to 350°F (180°C). Spray 2 (9-inch) round cake pans with baking spray with flour. Line bottom of pans with parchment paper.

2. In a 2-cup glass measuring cup, whisk together coffee and cocoa until completely combined. Let stand until mostly cooled, about 30 minutes.
3. In the bowl of a stand mixer, beat brown sugar and eggs at high speed until light and fluffy, stopping to scrape sides of bowl. Add mayonnaise, and beat until combined.
4. In a large bowl, sift together flour, baking soda, salt, and baking powder. With mixer on low speed, gradually add flour mixture to sugar mixture alternately with coffee mixture, beginning and ending with flour mixture, beating just until combined after each addition. Divide batter between prepared pans.
5. Bake until a wooden pick inserted in center comes out clean, 28 to 35 minutes. Let cool in pans for 10 minutes. Remove from pans, and let cool completely on wire racks.
6. Level cooled cake layers, if desired; discard parchment. Place a cake layer on a cake plate. Spread 1½ cups (412 grams) Creamy Chocolate Frosting on cake layer; top with remaining cake layer. Spread remaining frosting on top and sides of cake.

We used Blue Plate Mayonnaise and Swans Down Cake Flour.

CREAMY CHOCOLATE FROSTING
Makes about 5 cups

8 ounces (227 grams) 60% cacao bittersweet chocolate, finely chopped
¾ cup (170 grams) unsalted butter, cubed
7½ cups (900 grams) confectioners' sugar, sifted
1 cup (240 grams) sour cream, room temperature
1½ teaspoons (6 grams) vanilla extract

1. In the top of a double boiler, combine chocolate and butter. Cook over simmering water, stirring occasionally, until melted and smooth. Remove from heat; let cool for 5 minutes.
2. In the bowl of a stand mixer, beat confectioners' sugar, sour cream, and vanilla at low speed until smooth and well combined, stopping to scrape sides of bowl. Gradually beat in chocolate mixture until well combined, stopping to scrape sides of bowl. Increase mixer speed to medium, and beat until fluffy, about 2 minutes. Use immediately.

VANILLA LAYER CAKE WITH CREAMY VANILLA FROSTING

Makes 1 (9-inch) cake

Vanilla takes center stage in this showstopping naked layer cake, imparting bold, rich vanilla flavor to every bite. From the tender vanilla cake to that vanilla bean seed-speckled buttercream, this recipe proves that the simple things in life are sweetest.

1¼   cups (284 grams) unsalted butter, softened
2½   cups (500 grams) granulated sugar
5   large eggs (250 grams), room temperature
1½   tablespoons (19.5 grams) vanilla extract*
3¾   cups (469 grams) unbleached cake flour
1¾   teaspoons (8.75 grams) baking powder
1   teaspoon (3 grams) kosher salt
½   teaspoon (2.5 grams) baking soda
1½   cups (360 grams) whole buttermilk, room temperature
Creamy Vanilla Frosting (recipe follows)

1. Preheat oven to 350°F (180°C). Spray 2 (9-inch) round cake pans with baking spray with flour. Line bottom of pans with parchment paper.

2. In the bowl of a stand mixer fitted with the paddle attachment, beat butter and sugar at medium speed until fluffy, 3 to 4 minutes, stopping to scrape sides of bowl. Add eggs, one at a time, beating well after each addition. Beat in vanilla.

3. In a large bowl, whisk together flour, baking powder, salt, and baking soda. With mixer on low speed, gradually add flour mixture to butter mixture alternately with buttermilk, beginning and ending with flour mixture, beating until well combined after each addition. Divide batter between prepared pans, smoothing tops with a small offset spatula. Forcefully tap pans on a kitchen towel-lined counter several times to settle batter and release any air bubbles.

4. Bake until a wooden pick inserted in center comes out clean, about 35 minutes. Let cool in pans for 10 minutes. Remove from pans, and let cool completely, parchment side down, on wire racks.

5. Level cooled cake layers, if desired; discard parchment. Place a cake layer on a serving plate. Spoon 2½ cups (about 496 grams) Creamy Vanilla Frosting into a large pastry bag fitted with a ½-inch round piping tip (Wilton 1A). Pipe frosting evenly onto cake layer; using a small offset spatula, smooth into an even layer. Top with remaining cake layer. Spoon 2½ cups (about 496 grams) frosting into pastry bag. Pipe evenly on top of cake; using a small offset spatula, smooth into an even layer.

6. Spoon remaining frosting into pastry bag. Pipe all over sides of cake; holding a bench scraper or a large offset spatula against sides of cake, scrape off excess frosting until sides are smooth and layers are somewhat exposed. Pile excess frosting on top of cake; using the back of a spoon or a large offset spatula, spread and swirl frosting as desired. Using a bench scraper or a large offset spatula held against sides of cake, scrape frosting one more time to give sides a smooth, finished look.

*We used Heilala Pure Vanilla Extract.

CREAMY VANILLA FROSTING
Makes about 7 cups

2   cups (454 grams) unsalted butter, softened
½   teaspoon (1.5 grams) kosher salt
1   (2-pound) package (907 grams) confectioners' sugar
½   cup (120 grams) heavy whipping cream
1   tablespoon (18 grams) vanilla bean paste

1. In the bowl of a stand mixer fitted with the paddle attachment, beat butter and salt at medium speed until creamy, about 1 minute, stopping to scrape sides of bowl. With mixer on low speed, gradually add confectioners' sugar alternately with cream, beginning and ending with confectioners' sugar, beating just until combined after each addition. Beat in vanilla bean paste. Increase mixer speed to medium; beat until fluffy, about 2 minutes. Use immediately.

HOT CHOCOLATE MARSHMALLOW CAKE

Makes 1 (8-inch) cake

For this cake take on hot chocolate, we envisioned a cake packed with cocoa flavor in the form of rich chocolate cake layers and even richer Chocolate Meringue Buttercream. In order to do this, we had to adjust the 1-2-3-4 formula slightly, decreasing the flour to 2½ cups and making up the ½-cup deficit with cocoa powder. The final touches—a marshmallow-like Italian Meringue blanket and warming dose of coffee liqueur brushed onto the baked cake layers—bring the comfort of a cup of cocoa to the cake stand.

¾ cup (180 grams) whole milk, room temperature
3 tablespoons (30 grams) hot chocolate cocoa powder*
½ cup (120 grams) plus 3 tablespoons (45 grams) coffee liqueur*, divided
1 cup (227 grams) unsalted butter, softened
2 cups (400 grams) granulated sugar
4 large eggs (200 grams), room temperature
2 teaspoons (8 grams) vanilla extract
2½ cups (312 grams) cake flour
½ cup (43 grams) unsweetened cocoa powder
1 tablespoon (15 grams) baking powder
½ teaspoon (1.5 grams) kosher salt
Chocolate Meringue Buttercream (recipe follows)
4 cups (296 grams) Italian Meringue (recipe follows)

1. Preheat oven to 350°F (180°C). Spray 2 tall-sided 8-inch round cake pans with baking spray with flour.
2. In a small saucepan, heat milk over medium heat until steaming. (Do not boil.) Remove from heat, and whisk in hot chocolate powder until completely dissolved. Whisk in 3 tablespoons (45 grams) liqueur. Let cool slightly.
3. In the bowl of a stand mixer fitted with the paddle attachment, beat butter and sugar at medium speed until fluffy, 3 to 4 minutes, stopping to scrape sides of bowl. Add eggs, one at a time, beating well after each addition. Beat in vanilla.
4. In a medium bowl, whisk together flour, unsweetened cocoa, baking powder, and salt. With mixer on low speed, gradually add flour mixture to butter mixture alternately with milk mixture, beginning and ending with flour mixture, beating just until combined after each addition. Divide batter between prepared pans, smoothing tops with an offset spatula.
5. Bake until a wooden pick inserted in center comes out clean, 28 to 30 minutes. Let cool in pans for 10 minutes. Remove from pans, and let cool completely on wire racks.
6. Trim cooled cake layers flat, and brush layers with remaining ½ cup (120 grams) liqueur. Place a cake layer on a cake plate; spread Chocolate Meringue Buttercream on cake layer, and top with remaining cake layer. Spread Italian Meringue on top and sides

of cake. Using a handheld kitchen torch, carefully brown meringue. Store in an airtight container. Best served same day, but finished cake can be refrigerated for up to 2 days.

*We used Guittard Grand Cacao Drinking Chocolate and Kahlúa.

CHOCOLATE MERINGUE BUTTERCREAM
Makes 1⅔ cups

2 cups (148 grams) Italian Meringue (recipe follows)
⅔ cup (150 grams) unsalted butter, softened and cubed
2 ounces (57 grams) 70% cacao bittersweet chocolate, melted and cooled slightly

1. In the bowl of a stand mixer fitted with the whisk attachment, place Italian Meringue. With mixer on high speed, add butter, about 1 tablespoon (14 grams) at a time, beating until well combined after each addition. Fold in melted chocolate. Use immediately.

ITALIAN MERINGUE
Makes 6 cups

1½ cups (300 grams) granulated sugar
⅓ cup (80 grams) water
⅔ cup (160 grams) egg whites, room temperature (about 5 large egg whites)
¼ teaspoon cream of tartar
½ teaspoon (2 grams) vanilla extract

1. In a small saucepan, combine sugar and ⅓ cup (80 grams) water. Bring to a boil over high heat, being careful not to splash sides of pan, stirring to help sugar dissolve. (Do not stir once mixture starts to boil.) Cook until an instant-read thermometer registers 240°F (116°C).
2. Meanwhile, in the bowl of a stand mixer fitted with the whisk attachment, beat egg whites and cream of tartar at medium speed until soft peaks form.
3. With mixer on medium speed, pour hot sugar syrup between side of bowl and whisk attachment in a slow, steady stream. Increase mixer speed to high, and beat until bowl is cool to the touch, 4 to 5 minutes. Beat in vanilla. Use immediately.

PECAN PIE CAKE

Makes 1 (9-inch) cake

Combining the beloved flavor of a pecan pie with the delicate texture of a 1-2-3-4 layer cake, this cake offers the best of both desserts. Hidden beneath a generous coat of buttercream is a moist cake and a Pecan Pie Filling that'll call to mind your favorite deep-dish dessert.

1   cup (227 grams) unsalted butter, softened
2   cups (440 grams) firmly packed dark brown sugar
4   large eggs (200 grams), room temperature
2   teaspoons (8 grams) vanilla extract
3   cups (375 grams) cake flour
1   tablespoon (15 grams) baking powder
½   teaspoon (1.5 grams) kosher salt
1   cup (240 grams) whole milk, room temperature
Simple Syrup (recipe follows)
Brown Sugar Buttercream (recipe follows)
Pecan Pie Filling (recipe follows)
Garnish: finely chopped lightly toasted pecans

1. Preheat oven to 350°F (180°C). Spray 3 (9-inch) round cake pans with baking spray with flour.
2. In the bowl of a stand mixer fitted with the paddle attachment, beat butter and brown sugar at medium speed until fluffy, 3 to 4 minutes, stopping to scrape sides of bowl. Add eggs, one at a time, beating well after each addition. Beat in vanilla.
3. In a medium bowl, whisk together flour, baking powder, and salt. With mixer on low speed, gradually add flour mixture to butter mixture alternately with milk, beginning and ending with flour mixture, beating just until combined after each addition. Divide batter among prepared pans, smoothing tops with an offset spatula.
4. Bake until a wooden pick inserted in center comes out clean, 25 to 30 minutes. Let cool in pans for 10 minutes. Remove from pans, and let cool completely on wire racks.
5. Place a cooled cake layer on a cake plate. Brush layer with about 2½ tablespoons (45 grams) Simple Syrup. Place ½ cup (95 grams) Brown Sugar Buttercream in a small pastry bag; cut a ½-inch opening in tip. Pipe a border around edge of cake layer. Spoon half of Pecan Pie Filling (about 1¼ cups [about 337 grams]) on cake layer, and gently smooth until even and reaches piped border. Top with second cake layer. Place ½ cup (95 grams) buttercream in pastry bag; pipe a border around edge of cake layer. Spoon remaining Pecan Pie Filling on cake layer, and gently smooth until even and reaches piped border. Top with remaining cake layer, and brush with remaining Simple Syrup. Reserve 1½ cups (285 grams) Brown Sugar Buttercream to decorate top of cake. Spread remaining buttercream on top and sides of cake. Using a cake comb, comb sides of cake. Gently press pecans high on sides of cake and a few at bottom, if desired. Place reserved buttercream in a large pastry bag fitted with a ½-inch open star piping tip (Ateco #824), and pipe a border around edge of cake. Cover and refrigerate until ready to serve. Let come to room temperature before serving.

SIMPLE SYRUP
Makes ½ cup

⅓   cup (67 grams) granulated sugar
⅓   cup (80 grams) water

1. In a medium saucepan, heat sugar and ⅓ cup (80 grams) water over medium heat, stirring occasionally, just until sugar dissolves. Let cool completely before using.

BROWN SUGAR BUTTERCREAM
Makes about 7 cups

1½   cups (330 grams) firmly packed dark brown sugar
1   cup (240 grams) egg whites, room temperature (about 8 large egg whites)
⅔   cup (133 grams) granulated sugar
2⅔   cups (604 grams) unsalted butter, cubed and softened
2   teaspoons (8 grams) vanilla extract
½   teaspoon (1.5 grams) kosher salt

1. In the heatproof bowl of a stand mixer, whisk together brown sugar, egg whites, and granulated sugar by hand. Place bowl over a saucepan of simmering water. Cook, whisking occasionally, until sugars completely dissolve and an instant-read thermometer registers 120°F (49°C) to 130°F (54°C).
2. Carefully return bowl to stand mixer. Using the whisk attachment, beat at high speed until bowl is cool to the touch, about 8 minutes. Add butter, 2 tablespoons (28 grams) at a time, beating until combined after each addition. Beat in vanilla and salt. Use immediately, or refrigerate in an airtight container for up to 3 days. If refrigerating, let stand at room temperature for 2 hours and rewhip until smooth before using.

PECAN PIE FILLING
Makes about 2½ cups

1½   cups (170 grams) chopped pecans
⅔   cup (147 grams) firmly packed dark brown sugar
⅔   cup (226 grams) light corn syrup
⅓   cup (76 grams) unsalted butter, cubed
¼   cup (50 grams) granulated sugar
2   large eggs (100 grams)
1   teaspoon (4 grams) vanilla extract
¼   teaspoon kosher salt

1. In a medium saucepan, stir together all ingredients. Bring to a boil over medium-high heat, stirring frequently. Reduce heat to medium-low; simmer, stirring constantly, until thickened, 6 to 8 minutes. Let cool to room temperature before using.

VANILLA-RED VELVET LAYER CAKE

Makes 1 (8-inch) cake

One part vanilla, one part red velvet, full-on decadence. We adjusted the 1-2-3-4 cake formula slightly for the red velvet batter, replacing ¼ cup flour with ¼ cup cocoa powder. Styled with mesmerizing swirls of Cream Cheese Frosting, this is holiday cheer at its finest.

Vanilla layer:

½	cup (113 grams) unsalted butter, softened
1	cup (200 grams) granulated sugar
2	large eggs (100 grams), room temperature
2	teaspoons (12 grams) vanilla bean paste
1½	cups (187 grams) cake flour
1½	teaspoons (7.5 grams) baking powder
¼	teaspoon kosher salt
½	cup (120 grams) whole milk, room temperature

Red velvet layer:

½	cup (113 grams) unsalted butter, softened
1	cup (200 grams) granulated sugar
2	large eggs (100 grams), room temperature
1	teaspoon (4 grams) vanilla extract
1¼	cups (156 grams) cake flour
¼	cup (21 grams) unsweetened cocoa powder
1½	teaspoons (7.5 grams) baking powder
¼	teaspoon kosher salt
½	cup (120 grams) whole milk, room temperature
1	tablespoon (15 grams) red liquid food coloring

Vanilla Simple Syrup (recipe follows)
Cream Cheese Frosting (recipe follows)

1. Preheat oven to 350°F (180°C). Spray 2 tall-sided 8-inch round cake pans with baking spray wih flour.

2. For vanilla layer: In the bowl of a stand mixer fitted with the paddle attachment, beat butter and sugar at medium speed until fluffy, 3 to 4 minutes, stopping to scrape sides of bowl. Add eggs, one at a time, beating well after each addition. Beat in vanilla bean paste.

3. In a medium bowl, whisk together flour, baking powder, and salt. With mixer on low speed, gradually add flour mixture to butter mixture alternately with milk, beginning and ending with flour mixture, beating just until combined after each addition. Pour batter into a prepared pan, smoothing top with an offset spatula.

4. For red velvet layer: Clean bowl of stand mixer and paddle attachment. Using the paddle attachment, beat butter and sugar at medium speed until fluffy, 3 to 4 minutes, stopping to scrape sides of bowl. Add eggs, one at a time, beating well after each addition. Beat in vanilla extract.

5. In a medium bowl, whisk together flour, cocoa, baking powder, and salt. With mixer on low speed, gradually add flour mixture to butter mixture alternately with milk, beginning and ending with flour mixture, beating just until combined after each addition. Beat in food coloring. Pour batter into remaining prepared pan, smoothing top with an offset spatula.

6. Bake until a wooden pick inserted in center comes out clean, 35 to 40 minutes. Let cool in pans for 10 minutes. Remove from pans, and let cool completely on wire racks.

7. Trim cooled cake layers flat; cut each layer in half horizontally. Place a red velvet cake layer, cut side up, on a cake plate. Brush with 2 tablespoons (36 grams) Vanilla Simple Syrup; spread 1 cup (225 grams) Cream Cheese Frosting on cake layer. Place a vanilla cake layer on top of frosting, and brush with 2 tablespoons (36 grams) simple syrup; spread 1 cup (225 grams) frosting on cake layer. Repeat procedure with remaining red velvet layer. Top with remaining vanilla layer, and brush with remaining Vanilla Simple Syrup. Spread a thin layer of frosting on top and sides of cake to create a crumb coat. Refrigerate until crumb coat is set, about 45 minutes. Cover remaining frosting, and refrigerate until ready to use.

8. Using a spatula, fold remaining frosting until a spreadable consistency is reached. Reserve 3½ cups (788 grams) frosting. Spread remaining frosting on top of cake, swirling as desired. Place reserved frosting in a large pastry bag fitted with a ½-inch open star piping tip (Ateco #824). Pipe 1¼-inch-wide ribbons in a zigzag motion up sides of cake. Refrigerate until ready to serve.

VANILLA SIMPLE SYRUP

Makes about ½ cup

⅓	cup (67 grams) granulated sugar
⅓	cup (80 grams) water
1	teaspoon (4 grams) vanilla extract

1. In a medium saucepan, heat sugar and ⅓ cup (80 grams) water over medium heat, stirring occasionally, just until sugar dissolves. Stir in vanilla. Let cool completely before using.

CREAM CHEESE FROSTING

Makes about 9 cups

3	(8-ounce) packages (680 grams) cream cheese, softened
1½	cups (340 grams) unsalted butter, softened
1	tablespoon (13 grams) vanilla extract
½	teaspoon (1.5 grams) kosher salt
3	pounds (1,362 grams) confectioners' sugar

1. In the bowl of a stand mixer fitted with the paddle attachment, beat cream cheese and butter at medium-low speed until smooth and creamy, about 1 minute. Add vanilla and salt, beating until combined. With mixer on low speed, gradually add confectioners' sugar, beating until combined. Increase mixer speed to medium, and beat until fluffy, about 1 minute.

BUNDT AND
TUBE CAKES

From the fudgy 1966 superstar that kicked off the
Bundt cake craze to a *kugelhopf* fit for royalty, these
Bundt and tube cakes are destined for the spotlight

MILK CHOCOLATE TUNNEL OF FUDGE BUNDT CAKE

Makes 1 (15-cup) Bundt cake

Following its debut at the 1966 Pillsbury Bake-Off®, the Tunnel of Fudge Cake recipe became a hit. Two crucial elements give the "tunnel of fudge center": a large amount of sugar in the batter that prevents the center from completely baking through and nuts that help the batter set around the gooey middle. In our from-scratch take, we used milk chocolate instead of dark and swapped out the original walnuts for pecans.

1¾ cups (397 grams) unsalted butter, softened
1   cup (200 grams) granulated sugar
½   cup (110 grams) firmly packed light brown sugar
6   large eggs (300 grams)
1   teaspoon (4 grams) vanilla extract
1¾ cups (210 grams) confectioners' sugar
2¼ cups (281 grams) all-purpose flour
½   cup (84 grams) sweet ground cocoa*
1   teaspoon (3 grams) kosher salt
2   cups (226 grams) chopped pecans
Milk Chocolate Glaze (recipe follows)

1. Preheat oven to 350°F (180°C).
2. In the bowl of a stand mixer fitted with the paddle attachment, beat butter, granulated sugar, and brown sugar at medium speed until creamy, 3 to 4 minutes, stopping to scrape sides of bowl. Add eggs, one at a time, beating well after each addition. Beat in vanilla. Beat in confectioners' sugar.
3. In a medium bowl, stir together flour, ground cocoa, and salt. Add flour mixture and pecans to butter mixture, and beat at low speed until almost combined. Fold batter by hand just until combined.
4. Spray a 15-cup Bundt pan with baking spray with flour. Spoon batter into prepared pan. Tap pan on a kitchen towel-lined counter 3 to 4 times, and smooth with an offset spatula.
5. Bake until top is set and an instant-read thermometer inserted near center registers at least 160°F (71°C), 50 to 55 minutes. Let cool in pan for 2 hours. Invert cake onto a wire rack, and let cool completely.
6. Pour Milk Chocolate Glaze over cooled cake before serving. Serve slices with additional Milk Chocolate Glaze, if desired.

*We used Guittard Grand Cacao Drinking Chocolate Sweet Ground Cocoa, a mix of Dutch process cocoa powder and ground chocolate.

MILK CHOCOLATE GLAZE
Makes about 1⅔ cups

8   ounces (226 grams) milk chocolate, finely chopped
⅔   cup (160 grams) heavy whipping cream
1   tablespoon (21 grams) light corn syrup
3   tablespoons (42 grams) unsalted butter, cubed and softened

1. In a medium heatproof bowl, place chocolate.
2. In a medium saucepan, heat cream and corn syrup over medium heat just until bubbles form around edges of pan. (Do not boil.) Pour cream mixture over chocolate, and let stand until chocolate is melted, 2 to 3 minutes. Starting in center of bowl and using a rubber spatula, slowly stir mixture until well combined. Add butter, 1 tablespoon (14 grams) at a time, stirring until combined after each addition. Let cool for 10 minutes before using.

Note: *The glaze can be made ahead of time and refrigerated. Reheat in the top of a double boiler until fluid before using.*

BUTTERSCOTCH COFFEE CAKE

Makes 1 (10-inch) tube cake

This coffee cake gets its tender crumb from a rich Butterscotch Sauce mixed into the batter. A crunchy pecan streusel inside the cake and baked on top creates an addictive crunch.

½   cup (113 grams) unsalted butter, melted
2   cups (440 grams) firmly packed light brown sugar, divided
Butterscotch Sauce (recipe follows), divided
2   large eggs (100 grams)
1   teaspoon (4 grams) vanilla extract
2½   cups (313 grams) all-purpose flour
2¼   teaspoons (11.25 grams) baking powder
½   teaspoon (1.5 grams) kosher salt
¾   cup (180 grams) whole buttermilk
1   cup (113 grams) chopped pecans
2   teaspoons (4 grams) ground cinnamon

1. Preheat oven to 350°F (180°C). Spray a 10-inch tube pan with baking spray with flour.
2. In a medium bowl, place melted butter. Whisk in 1 cup (220 grams) brown sugar, ⅔ cup (180 grams) Butterscotch Sauce, eggs, and vanilla.

3. In another medium bowl, whisk together flour, baking powder, and salt. Add flour mixture to butter mixture, whisking until combined. Whisk in buttermilk just until combined.
4. In a small bowl, stir together pecans, cinnamon, and remaining 1 cup (220 grams) brown sugar.
5. Pour two-thirds of batter (about 745 grams) into prepared pan, smoothing with an offset spatula. Sprinkle with half of pecan mixture. Top with remaining batter (about 373 grams), smoothing with an offset spatula. Sprinkle with remaining pecan mixture.
6. Bake until a wooden pick inserted near center comes out clean, 40 to 45 minutes, covering with foil after 30 minutes of baking to prevent excess browning. Let cool in pan for 15 minutes. Remove from pan, and drizzle with Butterscotch Sauce. Serve warm or at room temperature with remaining Butterscotch Sauce.

BUTTERSCOTCH SAUCE

Makes 2 cups

½   cup (113 grams) unsalted butter
1   cup (220 grams) firmly packed light brown sugar
1   teaspoon (6 grams) vanilla bean paste
¼   teaspoon kosher salt
1   cup (240 grams) heavy whipping cream

1. In a small saucepan, melt butter over medium heat. Whisk in brown sugar, vanilla bean paste, and salt until dissolved. Add cream, and bring to a boil. Cook for 3 minutes. Transfer to a small bowl, and let cool to room temperature.

Note: *Butterscotch Sauce can be made ahead of time and stored in the refrigerator. Let it come to room temperature before making the cake or serving. (Alternatively, you can microwave it on high in 10-second intervals, stirring between each, until warm and fluid.)*

CREAM CHEESE POUND CAKE

Makes 1 (10-inch) tube cake

The original pound cake recipes rely on butter to create dense, velvety texture, but Southern bakers have been using cream cheese for years to introduce a new acidic note as well as an added dose of creamy milk fat. To drive home the superior cream cheese flavor, we covered the crisp, golden outer crust with Browned Butter Cream Cheese Glaze.

1½ cups (340 grams) unsalted butter, softened
8   ounces (226 grams) cream cheese, cubed and softened
2¾ cups (550 grams) granulated sugar
6   large eggs (300 grams), room temperature
1   tablespoon (13 grams) vanilla extract
¼   teaspoon (1 gram) almond extract
3   cups (375 grams) unbleached cake flour
1¼ teaspoons (3.75 grams) kosher salt
½   teaspoon (2.5 grams) baking powder
Browned Butter Cream Cheese Glaze (recipe follows)

1. Preheat oven to 325°F (170°C).
2. In the bowl of a stand mixer fitted with the paddle attachment, beat butter at medium speed until smooth and creamy, about 1 minute, stopping to scrape sides of bowl. Add cream cheese, beating until smooth and well combined, about 30 seconds; scrape sides of bowl. With mixer on medium-low speed, add sugar, beating just until combined. Increase mixer speed to medium, and beat until fluffy, about 2 minutes, stopping to scrape sides of bowl. Add eggs, one at a time, beating until well combined after each addition. Beat in extracts. (Mixture may look slightly curdled at this point, but batter will come together.)

3. In a large bowl, whisk together flour, salt, and baking powder. With mixer on low speed, gradually add flour mixture to butter mixture, beating just until combined and stopping to scrape sides of bowl.
4. Spray a 10-inch, straight-sided, light-colored metal tube pan with baking spray with flour. Line bottom of pan with parchment paper. Spoon batter into prepared pan. Forcefully tap pan on a kitchen towel-lined counter several times to settle batter and release as many air bubbles as possible.
5. Bake until a wooden pick inserted near center comes out with a few moist crumbs and an instant-read thermometer registers at least 200°F (93°C), 1 hour and 5 minutes to 1 hour and 15 minutes, loosely covering with foil and rotating pan during last 10 minutes of baking to prevent excess browning. Let cool in pan for 15 minutes. Using a large offset spatula, gently loosen edges of cake; remove from pan, and let cool completely on a wire rack.
6. Discard parchment paper, and transfer cake to a serving platter. Top with Browned Butter Cream Cheese Glaze, spreading and swirling with the back of a spoon as desired.

BROWNED BUTTER CREAM CHEESE GLAZE
Makes about 1 cup

⅓   cup (76 grams) unsalted butter, softened
4   ounces (113 grams) cream cheese, softened
1½ teaspoons (6 grams) vanilla extract
¼   teaspoon kosher salt
1   cup (120 grams) confectioners' sugar

1. In a small skillet, melt butter over medium heat. Cook, stirring frequently, until butter solids are browned and have a nutty aroma, 5 to 7 minutes. Remove from heat; let cool for 5 minutes.
2. In the bowl of a stand mixer fitted with the paddle attachment, beat cream cheese until smooth and creamy, about 2 minutes, stopping to scrape sides of bowl. Beat in vanilla and salt. With mixer on low speed, gradually add confectioners' sugar, beating just until combined. Increase mixer speed to medium-low; add browned butter, beating until well combined and stopping to scrape sides of bowl. Use immediately.

BUTTER PECAN POUND CAKE

Makes 1 (15-cup) Bundt cake

A buttery pound cake packed with nutty pecans, this Bundt is the definition of comfort baked from scratch. Sour cream in the batter gives it an extra-tender crumb while brown sugar brings out the warmth and richness of the pecans. We used both finely chopped pecans and pecan pieces to ensure that each bite of cake held a nutty morsel, big or small.

1½ cups (340 grams) unsalted butter, softened
1⅔ cups (333 grams) granulated sugar
1   cup (220 grams) firmly packed dark brown sugar
7   large eggs (350 grams)
1½ teaspoons (6 grams) vanilla extract
3¼ cups (406 grams) all-purpose flour
1   teaspoon (3 grams) kosher salt
1   cup (240 grams) sour cream
1¼ cups (141 grams) pecan pieces, divided
½   cup (57 grams) plus 2 tablespoons (14 grams) finely chopped pecans, divided
White Icing (recipe follows)

1. Preheat oven to 300°F (150°C).
2. In the bowl of a stand mixer fitted with the paddle attachment, beat butter and sugars at medium speed until fluffy, 6 to 7 minutes, stopping to scrape sides of bowl. Add eggs, one at a time, beating well after each addition. Stir in vanilla.
3. In a medium bowl, sift together flour and salt. With mixer on low speed, gradually add flour mixture to butter mixture alternately with sour cream, beginning and ending with flour mixture, beating just until combined after each addition. Add 1 cup (113 grams) pecan pieces and ½ cup (57 grams) chopped pecans, and beat until evenly distributed.
4. Spray a 15-cup Bundt pan with baking spray with flour. Spoon batter into prepared pan. Tap pan on a kitchen towel-lined counter several times to release any air bubbles. Smooth top.
5. Bake until a wooden pick inserted near center comes out clean, 1 hour and 35 minutes to 1 hour and 45 minutes. Let cool in pan for 20 minutes. Invert cake onto a wire rack, and let cool completely.

6. In a small bowl, combine remaining ¼ cup (28 grams) pecan pieces and remaining 2 tablespoons (14 grams) chopped pecans.
7. Spoon White Icing onto cooled cake; sprinkle pecan mixture on top of icing. Store in an airtight container for up to 3 days.

WHITE ICING
Makes about ⅔ cup

1¼ cups (150 grams) confectioners' sugar
4½ tablespoons (67.5 grams) heavy whipping cream
1   tablespoon (21 grams) light corn syrup

1. In a medium bowl, whisk together all ingredients until smooth.

APPLE DAPPLE CAKE

Makes 1 (15-cup) Bundt cake

A vintage jewel of a recipe, Apple Dapple Cake is "dappled" with apple chunks and soaked in a butter-and-brown sugar sauce while still hot from the oven. Tender and bursting with toffee notes, this richly spiced cake offers a delightfully warm finish to any autumn day.

1⅓ cups (267 grams) granulated sugar
¾ cup (160 grams) vegetable oil
3 large eggs (150 grams), room temperature
⅔ cup (150 grams) unsalted butter, melted
1⅓ cups (293 grams) firmly packed dark brown sugar, divided
1 tablespoon (13 grams) plus 1 teaspoon (4 grams) vanilla extract, divided
3 cups (375 grams) plus 2 tablespoons (16 grams) all-purpose flour, divided
2¼ teaspoons (6.75 grams) kosher salt, divided
1½ teaspoons (3 grams) ground cinnamon
1 teaspoon (5 grams) baking soda
½ teaspoon (1 gram) ground nutmeg
¼ teaspoon ground allspice
¼ teaspoon ground cardamom
3½ cups (438 grams) ⅓- to ½-inch-chopped peeled Golden Delicious apples
1½ cups (170 grams) chopped toasted pecans
¾ cup (170 grams) unsalted butter, softened
¼ cup (60 grams) heavy whipping cream
2 tablespoons (26 grams) dark spiced rum
Garnish: chopped toasted pecans

1. Preheat oven to 350°F (180°C).
2. In the bowl of a stand mixer fitted with the paddle attachment, beat granulated sugar, oil, eggs, melted butter, ⅓ cup (73 grams) brown sugar, and 1 tablespoon (13 grams) vanilla at medium-low speed until well combined, about 2 minutes, stopping to scrape sides of bowl.
3. In a medium bowl, whisk together 3 cups (375 grams) flour, 1¾ teaspoons

(5.25 grams) salt, cinnamon, baking soda, nutmeg, allspice, and cardamom. With mixer on low speed, gradually add flour mixture to sugar mixture, beating until combined and stopping to scrape sides of bowl. (Batter will be quite thick.)
4. In a medium bowl, stir together apples, pecans, and remaining 2 tablespoons (16 grams) flour. Fold apple mixture into batter.
5. Spray a 15-cup Nordic Ware Anniversary Bundt Pan with baking spray with flour. Spoon batter into prepared pan. Tap pan on a kitchen towel-lined counter several times to settle batter and release any air bubbles.
6. Bake until a wooden pick inserted near center comes out clean, 50 minutes to 1 hour, rotating pan halfway through baking and loosely covering with foil to prevent excess browning, if necessary.
7. Meanwhile, in a medium saucepan, combine softened butter, cream, remaining 1 cup (220 grams) brown sugar, and

remaining ½ teaspoon (1.5 grams) salt. Bring to a boil over medium-high heat, stirring frequently; cook, stirring constantly, for 2 minutes. Remove from heat; stir in rum and remaining 1 teaspoon (4 grams) vanilla.
8. Poke hot cake all over with a wooden pick; pour ¾ cup (about 195 grams) butter mixture over top, spreading evenly with a small offset spatula. Let cake cool completely in pan on a wire rack. Transfer remaining butter mixture to a small microwave-safe bowl; cover and refrigerate.
9. When ready to serve, using a small offset spatula, gently loosen cooled cake from center and edges of pan. Remove from pan, and place, flat side up, on a serving plate.
10. Heat remaining butter mixture on high in 10-second intervals, stirring between each, until melted and smooth. Spoon butter mixture over top of cooled cake, smoothing and spreading as needed. Garnish with pecans, if desired.

BASQUE BUNDT CAKE

Makes 1 (10-cup) Bundt cake

The gâteau Basque, a classic French cake filled with luxurious pastry cream, is one of my favorites. When I saw a loaf cake take on the menu at one of my favorite restaurants, Highlands Bar & Grill in Birmingham, Alabama, I was thrilled. When I tasted the cake, I found that rather than having a pastry cream filling, it had the pastry cream mixed right into the batter, and I was inspired to take the innovation one step further with a beautiful Bundt cake. We made a Basque Custard that we then stirred into a plain pound cake base, creating a cake that tastes of pastry cream but has the texture of a tender pound cake.

1½ cups (340 grams) unsalted butter, softened
2   cups (400 grams) granulated sugar
5   large eggs (250 grams), room temperature
3   cups (375 grams) all-purpose flour
1   teaspoon (3 grams) kosher salt
½   teaspoon (1 gram) cream of tartar
1⅔ cups (360 grams) Basque Custard (recipe follows)
Confectioners' sugar, for dusting

1. Preheat oven to 350°F (180°C).
2. In the bowl of a stand mixer fitted with the paddle attachment, beat butter and granulated sugar at low speed just until combined; increase mixer speed to medium, and beat until fluffy, 3 to 4 minutes, stopping to scrape sides of bowl. Add eggs, one at time, beating well after each addition.
3. In a medium bowl, whisk together flour, salt, and cream of tartar. With mixer on low speed, gradually add flour mixture to butter mixture alternately with Basque Custard, beginning and ending with flour mixture, beating just until combined after each addition and stopping to scrape sides of bowl.
4. Spray a 10-cup Bundt pan with baking spray with flour. Spoon and spread batter evenly into prepared pan. Tap pan on a kitchen towel-lined counter a few times to settle batter and release any air bubbles.

5. Bake until golden brown and a wooden pick inserted near center comes out clean, 1 hour to 1 hour and 10 minutes, loosely covering with foil to prevent excess browning, if necessary. Let cool in pan for 10 minutes. Invert cake onto a wire rack. Serve warm or at room temperature. Dust with confectioners' sugar just before serving.

> **PRO TIP**
> If your oven runs hot and browns your cakes easily, try baking your cake at 325°F (170°C) for the same bake time (1 hour to 1 hour and 10 minutes). It'll yield the same results but with a lighter crust.

BASQUE CUSTARD
Makes about 2 cups

2   cups (480 grams) whole milk
1   vanilla bean, split lengthwise, seeds scraped and reserved
⅓   cup (67 grams) granulated sugar
⅓   cup (40 grams) cornstarch
4   large egg yolks (74 grams)
1   large egg (50 grams)
2   tablespoons (16 grams) all-purpose flour
½   teaspoon (1.5 grams) kosher salt

1. Place a fine-mesh sieve over a medium bowl.
2. In a medium saucepan, heat milk and reserved vanilla bean seeds over medium heat until steaming. (Do not boil.)
3. In a medium bowl, whisk together sugar, cornstarch, egg yolks, egg, flour, and salt. Gradually whisk hot milk mixture into sugar mixture. Return mixture to saucepan, and cook, whisking constantly, until bubbly and very thick, 2 to 6 minutes. Strain through prepared sieve. Cover with a piece of plastic wrap, pressing wrap directly onto surface of custard to prevent a skin from forming. Use warm.

POLISH BABKA

Makes 8 to 12 servings

Polish babka is traditionally a round yeasted cake and, thus, destined to end up in the shape of the brilliant Anniversary Bundt Pan. Golden raisins, candied oranges, and dried cranberries are folded into the batter for a fruity sweetness, and a Sparkling Wine Syrup and glaze impart a taste of celebration.

3¾ cups (469 grams) all-purpose flour, divided
⅓   cup (67 grams) granulated sugar
3½ teaspoons (10.5 grams) instant yeast
2   teaspoons (6 grams) kosher salt
1   cup (240 grams) whole milk
¾   cup (170 grams) unsalted butter, cubed and softened
5   large eggs (250 grams), room temperature
1   tablespoon (10 grams) tightly packed orange zest
2   teaspoons (12 grams) vanilla bean paste
⅓   cup (56 grams) lightly packed chopped golden raisins
⅓   cup (55 grams) lightly packed ¼-inch-chopped candied oranges
⅓   cup (52 grams) lightly packed chopped dried sweetened cranberries
Sparkling Wine Syrup (recipe follows)
Confectioners' sugar, for dusting
Sparkling Wine Glaze (recipe follows)

1. In the bowl of a stand mixer fitted with the paddle attachment, beat 1 cup (125 grams) flour, granulated sugar, yeast, and salt at low speed just until combined.
2. In a medium saucepan, heat milk and butter over medium heat, stirring occasionally, until butter is melted and an instant-read thermometer registers 120°F (49°C) to 130°F (54°C). Add warm milk mixture to flour mixture; beat at medium-low speed for 2 minutes, stopping to scrape sides of bowl. Add eggs, orange zest, vanilla bean paste, and remaining 2¾ cups (344 grams) flour; beat at low speed just until combined. Increase mixer speed to high, and beat for 2 minutes, stopping to scrape sides of bowl. (Mixture consistency will be a cross between a thick cake batter and a very wet dough.) Fold in raisins, candied oranges, and cranberries just until combined. Cover with a sheet of greased plastic wrap, and let rise in a warm, draft-free place (75°F/24°C) until doubled in size, about 1 hour.
3. Preheat oven to 350°F (180°C). Spray a 15-cup Nordic Ware Anniversary Bundt Pan with baking spray with flour.

4. Stir down batter, releasing as many air bubbles as possible; spoon batter into prepared pan. Tap pan on a kitchen towel-lined counter several times to settle batter and release any air bubbles. Cover with a sheet of greased plastic wrap, and let rise in a warm, draft-free place (75°F/24°C) until doubled in size, about 30 minutes. (Pan will look quite full, but batter will not overflow while baking.)
5. Bake until golden and an instant-read thermometer inserted near center registers 190°F (88°C), 25 to 35 minutes, rotating pan halfway through baking and loosely covering with foil to prevent excess browning, if necessary. Let cool in pan for 10 minutes. Using a small offset spatula or a butter knife, loosen babka from center of pan; invert onto a wire rack.
6. Pour half of Sparkling Wine Syrup into pan, and carefully return babka to pan. Pour remaining Sparkling Wine Syrup over babka; let stand for 5 minutes. Invert babka onto a lightly greased wire rack placed over a rimmed baking sheet; let cool completely.
7. Dust cooled babka with confectioners' sugar, and serve with Sparkling Wine Glaze.

SPARKLING WINE SYRUP
Makes 2¼ cups

1¼ cups (250 grams) granulated sugar
1⅔ cups (378 grams) dry sparkling white wine, divided

1. In a small saucepan, combine sugar and ⅔ cup (152 grams) wine; cook over medium-high heat, stirring frequently, until mixture just comes to a boil and sugar dissolves. Remove from heat; transfer sugar mixture to a small bowl. Stir in remaining 1 cup (226 grams) wine.

SPARKLING WINE GLAZE
Makes about 1 cup

2½ cups (300 grams) confectioners' sugar
¼   cup (56 grams) dry sparkling white wine
½   teaspoon (1.5 grams) kosher salt

1. In a medium bowl, stir together all ingredients until smooth and well combined. Use immediately.

PEAR-CRÈME FRAÎCHE POUND CAKE

Makes 1 (15-cup) Bundt cake

Delicate Bosc pears stud this beautiful pound cake while crème fraîche enriches the batter and punctuates the tangy glaze. Flecked with vanilla bean seeds and perfumed with almond extract, each bite of this Bundt cake promises complex texture and taste.

1½ cups (340 grams) unsalted butter, softened
2¾ cups (550 grams) granulated sugar
6   large eggs (300 grams), room temperature
2   teaspoons (12 grams) vanilla bean paste
1½ teaspoons (6 grams) almond extract
3   cups (375 grams) all-purpose flour
1½ teaspoons (4.5 grams) kosher salt
½   teaspoon (2.5 grams) baking soda
1¼ cups (300 grams) crème fraîche, room temperature
2½ cups (400 grams) ½-inch-diced Bosc pears* (about 3 large pears)
Vanilla-Crème Fraîche Glaze (recipe follows)

1. Preheat oven to 325°F (170°C).
2. In the bowl of a stand mixer fitted with the paddle attachment, beat butter and sugar at low speed just until combined; increase mixer speed to medium, and beat until fluffy, about 3 minutes, stopping to scrape sides of bowl. Add eggs, one at a time, beating well after each addition and stopping to scrape sides of bowl. Beat in vanilla bean paste and almond extract. (Mixture may look slightly curdled at this point, but batter will come together.)
3. In a medium bowl, whisk together flour, salt, and baking soda. With mixer on low speed, gradually add flour mixture to butter mixture alternately with crème fraîche, beginning and ending with flour mixture, beating just until combined after each addition and stopping to scrape sides of bowl. Fold in pears.
4. Generously spray a 15-cup Nordic Ware Anniversary Bundt Pan with baking spray with flour. Spoon batter into prepared pan. Tap pan on a kitchen towel-lined counter several times to settle batter and release any air bubbles. (Pan will be quite full, but batter will not overflow during baking.)
5. Bake until a wooden pick inserted near center comes out clean and an instant-read thermometer inserted near center registers 205°F (96°C) to 210°F (98°C), 1 hour and 10 minutes to 1 hour and 15 minutes, rotating pan halfway through baking and loosely covering with foil to prevent excess browning, if necessary. Let cool in pan for 20 minutes. Using a small offset spatula, gently loosen cake from center and edges of pan. Invert cake onto a wire rack, and let cool completely.
6. Spoon and spread Vanilla-Crème Fraîche Glaze onto cooled cake as desired. Serve immediately, or let stand until glaze is set, about 15 minutes.

Be sure to use ripe but firm, room temperature Bosc pears for this recipe.

VANILLA-CRÈME FRAÎCHE GLAZE

Makes ¾ cup

1½ cups (180 grams) confectioners' sugar
3   tablespoons (45 grams) crème fraîche
4   teaspoons (20 grams) heavy whipping cream
1   teaspoon (6 grams) vanilla bean paste
¼   teaspoon kosher salt

1. In a medium bowl, stir together all ingredients until smooth and well combined. Use immediately.

KUGELHOPF

Makes 1 (10-cup) kugelhopf

Our brioche-like cake gets an aromatic boost from orange zest and amaretto-soaked raisins. A final dusting of confectioners' sugar over the sliced almonds resembles fresh-fallen snow on a shingled roof. Yet under it all, the elegant crown shape reigns supreme—rivaled by none.

3½ cups (438 grams) all-purpose flour, divided
⅓ cup (67 grams) plus ¼ cup (50 grams) granulated sugar, divided
½ cup (120 grams) plus ⅓ cup (80 grams) warm whole milk (110°F/43°C to 115°F/46°C), divided
2¼ teaspoons (7 grams) active dry yeast
¼ cup (60 grams) amaretto
1 cup (128 grams) golden raisins
1 cup (227 grams) unsalted butter, room temperature*
1 tablespoon (15 grams) tightly packed orange zest
1 teaspoon (3 grams) kosher salt
¾ teaspoon (3 grams) almond extract
½ teaspoon (1 gram) ground cinnamon
½ teaspoon (2 grams) vanilla extract
2 large eggs (100 grams), room temperature
⅓ cup (38 grams) sliced almonds
Confectioners' sugar, for dusting

1. In the bowl of a stand mixer, whisk together ¾ cup (94 grams) flour and ¼ cup (50 grams) granulated sugar.

2. In a small bowl, whisk together ½ cup (120 grams) warm milk and yeast until yeast dissolves. Add yeast mixture to flour mixture, and whisk by hand until smooth and well combined. Cover and let stand until bubbles form, about 30 minutes.

3. In a small saucepan, heat amaretto over medium-low heat until steaming. (Do not boil.) Remove from heat, and add raisins; cover and let stand for 30 minutes, stirring occasionally. Drain.

4. Add butter, orange zest, salt, almond extract, cinnamon, vanilla, and remaining ⅓ cup (67 grams) granulated sugar to flour mixture. Using the paddle attachment, beat at medium-low speed until combined. Beat in eggs. With mixer on low speed, add remaining 2¾ cups (344 grams) flour in three additions alternately with remaining ⅓ cup (80 grams) warm milk, beginning and ending with flour, beating just until combined after each addition. Increase mixer speed to medium-high, and beat until smooth, shiny, and elastic and dough pulls completely away from sides of bowl, about 9 minutes. (It is best not to stop mixing during this time). Scrape paddle; add raisins, and beat at low speed just until combined.

5. Spray a 10-cup kugelhopf pan with baking spray with flour. Sprinkle bottom and sides of pan with almonds; using a wooden pick, move almonds around to fill any holes.

6. Using lightly floured hands or a bowl scraper, pinch off small pieces of dough, and place in prepared pan. Using lightly floured fingers, press dough even and flat. Gently tap pan on a kitchen towel-lined counter a few times. Cover and let rise in a warm, draft-free place (75°F/24°C) until dough almost reaches top of pan, 1½ to 2 hours.

7. Preheat oven to 350°F (180°C).

8. Bake until golden and an instant-read thermometer inserted near center registers 190°F (88°C), 30 to 35 minutes. Let cool in pan for 10 minutes. Invert kugelhopf onto a wire rack, and let cool completely. Before serving, using a fine-mesh sieve, lightly dust with confectioners' sugar.

Unlike softened butter, room temperature butter should provide no resistance when pressed with a finger. At this point, the butter is softened enough to easily incorporate into this dough.

ONE-LAYER
CAKES

Spice things up with a stunningly swirled chai-spiced cheesecake or strike it rich with a dark chocolate sheet cake piled with creamy Peanut Butter Frosting. Each of our one-layer cakes is a one of a kind.

KUCHEN DE MIGAS

Makes 1 (9-inch) cake

A hybrid of Chilean and German descent, Kuchen (the German word for "cake") de migas (the Spanish word for "crumbs") has a generous spiced streusel topping and is strewn with apple chunks. Germans began to settle in Chile in the 1850s, bringing over many baked goods that the Chileans adapted, such as berlines, German-style doughnuts filled with dulce de leche. But perhaps most beloved is their Kuchen de migas, a marriage of German pastry and Chilean-grown apples, like Pink Lady and Granny Smith.

5½	cups (670 grams) 1- to 1½-inch-chopped peeled Pink Lady apples
4¼	cups (520 grams) 1- to 1½-inch-chopped peeled Granny Smith apples
1¼	cups (250 grams) granulated sugar, divided
¾	cup (165 grams) firmly packed light brown sugar, divided
¾	teaspoon (3 grams) tightly packed orange zest
1	tablespoon (15 grams) fresh orange juice
1	teaspoon (2 grams) ground cinnamon
1½	teaspoons (4.5 grams) kosher salt, divided
¼	teaspoon ground allspice
4	tablespoons (32 grams) cornstarch, divided
¾	cup (170 grams) plus 2 tablespoons (28 grams) unsalted butter, softened and divided
2	large eggs (100 grams), room temperature
1½	teaspoons (6 grams) vanilla extract
2	cups (250 grams) all-purpose flour
1	teaspoon (5 grams) baking powder

Cinnamon Crumb Topping (recipe follows)

1. Line a rimmed baking sheet with parchment paper.
2. In a large bowl, stir together apples, ½ cup (100 grams) granulated sugar, ½ cup (110 grams) brown sugar, orange zest and juice, cinnamon, ½ teaspoon (1.5 grams) salt, and allspice. Let stand for 30 minutes, stirring occasionally. Stir in 2 tablespoons (16 grams) cornstarch.
3. In a large Dutch oven, melt 2 tablespoons (28 grams) butter over medium-high heat. Add apple mixture. Reduce heat to medium; cover and cook, stirring frequently, until apples are just softened, 25 to 30 minutes. Uncover and cook, stirring frequently, until liquid has thickened and apples are softened, about 5 minutes. Transfer apple mixture to prepared pan,

spreading into an even layer. Let cool to room temperature, about 30 minutes.
4. Preheat oven to 350°F (180°C).
5. In the bowl of a stand mixer fitted with the paddle attachment, beat remaining ¾ cup (170 grams) butter, remaining ¾ cup (150 grams) granulated sugar, and remaining ¼ cup (55 grams) brown sugar at medium speed until fluffy, 2 to 3 minutes, stopping to scrape sides of bowl. Add eggs, one at a time, beating until well combined after each addition. Beat in vanilla.
6. In a medium bowl, whisk together flour, baking powder, remaining 2 tablespoons (16 grams) cornstarch, and remaining 1 teaspoon (3 grams) salt. Add flour mixture to butter mixture all at once; beat at low speed just until combined, stopping to scrape sides of bowl. (Mixture will resemble very soft drop cookie dough.)
7. Spray a 9-inch springform pan with baking spray with flour. Line bottom of pan with parchment paper. Transfer dough to prepared pan; using a sheet of plastic wrap pressed directly on surface, press dough evenly into bottom and up to 1¼ inches from top edge of pan. Carefully remove plastic wrap; using fingertips, gently seal any holes or bubbles left in dough. Spoon cooled apple mixture onto dough, spreading into an even layer. Sprinkle clumps of Cinnamon Crumb Topping on top.
8. Bake until edges are deep golden brown, 1 hour to 1 hour and 20 minutes, loosely covering with foil to prevent excess browning, if necessary. Let cool in pan for 10 minutes. Carefully remove sides of pan; let cool completely on base of pan on a wire rack. (Center of cake will sink slightly as filling cools.)

CINNAMON CRUMB TOPPING
Makes about 1 cup

½	cup (100 grams) granulated sugar
⅓	cup (76 grams) unsalted butter, melted
⅛	teaspoon kosher salt
1	cup (125 grams) all-purpose flour
¾	teaspoon (1.5 grams) ground cinnamon

1. In a medium bowl, stir together sugar, melted butter, and salt until well combined. Stir in flour and cinnamon until well combined.

STRAWBERRY ALMOND POPPY SEED CAKE

Makes 1 (9-inch) cake

A tender almond cake speckled with earthy poppy seeds and a strawberry-dappled top dusted with confectioners' sugar, this simple yet chic one-layer stunner embodies the flavors of spring. We call it "a counter cake" because you'll want to keep it on your counter all season long.

½ cup (100 grams) granulated sugar
½ cup (110 grams) firmly packed light brown sugar
½ cup (120 grams) sour cream, room temperature
½ cup (120 grams) heavy whipping cream, room temperature
⅓ cup (76 grams) unsalted butter, melted and cooled for 5 minutes
1 large egg (50 grams), room temperature
1 large egg yolk (19 grams), room temperature

1 tablespoon (6 grams) packed orange zest
1 tablespoon (13 grams) vanilla extract
¼ teaspoon (1 gram) almond extract
1½ cups (188 grams) all-purpose flour
¾ cup (72 grams) blanched almond flour
4 teaspoons (12 grams) poppy seeds
2 teaspoons (10 grams) baking powder
1 teaspoon (3 grams) kosher salt
2 cups (291 grams) halved fresh strawberries (quartered if large), divided
⅓ cup (26 grams) sliced almonds
Garnish: confectioners' sugar

1. Preheat oven to 350°F (180°C).
2. In the bowl of a stand mixer fitted with the paddle attachment, beat granulated sugar, brown sugar, sour cream, heavy cream, melted butter, egg, egg yolk, orange zest, and extracts at medium speed until well combined, about 2 minutes, stopping to scrape sides of bowl.

3. In a large bowl, whisk together flours, poppy seeds, baking powder, and salt. With mixer on low speed, gradually add flour mixture to sugar mixture, beating just until combined and stopping to scrape sides of bowl. Fold in 1 cup (145.5 grams) strawberries.
4. Spray a 9-inch springform pan with baking spray with flour. Line bottom of pan with parchment paper. Spoon batter into prepared pan; spread into an even layer using a small offset spatula.
5. Bake for 25 minutes. Gently press remaining 1 cup (145.5 grams) strawberries into top of cake; sprinkle with almonds. Bake until a wooden pick inserted in center comes out clean, 25 to 30 minutes more. Let cool in pan on a wire rack for 10 minutes. Carefully remove sides of pan; let cake cool completely on base of pan on a wire rack. Transfer to a serving plate, discarding parchment. Just before serving, garnish with confectioners' sugar, if desired.

BLUEBERRY SOUR CREAM COFFEE CAKE

Makes 1 (9-inch) cake

This endlessly customizable classic comes together in a flash. The warm notes of vanilla complement the subtle tanginess from the sour cream beautifully in the irresistibly tender crumb. We finished it off with plump blueberries folded into the batter and sprinkled on top with an almond-cinnamon streusel.

1 cup (200 grams) granulated sugar
½ cup (113 grams) unsalted butter, melted
2 large eggs (100 grams)
2 teaspoons (8 grams) vanilla extract
1½ cups (188 grams) all-purpose flour
1½ teaspoons (7.5 grams) baking powder
½ teaspoon (1.5 grams) kosher salt
½ cup (120 grams) sour cream
¼ cup (60 grams) whole milk
1 cup (148 grams) fresh blueberries, divided
Almond Streusel (recipe follows)
Sour Cream Glaze (recipe follows)

1. Preheat oven to 350°F (180°C). Spray a 9-inch springform pan with baking spray with flour.
2. In a medium bowl, whisk together sugar, melted butter, eggs, and vanilla.
3. In another medium bowl, whisk together flour, baking powder, and salt. Whisk flour mixture into butter mixture. Add sour cream and milk, whisking just until combined. Fold in ½ cup (74 grams) blueberries. Pour into prepared pan, smoothing top with an offset spatula. Sprinkle with remaining ½ cup (74 grams) blueberries; sprinkle with Almond Streusel.
4. Bake for 30 minutes. Loosely cover with foil, and bake for 15 to 20 minutes more. Let cool in pan for 15 minutes. Remove from pan, and drizzle with Sour Cream Glaze. Serve warm or at room temperature.

ALMOND STREUSEL
Makes about 1 cup

½ cup (63 grams) all-purpose flour
¼ cup (50 grams) granulated sugar
½ teaspoon (1 gram) ground cinnamon
¼ teaspoon kosher salt
½ cup (57 grams) sliced almonds
3 tablespoons (42 grams) unsalted butter, melted

1. In a medium bowl, stir together flour, sugar, cinnamon, and salt. Stir in almonds. Stir in melted butter until mixture is crumbly. Crumble with your fingertips until desired consistency is reached.

SOUR CREAM GLAZE
Makes about ½ cup

1 cup (120 grams) confectioners' sugar
2 tablespoons (30 grams) sour cream
1 tablespoon (15 grams) whole milk
½ teaspoon (2 grams) vanilla extract

1. In a small bowl, whisk together all ingredients until smooth.

CLASSIC CHEESECAKE

Makes 1 (9-inch) cake

Our Classic Cheesecake has an uber creamy, dreamy texture thanks to a triple-threat dairy base comprised of heavy cream, sour cream, and cream cheese. The vanilla bean seed-speckled filling covers a buttery crumb crust, and a final veil of sour cream gets baked into the top at the very end, creating a dramatic snow-white cap.

2   cups (224 grams) graham cracker crumbs
¼   cup (57 grams) unsalted butter, melted
1½ cups (300 grams) plus 5½ tablespoons (66 grams) granulated sugar, divided
½   teaspoon kosher salt, divided
¼   teaspoon ground cinnamon
3   (8-ounce) packages (680 grams) cream cheese, cubed and room temperature
3   tablespoons (24 grams) all-purpose flour
2   teaspoons (12 grams) vanilla bean paste
4   large eggs (200 grams), room temperature
2¼ cups (540 grams) sour cream, room temperature and divided
¼   cup (60 grams) heavy whipping cream, room temperature

1. Preheat oven to 350°F (180°C). Spray bottom of a 9-inch springform pan with baking spray with flour. Line bottom of pan with parchment paper.

2. In a large bowl, stir together graham cracker crumbs, melted butter, 2½ tablespoons (30 grams) sugar, ¼ teaspoon salt, and cinnamon until well combined; using a small straight-sided measuring cup, press crumb mixture into bottom and 1 inch up sides of prepared pan.

3. Bake until set and fragrant, 8 to 10 minutes. Let cool on a wire rack for 30 minutes. Wrap bottom and sides of pan in a double layer of heavy-duty foil; place in a large oven bag, tucking ends so bag is flush with top edge of pan. Reduce oven temperature to 325°F (170°C).

4. In the bowl of a stand mixer fitted with the paddle attachment, beat cream cheese at medium speed until smooth and creamy, 2 to 3 minutes, stopping to scrape sides of bowl. Add 1½ cups (300 grams) sugar, flour, vanilla bean paste, and remaining ¼ teaspoon salt; beat at low speed just until combined. Increase mixer speed to medium, and beat until well combined, 1 to 2 minutes, stopping to scrape sides of bowl. Add eggs, one at a time, beating just until combined after each addition. Add ¾ cup (180 grams) sour cream and heavy cream; beat at medium-low speed until well combined, 1 to 2 minutes, stopping to scrape sides of bowl.

5. Spray sides of prepared pan with baking spray with flour. Pour cream cheese mixture into prepared crust, spreading into an even layer with a small offset spatula. Carefully place springform pan in a large roasting pan. Position oven rack so top of springform pan is 5 to 5½ inches from top heating element; place roasting pan in oven, and add hot water to come 1 inch up sides of springform pan.

6. Bake until edges are set, top looks dry, center is almost set, and an instant-read thermometer inserted in center registers 150°F (66°C) to 155°F (68°C), 1½ hours to 1 hour and 45 minutes, loosely covering with foil to prevent excess browning, if necessary.

7. Meanwhile, clean bowl of a stand mixer and paddle attachment. Using the paddle attachment, beat remaining 1½ cups (360 grams) sour cream and remaining 3 tablespoons (36 grams) sugar at medium-low speed until well combined, 1 to 2 minutes, stopping to scrape sides of bowl.

8. Carefully spoon sour cream mixture onto hot cheesecake; using a small offset spatula or the back of a spoon, spread into an even layer and swirl as desired. Bake for 8 minutes more.

9. Carefully remove oven bag and foil from pan. Let cool in pan on a wire rack for 1½ to 2 hours. Refrigerate in pan on a wire rack overnight, loosely covering with foil only when completely cool to prevent condensation from forming on top of cheesecake. Carefully remove from pan, and transfer to a serving plate. Use a warm dry knife to slice when ready to serve.

THE MAGIC WATER BATH
Master the secret to a perfectly baked cheesecake

WHY WE DO IT: Think of cheesecake as a custard-based dish like crème brûlée. Heavy on eggs and dairy, the cheesecake filling needs a humid bake to keep the egg proteins from drying out or overcooking. Enter the water bath, a homemade humidifier that'll help you create the most luxuriously textured cheesecake.

HOW WE DO IT: After wrapping the springform pan and adding your filling, place the springform pan in a large roasting pan (a disposable one works fine). Then place your roasting pan into the preheated oven. Using a large measuring cup, pour hot water into roasting pan to 1 inch up the sides of the springform pan.

BATTER UP

From pressing in the crust to pouring the filling, here's how to get an ideal cheesecake from mixer to oven

Use the bottom of a glass or metal measuring cup to smooth and tamp down your crumb crust in the springform pan. It should be a tight fit, with no loose crumbs lingering. Prebaking your crust will help create a sealed barrier between crust and filling, sidestepping the soggy bottom issue.

For the smoothest batter, make sure your ingredients are room temperature before starting. Also, scrape the sides of the bowl periodically throughout mixing. If you skip these steps, pieces of cream cheese and other dairy will remain unincorporated and stick around as little globs in your otherwise perfectly smooth filling.

Before pouring your filling into the prebaked crust, wrap your springform pan in a double layer of heavy-duty foil and then place it in a large oven bag, tucking the ends so the bag is flush with the top edge of the pan. The foil will protect your cheesecake from uneven amounts of heat while the oven bag should act as an added barrier between the water bath and the springform pan.

BLUEBERRY-TOPPED CHEESECAKE

Makes 1 (9-inch) cake

Cheesecake is a dessert for all seasons, but this one is geared directly toward warmer months. We traded the traditional graham cracker crust for a spicy gingersnap crumb base that complements a sunny citrus cheesecake filling. But the coup de grâce is the bright and beautiful blueberry topping, a glistening crown that offers jammy berries in every bite.

2	cups (274 grams) gingersnap cookie crumbs
¼	cup (57 grams) unsalted butter, melted
½	teaspoon kosher salt, divided
3	(8-ounce) packages (680 grams) cream cheese, cubed and room temperature
2	cups (400 grams) granulated sugar, divided
3	tablespoons (24 grams) all-purpose flour
2	tablespoons (9 grams) packed lemon zest
1	teaspoon (4 grams) vanilla extract
4	large eggs (200 grams), room temperature
¾	cup (180 grams) sour cream, room temperature
¼	cup (60 grams) heavy whipping cream, room temperature
1	tablespoon (8 grams) cornstarch
¼	cup (60 grams) water
2	tablespoons (30 grams) fresh lemon juice
2	cups (294 grams) fresh blueberries, divided

Whipped cream, to serve

1. Preheat oven to 350°F (180°C). Spray bottom of a 9-inch springform pan with baking spray with flour. Line bottom of pan with parchment paper.

2. In a large bowl, stir together gingersnap crumbs, melted butter, and ¼ teaspoon salt until well combined; using a small straight-sided measuring cup, press crumb mixture into bottom of prepared pan.

3. Bake until set and fragrant, 8 to 10 minutes; let cool on a wire rack for 30 minutes. Wrap bottom and sides of pan in a double layer of heavy-duty foil; place in a large oven bag, tucking ends so bag is flush with top edge of pan. Reduce oven temperature to 325°F (170°C).

4. In the bowl of a stand mixer fitted with the paddle attachment, beat cream cheese at medium speed until smooth and creamy, 2 to 3 minutes, stopping to scrape sides of bowl. Add 1½ cups (300 grams) sugar, flour, lemon zest, vanilla, and remaining ¼ teaspoon salt; beat at low speed just until combined. Increase mixer speed to medium, and beat until well combined, 1 to 2 minutes, stopping to scrape sides of bowl. Add eggs, one at a time, beating just until combined after each addition. Add sour cream and heavy cream; beat at medium-low speed just until combined, 1 to 2 minutes, stopping to scrape sides of bowl.

5. Spray sides of prepared pan with baking spray with flour. Pour cream cheese mixture into prepared crust, spreading into an even layer with a small offset spatula. Carefully place springform pan in a large roasting pan. Position oven rack so top of springform pan is 5 to 5½ inches from top heating element; place roasting pan in oven, and add hot water to come 1 inch up sides of springform pan.

6. Bake until edges are set, top looks dry, center is almost set, and an instant-read thermometer inserted in center registers 150°F (66°C) to 155°F (68°C), 1½ hours to 1 hour and 45 minutes, loosely covering with foil to prevent excess browning, if necessary. Carefully remove oven bag and foil from pan. Let cool in pan on a wire rack for 1½ to 2 hours.

7. In a medium saucepan, whisk together cornstarch and remaining ½ cup (100 grams) sugar. Stir in ¼ cup (60 grams) water and lemon juice until well combined; stir in 1 cup (147 grams) blueberries. Bring to a boil over medium heat, stirring frequently; cook until mixture is thickened, some blueberries have burst, and an instant-read thermometer registers 190°F (88°C), about 4 minutes. Stir in remaining 1 cup (147 grams) blueberries; remove from heat, and let cool for 5 minutes.

8. Spread blueberry mixture on top of cooled cheesecake as desired. Refrigerate in pan on a wire rack overnight, loosely covering with foil only when completely cool to prevent condensation from forming on top of cheesecake.

9. Remove from pan, and transfer to a serving plate. Use a warm dry knife to slice when ready to serve. Serve with whipped cream.

CRACKING THE CASE

The reasons why cheesecake cracks—and how best to avoid them

THE CAUSE: Overmixing the batter. When making your filling, overmixing can lead to incorporating too much air into the batter. Once baked, the air bubbles will burst, and the cheesecake will fall and crack.

THE FIX: The number one reason why you'd overbeat your batter is because you're having difficulty incorporating cold ingredients. Bring your ingredients to room temperature beforehand so the batter will need minimal mixing.

THE CAUSE: Overbaking. Perhaps the jiggly center made you nervous or you accidentally forgot to set the timer, but no matter what, if you overbake your cheesecake, the egg proteins will overcook and cause cracks.

THE FIX: Using a water bath helps the cheesecake bake at a gentle, steady temperature. Plus, you can use an instant-read thermometer to see when your cheesecake is truly ready (when it registers 150°F [66°C] to 155°F [68°C]).

THE CAUSE: Cheesecake sticking to the sides of the springform pan. As the cheesecake cools, the filling shrinks slightly, creating a tug-of-war between the filling stuck to the sides of the pan and the cheesecake center.

THE FIX: Make sure you've properly greased or sprayed your springform pan before pouring in the filling. This will keep your cheesecake from sticking to the sides.

THE CAUSE: Drastic temperature changes. You might have opened the oven door too soon, letting in a cold draft. Or once you removed your cheesecake from the oven, you were tempted to rush it into the refrigerator for the overnight chill. Either way, the shock of cold to a still-warm cheesecake causes cracks.

THE FIX: Resist opening your oven door until your cheesecake is close to completing its baking time. Then let your cheesecake cool completely at room temperature before putting it into the refrigerator to chill overnight.

CRACKS HAPPEN. Perhaps your kitchen is colder because of weather or your oven has a hot spot. For whatever reason, the cheesecake has cracked despite your best efforts. Remember, your cheesecake is still delicious, so instead of calling it a failed experiment, cover the crack with a delicious topping, like a sour cream coat.

PEAR-ALMOND OLIVE OIL CAKE

Makes 1 (9-inch) cake

All you need is a single pear to create the beautiful fanned design on top of this stunning cake, and it's so easy to do. You'll love the extra punch of almond flavor from the almond flour and sliced almonds on top.

2   large eggs (100 grams), room temperature
1   cup (200 grams) granulated sugar
½   cup (112 grams) extra-virgin olive oil
⅔   cup (64 grams) blanched almond flour
⅓   cup (80 grams) whole milk
1   tablespoon (15 grams) tightly packed lemon zest
1   teaspoon (4 grams) vanilla extract
¼   teaspoon (1 gram) almond extract
1⅓   cups (167 grams) all-purpose flour
1½   teaspoons (7.5 grams) baking powder
¾   teaspoon (2.25 grams) kosher salt
1   large Anjou or Bosc pear (230 grams)
2   teaspoons (10 grams) fresh lemon juice
½   cup (46 grams) sliced almonds
Garnish: confectioners' sugar

1. Preheat oven to 350°F (180°C). Spray a 9-inch springform pan with baking spray with flour. Line bottom of pan with parchment paper.
2. In the bowl of a stand mixer fitted with the whisk attachment, beat eggs at high speed until uniform in color and foamy, about 1 minute. With mixer on medium speed, add granulated sugar in a slow, steady stream. Increase mixer speed to high, and beat until thick and pale, about 2 minutes. With mixer on low speed, gradually add oil in a slow, steady stream, beating until combined; scrape sides of bowl. Add almond flour, milk, lemon zest, and extracts, and beat at medium speed until combined.
3. In a medium bowl, whisk together all-purpose flour, baking powder, and salt. Fold all-purpose flour mixture into egg mixture just until combined. Pour batter into prepared pan.
4. Cut pear in half. Core each half, and cut off top part of pear and stem. Cut pear halves into ⅛-inch-thick slices. Divide slices into groups of 4 to 5. Fan slices, and gently place on top of cake batter. (See Note.) Gently brush lemon juice onto pear slices. Sprinkle almonds around edge of batter and between groups of fanned pears.
5. Bake until a wooden pick inserted in center comes out with a few moist crumbs, 50 to 55 minutes. Let cool in pan for 15 minutes. Remove sides of pan. Serve warm, or let cool completely on base of pan on a wire rack.
6. Before serving, cut a 7-inch circle from parchment paper; place in center of cake. Using a fine-mesh sieve, sift confectioners' sugar onto edges of cake, if desired.

Note: *It is very difficult to move the pear slices once they've been placed on the batter, so be intentional about the placement.*

ORANGE-ANISE BASQUE CHEESECAKE

Makes 1 (9-inch) cake

This cheesecake is all custard, no filler. An iconic crustless cheesecake from the Basque region of Spain, the Basque cheesecake has a starkly scorched top with a creamy, just-set interior thanks to a high-temperature bake. We infused our custard with orange zest and star anise, aromatics that often make their way into mulled wine, for a holiday twist.

1	large orange (184 grams)
2¼	cups (540 grams) heavy whipping cream
3	whole star anise (3 grams), lightly crushed
3	(8-ounce) packages (680 grams) cream cheese, softened
1⅓	cups (267 grams) granulated sugar
½	teaspoon (1.5 grams) kosher salt
5	large eggs (250 gram), room temperature
2	teaspoons (10 grams) tightly packed orange zest
1	teaspoon (6 grams) vanilla bean paste
¼	cup (31 grams) all-purpose flour

1. Using a peeler, remove zest from orange in 1-inch strips.

2. In a medium saucepan, heat zest strips, cream, and star anise over medium-low heat just until steaming and a film forms on top. (Do not boil.) Remove from heat, and let stand for 30 minutes, stirring occasionally. Strain through a fine-mesh sieve, discarding solids. Pour 1⅔ cups (400 grams) infused cream into a small bowl; discard any remaining liquid.

3. Preheat oven to 400°F (200°C). Line a 9-inch springform pan with 2 (16¼x12¼-inch) sheets of parchment paper placed perpendicular to each another; spray parchment with cooking spray. Place prepared pan on a rimmed baking sheet.

4. In the bowl of a stand mixer fitted with the paddle attachment, beat cream cheese at medium speed until smooth and creamy, 2 to 3 minutes, stopping to scrape sides of bowl. Add sugar and salt; beat at low speed just until combined. Increase mixer speed to medium, and beat until well combined, about 1 minute, stopping to scrape sides of bowl. Add eggs, one at a time, beating until combined after each addition. Beat in orange zest and vanilla bean paste. With mixer on low speed, add infused cream in a slow, steady stream; increase mixer speed to medium-low, and beat until well combined, about 1 minute, stopping to scrape sides of bowl. Sift flour over batter; beat at low speed until combined and smooth. Pour batter into prepared springform pan. Gently tap sides of pan 2 to 3 times to release any large air bubbles.

5. Bake until deep golden brown, center is very jiggly, and an instant-read thermometer inserted in center registers 170°F (77°C) to 175°F (79°C), 50 minutes to 1 hour. Place baking sheet on a wire rack, and let cheesecake cool to room temperature, about 2 hours. Serve immediately, or refrigerate in pan on wire rack until chilled, 4 to 5 hours or up to overnight. (If refrigerating overnight, cover loosely with foil once cooled to room temperature.) Carefully remove from pan, and transfer to a serving plate. If chilled, let stand until room temperature, at least 30 minutes, before serving.

MEYER LEMON SNACK CAKE WITH CRÈME FRAÎCHE GLAZE

Makes 1 (9-inch) cake

This zesty poppy seed-speckled cake is just as at home on the breakfast table as it is served as the finale of an elegant dinner. A mix of whole milk and Meyer lemon juice gives it an unbelievably tender crumb while imbuing every bite with the Meyer lemon's unique floral flavor. Our Crème Fraîche Glaze rounds out this cake's sweet notes with welcome tanginess.

¾   cup (170 grams) unsalted butter, softened
1½   cups (300 grams) granulated sugar
2½   tablespoons (11 grams) packed Meyer lemon zest
3   large eggs (150 grams), room temperature
½   teaspoon (2 grams) vanilla extract
2¼   cups (281 grams) unbleached cake flour
1   tablespoon (9 grams) poppy seeds
1   teaspoon (5 grams) baking powder
¾   teaspoon (2.25 grams) kosher salt
½   teaspoon (2.5 grams) baking soda
1   cup (240 grams) whole milk, room temperature
3   tablespoons (45 grams) fresh Meyer lemon juice
Crème Fraîche Glaze (recipe follows)
Garnish: poppy seeds, Meyer lemon zest

1. Preheat oven to 350°F (180°C). Spray a 9-inch square baking pan with baking spray with flour. Line with parchment paper, letting excess extend over sides of pan; lightly spray parchment.
2. In the bowl of a stand mixer fitted with the paddle attachment, beat butter, sugar, and lemon zest at medium speed until fluffy, 3 to 4 minutes, stopping to scrape sides of bowl.

Add eggs, one at a time, beating well after each addition. Beat in vanilla. (Mixture may look slightly broken at this point, but batter will come together.)
3. In a medium bowl, whisk together flour, poppy seeds, baking powder, salt, and baking soda. In a small bowl, whisk together milk and lemon juice. (Juice will cause milk to curdle slightly, and that is OK.) With mixer on low speed, gradually add flour mixture to butter mixture alternately with milk mixture, beginning and ending with flour mixture, beating just until combined after each addition. Spoon batter into prepared pan, smoothing into an even layer. Tap pan on a kitchen towel-lined counter several times to settle batter and release any air bubbles.
4. Bake until a wooden pick inserted in center comes out clean, 30 to 40 minutes. Let cool in pan for 10 minutes. Using excess parchment as handles, remove from pan, and let cool completely on a wire rack.
5. Pour Crème Fraîche Glaze onto cooled cake; using a small offset spatula, spread into an even layer. Garnish with poppy seeds and lemon zest, if desired.

Notes: *Adding fresh Meyer lemon juice to milk creates a buttermilk-like mixture, which means more Meyer lemon flavor in this deliciously moist cake.*

Meyer lemons have a distinct, slightly floral flavor profile. Therefore, if substituting regular lemons, note that the final product will taste different.

CRÈME FRAÎCHE GLAZE
Makes about 1 cup

2   cups (240 grams) confectioners' sugar
¼   cup (60 grams) crème fraîche
1½   tablespoons (22.5 grams) fresh Meyer lemon juice
¼   teaspoon kosher salt

1. In a medium bowl, stir together all ingredients until smooth. Use immediately.

ORANGE COFFEE CAKE

Makes 1 (10-inch) cake

With a rich layer of cream cheese, crunchy streusel topping, and beautiful golden crust (thank you, cast iron!), it's hard to beat this hefty coffee cake. Yogurt and a double dose of orange zest and juice in the batter keep the flavor fresh and the crumb extra tender.

1½   cups (300 grams) granulated sugar, divided
½   cup (113 grams) unsalted butter, melted
3   large eggs (150 grams), divided
2½   tablespoons (23 grams) tightly packed orange zest, divided
2   tablespoons (30 grams) fresh orange juice, divided
2   teaspoons (8 grams) vanilla extract
2   cups (250 grams) all-purpose flour
2   teaspoons (10 grams) baking powder
½   teaspoon (1.5 grams) kosher salt
½   cup (120 grams) whole Greek yogurt
¼   cup (60 grams) whole milk
8   ounces (226 grams) cream cheese, softened
Almond Streusel (recipe follows)

1. Preheat oven to 350°F (180°C). Spray a 10-inch cast-iron skillet with baking spray with flour.

2. In a large bowl, whisk together 1 cup (200 grams) sugar, melted butter, 2 eggs (100 grams), 1½ tablespoons (14 grams) orange zest, 1 tablespoon (15 grams) orange juice, and vanilla until combined.

3. In a medium bowl, whisk together flour, baking powder, and salt. In a small bowl, whisk together yogurt and milk. Gradually add flour mixture to butter mixture alternately with yogurt mixture, beginning and ending with flour mixture, whisking just until combined after each addition. Spoon two-thirds of batter (about 582 grams) into prepared skillet, smoothing with an offset spatula; slightly push outside edges up sides of skillet.

4. In another medium bowl, beat cream cheese with a mixer at medium speed until smooth. Add remaining ½ cup (100 grams) sugar, remaining 1 egg (50 grams), remaining 1 tablespoon (9 grams) orange zest, and remaining 1 tablespoon (15 grams) orange juice, beating until well combined. Pour on top of batter in skillet, keeping cream cheese mixture from touching sides of skillet. Spoon remaining batter along outside edge of skillet; using an offset spatula, gently smooth batter flat over cream cheese mixture. (Batter will not cover cream cheese mixture completely in center.) Sprinkle with Almond Streusel.

5. Bake until center is almost set and an instant-read thermometer inserted in center registers 175°F (79°C) to 180°F (82°C), 45 to 50 minutes. Let cool in skillet for at least 30 minutes. Serve warm or at room temperature.

ALMOND STREUSEL

Makes about 1 cup

½   cup (63 grams) all-purpose flour
⅓   cup (67 grams) granulated sugar
2   teaspoons (6 grams) tightly packed orange zest
¼   teaspoon kosher salt
½   cup (57 grams) sliced almonds
3   tablespoons (42 grams) unsalted butter, melted

1. In a medium bowl, stir together flour, sugar, orange zest, and salt. Stir in almonds. Stir in melted butter until mixture is crumbly. Crumble with your fingertips until desired consistency is reached.

PRO TIP

When choosing a skillet for baking, you have two main choices: an enamel-coated cast-iron skillet or a traditional black cast-iron skillet. The difference is in the coating, but the results will remain the same as long as you have a well-seasoned skillet. You can also bake this recipe using a tall-sided 10-inch round cake pan.

GÂTEAU BASQUE LOAF

Makes 1 (9x5-inch) cake

We took the classic French one-layer cake (our editor-in-chief's favorite!) from round to rectangle. A tender, golden crust encases a surprise center of thick, velvety Custard Filling, a defining factor of the original gâteau Basque, with a thin layer of fresh blueberries to bring brightness to every slice.

¾   cup (170 grams) unsalted butter, softened
1⅔   cups (333 grams) granulated sugar
3   large eggs (150 grams), divided
2   large egg yolks (37 grams)
3¼   cups (406 grams) all-purpose flour
2¼   teaspoons (11.25 grams) baking powder
1¼   teaspoons (3.75 grams) kosher salt
Custard Filling (recipe follows)
¾   cup (128 grams) fresh blueberries
1   tablespoon (15 grams) water
Garnish: confectioners' sugar

1. In the bowl of a stand mixer fitted with the paddle attachment, beat butter and granulated sugar at medium speed until fluffy, 3 to 4 minutes, stopping to scrape sides of bowl. Add 2 eggs (100 grams) and egg yolks, one at a time, beating well after each addition.

2. In a medium bowl, whisk together flour, baking powder, and salt. With mixer on low speed, gradually add flour mixture to butter mixture, beating just until combined. Turn out dough, and shape into a disk. Wrap in plastic wrap, and refrigerate until firm, about 2 hours or up to overnight.

3. Line a 9x5-inch loaf pan with parchment paper, letting excess extend over sides of pan.

4. On a heavily floured surface, roll dough to ¼-inch thickness. Cut a 9-inch square from dough. Gently transfer to prepared pan, placing in bottom and up long sides. Cut 2 (4½x3-inch) rectangles from remaining dough, and place widthwise on short sides of prepared pan. Press dough together in corners to seal. (See Note.)

5. Reroll remaining dough to ¼-inch thickness, and cut a 9x5-inch rectangle from dough. Transfer to a sheet of parchment paper, and refrigerate.

6. In bottom of pan, place blueberries in a single layer. Spoon Custard Filling on top of blueberries, smoothing flat, and tap pan on a kitchen towel-lined counter 3 times to release any air bubbles. Trim dough to ⅛ inch above Custard Filling.

7. In a small bowl, whisk together 1 tablespoon (15 grams) water and remaining 1 egg (50 grams). Brush top of dough in pan with egg wash. Place 9x5-inch dough rectangle on top, pressing around edges to seal. Freeze until set, 30 to 45 minutes.

8. Preheat oven to 400°F (200°C).

9. Brush dough with egg wash.

10. Bake for 20 minutes. Reduce oven temperature to 350°F (180°C), and bake until top is deep golden brown and a wooden pick inserted in top (but not in custard) comes out clean, about 40 minutes more, covering with foil after 20 minutes of baking to prevent excess browning. Let cool in pan for 15 minutes. Using excess parchment as handles, remove from pan, and let cool completely on a wire rack. Just before serving, garnish with confectioners' sugar, if desired. Refrigerate in an airtight container for up to 4 days.

Note: *This dough is very forgiving. Reroll when needed, and if it tears, just press it back together. If the dough gets too soft while working with it, refrigerate it for a few minutes. If you refrigerate the dough overnight, let it stand for 5 to 10 minutes before rolling it out.*

CUSTARD FILLING
Makes about 3 cups

2½   cups (600 grams) whole milk
½   cup (100 grams) granulated sugar, divided
1   vanilla bean, split lengthwise, seeds scraped and reserved
6   large egg yolks (112 grams)
⅓   cup (40 grams) cornstarch

1. In a medium saucepan, heat milk, ¼ cup (50 grams) sugar, and reserved vanilla bean seeds over medium heat until steaming. (Do not boil.)

2. In a medium bowl, whisk together egg yolks, cornstarch, and remaining ¼ cup (50 grams) sugar. Whisk hot milk mixture into egg yolk mixture. Return mixture to saucepan, and cook, whisking constantly, until mixture starts to boil. Cook, whisking constantly, until cornstarch flavor is cooked out, 2 to 3 minutes. Remove from heat, and strain through a fine-mesh sieve into a medium heatproof bowl. Cover with plastic wrap, pressing wrap directly onto surface of custard to prevent a skin from forming. Let stand at room temperature until just warm, about 30 minutes. Use immediately.

COCONUT-ALMOND RICE CAKE

Makes 1 (9-inch) cake

For Chinese New Year, a number of rituals ensure luck and fortune: wearing red, not cleaning, burning fake money and coins, and, most deliciously, eating nian gao. This traditionally steamed rice cake is almost 2,000 years old, first coming to prominence around AD 200. Our nian gao doesn't require a steamer basket—it's baked in the oven. And though there are thousands of variations, ours shares DNA with all the others through the use of gelatinous rice flour, the secret to its signature sticky texture.

16 ounces (454 grams) mochiko sweet rice flour*
2¼ cups (450 grams) granulated sugar
¼ cup (55 grams) firmly packed light brown sugar
½ teaspoon (1.5 grams) kosher salt
1⅔ cups (400 grams) unsweetened full-fat coconut milk
1⅓ cups (320 grams) whole milk, room temperature
4 large eggs (200 grams), room temperature and lightly beaten
3 tablespoons (42 grams) unsalted butter, melted and cooled
½ teaspoon (2 grams) almond extract
¼ teaspoon (1 gram) vanilla extract
¼ cup (21 grams) lightly toasted sweetened flaked coconut
3 tablespoons (21 grams) lightly toasted sliced almonds

1. Preheat oven to 325°F (170°C). Spray a 9-inch round cake pan with baking spray with flour. Line bottom of pans with parchment paper; lightly spray parchment. Place a fine-mesh sieve over a large bowl.
2. In another large bowl, whisk together flour, sugars, and salt.
3. In a medium bowl, whisk together milks, eggs, melted butter, and extracts. Gradually add milk mixture to flour mixture, whisking until smooth and well combined. (Batter will be very thin.) Pour through prepared sieve; discard any solids. Pour strained mixture into prepared pan. (Pan will be very full, but batter will not overflow.)
4. Bake until top is just nearly set, 50 to 55 minutes. Sprinkle with coconut and almonds. Bake until set and lightly golden, about 40 minutes more, lightly covering with foil halfway through baking to prevent excess browning, if necessary. (Trapped steam may cause cake to puff slightly out of pan while baking; run a small offset spatula around edges to gently release steam and push cake back into pan.) Let cool in pan for 15 minutes. Invert cake onto a large flat plate; discard parchment. Invert cake onto a wire rack, and let cool to room temperature before serving.

*You can find mochiko sweet rice flour at local specialty Asian markets or online at amazon.com.

DARK CHOCOLATE LAVA CAKES

Makes 2 servings

Cakey on the outside and filled with a mouthwatering center of molten dark chocolate, these lava cakes are the ultimate romantic dessert for two.

¼	cup (57 grams) unsalted butter
2	ounces (55 grams) 60% cacao bittersweet chocolate, chopped
¼	cup (50 grams) granulated sugar
1	large egg (50 grams)
1	large egg yolk (19 grams)
¼	teaspoon (1 gram) vanilla extract
⅛	teaspoon kosher salt
2	teaspoons (6 grams) all-purpose flour

Dutch process cocoa powder, for dusting

1. Preheat oven to 425°F (220°C). Lightly spray 2 (8-ounce) ramekins with baking spray with flour.

2. In the top of a double boiler, place butter and chocolate. Cook over simmering water until melted. Whisk until smooth.

3. In medium bowl, beat sugar, egg, egg yolk, vanilla, and salt with a mixer at high speed until thickened and pale and has a ribbon-like consistency. Quickly whisk sugar mixture and flour into butter mixture by hand just until combined. Divide batter between prepared ramekins (about 114 grams each). Tap ramekins on a kitchen towel-lined counter twice, and place on a rimmed baking sheet; let stand for 15 minutes at room temperature.

4. Bake until tops are barely set and cakes jiggle slightly when shaken, 12 to 13 minutes. Let cool in ramekins for 1 minute. Run an offset spatula around edges of cakes. Carefully invert each ramekin onto a dessert plate. Let stand for 30 seconds, and remove ramekins. Dust cakes with cocoa, and serve immediately.

PRO TIP
Need to serve more than two? Simply double the recipe. It works just as beautifully.

DARK CHOCOLATE SHEET CAKE WITH PEANUT BUTTER FROSTING

Makes 1 (13x9-inch) cake

The classic pairing of chocolate and peanut butter is back and more indulgent than ever. We coated an incredibly fudgy dark chocolate cake with a generous slather of Peanut Butter Frosting.

4   ounces (113 grams) 60% cacao semisweet chocolate, chopped
6   tablespoons (84 grams) unsalted butter
1½   cups (360 grams) water
1   cup (200 grams) granulated sugar
1   cup (220 grams) firmly packed light brown sugar
¼   cup (21 grams) unsweetened cocoa powder
⅔   cup (160 grams) sour cream
1   teaspoon (4 grams) vanilla extract
2   large eggs (100 grams), lightly beaten
2   cups (250 grams) all-purpose flour
2   teaspoons (10 grams) baking powder
2   teaspoons (10 grams) baking soda
1   teaspoon (3 grams) kosher salt
Peanut Butter Frosting (recipe follows)
Garnish: chopped semisweet chocolate

1. Preheat oven to 350°F (180°C). Line a 13x9-inch baking pan with parchment paper, letting parchment extend over sides of pan. Spray parchment with baking spray with flour.
2. In a large bowl, place chocolate and butter.
3. In a medium saucepan, whisk together 1½ cups (360 grams) water and sugars; bring to a boil over medium-high heat, stirring occasionally, until sugar dissolves. Whisk in cocoa. Pour over chocolate mixture, and let stand for 2 minutes. Stir until chocolate and butter are melted and mixture is combined. Stir in sour cream and vanilla. Whisk in eggs.

4. In a medium bowl, whisk together flour, baking powder, baking soda, and salt. Slowly add flour mixture to chocolate mixture, whisking just until combined. Pour batter into prepared pan.
5. Bake until a wooden pick inserted in center comes out clean, 30 to 35 minutes. Let cool completely in pan.
6. Using excess parchment as handles, removed from pan. Spread Peanut Butter Frosting on top of cooled cake, swirling as desired. Garnish with chocolate, if desired.

PEANUT BUTTER FROSTING
Makes about 5 cups

1   cup (227 grams) unsalted butter, softened
1   cup (225 grams) cream cheese, softened
1½   cups (384 grams) creamy peanut butter
1   tablespoon (13 grams) vanilla extract
2   cups (240 grams) confectioners' sugar
2   tablespoons (30 grams) whole milk

1. In the bowl of a stand mixer fitted with the paddle attachment, beat butter and cream cheese at low speed until smooth. Add peanut butter and vanilla, beating until combined. Gradually add confectioners' sugar alternately with milk, beating until smooth. Increase mixer speed to medium, and beat until fluffy, 1 to 2 minutes.

CHOCOLATE CHUNK COFFEE CAKE WITH STREUSEL TOPPING

Makes 1 (9-inch) cake

Recipe by Erin Clarkson

Erin Clarkson of the blog Cloudy Kitchen, a Kiwi expat living and baking in New York City, knew she wanted to take on a classic New York treat: the coffee cake. Her version is a perfectly dense chocolate chip coffee cake with a little tang from yogurt, topped with a generous amount of streusel.

Cocoa vanilla extract streusel topping:

½ cup (100 grams) vanilla sugar*
⅓ cup plus 2 tablespoons (100 grams) firmly packed light or dark brown sugar
2 cups (250 grams) all-purpose flour
½ teaspoon (1.5 grams) kosher salt
1½ teaspoons (6 grams) cocoa vanilla extract*
⅔ cup (150 grams) unsalted butter, melted and cooled slightly

Chocolate chip coffee cake:

½ cup (115 grams) unsalted butter, room temperature
¾ cup (150 grams) granulated sugar
1 large egg (50 grams), room temperature
1½ teaspoons (6 grams) cocoa vanilla extract*
2 cups (250 grams) all-purpose flour
2 teaspoons (10 grams) baking powder
½ teaspoon (1.5 grams) kosher salt
⅔ cup plus ¼ cup (220 grams) Greek yogurt or sour cream, room temperature
⅔ cup plus 1 tablespoon (120 grams) chopped 74% cacao dark chocolate

1. For streusel: In a medium bowl, whisk together Heilala Vanilla Sugar, brown sugar, flour, and salt. Add the Heilala Cocoa Vanilla Extract and the melted butter, and stir with a spatula until clumps form. Set aside.
2. Preheat the oven to 325°F (165°C). Grease a 9-inch square baking pan, and line it with parchment paper.

3. For cake: In the bowl of a stand mixer fitted with the paddle attachment, cream the butter and sugar together on high speed until light and fluffy, about 3 to 5 minutes. Add the egg and Heilala Cocoa Vanilla Extract and mix to combine.
4. In a medium bowl, sift together the flour, baking powder, and salt. With the mixer on low, add about a third of the flour mixture, followed by half of the yogurt and another third of the flour and then the rest of the yogurt, followed by the remainder of the flour. Mix on low until almost combined—you want to see some flour remaining in the bowl.
5. Remove the bowl from the mixer and add in the chopped chocolate. Finish mixing the cake batter by hand to finish off the mixing process and incorporate the chocolate.

Transfer the cake batter in a few large dollops to the prepared pan, and smooth it down with an offset spatula.
6. Sprinkle the prepared streusel evenly over the surface of the cake, breaking up any large clumps with your fingers, and pressing down lightly to help adhere.
7. Bake the coffee cake for 50 minutes to an hour, or until a instant read thermometer inserted into the center of cake reads 190°F (93°C).
8. Allow to cool in the pan before slicing into squares. Store leftovers in an airtight container at room temperature.

We used Heilala Vanilla Sugar and Hielala Cocoa Vanilla Extract.

Photo by Erin Clarkson

CHOCOLATE CARROT CAKE LOAF

Makes 1 (8½x4½-inch) cake

We love the stark, swirly contrast between this cake's chocolate and plain layers.

Plain batter:
½   cup (100 grams) granulated sugar
⅓   cup (76 grams) unsalted butter, melted
1   large egg (50 grams)
2   tablespoons (30 grams) vanilla yogurt
⅔   cup (83 grams) all-purpose flour
¾   teaspoon (2.25 grams) kosher salt
¾   teaspoon (1.5 grams) ground cinnamon
½   teaspoon (2.5 grams) baking powder
¼   teaspoon ground ginger
⅛   teaspoon ground nutmeg
½   cup (54 grams) lightly packed grated carrot
¼   cup (43 grams) chopped 60% cacao bittersweet chocolate

Chocolate batter:
½   cup (100 grams) granulated sugar
⅓   cup (76 grams) unsalted butter, melted
¼   cup (60 grams) vanilla yogurt
1   large egg (50 grams)
½   cup (63 grams) all-purpose flour
2   tablespoons (10 grams) unsweetened cocoa powder
¾   teaspoon (2.25 grams) kosher salt
¾   teaspoon (1.5 grams) ground cinnamon
½   teaspoon (2.5 grams) baking powder
¼   teaspoon ground ginger
⅛   teaspoon ground nutmeg
½   cup (54 grams) lightly packed grated carrot
¼   cup (43 grams) chopped 60% cacao bittersweet chocolate

Vanilla Yogurt Glaze (recipe follows)

1. Preheat oven to 350°F (180°C). Spray an 8½x4½-inch loaf pan with baking spray with flour.
2. For plain batter: In a large bowl, whisk together sugar, melted butter, egg, and yogurt until well combined.
3. In a medium bowl, whisk together flour, salt, cinnamon, baking powder, ginger, and nutmeg. Gradually add flour mixture to sugar mixture, whisking just until combined. Fold in carrot and chocolate. Pour batter into prepared pan, and smooth top with an offset spatula.
4. For chocolate batter: In a large bowl, whisk together sugar, melted butter, yogurt, and egg until well combined.
5. In a medium bowl, whisk together flour, cocoa, salt, cinnamon, baking powder, ginger, and nutmeg. Gradually add flour mixture to sugar mixture, whisking just until combined. Fold in carrot and chocolate. Spoon batter in small dollops on top of plain batter; gently smooth top with an offset spatula.
6. Bake until a wooden pick inserted in center comes out clean, 1 hour to 1 hour and 5 minutes, covering with foil halfway through baking to prevent excess browning on edges. Let cool in pan for 15 minutes. Remove from pan, and let cool completely on a wire rack. Top with Vanilla Yogurt Glaze before serving.

VANILLA YOGURT GLAZE
Makes about ½ cup

½   cup (120 grams) vanilla yogurt
3   tablespoons (21 grams) confectioners' sugar
1   teaspoon (5 grams) whole milk

1. In a medium bowl, whisk together all ingredients until smooth. Refrigerate until ready to use.

DUTCH BUTTER CAKE (BOTERKOEK)

Makes 1 (9-inch) cake

This homey one-layer cake is a dense, rich treat that's a classic of Dutch cuisine. Made of mostly butter and flour, it's a stick-to-your-ribs kind of recipe that's best enjoyed in true Amsterdam style: served alongside a hot cup of coffee or afternoon tea.

1½ cups (340 grams) unsalted butter, softened
1¼ cups (250 grams) granulated sugar
¼   cup (55 grams) firmly packed dark brown sugar
2   teaspoons (7 grams) tightly packed orange zest
1   large egg (50 grams), room temperature
1   large egg yolk (19 grams), room temperature
1½ teaspoons (9 grams) vanilla bean paste

2½ cups (313 grams) all-purpose flour
½   cup (62 grams) unbleached cake flour
1   teaspoon (3 grams) kosher salt
¼   teaspoon ground nutmeg
1   large egg white (30 grams), lightly beaten

1. Preheat oven to 350°F (180°C).
2. In the bowl of a stand mixer fitted with the paddle attachment, beat butter, sugars, and orange zest at low speed just until combined. Increase mixer speed to medium, and beat until fluffy, 2 to 3 minutes, stopping to scrape sides of bowl. Add egg and egg yolk, one at a time, beating until well combined after each addition. Beat in vanilla bean paste.
3. In a large bowl, whisk together flours, salt, and nutmeg until well combined. With mixer on low speed, gradually add flour mixture to butter mixture, beating just until combined

and stopping to scrape sides of bowl. (Dough will be quite thick.)
4. Spray a 9-inch springform pan with baking spray with flour. Line bottom of pan with parchment paper. Transfer dough to prepared pan; using a sheet of plastic wrap pressed directly on surface, spread and press dough into an even layer; discard plastic wrap. Gently brush top of dough with egg white; using the tines of a fork, make a crosshatch pattern over surface of dough.
5. Bake for 25 minutes. Rotate pan, and bake until golden brown and a wooden pick inserted in center comes out clean, 10 to 15 minutes more. Let cool in pan for 5 minutes. Carefully remove sides of pan. Let cool completely on base of pan on a wire rack. Remove from base of pan and discard parchment before serving.

GLAZED CITRUS LOAF (CITROENCAKE)

Makes 1 (9x5-inch) cake

Inspired by the signature citroencake served on KLM Royal Dutch Airline flights, this tender citrus loaf cake is studded with candied oranges and topped with a Vanilla Glaze. Each slice is guaranteed to fill you with the warmth and comfort that's characteristic of Dutch home-baked sweets.

1   cup (227 grams) unsalted butter, softened
1¼ cups (250 grams) granulated sugar
1   tablespoon (3 grams) lemon zest
2   teaspoons (7 grams) tightly packed orange zest
4   large eggs (200 grams), room temperature
2   teaspoons (12 grams) vanilla bean paste
2   cups (250 grams) plus 1 teaspoon (3 grams) unbleached cake flour, divided
¾   teaspoon (2.25 grams) kosher salt
¼   teaspoon (1.25 grams) baking powder
⅓   cup (80 grams) whole milk, room temperature

½   cup (70 grams) finely chopped candied orange slices
Vanilla Glaze (recipe follows)

1. Preheat oven to 325°F (170°C). Spray a 9x5-inch loaf pan with baking spray with flour. Line pan with parchment paper, letting excess extend over sides of pan.
2. In the bowl of a stand mixer fitted with the paddle attachment, beat butter, sugar, and zests at medium speed until fluffy, 3 to 4 minutes, stopping to scrape sides of bowl. Add eggs, one at a time, beating until combined after each addition. Beat in vanilla bean paste. (Mixture may look slightly curdled at this point, but batter will come together.)
3. In a medium bowl, whisk together 2 cups (250 grams) flour, salt, and baking powder. With mixer on low speed, gradually add flour mixture to butter mixture alternately with milk, beginning and ending with flour mixture, beating just until combined after each addition. (Batter will be thick.)
4. In a small bowl, stir together candied orange and remaining 1 teaspoon (3 grams) flour until well combined; fold into batter. Spoon batter into prepared pan; using a small

offset spatula, smooth into an even layer.
5. Bake until a wooden pick inserted in center comes out clean, 1 hour and 20 minutes to 1 hour and 25 minutes, rotating pan halfway through baking. Let cool in pan for 5 minutes. Using excess parchment as handles, remove from pan, and let cool completely on a wire rack.
6. Spoon Vanilla Glaze onto cooled cake, and spread as desired. Serve immediately, or let stand until glaze is set, about 30 minutes.

VANILLA GLAZE
Makes about ⅔ cup

1¼ cups (150 grams) confectioners' sugar, sifted
3   tablespoons (45 grams) heavy whipping cream
2   tablespoons (28 grams) unsalted butter, melted
1   teaspoon (4 grams) vanilla extract
¼   teaspoon kosher salt

1. In a medium bowl, stir together all ingredients until smooth and well combined. Use immediately.

APPLE SLICE TRAYBAKE

Makes 8 to 12 servings

Hailing from County Kerry, the famous producer of the brilliant yellow butter beloved by the global baking community, this Kerry apple slice is a celebration of both rich, golden butter and tender, juicy apples. We transformed this definitive baked good—traditionally baked in a bastible, a cast-iron baking pot, over an open fire—into another Irish classic: the traybake. So-called because they're baked in a "tray" (a 13x9- or 9-inch square baking pan), these simple yet decadent desserts are a common source of comfort in the Irish home.

1¼	cups (284 grams) unsalted butter, softened
1½	cups (300 grams) plus 1 tablespoon (12 grams) castor sugar, divided
4	large eggs (200 grams), room temperature
1½	teaspoons (9 grams) vanilla bean paste
3⅓	cups (417 grams) self-rising flour
½	teaspoon (1 gram) ground cinnamon
⅛	teaspoon ground allspice
4	cups (440 grams) ¼-inch-sliced Honeycrisp apples
1	tablespoon (15 grams) fresh lemon juice
2	tablespoons (24 grams) turbinado sugar

Confectioners' sugar, for dusting
Vanilla Custard Sauce (recipe follows)

1. Preheat oven to 350°F (180°C). Spray a light-colored 9-inch square baking pan with cooking spray. Line pan with parchment paper, letting excess extend over sides of pan.
2. In the bowl of a stand mixer fitted with the paddle attachment, beat butter and 1½ cups (300 grams) castor sugar at medium speed until well combined, about 2 minutes, stopping to scrape sides of bowl. Add eggs, one at a time, beating well after each addition. Beat in vanilla bean paste. (Mixture may look slightly curdled at this point, but batter will come together.)
3. In a large bowl, whisk together flour, cinnamon, and allspice. With mixer on low speed, gradually add flour mixture to butter mixture, beating just until combined and stopping to scrape sides of bowl. Spread half of batter (about 596 grams) into prepared pan, smoothing into an even layer with the back of a spoon.
4. In a large bowl, toss together apple slices, lemon juice, and remaining 1 tablespoon (12 grams) castor sugar. Arrange apple slices, flat side down, on top of batter in pan. Top apple slices with remaining batter, spreading and swirling into an even layer with the back of a spoon. Sprinkle with turbinado sugar.

5. Bake until a wooden pick inserted in center comes out clean and an instant-read thermometer inserted in center registers 200°F (93°C), 1 hour to 1 hour and 15 minutes, rotating pan and loosely covering with foil after 30 minutes of baking. Let cool in pan for 10 minutes. Using excess parchment as handles, remove from pan. Using a serrated knife, cut into pieces as desired. Dust with confectioners' sugar, and serve warm with Vanilla Custard Sauce.

VANILLA CUSTARD SAUCE
Makes about 2 cups

⅓	cup (67 grams) castor sugar
3	large egg yolks (56 grams)
¼	teaspoon kosher salt
1½	cups (360 grams) whole milk
1	teaspoon (6 grams) vanilla bean paste

1. Place a fine-mesh sieve over a medium metal bowl. Fill a large bowl with ice water.
2. In another medium bowl, whisk together castor sugar, egg yolks, and salt.
3. In a medium saucepan, heat milk over medium heat until steaming. (Do not boil.) Gradually whisk warm milk into sugar mixture. Return mixture to saucepan, and cook over medium heat, stirring constantly, until mixture is thickened, coats the back of a wooden spoon, and holds a trail when a finger is dragged through, 10 to 20 minutes.
4. Strain mixture through prepared sieve, and place in prepared ice water bath; whisk until an instant-read thermometer registers 70°F (21°C). Stir in vanilla bean paste. Loosely cover and refrigerate until completely chilled, 3 to 4 hours.

TRIPLE-MARBLE POUND CAKE

Makes 1 (8½x4½-inch) cake

We call this sour cream pound cake a triple marble because it's marbled with three epic batters—vanilla, chocolate, and dulce de leche. All three are crave-worthy on their own, but swirled together? Game changer.

- ¾ cup (170 grams) unsalted butter, softened
- 1½ cups (300 grams) granulated sugar
- 3 large eggs (150 grams), room temperature
- 1¾ cups (219 grams) all-purpose flour
- ½ teaspoon (1.5 grams) kosher salt
- ¼ teaspoon (1.25 grams) baking powder
- ½ cup (120 grams) sour cream, room temperature
- ¼ cup (80 grams) dulce de leche
- ⅓ cup (57 grams) chopped 66% cacao dark chocolate, melted and cooled slightly
- 1 tablespoon (5 grams) Dutch process cocoa powder
- 2 teaspoons (8 grams) vanilla extract

1. Preheat oven to 300°F (150°C). Spray an 8½x4½-inch loaf pan with baking spray with flour. Line pan with parchment paper, letting excess extend over sides of pan.

2. In the bowl of a stand mixer fitted with the paddle attachment, beat butter and sugar at medium speed until fluffy, 5 to 6 minutes, stopping to scrape sides of bowl. Add eggs, one at a time, beating well after each addition.

3. In a medium bowl, whisk together flour, salt, and baking powder. With mixer on low speed, add flour mixture to butter mixture in three additions alternately with sour cream, beginning and ending with flour mixture, beating just until combined after each addition. Divide batter into 3 portions (about 1⅓ cups [316 grams] each).

4. In a small microwave-safe bowl, heat dulce de leche for 15 to 20 seconds to soften slightly. Fold into 1 portion of batter. To second portion, add melted chocolate and cocoa, and fold until combined. To remaining portion, add vanilla, and fold until combined.

5. Using 1½-tablespoon spring-loaded scoops, scoop vanilla and chocolate batters in a checkerboard pattern into bottom of prepared pan (10 scoops total). Scoop a row of dulce de leche batter down center of pan on top of vanilla/chocolate layer (5 scoops). Tap pan 2 to 3 times to help level batter and fill pan. Create another layer in a checkerboard pattern using dulce de leche and chocolate batters, being sure to place chocolate on top of vanilla batter from first layer. Scoop a row of vanilla batter down center of pan on top of dulce de leche/chocolate layer. Tap pan again. Scoop remaining batter randomly on top. Using a wooden pick, swirl batters together well. Tap pan again to help level batter and fill in any gaps.

6. Bake until a wooden pick inserted in center comes out clean, 1 hour and 40 minutes to 1 hour and 50 minutes. Let cool in pan for 10 minutes. Using excess parchment as handles, remove from pan. Serve warm, or let cool completely on wire rack.

PEACH STREUSEL SNACK CAKE

Makes 1 (9-inch) cake

This spiced snack cake has it all: sweetness from the peaches, tang from the sour cream, and just the right amount of crunch from the Oat Streusel.

½   cup (113 grams) unsalted butter, softened
1   cup (200 grams) granulated sugar, divided
⅓   cup (73 grams) firmly packed light brown sugar
2   large eggs (100 grams), room temperature
1½ teaspoons (9 grams) vanilla bean paste
2   cups (250 grams) all-purpose flour
1   tablespoon (15 grams) baking powder
¾   teaspoon (2.25 grams) kosher salt
¾   teaspoon (1.5 grams) ground ginger
1   cup (240 grams) sour cream, room temperature
½   teaspoon (1 gram) ground cardamom
2½ cups (448 grams) ¾-inch-chopped peeled fresh or frozen* peaches, divided (about 4 to 5 medium peaches)
Oat Streusel (recipe follows)
Garnish: confectioners' sugar

1. Preheat oven to 350°F (180°C). Spray a 9-inch square baking pan with cooking spray. Line pan with parchment paper, letting excess extend over sides of pan.
2. In the bowl of a stand mixer fitted with the paddle attachment, beat butter, ⅔ cup (133 grams) granulated sugar, and brown sugar at medium speed until fluffy, 3 to 4 minutes, stopping to scrape sides of bowl. Add eggs, one at a time, beating well after each addition. Beat in vanilla bean paste.
3. In a medium bowl, whisk together flour, baking powder, salt, and ginger. With mixer on low speed, gradually add flour mixture to butter mixture alternately with sour cream, beginning and ending with flour mixture, beating just until combined after each addition. Spoon half of batter (about 438 grams) into prepared pan; using a small offset spatula, smooth into an even layer.

4. In a medium bowl, stir together cardamom and remaining ⅓ cup (67 grams) granulated sugar; add 1¼ cups (224 grams) peaches, tossing until well combined. Spoon peach mixture evenly onto batter in pan. Spoon remaining batter onto peach mixture, smoothing into an even layer. (It's OK if some peaches peek through.) Top with Oat Streusel and remaining 1¼ cups (224 grams) peaches.
5. Bake until a wooden pick inserted in center comes out clean, 50 minutes to 1 hour, rotating pan halfway through baking and loosely covering with foil to prevent excess browning, if necessary. Let cool in pan on a wire rack for 10 minutes. Run a sharp knife around sides of pan between paper and pan. Using excess parchment as handles, remove cake from pan. Garnish with confectioners' sugar, if desired. Serve warm or at room temperature.

*If using frozen peaches, be sure to thaw, drain, and pat dry before using in this recipe.

Oat Streusel
Makes ½ cup

⅓   cup (73 grams) firmly packed light brown sugar
2   tablespoons (28 grams) unsalted butter, melted
⅛   teaspoon kosher salt
⅓   cup (42 grams) all-purpose flour
¼   cup (23 grams) old-fashioned oats
¼   teaspoon ground cinnamon

1. In a small bowl, stir together brown sugar, melted butter, and salt until well combined. Stir in flour, oats, and cinnamon until well combined. Use immediately, or refrigerate until ready to use.

TROPICAL CARROT CAKE

Makes 1 (9-inch) cake

A less fussy, tropical take on the traditional cake, this one-layer stir-together comes together in a flash. Piled high with luscious swoops of Crème Fraîche Frosting and a halo of electric-orange sugared carrots, this beauty is just as eye-catching as the original.

1¼ cups (250 grams) granulated sugar
1 (8-ounce) can (227 grams) crushed pineapple
½ cup (112 grams) canola oil
2 large eggs (100 grams)
1 teaspoon (4 grams) vanilla extract
1½ cups (188 grams) all-purpose flour
1½ teaspoons (3 grams) ground cinnamon
1 teaspoon (5 grams) baking powder
¾ teaspoon (2.25 grams) kosher salt
½ teaspoon (1 gram) ground ginger
½ teaspoon (1 gram) ground nutmeg
¼ teaspoon (1.25 grams) baking soda
1½ cups (161 grams) lightly packed grated carrot
½ cup (64 grams) golden raisins
½ cup (57 grams) chopped walnuts
½ cup (42 grams) sweetened flaked coconut
Crème Fraîche Frosting (recipe follows)
Garnish: Candied Carrots (recipe follows)

1. Preheat oven to 350°F (180°C). Spray a 9-inch springform pan with baking spray with flour. Line bottom of pan with parchment paper.
2. In a large bowl, whisk together sugar, pineapple, oil, eggs, and vanilla.
3. In a medium bowl, stir together flour, cinnamon, baking powder, salt, ginger, nutmeg, and baking soda. Add flour mixture to sugar mixture, whisking just until combined. Add carrot, raisins, walnuts, and coconut, and fold just until combined. Pour batter into prepared pan. Smooth top with an offset spatula.
4. Bake until a wooden pick inserted in center comes out clean, 40 to 45 minutes. Let cool in pan for 15 minutes. Remove from pan, and let cool completely on a wire rack.
5. Spread Crème Fraîche Frosting on top of cooled cake. Refrigerate until ready to serve. Garnish with Candied Carrots before serving, if desired.

Crème Fraîche Frosting
Makes about 1⅓ cups

½ cup (100 grams) granulated sugar
2 large egg whites (60 grams), room temperature
⅛ teaspoon kosher salt
⅔ cup (150 grams) unsalted butter, cubed and softened
¼ cup (60 grams) cold crème fraîche

1. In the heatproof bowl of a stand mixer, whisk together sugar and egg whites by hand. Place bowl over a saucepan of simmering water. Cook, whisking occasionally, until an instant-read thermometer registers 150°F (65°C) to 155°F (68°C).
2. Carefully return bowl to stand mixer. Using the whisk attachment, beat at high speed until stiff peaks form and bowl is cool to the touch, 4 to 5 minutes. Beat in salt. Add butter, 2 tablespoons (28 grams) at a time, beating until combined after each addition. Gently fold in cold crème fraîche by hand just until combined. Use immediately.

Candied Carrots
Makes about 1 cup

½ cup (54 grams) lightly packed grated carrot, patted dry
1 cup (200 grams) granulated sugar
4 tablespoons (60 grams) water, divided

1. On a nonstick baking mat or rimmed baking sheet, sprinkle carrots evenly in center.
2. In a medium saucepan, stir together sugar and 3 tablespoons (45 grams) water (it should be the consistency of wet sand), and cook over medium heat, being careful not to splash sides of pan and stirring occasionally to help sugar dissolve; use remaining 1 tablespoon (15 grams) water to brush down sides of pan. Once it starts to boil, increase heat to high and do not stir. Cook until light amber color is reached. Remove from heat; immediately pour over carrots. Let stand until cool and set. Place on a cutting board, and using a chef's knife, cut into small pieces.

PINEAPPLE-RASPBERRY UPSIDE-DOWN CAKE

Makes 1 (9x5-inch) cake

With raspberries mixed into the batter, this upside-down cake is the perfect fruity finale to any summertime meal.

½   cup (113 grams) plus 3 tablespoons (42 grams) unsalted butter, melted and divided
⅓   cup (73 grams) plus ¼ cup (55 grams) firmly packed light brown sugar, divided
5   pineapple rings* (184 grams)
4   whole fresh raspberries (8 grams)
1   cup (200 grams) granulated sugar
2   large eggs (100 grams)
1½ teaspoons (6 grams) vanilla extract
2   cups (250 grams) all-purpose flour
2½ teaspoons (12.5 grams) baking powder
½   teaspoon (1.5 grams) kosher salt
½   cup (120 grams) whole milk
1   cup (130 grams) halved fresh raspberries

1. Preheat oven to 350°F (180°C). Spray sides of a 9x5-inch loaf pan with baking spray with flour. Line bottom of pan with parchment paper.

2. In a small bowl, stir together 3 tablespoons (42 grams) melted butter and ⅓ cup (73 grams) brown sugar. Pour into bottom of prepared pan, spreading evenly. Arrange pineapple slices in a single layer in bottom of pan, trimming slices as needed. Place 1 whole raspberry in center of each pineapple slice, pressing raspberry flat to fill entire hole of pineapple.

3. In a large bowl, whisk together granulated sugar, remaining ½ cup (113 grams) melted butter, and remaining ¼ cup (55 grams) brown sugar; whisk in eggs and vanilla.

4. In a medium bowl, whisk together flour, baking powder, and salt. Add flour mixture to sugar mixture in three additions alternately with milk, beginning and ending with flour mixture, stirring just until combined after each addition. Fold in halved raspberries. Spoon batter onto pineapple rings in pan, smoothing with an offset spatula.

5. Bake until a wooden pick inserted in center comes out clean, 1 hour to 1 hour and 5 minutes, covering with foil to prevent excess browning, if necessary. Let cool in pan for 5 minutes; carefully invert cake onto a flat serving plate, and discard parchment. Serve warm or at room temperature.

Use pineapple rings in juice, not in syrup.

LEMON POPPY SEED COFFEE CAKE

Makes 1 (9-inch) cake

This coffee cake is summer's sweetest wake-up call. Buttermilk in the batter gives this one-layer wonder a cakey crumb that contrasts beautifully with the crumbly streusel topping.

1½   cups (300 grams) granulated sugar
¾   cup (170 grams) unsalted butter, melted
3   large eggs (150 grams)
1½   tablespoons (7.5 grams) packed lemon zest
3   tablespoons (45 grams) fresh lemon juice
1½   teaspoons (9 grams) vanilla bean paste
2¼   cups (281 grams) all-purpose flour
1½   tablespoons (14 grams) poppy seeds
2   teaspoons (10 grams) baking powder
¾   teaspoon (2.25 grams) kosher salt
¼   teaspoon (1.25 grams) baking soda
1   cup (240 grams) whole buttermilk
Lemon Poppy Seed Streusel (recipe follows)
Buttermilk Glaze (recipe follows)

1. Preheat oven to 325°F (170°C). Spray a 9-inch springform pan with baking spray with flour. Line bottom of pan with parchment paper.
2. In a large bowl, whisk together sugar and melted butter; add eggs, lemon zest and juice, and vanilla bean paste, whisking until combined.
3. In a medium bowl, whisk together flour, poppy seeds, baking powder, salt, and baking soda. Add flour mixture to sugar mixture, whisking until combined. Whisk in buttermilk just until combined. Pour into prepared pan, smoothing with an offset spatula. Sprinkle evenly with Lemon Poppy Seed Streusel.
4. Bake until a wooden pick inserted in center comes out with a few moist crumbs, 50 minutes to 1 hour. Let cool in pan for 15 minutes. Remove from pan, and drizzle with Buttermilk Glaze. Serve warm or at room temperature.

LEMON POPPY SEED STREUSEL

Makes about 1 cup

½   cup (63 grams) all-purpose flour
⅓   cup (67 grams) granulated sugar
2   teaspoons (3.5 grams) packed lemon zest
1   teaspoon (3 grams) poppy seeds
¼   teaspoon kosher salt
3   tablespoons (42 grams) cold unsalted butter, cubed

1. In a medium bowl, stir together flour, sugar, lemon zest, poppy seeds, and salt. Using your fingers, cut in cold butter until mixture is crumbly. Crumble with your fingertips until desired consistency is reached. Refrigerate until ready to use.

BUTTERMILK GLAZE

Makes about ¾ cup

1½   cups (180 grams) confectioners' sugar
3   tablespoons (45 grams) whole buttermilk
1   teaspoon (2 grams) packed lemon zest

1. In a small bowl, whisk together all ingredients until smooth.

TWICE-BAKED MERINGUE BROWNIE LOAF

Makes 10 to 12 servings

What's better than a fudgy brownie? A fudgy brownie topped with crisp, chocolate-swirled meringue. We baked the brownie base first and then topped it with generous swoops of meringue before baking a second time to sweet perfection.

5   ounces (141 grams) 60% cacao bittersweet chocolate baking bars, chopped and divided
½   cup (113 grams) unsalted butter, cubed
2   teaspoons (4 grams) instant espresso powder
1½   cups (300 grams) granulated sugar, divided
½   cup (110 grams) firmly packed dark brown sugar
1   cup (125 grams) all-purpose flour
¼   cup (21 grams) Dutch process cocoa powder
1   teaspoon (3 grams) kosher salt
3   large eggs (150 grams), lightly beaten
1½   teaspoons (6 grams) vanilla extract
3   large egg whites (90 grams)
1½   teaspoons (4.5 grams) cornstarch
¾   teaspoon (3.75 grams) distilled white vinegar

1. Position oven rack in center of oven. Preheat oven to 325°F (170°C). Line a 9x5-inch loaf pan with parchment paper, letting excess extend over sides of pan; spray parchment with cooking spray.

2. In the top of a double boiler, combine 4 ounces (113 grams) chocolate, butter, and espresso powder. Cook over simmering water, stirring occasionally, until mixture is smooth. Turn off heat, and whisk in ¾ cup (150 grams) granulated sugar and brown sugar. (Mixture will look granular.) Remove from heat, and let cool slightly.

3. In a medium bowl, whisk together flour, cocoa, and salt.

4. Add eggs to chocolate mixture, whisking until combined. Whisk in vanilla. Fold in flour mixture until a few bits of flour remain. Spread batter into prepared pan.

5. Bake until top is shiny and set, 50 to 55 minutes.

6. Meanwhile, in the heatproof bowl of a stand mixer, whisk together egg whites and remaining ¾ cup (150 grams) granulated sugar by hand. Place bowl over a saucepan of simmering water. Cook, whisking frequently, until sugar dissolves and an instant-read thermometer registers

120°F (49°C) to 130°F (54°C). Carefully return bowl to stand mixer. Using the whisk attachment, beat at high speed until stiff peaks form and bowl is cool to the touch, 4 to 5 minutes.

7. In a small bowl, whisk together cornstarch and vinegar. Add to egg white mixture, and beat until combined, about 30 seconds.

8. In a small microwave-safe bowl, heat remaining 1 ounce (28 grams) chocolate on high in 30-second intervals, stirring between each, until melted and smooth.

9. Spoon meringue on top of hot brownies. Drizzle with melted chocolate, and swirl gently until desired look is reached. Position oven rack in bottom third of oven; return brownie to oven. Immediately reduce oven temperature to 275°F (140°C).

10. Bake until meringue is dry to the touch and an instant-read thermometer inserted in meringue registers at least 160°F (71°C), 35 to 40 minutes. Let cool in pan for 20 minutes. Using excess parchment as handles, remove from pan, and let cool completely on a wire rack. Store in an airtight container at room temperature.

BUTTER PECAN POKE CAKE

Makes 1 (13x9-inch) cake

Studded with pecans, this sheet cake has an indulgent dulce de leche-bourbon soak.

1¾ cups (385 grams) firmly packed light brown sugar
¾   cup (170 grams) unsalted butter, melted
3   large eggs (150 grams)
1   tablespoon (13 grams) vanilla extract
3   cups (375 grams) all-purpose flour
1   tablespoon (15 grams) baking powder
1   teaspoon (5 grams) baking soda
1   teaspoon (3 grams) kosher salt
1   cup (240 grams) sour cream
1½ cups (360 grams) whole milk, divided
1   cup (113 grams) pecan pieces
1   (13.4-ounce) can (380 grams) dulce de leche
2   tablespoons (30 grams) bourbon
Cream Cheese Frosting (recipe follows)
Garnish: chopped candied pecans

1. Preheat oven to 350°F (180°C). Line a 13x9-inch baking pan with parchment paper, letting excess extend over sides of pan.

2. In a large bowl, whisk together brown sugar and melted butter until combined. Add eggs and vanilla, whisking until well combined.

3. In a medium bowl, whisk together flour, baking powder, baking soda, and salt. In a small bowl, whisk together sour cream and ½ cup (120 grams) milk. Gradually add flour mixture to sugar mixture alternately with sour cream mixture, beginning and ending with flour mixture, stirring just until combined after each addition. Fold in pecan pieces. Pour batter into prepared pan, smoothing top with an offset spatula.

4. Bake until a wooden pick inserted in center comes out clean, 35 to 40 minutes. Let cool in pan for 20 minutes.

5. In a small saucepan, heat dulce de leche and remaining 1 cup (240 grams) milk over medium heat, stirring occasionally, just until steaming, smooth, and combined. (Do not boil.) Remove from heat, and stir in bourbon.

6. Using a wooden skewer, poke warm cake all over at about ½-inch intervals. Slowly pour dulce de leche mixture, about ½ cup at a time, over cake. Refrigerate for 3 to 4 hours.

7. Invert cake onto a wire rack; discard parchment paper, and invert cake onto a serving platter or baking sheet. Top with Cream Cheese Frosting, and garnish with candied pecans, if desired. Refrigerate until ready to serve.

CREAM CHEESE FROSTING
Makes about 5 cups

12   ounces (340 grams) cream cheese, softened
¾   cup (170 grams) unsalted butter, softened
1½   teaspoons (6 grams) vanilla extract
¼   teaspoon kosher salt
5⅔   cups (680 grams) confectioners' sugar

1. In the bowl of a stand mixer fitted with the paddle attachment, beat cream cheese and butter at medium-low speed until smooth and creamy, about 1 minute. Beat in vanilla and salt until combined. Reduce mixer speed to low, and gradually add confectioners' sugar, beating until combined. Increase mixer speed to medium, and beat until fluffy, about 1 minute.

CHAI MARBLE CHEESECAKE

Makes 1 (9-inch) cake

This cheesecake has all the familiar cheesecake characteristics you love—thick, creamy filling blanketing a crisp gingersnap crust—but with twice the visual appeal and an extra dose of fall flavor thanks to the aromatic homemade Chai Spice Mix we added to the chocolate batter.

⅔ cup (160 grams) heavy whipping cream
1 tablespoon (6 grams) loose-leaf chai tea
2 cups (268 grams) finely ground gingersnap cookies
¼ cup (57 grams) unsalted butter, melted
1½ cups (300 grams) plus 2 tablespoons (24 grams) granulated sugar, divided
½ teaspoon kosher salt, divided
3 (8-ounce) packages (680 grams) cream cheese, cubed and softened
3 tablespoons (24 grams) all-purpose flour
1½ teaspoons (6 grams) vanilla extract
3 large eggs (150 grams), room temperature
½ cup (120 grams) sour cream, room temperature
2 teaspoons (4 grams) Chai Spice Mix (recipe follows)
1 teaspoon (2 grams) Dutch process cocoa powder

1. In a small saucepan, heat cream over medium heat, stirring occasionally, until a film starts to form on top and an instant-read thermometer registers 180°F (82°C). Remove from heat, and stir in tea. Let stand for 5 minutes. Stain through a fine-mesh sieve, discarding solids. Pour ½ cup (120 grams) chai cream into a small bowl, and let cool to room temperature; discard any remaining cream.

2. Preheat oven to 350°F (180°C). Spray bottom of a 9-inch springform pan with baking spray with flour. Line bottom of pan with parchment paper.

3. In a large bowl, stir together ground gingersnap cookies, melted butter, 2 tablespoons (24 grams) sugar, and ¼ teaspoon salt until well combined; using a small straight-sided measuring cup, press mixture into bottom of prepared pan.

4. Bake until set and fragrant, 10 to 12 minutes. Let cool on a wire rack for 30 minutes. Wrap bottom and sides of pan in a double layer of heavy-duty foil; place in a large oven bag, tucking ends so bag is flush with top edge of pan. Reduce oven temperature to 325°F (170°C).

5. In the bowl of a stand mixer fitted with the paddle attachment, beat cream cheese at medium speed until smooth and creamy,

2 to 3 minutes, stopping to scrape sides of bowl. Add flour, vanilla, remaining 1½ cups (300 grams) sugar, and remaining ¼ teaspoon salt; beat at low speed just until combined. Increase mixer speed to medium, and beat until well combined, 1 to 2 minutes, stopping to scrape sides of bowl. Add eggs, one at a time, beating until combined after each addition. Add chai cream and sour cream; beat at medium-low speed until well combined, 1 to 2 minutes, stopping to scrape sides of bowl. Transfer 2¼ cups (about 470 grams) batter to a medium bowl; add Chai Spice Mix and cocoa, folding just until combined.

6. Spray sides of prepared pan with baking spray with flour. Pour 2¼ cups (about 470 grams) plain batter onto prepared crust. Pour 1 cup (about 208 grams) chai batter in center of plain batter in pan. Using a spoon, dollop both remaining batters randomly onto surface of batter in pan. Using the tip of a knife, swirl batters together. (To get full marbled effect throughout cake, place knife almost to crust when swirling. Be careful not to bring knife in and out of batter too much; it will create air bubbles on top of cheesecake.)

7. Position oven rack in bottom third of oven. Place a roasting pan in oven; place springform pan in center of roasting pan. Add hot water to come 1 inch up sides of springform pan.

8. Bake until edges are set, top looks dry, center is almost set, and an instant-read thermometer inserted in center registers 150°F (66°C) to 155°F (68°C), 1½ hours to 1 hour and 40 minutes. Let cool in pan on a wire rack for 1½ to 2 hours. Refrigerate in pan on a wire rack overnight, loosely covering with foil only when completely cool to prevent condensation from forming on top of cheesecake. Carefully remove from pan, and transfer to a serving plate. Use a warm dry knife to slice when ready to serve.

CHAI SPICE MIX
Makes about ⅓ cup

3 tablespoons (18 grams) ground cinnamon
1½ tablespoons (9 grams) ground ginger
1 tablespoon (6 grams) ground cloves
½ tablespoon (3 grams) ground cardamom
½ tablespoon (3 grams) finely ground black pepper

1. In a small bowl, stir together all ingredients. Store in an airtight container for up to 2 months.

VANILLA BEAN BERRY POUND CAKE WITH SOUR CREAM VANILLA GLAZE

Makes 1 (8½x4½-inch) cake

Vanilla brings a warm richness to this berry-studded loaf cake, perfect for summertime.

2 cups (223 grams) fresh berries, such as raspberries, blackberries, and blueberries (see Note), patted dry
1¼ cups (156 grams) plus 1 tablespoon (8 grams) all-purpose flour, divided
½ cup (113 grams) unsalted butter, softened
1 cup (200 grams) granulated sugar
2 large eggs (100 grams), room temperature
2 teaspoons (12 grams) vanilla bean paste*
1 teaspoon (1 gram) lemon zest
¾ teaspoon (3.75 grams) baking powder
½ teaspoon (1.5 grams) kosher salt
⅓ cup (80 grams) sour cream
Sour Cream Vanilla Glaze (recipe follows)
Garnish: fresh berries, fresh mint leaves

1. Preheat oven to 350°F (180°C). Spray an 8½x4½-inch loaf pan with baking spray with flour. Line pan with parchment paper, letting ends extend over sides of pan.
2. In a medium bowl, toss together berries and 1 tablespoon (8 grams) flour; set aside.
3. In the bowl of a stand mixer fitted with the paddle attachment, beat butter and sugar at medium speed until fluffy, 3 to 4 minutes, stopping to scrape sides of bowl. Add eggs, one at time, beating well after each addition. Beat in vanilla bean paste and lemon zest.
4. In a medium bowl, whisk together baking powder, salt, and remaining 1¼ cups (156 grams) flour. With mixer on low speed, gradually add baking powder mixture to butter mixture alternately with sour cream, beginning and ending with baking powder mixture, beating just until combined after each addition. Gently fold in berry mixture. (Batter will be thick.) Spoon batter into prepared pan, spreading evenly.
5. Bake until a wooden pick inserted in center comes out clean, about 1 hour and 15 minutes. Let cool in pan for 15 minutes. Using excess parchment as handles, remove from pan, and let cool completely on a wire rack.
6. Spread Sour Cream Vanilla Glaze onto cooled cake. Garnish with berries and mint, if desired.

We used Heilala Vanilla Bean Paste.

Note: *Avoid using strawberries in this loaf, as they lose their color when baked and may leave wet spots in the cake crumb.*

SOUR CREAM VANILLA GLAZE
Makes about ⅓ cup

1 cup (120 grams) confectioners' sugar
2 tablespoons (30 grams) sour cream
½ teaspoon (2 grams) vanilla extract*
Water, as needed

1. In a small bowl, stir together confectioners' sugar, sour cream, and vanilla with a fork until smooth. (Mixture will seem too dry at first, but it should come together.) Stir in water, a few drops at a time, until desired consistency is reached. Use immediately.

We used Heilala Pure Vanilla Extract.

IRISH CREAM CAKE

Makes 1 (9-inch) cake

Walking County Cork's misty seaside cliffs and the rolling green pastures where the cows that make some of Ireland's best Irish cream graze was the experience of a lifetime. After meeting the founder and experiencing the artisan nature of Five Farms Irish Cream Liqueur, I was so in love, I carried a bottle all the way home to Alabama with me. It was worth it— not only for the sipping but also because it was destined to be featured in this marble cake frosted with a buttercream that showcases the liqueur's delicate flavor and incomparable quality.

½ cup (113 grams) unsalted butter, softened
1 cup plus 2 tablespoons (224 grams) granulated sugar
2 large eggs (100 grams), room temperature
1¾ cups (219 grams) cake flour
2 teaspoons (10 grams) baking powder
½ teaspoon (1.5 grams) kosher salt
⅔ cup (160 grams) Irish cream liqueur*
1 teaspoon (4 grams) vanilla extract
¼ cup (35 grams) 66% cacao semisweet chocolate baking wafers
1 tablespoon (15 grams) whole milk
Irish Cream Buttercream Frosting (recipe follows)

1. Preheat oven to 350°F (180°C). Spray a 9-inch round cake pan with baking spray with flour.
2. In the bowl of a stand mixer fitted with the paddle attachment, beat butter and sugar at medium speed until fluffy, 3 to 4 minutes, stopping to scrape sides of bowl. Add eggs, one at a time, beating well after each addition.
3. In a medium bowl, sift together flour, baking powder, and salt. In a small bowl, combine liqueur and vanilla. With mixer on low speed, gradually add flour mixture to butter mixture alternately with liqueur mixture, beginning and ending with flour mixture, beating just until combined after each addition. Reserve ½ cup (about 135 grams) batter in another small bowl. Pour remaining batter into prepared pan, smoothing top with an offset spatula.
4. In a small microwave-safe bowl, heat chocolate on high in 15-second intervals, stirring between each, until melted and smooth. Stir in reserved batter and milk until combined. Drop tablespoonfuls of chocolate batter on top of batter in pan. Using the tip of an offset spatula or butter knife, swirl batters.
5. Bake until a wooden pick inserted in center comes out clean, 25 to 30 minutes. Let cool in pan for 15 minutes. Remove from pan, and let cool completely on a wire rack.
6. Using an offset spatula, spread Irish Cream Buttercream Frosting on cooled cake, swirling as desired.

We used Five Farms Irish Cream Liqueur.

IRISH CREAM BUTTERCREAM FROSTING
Makes about 1½ cups

¾ cup (170 grams) unsalted butter, softened
3 cups (360 grams) confectioners' sugar
3 tablespoons (45 grams) Irish cream liqueur
¾ teaspoon (2.25 grams) kosher salt
¾ teaspoon (4.5 grams) vanilla bean paste

1. In the bowl of a stand mixer fitted with the paddle attachment, beat butter at medium speed until creamy, about 3 minutes. Gradually add confectioners' sugar, beating until combined. Add liqueur, salt, and vanilla bean paste, and beat at medium-high speed until smooth, 1 to 2 minutes. (Do not overbeat.) Use immediately.

RHUBARB & GINGER UPSIDE-DOWN CAKE

Makes 1 (9-inch) cake

Recipe by Clodagh McKenna

Simple and sweet, with a hint of ginger spice, this upside-down cake is the perfect summer dessert.

3   tablespoons (42 grams) unsalted butter
⅔   cup plus 2 tablespoons (202 grams) firmly packed light brown sugar, divided
6   teaspoons (21 grams) finely chopped crystallized ginger, divided
12 ounces (340 grams) fresh rhubarb, trimmed and cut into 1-inch pieces
1½ cups plus 1 tablespoon (196 grams) all-purpose flour
1   teaspoon (5 grams) baking powder
½   teaspoon (1.5 grams) kosher salt
¼   teaspoon (1.25 grams) baking soda
¾   cup plus 1 tablespoon (195 grams) whole buttermilk
2   medium eggs (94 grams)
⅓   cup plus 2 teaspoons (85 grams) canola oil
Crème fraîche, to serve

1. Preheat oven to 350°F (180°C).
2. In a 9-inch ovenproof skillet, melt butter over medium heat. Stir in ⅓ cup plus 2 tablespoons (101 grams) brown sugar, and cook, stirring occasionally, until sugar is melted and combined, about 2 minutes. Add 2 teaspoons (7 grams) ginger, stirring to combine. Remove from heat. Arrange rhubarb in a single layer in skillet.
3. In a medium bowl, sift together flour, baking powder, salt, and baking soda.
4. In a large bowl, whisk together buttermilk, eggs, oil, remaining ⅓ cup plus 2 tablespoons (101 grams) brown sugar, and remaining 4 teaspoons (14 grams) ginger. Whisk in flour mixture just until combined. Pour over rhubarb in pan, smoothing with an offset spatula.
5. Bake until cake springs back when pressed in center, 30 to 45 minutes. Let cool in skillet on a wire rack for 5 minutes. Invert cake onto a serving plate. Serve with crème fraîche.

BARMBRACK

Makes 1 (9-inch) cake

Recipe courtesy of Gemma Stafford

Barmbrack, also known as tea brack or just called "brack" for short, is a cake synonymous with Halloween in Ireland, but it's really baked year-round. Often symbolic charms are baked into the bread, meant to indicate the different fortunes of the recipient. A ring, which is the most common charm used today, means the person will be married within the year. Barmbrack is delicious toasted and smeared with butter. Brushing the just-baked cake with honey gives it extra shine and sweetness.

1⅓   cups (293 grams) firmly packed dark brown sugar
2   cups plus 4 teaspoons (500 grams) hot strong-brewed black Irish breakfast tea*
1¼   cups (200 grams) dried cherries
1   cup (128 grams) raisins
1   cup (128 grams) golden raisins
¼   cup (32 grams) candied citrus peel
3   cups (375 grams) all-purpose flour
2   teaspoons (10 grams) baking powder
1   teaspoon (2 grams) mixed spice or pumpkin pie spice
½   teaspoon (1.5 grams) kosher salt
2   large eggs (100 grams), lightly beaten
2   tablespoons (42 grams) honey
Unsalted butter and honey, to serve

1. In a medium bowl, place brown sugar. Pour hot tea over sugar, and stir until sugar is completely melted. Add cherries, raisins, golden raisins, and citrus peel, stirring to combine. Cover with a piece of plastic wrap, and let stand at room temperature overnight to soak.

2. Preheat oven to 325°F (170°C). Butter a tall-sided 9-inch round cake pan or springform pan. Line bottom of pan with parchment paper.

3. In a large bowl, whisk together flour, baking powder, spice, and salt. Gradually add fruit mixture to flour mixture alternately with eggs. Stir until well combined and no dry streaks remain. (See Note.) Pour batter into prepared pan.

4. Bake until golden and a wooden pick inserted in center comes out clean, 1 hour and 20 minutes to 1½ hours, covering with foil after 1 hour of baking to prevent excess browning. Let cool in pan for 20 minutes. Remove from pan, and place on a wire rack. Using a pastry brush, brush honey onto warm cake. Let cool completely. Store in an airtight container for up to 1 week. Serve with butter and honey.

*Use 2 teabags to get extra-strong flavor.

Note: *If you want to include a trinket in your barmbrack, wrap it in parchment, and add it to the batter before pouring the batter into the pan.*

BERRIES & IRISH CREAM COFFEE CAKE

Makes 1 (9-inch) cake

Like your coffee cake with a little kick? Irish cream liqueur gives this cake, brimming with strawberries, blueberries, and blackberries, an extra-fluffy crumb and rich flavor.

½   cup (113 grams) unsalted butter, softened
¾   cup (150 grams) granulated sugar
¼   cup (55 grams) firmly packed light brown sugar
2   large eggs (100 grams), room temperature
1   large egg yolk (19 grams), room temperature
½   teaspoon (3 grams) vanilla bean paste
1⅔ cups (208 grams) plus 1 teaspoon (3 grams) all-purpose flour, divided
2¼ teaspoons (11.25 grams) baking powder
¾   teaspoon (2.25 grams) kosher salt
¾   cup (180 grams) sour cream, room temperature
¼   cup (60 grams) Irish cream liqueur*
⅓   cup (52 grams) plus 2 tablespoons (21 grams) fresh blueberries, divided
½   cup (84 grams) quartered fresh strawberries, divided
½   cup (90 grams) halved fresh blackberries, divided
Spiced Streusel (recipe follows)
Irish Cream Glaze (recipe follows)

1. Preheat oven to 325°F (170°C). Spray a light-colored 9-inch springform pan with baking spray with flour. Line bottom of pan with parchment paper.
2. In the bowl of a stand mixer fitted with the paddle attachment, beat butter and sugars at medium speed until fluffy, about 3 minutes, stopping to scrape sides of bowl. Add eggs and egg yolk, one at a time, beating well after each addition. Beat in vanilla bean paste.
3. In a medium bowl, whisk together 1⅔ cups (208 grams) flour, baking powder, and salt. In a small bowl, stir together sour cream and liqueur. With mixer on low speed, gradually add flour mixture to butter mixture alternately with sour cream mixture, beginning and ending with flour mixture, beating just until combined after each addition.
4. In another medium bowl, combine ⅓ cup (52 grams) blueberries, ¼ cup (42 grams) strawberries, and ¼ cup (45 grams) blackberries. Add remaining 1 teaspoon (3 grams) flour, tossing until well combined. Fold berry mixture into batter. Spoon batter into prepared pan, smoothing into an

even layer with a small offset spatula. Sprinkle Spiced Streusel onto batter; top with remaining 2 tablespoons (20 grams) blueberries, remaining ¼ cup (42 grams) strawberries, and remaining ¼ cup (45 grams) blackberries.
5. Bake until a wooden pick inserted in center comes out clean, 1 hour to 1 hour and 5 minutes, rotating pan halfway through baking and loosely covering with foil to prevent excess browning, if necessary. Let cool in pan for 10 minutes. Remove sides of pan; let cool completely on base of pan on a wire rack. Drizzle with Irish Cream Glaze before serving.

We used Five Farms Irish Cream Liqueur.

SPICED STREUSEL
Makes 1⅓ cups

⅓   cup (67 grams) granulated sugar
¼   cup (55 grams) firmly packed light brown sugar
¼   teaspoon kosher salt
½   cup (113 grams) unsalted butter, melted
1⅓ cups (167 grams) all-purpose flour
¾   teaspoon (1.5 grams) ground cinnamon
½   teaspoon (2.5 grams) baking powder
¼   teaspoon ground ginger

1. In a medium bowl, stir together sugars and salt until well combined. Stir in melted butter until well combined.
2. In another medium bowl, whisk together flour, cinnamon, baking powder, and ginger. Add flour mixture to sugar mixture, stirring until well combined.

IRISH CREAM GLAZE
Makes ⅓ cup

¾   cup (90 grams) confectioners' sugar
2½ tablespoons (37.5 grams) Irish cream liqueur
⅛   teaspoon kosher salt

1. In a small bowl, stir together all ingredients until smooth and well combined. Use immediately.

SHARLOTKA (RUSSIAN APPLE CAKE)

Makes 1 (9-inch) cake

Despite its Russian name, the Sharlotka (Russian for "Charlotte") is actually British in origin but was served to a very important Russian guest during his visit. Czar Alexander I dined in London, England, on an apple dish that French pastry chef Marie-Antoine Carême had just invented, made with ladyfingers, Bavarian cream, and apples. Sometimes known by its more famous moniker charlotte russe, Sharlotka changed when it came to Russia, taking on a less complicated form of apples intermittently layered with a fluffy cake batter, creating a recipe that is both seductively simple and satisfying.

3   cups (330 grams) ¼-inch-sliced peeled Granny Smith apples
2   cups (220 grams) ¼-inch-sliced peeled Golden Delicious apples
1   cup (200 grams) plus 1 tablespoon (12 grams) granulated sugar, divided
¼   teaspoon packed lemon zest
2   teaspoons (10 grams) fresh lemon juice
4   large eggs (200 grams), room temperature
1½   teaspoons (6 grams) vanilla extract
¾   teaspoon (2.25 grams) kosher salt
1¼   cups (156 grams) all-purpose flour
1½   teaspoons (7.5 grams) baking powder
¼   teaspoon ground cinnamon
¼   teaspoon ground cardamom
Confectioners' sugar, for dusting

1. Preheat oven to 350°F (180°C). Butter a 9-inch springform pan. Line bottom of pan with parchment paper.

2. In a large bowl, stir together apples, 1 tablespoon (12 grams) granulated sugar, and lemon zest and juice. Set aside.

3. In the bowl of a stand mixer fitted with the whisk attachment, beat eggs, vanilla, salt, and remaining 1 cup (200 grams) granulated sugar at medium-high speed until thickened and pale and ribbons form when whisk attachment is lifted, 6 to 7 minutes. Remove bowl from stand mixer.

4. In a medium bowl, whisk together flour, baking powder, cinnamon, and cardamom. Using a fine-mesh sieve, gradually sift flour mixture over egg mixture, gently folding after each addition; fold just until combined and no dry streaks remain.

5. In prepared pan, place half of apple mixture (about 281 grams). Pour half of batter (about 279 grams) over apple mixture; gently smooth with a small offset spatula to ensure batter is spread over and between apple mixture. Scatter remaining apple mixture evenly on top of batter in pan; pour remaining batter over apple mixture, gently smoothing with a small offset spatula. Let stand for 2 minutes, tapping sides of pan forcefully to release as many air bubbles as possible; pop any bubbles that rise to the surface, smoothing batter as needed.

6. Bake until top is golden brown, cake springs back when touched in center, and a wooden pick inserted in center comes out clean, 35 to 45 minutes, loosely covering with foil to prevent excess browning, if necessary. Let cool in pan for 15 minutes. Carefully remove sides of pan. Serve warm, or let cool to room temperature on base of pan on a wire rack. Dust with confectioners' sugar before serving.

PRO TIP
Feel free to customize your Sharlotka with different flavor twists. Add orange zest and juice instead of lemon, or stir a bit of your favorite baking spices into the batter or the apples.

FRENCH APPLE CAKE

Makes 1 (9-inch) cake

In Normandy, France, more than 800 different varieties of apples grow and have flourished since the eighth century. From this land of a thousand orchards comes the French version of apple cake, often spiked with rum and so jam-packed with apples, it'll always boast a custard-like texture.

4⅓	cups (542 grams) ¾- to 1-inch-chopped peeled Honeycrisp apples
3	cups (375 grams) ¾- to 1-inch-chopped peeled Pink Lady apples
2	teaspoons (10 grams) fresh lemon juice
3	large eggs (150 grams), room temperature
¾	cup (150 grams) granulated sugar
3	tablespoons (39 grams) dark spiced rum
1	teaspoon (6 grams) vanilla bean paste
1	cup (125 grams) all-purpose flour
1½	teaspoons (7.5 grams) baking powder
1	teaspoon (3 grams) kosher salt
⅔	cup (150 grams) unsalted butter, melted and cooled for 15 minutes
1	tablespoon (12 grams) sparkling sugar

Garnish: sparkling sugar, confectioners' sugar

1. Position an oven rack in center of oven. Place a sheet of foil on lowest oven rack to catch any drips. Preheat oven to 350°F (180°C).

2. In a large bowl, toss together apples and lemon juice. Set aside.

3. In another large bowl, whisk eggs until pale and foamy, about 2 minutes. Add granulated sugar, rum, and vanilla bean paste, whisking until well combined.

4. In a medium bowl, whisk together flour, baking powder, and salt. Gradually add flour mixture to egg mixture alternately with melted butter, beginning and ending with flour mixture, whisking until combined and stopping to scrape sides of bowl.

5. Spray a light-colored 9-inch springform pan with baking spray with flour. Line bottom of pan with parchment paper.

6. Reserve 1 cup (125 grams) apples. Using a large silicone spatula, fold remaining apples into batter. Using a small offset spatula, spread batter in prepared pan, pressing down to distribute batter between apples and into edges of pan; smooth into an even layer. Arrange reserved apples on top as desired, pressing into batter and smoothing as needed.

7. Bake for 20 minutes. Sprinkle with sparkling sugar, and bake until a wooden pick inserted in center comes out clean and an instant-read thermometer registers 200°F (93°C) to 205°F (96°C), 36 to 42 minutes, rotating pan halfway through baking and loosely covering with foil to prevent excess browning, if necessary. Let cool in pan for 10 minutes. Carefully remove sides of pan; let cool completely on base on a wire rack. Garnish with sparkling sugar and confectioners' sugar, if desired.

PRO TIPS

The dark spiced rum in this recipe gives this cake its depth of flavor. Calvados, an apple brandy produced in Normandy, is another great option to swirl into your batter.

PEARL SUGAR STREUSEL COFFEE-FRUITCAKE

Makes 1 (9-inch) cake

Coffee cake meets fruitcake in a chic rendition of flavors. Dried cranberries, candied orange, and candied ginger get a luxurious bath in fragrant brandy while spices reminiscent of the holidays infuse the silky batter. We swapped out the usual sour cream for tangy crème fraîche to create an extra-elegant crumb. To top it all off, Swedish pearl sugar adds a surprise crunch to the crispy streusel that will have your cup of coffee begging for more.

1   cup (210 grams) brandy
⅓   cup (53 grams) lightly packed sweetened dried cranberries, roughly chopped
⅓   cup (50 grams) lightly packed finely chopped candied orange
3   tablespoons (40 grams) lightly packed finely chopped candied ginger
⅔   cup (150 grams) unsalted butter, softened
⅔   cup (147 grams) firmly packed dark brown sugar
¼   cup (50 grams) granulated sugar
2   large eggs (100 grams), room temperature
1⅔   cups (208 grams) plus 1 tablespoon (8 grams) all-purpose flour, divided
2   teaspoons (10 grams) baking powder
1   teaspoon (2 grams) ground cinnamon
¾   teaspoon (2.25 grams) kosher salt
¾   teaspoon (1.5 grams) ground ginger
¼   teaspoon ground nutmeg
¼   teaspoon ground cloves
⅔   cup (160 grams) crème fraîche, room temperature
2   teaspoons (8 grams) vanilla extract
Pearl Sugar Streusel (recipe follows)
¼   cup (48 grams) Swedish pearl sugar
Garnish: confectioners' sugar

1. In a small saucepan, bring brandy just to a boil over medium-high heat. Remove from heat; stir in cranberries, candied orange, and candied ginger. Cover and let stand for 30 minutes, stirring occasionally. Drain fruit mixture, reserving brandy.
2. Preheat oven to 350°F (180°C). Spray a 9-inch springform pan with baking spray with flour. Line bottom of pan with parchment paper.
3. In the bowl of a stand mixer fitted with the paddle attachment, beat butter, brown sugar, and granulated sugar at medium speed until fluffy, 3 to 4 minutes, stopping to scrape sides of bowl. Add eggs, one at a time, beating well after each addition.

4. In a medium bowl, whisk together 1⅔ cups (208 grams) flour, baking powder, cinnamon, salt, ground ginger, nutmeg, and cloves. In a small bowl, stir together crème fraîche, 1 tablespoon (13 grams) reserved brandy, and vanilla. With mixer on low speed, gradually add flour mixture to butter mixture alternately with crème fraîche mixture, beginning and ending with flour mixture, beating just until combined after each addition.
5. In a small bowl, stir together fruit mixture and remaining 1 tablespoon (8 grams) flour; fold into batter. Spread batter in prepared pan. Crumble Pearl Sugar Streusel on top. (Crumble layer will be quite thick.) Sprinkle with pearl sugar.
6. Bake until golden brown and a wooden pick inserted in center comes out clean, 40 to 45 minutes, rotating pan halfway through baking and loosely covering with foil to prevent excess browning, if necessary. Let cool in pan for 10 minutes. Remove sides of pan. Let cool completely on base of pan on a wire rack. Garnish with confectioners' sugar, if desired.

> **PRO TIP**
> The leftover strained brandy can be used as a boozy flavoring for other cakes and baked goods. It also makes a great addition to cocktails, coffee, and more!

PEARL SUGAR STREUSEL
Makes 1½ cups

½   cup plus 2 tablespoons (124 grams) granulated sugar
½   cup (113 grams) unsalted butter, melted
1   teaspoon (4 grams) vanilla extract
¼   teaspoon kosher salt
1⅓   cups (167 grams) all-purpose flour
½   teaspoon (2.5 grams) baking powder
⅓   cup (64 grams) Swedish pearl sugar

1. In a medium bowl, stir together granulated sugar, melted butter, vanilla, and salt until well combined. Add flour and baking powder; stir until well combined. Fold in pearl sugar.

BREADS

QUICK BREADS

Short on time but not on flavor, our quick breads will have you baking in a flash. From soda breads that take you straight to Ireland to banana bread that is a caramelized dream, these recipes add comfort on demand.

CHEDDAR-PECAN SCONES

Makes 8 scones

Cheesy and nutty, with just the right amount of peppery kick, these savory scones are tender perfection. Baking them in the cast-iron wedge skillet makes these scones thicker, with straight, symmetrical edges.

2 cups (250 grams) all-purpose flour
2 tablespoons (24 grams) granulated sugar
1 tablespoon (15 grams) baking powder
½ teaspoon (1.5 grams) kosher salt
¼ teaspoon ground red pepper
¼ teaspoon ground black pepper
⅓ cup (76 grams) cold unsalted butter, cubed
¾ cup (71 grams) shredded extra-sharp Cheddar cheese
½ cup (57 grams) finely chopped pecans
¾ cup (180 grams) plus 1 tablespoon (15 grams) cold heavy whipping cream, divided

1. Preheat oven to 375°F (190°C). Spray an 8-well cast-iron wedge pan with baking spray with flour. (See Note.)
2. In a large bowl, whisk together flour, sugar, baking powder, salt, red pepper, and black pepper. Using a pastry blender or 2 forks, cut in cold butter until mixture is crumbly. Stir in cheese and pecans. Add ¾ cup (180 grams) cold cream, stirring with a fork just until dry ingredients are moistened. Working gently, bring mixture together with hands until a dough forms.
3. Turn out dough onto a lightly floured surface, and pat into 7-inch circle. Using a bench scraper or sharp knife, cut into 8 wedges. Place a wedge in each well of prepared pan. Brush tops with remaining 1 tablespoon (15 grams) cold cream.
4. Bake until golden brown, 20 to 25 minutes. Let cool in pan for 10 minutes. Remove from pan, and serve warm or at room temperature.

Note: *You can also bake these scones in a regular 10-inch cast-iron skillet or on a baking sheet lined with parchment paper. After you cut the circle of dough into 8 wedges in step 3, place scones about 1½ inches apart on prepared baking sheet, and proceed with recipe. If using a regular skillet, transfer dough to skillet, and proceed with recipe.*

HAZELNUT-BANANA SOUR CREAM MUFFINS

Makes 12 muffins

With a toasty Hazelnut Streusel topping and the tender crumb of banana bread, these muffins are a welcome treat for cold winter mornings.

½   cup (113 grams) unsalted butter, melted
1   cup (200 grams) granulated sugar
¾   cup (150 grams) mashed ripe banana (about 2 medium bananas)
1   large egg (50 grams)
2   teaspoons (8 grams) vanilla extract
1⅔ cups (208 grams) all-purpose flour
1½ teaspoons (7.5 grams) baking powder
1   teaspoon (2 grams) ground cinnamon
½   teaspoon (1.5 grams) kosher salt
¼   teaspoon (1.25 grams) baking soda
½   cup (120 grams) sour cream
¼   cup (60 grams) whole milk
¾   cup (85 grams) chopped hazelnuts
Hazelnut Streusel (recipe follows)

1. Preheat oven to 375°F (190°C). Spray a 12-cup muffin pan with baking spray with flour.
2. In a large bowl, place melted butter. Whisk in sugar, banana, egg, and vanilla until combined.
3. In a medium bowl, whisk together flour, baking powder, cinnamon, salt, and baking soda. Whisk flour mixture into butter mixture. Add sour cream and milk, whisking just until combined. Fold in hazelnuts. Divide batter among prepared muffin cups. Sprinkle with Hazelnut Streusel.
4. Bake until a wooden pick inserted in center comes out clean, 15 to 20 minutes. Let cool in pan for 10 minutes. Remove from pan, and serve warm or at room temperature.

HAZELNUT STREUSEL

Makes about 1 cup

⅓   cup (42 grams) all-purpose flour
¼   cup (50 grams) granulated sugar
½   teaspoon (1 gram) ground cinnamon
¼   teaspoon kosher salt
½   cup (57 grams) chopped hazelnuts
2   tablespoons (28 grams) unsalted butter, melted

1. In a medium bowl, stir together flour, sugar, cinnamon, and salt. Stir in hazelnuts. Stir in melted butter until mixture is crumbly. Crumble with your fingertips until desired consistency is reached.

BANANAS FOSTER UPSIDE-DOWN BANANA BREAD

Makes 1 (9-inch) loaf

In this showstopper, halved bananas are caramelized in brown sugar, rum, and vanilla bean paste and then covered with a luscious banana-packed batter. Once baked, it becomes the perfect blend of tender banana bread and aromatic, boozy bananas Foster.

¼   cup (57 grams) unsalted butter
1½   cups (330 grams) firmly packed dark brown sugar, divided
5   tablespoons (75 grams) dark spiced rum, divided
2   teaspoons (10 grams) banana liqueur (optional)
1   teaspoon (6 grams) vanilla bean paste
1   teaspoon (1.5 grams) ground cinnamon, divided
3   firm large bananas (408 grams), halved lengthwise
2   cups (250 grams) all-purpose flour
2   teaspoons (10 grams) baking powder
½   teaspoon (1.5 grams) kosher salt
1   cup (227 grams) mashed ripe banana (about 3 medium bananas)
½   cup (113 grams) unsalted butter, melted
2   large eggs (100 grams)
¼   cup (60 grams) whole milk
½   cup (57 grams) chopped walnuts

1. Preheat oven to 350°F (180°C). Spray sides of a 9-inch round cake pan with baking spray with flour.

2. In a medium saucepan, melt butter. Whisk in ½ cup (110 grams) brown sugar, and cook, stirring occasionally, until it starts to smell like caramel, 4 to 5 minutes. Slowly add 2 tablespoons (30 grams) rum and liqueur (if using), whisking until smooth and combined. Whisk in vanilla bean paste and ¼ teaspoon cinnamon. Pour into prepared pan. Place banana halves, cut side down, on top of caramel, cutting bananas to fit, if necessary.

3. In a medium bowl, whisk together flour, baking powder, and salt.

4. In a large bowl, whisk together mashed banana, melted butter, eggs, milk, remaining 1 cup (220 grams) brown sugar, remaining 3 tablespoons (45 grams) rum, and remaining ¾ teaspoon (1.5 grams) cinnamon. Whisk flour mixture into mashed banana mixture just until combined. Fold in walnuts. Pour into prepared pan.

5. Bake until a wooden pick inserted in center comes out clean, 55 minutes to 1 hour. Let cool in pan for 5 minutes. Invert bread onto a rimmed serving platter. Serve warm or at room temperature.

CHEDDAR-PECAN LOAF

Makes 1 (8½x4½-inch) loaf

Packed with Cheddar cheese and flavored with dill, this quick bread recipe has fresh springtime flavor that highlights the richness of pecans. Made all the more tender from buttermilk in the batter, this loaf is delicious served warm from the oven and slathered in butter.

2½ cups (313 grams) all-purpose flour
3 tablespoons (36 grams) granulated sugar
1½ teaspoons (7.5 grams) baking powder
1 teaspoon (3 grams) kosher salt
1 teaspoon (2 grams) garlic powder
¼ teaspoon (1.25 grams) baking soda
1⅓ cups (320 grams) whole buttermilk, room temperature
¼ cup (56 grams) canola oil
1 large egg (50 grams), room temperature

1 cup (113 grams) roughly chopped toasted pecans*
⅔ cup (75 grams) plus 3 tablespoons (22 grams) firmly packed shredded extra-sharp Cheddar cheese, divided
½ cup (56 grams) finely chopped green onion
¼ cup (10 grams) lightly packed finely chopped fresh dill
¼ cup (28 grams) roughly chopped raw pecans*
Softened butter, to serve

1. Preheat oven to 350°F (180°F). Spray an 8½x4½-inch loaf pan with baking spray with flour. Line pan with parchment paper, letting excess extend over sides of pan.
2. In a large bowl, whisk together flour, sugar, baking powder, salt, garlic powder, and baking soda.

3. In a medium bowl, whisk together buttermilk, oil, and egg. Add buttermilk mixture to flour mixture; stir until well combined. (Batter will be very thick.) Fold in toasted pecans, ⅔ cup (75 grams) cheese, green onion, and dill until well combined. Spoon batter into prepared pan; using a small offset spatula, smooth into an even layer. Sprinkle top with raw pecans and remaining 3 tablespoons (22 grams) cheese.
4. Bake until a wooden pick inserted in center comes out clean and an instant-read thermometer inserted in center registers 200°F (93°C), 1 hour to 1 hour and 5 minutes. Let cool in pan for 5 minutes. Using excess parchment as handles, remove from pan, and let cool completely on a wire rack. Serve with softened butter.

We used Sunnyland Farms Raw Georgia Pecan Halves.

STRAWBERRY-PECAN SCONES

Makes 8 scones

Capture the essence of strawberry season with these tender pecan-studded scones that highlight the sweetness of the strawberries with rich, buttery notes while lending irresistible crunch to every bite. Topped with a velvety vanilla glaze, these scones are next-level delicious.

2   cups (250 grams) all-purpose flour
⅓   cup (73 grams) firmly packed light brown sugar
2   teaspoons (10 grams) baking powder
1   teaspoon (3 grams) kosher salt
¼   teaspoon ground cinnamon
¼   cup (57 grams) cold unsalted butter, cubed
¾   cup (180 grams) cold heavy whipping cream
1   teaspoon (6 grams) vanilla bean paste
¼   teaspoon (1 gram) tightly packed orange zest
½   cup (85 grams) ½-inch-chopped fresh strawberries, patted dry
½   cup (57 grams) chopped toasted pecans*
2   tablespoons (14 grams) chopped raw pecans*
1   large egg (50 grams), lightly beaten
Sparkling sugar, for sprinkling
Vanilla Bean Glaze (recipe follows)

1. Preheat oven to 375°F (190°C). Line a baking sheet with parchment paper.
2. In a large bowl, whisk together flour, brown sugar, baking powder, salt, and cinnamon, breaking up any clumps by hand if needed. Using a pastry blender or 2 forks, cut in cold butter until mixture resembles coarse crumbs.
3. In a small bowl, stir together cold cream, vanilla bean paste, and orange zest. Gradually add cream mixture to flour mixture, stirring with a fork until dry ingredients are moistened. Gently stir in strawberries and toasted pecans. (It's OK if dough is crumbly or shaggy in parts.)
4. Turn out dough onto a very lightly floured surface; knead gently 4 to 6 times to bring dough together. Roll or pat dough into a 7-inch circle (1-inch thickness), lightly flouring surface as needed to prevent sticking. Using a bench scraper or a thin-bladed knife, cut dough circle into 8 wedges; gently press raw pecans into tops of scones as desired. Place scones at least 2 inches apart on prepared pan. Freeze for 15 minutes.
5. Brush tops of scones with egg wash, and sprinkle with sparkling sugar.
6. Bake until golden brown and a wooden pick inserted in center comes out clean, 20 to 22 minutes. Let cool to room temperature. Spoon Vanilla Bean Glaze into a small pastry bag; cut a ¼-inch opening in tip. Drizzle onto scones as desired.

We used Sunnyland Farms Raw Georgia Pecan Halves.

VANILLA BEAN GLAZE
Makes about ⅓ cup

⅔   cup (80 grams) confectioners' sugar
2½   tablespoons (37.5 grams) heavy whipping cream
½   teaspoon (3 grams) vanilla bean paste
¼   teaspoon kosher salt

1. In a small bowl, stir together all ingredients until smooth. Use immediately.

DOUBLE-CHOCOLATE ZUCCHINI MUFFINS

Makes 12 muffins

Why go for tried-and-true zucchini bread when you could have these indulgent muffins? Owing their soft texture to juicy zucchini, these muffins get a dose of decadence from white chocolate chips embedded in the cocoa-rich batter.

1   cup (200 grams) granulated sugar
½   cup (120 grams) sour cream, room temperature
⅓   cup (76 grams) unsalted butter, melted
⅓   cup (80 grams) whole milk
2   large eggs (100 grams), room temperature
1   teaspoon (4 grams) vanilla extract

2   cups (250 grams) all-purpose flour
½   cup (43 grams) Dutch process cocoa powder
1½ teaspoons (7.5 grams) baking powder
½   teaspoon (2.5 grams) baking soda
½   teaspoon (1.5 grams) kosher salt
1   cup (120 grams) shredded zucchini, patted dry
1   cup (170 grams) white chocolate chips

1. Preheat oven 350°F (180°C). Line a 12-cup muffin pan with parchment paper liners.

2. In a large bowl, whisk together sugar, sour cream, melted butter, and milk; whisk in eggs and vanilla.

3. In a medium bowl, whisk together flour, cocoa, baking powder, baking soda, and salt. Add flour mixture to sugar mixture, whisking just until combined. Fold in zucchini and white chocolate chips. Divide batter among prepared muffin cups.

4. Bake until a wooden pick inserted in center comes out clean, 20 to 25 minutes. Let cool in pan for 10 minutes. Remove from pan, and serve warm, or let cool completely on a wire rack.

CHOCOLATE CHUNK BANANA SCONES

Makes 8 scones

Time to shake up your scone game. Mashed banana in the dough gives these scones an irresistibly tender crumb and pairs perfectly with the chocolate chunks speckled throughout.

3   cups (375 grams) all-purpose flour
¼   cup (50 grams) granulated sugar
4   teaspoons (20 grams) baking powder
1½   teaspoons (4.5 grams) kosher salt
½   cup (113 grams) cold unsalted butter, cubed
⅔   cup (160 grams) cold heavy whipping cream
⅔   cup (151 grams) mashed ripe banana
¾   cup (128 grams) chopped 60% cacao bittersweet chocolate
1   large egg (50 grams)
1   tablespoon (15 grams) water
1   cup (120 grams) confectioners' sugar
2   tablespoons (30 grams) crème fraîche
1   tablespoon (15 grams) warm water (90°F/32°C to 110°F/43°C)

Garnish: grated chocolate

1. Line a baking sheet with parchment paper.
2. In a large bowl, whisk together flour, granulated sugar, baking powder, and salt. Using a pastry blender or 2 forks, cut in cold butter until mixture is crumbly.
3. In a small bowl, whisk together cold cream and banana. Add cream mixture to flour mixture, stirring with a fork until mixture just starts to come together. Using your hands, knead dough until it almost comes together. Add chocolate, and knead just until chocolate is evenly distributed and no pockets of flour remain.
4. Turn out dough onto a lightly floured surface, and pat or roll into an 8-inch circle (1 inch thick). Using a bench scraper or a sharp knife dipped in flour, cut into 8 wedges. Place scones on prepared pan. Cover and refrigerate until firm, 1 hour or up to overnight.
5. Preheat oven to 375°F (190°C).
6. In a small bowl, whisk together egg and 1 tablespoon (15 grams) water. Brush tops of scones with egg wash.
7. Bake until golden brown, 20 to 25 minutes. Let cool on pan for 5 minutes.
8. In a medium bowl, whisk together confectioners' sugar, crème fraîche, and 1 tablespoon (15 grams) warm water until smooth. Just before serving, dip tops of scones in glaze. Garnish with grated chocolate, if desired. Serve immediately. Store in airtight container at room temperature for up to 4 days.

BLUEBERRY BISCUITS

Makes about 12 biscuits

Flaky buttermilk biscuits get a bright blueberry update in these sweet meets savory treats.

¾   cup (111 grams) fresh blueberries, patted dry
3   cups (375 grams) all-purpose flour
3   tablespoons (36 grams) granulated sugar
3¾ teaspoons (19 grams) baking powder
1   tablespoon (3 grams) lemon zest
2   teaspoons (6 grams) kosher salt
¾   cup (170 grams) cold unsalted butter, cubed
1   cup (240 grams) cold whole buttermilk
1   large egg (50 grams)
1   tablespoon (15 grams) water
Lemon Whipped Cream (recipe follows)
Garnish: fresh blueberries, lemon zest strips

1. On a baking sheet, arrange blueberries in a single layer, or place in a resealable plastic freezer bag. Freeze until firm, about 1 hour.

2. Preheat oven to 400°F (200°C). Line a baking sheet with parchment paper.

3. In a large bowl, stir together flour, sugar, baking powder, lemon zest, and salt. Using a pastry blender or 2 forks, cut in cold butter until mixture is crumbly. Stir in cold buttermilk until a shaggy dough forms.

4. Turn out dough onto a lightly floured surface. Pat into a ¾-inch-thick rectangle, and cut into thirds. Sprinkle with one-third of frozen blueberries, pressing blueberries into dough. Stack thirds on top of each other, placing top third blueberry side down. Pat into a ¾-inch-thick rectangle. Repeat procedure twice using remaining frozen blueberries, flouring work surface as needed. Pat or roll dough to ¾-inch thickness. Using a 2½-inch round cutter dipped in flour, cut dough without twisting cutter, rerolling scraps once, and place at least 1 inch apart on prepared pan.

5. In a small bowl, whisk together egg and 1 tablespoon (15 grams) water. Brush tops of biscuits with egg wash.

6. Bake until golden brown, 15 to 20 minutes. Let cool completely on pan. Serve with Lemon Whipped Cream. Garnish with blueberries and zest strips, if desired.

LEMON WHIPPED CREAM
Makes about 2 cups

1   cup (240 grams) cold heavy whipping cream
2   tablespoons (24 grams) granulated sugar
2   teaspoons (2 grams) lemon zest
2   teaspoons (10 grams) fresh lemon juice

1. In a large bowl, whisk together all ingredients until soft to medium peaks form. Refrigerate until ready to use.

IRISH CHEDDAR WHITE SODA BREAD

Makes 1 (10-inch) loaf

The grand symbol of Ireland's baking, Irish soda bread is defined not by the baking soda but by the soft white wheat that grows in Ireland. Low in gluten and protein, the soft Irish wheat receives a boost from baking soda, invented in the 1800s and an immediate game changer for Irish baking. Slashed with a cross and pricked to release heat—or fairies?—our traditional soda bread is enhanced with strong Irish Cheddar, fresh dill, and ground black pepper.

3⅔   cups (458 grams) all-purpose flour
1½   teaspoons (4.5 grams) kosher salt
½   teaspoon (2.5 grams) baking soda
1   cup (113 grams) coarsely grated aged white Irish Cheddar cheese, divided
1   tablespoon (2 grams) chopped fresh dill
½   teaspoon (1 gram) ground black pepper
2   cups (480 grams) whole buttermilk

1. Preheat oven to 450°F (230°C). Line a baking sheet with parchment paper.
2. In a large bowl, whisk together flour, salt, and baking soda until well combined. Stir in ⅔ cup (75 grams) cheese, dill, and pepper. Make a well in center, and add buttermilk. Using your hand like a claw, mix buttermilk into dry ingredients, working from center to outside of bowl, just until combined and a ball of dough forms. (Dough should be sticky and slightly clumpy.)
3. Turn out dough onto a lightly floured surface. Using floured hands, gently shape into a round. Turn dough over, and tuck and rotate dough until edges are rounded and even. Transfer to prepared pan, and pat into a 1½-inch-thick disk. Using a knife dipped in flour, cut a 1-inch-deep "X" across top of dough. Using tip of knife, prick a hole into each of the four sections of dough. Sprinkle remaining ⅓ cup (38 grams) cheese on top.
4. Bake for 15 minutes. Reduce oven temperature to 400°F (200°C), and bake until golden brown and an instant-read thermometer inserted in a section of bread registers 200°F (93°C), 15 to 20 minutes more. (If you tap bottom of loaf, it should sound hollow.) Remove from pan, and place on a wire rack. Let cool enough to handle, about 30 minutes. Best served warm.

Our soda bread dough can be a little sticky to work with, so use floured hands to help shape it. As you tuck and rotate the dough, keep in mind that it should be a rustic round—not perfect. If you try to make it pristine, you risk overhandling the dough, making it tough.

Use a floured knife to keep the sticky dough from tearing while you make your incision. Though you may think of it as mere decoration, make sure your cross is 1 inch deep, as this deep scoring allows the hot steam to be released from the bread while baking.

As an added bonus to the good luck from the cross-scoring on top, this pricking in the four corners of the dough allows both fairies and heat to escape from the bread. This helps the bread rise and cook evenly.

SODA FARLS

Makes 4 farls

Northern Ireland has its own signature take on soda bread in the form of farl wedges, derived from the Gaelic word fardel, which roughly translates to "four part." Though they're traditionally baked on an open-hearth flame, we baked our farls on the more modern griddle. In keeping with the methods of the Old World, though, we harned the dough—turning and cooking the sides of the farl to make sharp, crisp edges.

1⅔ cups (208 grams) all-purpose flour
¾ teaspoon (2.25 grams) kosher salt
½ teaspoon (2.5 grams) baking soda
3 tablespoons (42 grams) cold unsalted butter, cubed and divided
¾ cup plus 3 tablespoons (225 grams) whole buttermilk
Herb Compound Butter (recipe follows)

1. In a medium bowl, whisk together flour, salt, and baking soda until well combined. Using your fingers, cut in 2 tablespoons (28 grams) cold butter until mixture resembles bread crumbs. Make a well in center, and add buttermilk. Using a wooden spoon, stir buttermilk into dry ingredients, working from center to outside of bowl, just until combined and a dough forms.
2. Turn out dough onto a heavily floured surface, and flour top of dough. Using floured hands, tuck and rotate dough until edges are rounded and even. Pat into an 8-inch circle (½-inch thickness). Using a knife dipped in flour, cut into quarters.
3. Preheat a cast-iron griddle to medium heat. (See Note.) Add remaining 1 tablespoon (14 grams) butter to griddle.
4. Brush and shake off any excess flour from dough quarters, and place, not touching, on hot griddle. Cook until golden brown, 7 to 10 minutes. (Bread will double in size and puff up; if you want a neater look, use a knife or bench scraper to keep edges straight.) Turn, and cook until golden brown, 7 to 10 minutes. (If you tap bottom of bread, it should sound hollow.) Stand each farl on its side, and place side by side. Cook for 1 to 2 minutes; repeat with remaining 2 sides. Serve warm with Herb Compound Butter.

Note: *A 12-inch cast-iron skillet will work, too. Cook farls in batches until golden brown, 5 to 7 minutes per side.*

HERB COMPOUND BUTTER
Makes ½ cup

½ cup (113 grams) salted butter, softened
1 tablespoon (2 grams) chopped fresh dill
1 tablespoon (2 grams) chopped fresh tarragon
1 teaspoon (1 gram) lemon zest

1. In a small bowl, stir together all ingredients until well combined. Use immediately, or cover and refrigerate until ready to use. Let stand until softened before serving.

Like our other soda bread dough, this one is quite sticky too, so flour your bench scraper or knife when dividing into four equal wedges.

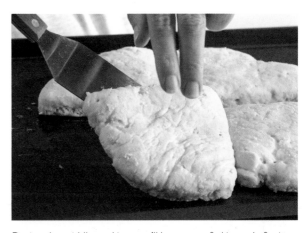

During the griddle cooking, you'll know your farl is ready for its first turn once the bread has nearly doubled and is markedly puffy. This will take 7 to 10 minutes on each side.

Now for the "harning." You'll turn the dough and allow it to cook while standing on its side (holding in place with two spatulas, if necessary) for 1 to 2 minutes. Repeat with remaining sides for a perfectly sharp-edged golden triangle of a farl.

BROWN SODA BREAD

Makes 1 (8½x4½-inch) loaf

Like all other Irish soda breads, Irish brown soda bread needs the leavening power of baking soda to help make it rise to the occasion. Yet this take receives an earthy boost from whole wheat flour and a touch of sweetness from molasses while steel-cut oats, a staple of Irish agriculture, bring a bit of textured crunch to the top.

2¼ cups (281 grams) stone-ground whole
    wheat flour
1¼ cups (156 grams) all-purpose flour
1½ teaspoons (4.5 grams) kosher salt
¾ teaspoon (3.75 grams) baking soda
2 cups (480 grams) whole buttermilk
¼ cup (85 grams) unsulphured molasses
1 large egg (50 grams)
3 tablespoons (33 grams) steel-cut oats

1. Preheat oven to 325°F (170°C). Spray an 8½x4½-inch loaf pan with cooking spray.
2. In a large bowl, whisk together flours, salt, and baking soda until well combined. Make a well in center.
3. In a medium bowl, whisk together buttermilk, molasses, and egg. Add buttermilk mixture to flour mixture. Using one hand like a claw, mix buttermilk mixture into dry ingredients, working from center to outside of bowl, just until combined. Spoon dough into prepared pan, and spread until even. Sprinkle with oats.
4. Bake until deep golden brown and an instant-read thermometer inserted in center registers 200°F (93°C), 1 hour to 1 hour and 5 minutes. Let cool in pan for 15 minutes. Remove from pan; wrap in a clean tea towel, and let cool on a wire rack. Best served warm.

Overmixing leads to tough baked goods. Recipes that are sensitive to overmixing the dough, like muffins, biscuits, and each of our soda breads, require you to make a flour well. This allows you to mix the wet ingredients into the dry ingredients in a uniform manner.

Think of your hand as your most prized baking tool for soda bread. Forming it into a claw and working from the center to the outside of the bowl helps combine the wet and dry ingredients with minimal risk of overworking your dough.

Brown soda bread has a softer crust than your traditional yeast-leavened or sourdough bread. To add an extra note of chew to the crust, we sprinkled the top with steel-cut oats before baking.

IRISH POTATO FARLS

Makes 12 farls

Recipe courtesy of Tracey Jeffrey

A 17th-century thatched cottage on the shores of the Celtic Sea surrounded by the Mourne Mountains, there are few places more scenic to learn to make the breads of Northern Ireland than at Tracey's Farmhouse Kitchen. This recipe comes straight from head instructor Tracey Jeffrey and highlights a Northern Ireland icon: the farl. This is the classic potato-filled version and is delicious smeared with Irish butter.

1½ pounds (680 grams) russet potatoes, peeled and cut into 1- to 1¼-inch cubes
2   tablespoons (28 grams) unsalted butter
1   teaspoon (3 grams) kosher salt
¼   teaspoon ground black pepper
¾   cup (94 grams) all-purpose flour, divided

1. In a small saucepan, combine potatoes and water to cover by 1 inch. Bring to a boil over high heat. Reduce heat to medium-high, and cook until potatoes are tender, 12 to 15 minutes. Drain potatoes, and return to saucepan. Add butter, salt, and pepper, and mash potatoes until smooth. Let cool slightly.
2. On a heavily floured surface, place 2 cups (446 grams) mashed potatoes, reserving remaining mashed potatoes for another use. Add ½ cup (63 grams) flour, and knead until a stiff, pliable dough forms. Add up to remaining ¼ cup (31 grams) flour, if necessary. Divide dough in half. Flour work surface again, and roll or pat each dough portion to ⅓-inch thickness. Using a knife, cut each portion into 6 pieces (12 total).
3. Lightly butter a cast-iron griddle or skillet, and heat over medium heat.
4. Shake or brush any excess flour off dough pieces. Working in batches, cook farls until golden brown, slightly puffed, and crisp, 3 to 4 minutes per side. (The farls should have patchy brown spots when nearly done.)

Photo by Joann Pai

> **PRO TIP**
> For extra flavor and deep golden color, spread butter onto cooked side of farls after turning and then again before removing from griddle or skillet.

OATEN BREAD

Makes 4 servings

Warmed with a touch of allspice and sweetened with a bit of honey, this tender bread has hearty oats mixed into the dough and sprinkled on top for an extra-toasty and textured exterior.

1½ cups (188 grams) all-purpose flour
1 teaspoon (3 grams) kosher salt
¾ teaspoon (3.75 grams) baking powder
¼ teaspoon (1.25 grams) baking soda
¼ teaspoon ground allspice
3 tablespoons (42 grams) cold unsalted butter, cubed
¾ cup (70 grams) plus 1 tablespoon (6 grams) old-fashioned oats, divided
½ cup (120 grams) whole buttermilk
2 large eggs (100 grams), divided
1 tablespoon (21 grams) clover honey

1 tablespoon (15 grams) water
Softened butter and preserves, to serve

1. Preheat oven to 425°F (220°C). Line a baking sheet with parchment paper.
2. In a large bowl, whisk together flour, salt, baking powder, baking soda, and allspice. Using a pastry blender or 2 forks, cut in cold butter until mixture resembles coarse crumbs. Stir in ¾ cup (70 grams) oats. Make a well in center.
3. In a small bowl, whisk together buttermilk, 1 egg (50 grams), and honey until well combined. Add buttermilk mixture to flour mixture, stirring until well combined and a dough forms.
4. Turn out dough onto a heavily floured surface; knead until dough is relatively smooth, about 25 times, lightly flouring dough and work surface as needed. Shape dough into a 7-inch round. Using a bench knife, cut dough round into fourths, and place at least 2 inches apart on prepared pan.
5. In a small bowl, whisk together 1 tablespoon (15 grams) water and remaining 1 egg (50 grams). Brush top of dough with egg wash; sprinkle with remaining 1 tablespoon (6 grams) oats.
6. Bake until golden brown and a wooden pick inserted in center comes out clean, 12 to 14 minutes. Let cool completely on pan on a wire rack. Serve with softened butter and preserves.

SWEET WHITE SCONES

Makes 9 scones

Recipe courtesy of Darina Allen

If I could teach you how to make one thing, if you had never baked or cooked anything, this dough is where I'd start. Our Sweet White Scones are made with our soda bread dough. You don't have to stamp them out using a cutter; you can cut them into whatever shape you like using a knife. Brush the top with buttermilk or egg wash and dip it into grated cheese or put some scallions or chopped seaweed, curry powder, raisins, or rosemary into the mix. This recipe is an incredibly versatile thing.

¼ cup (50 grams) demerara or other coarse sugar
1½ large eggs (75 grams)

1 cup (240 grams) whole milk
3½ cups plus 2 tablespoons (454 grams) all-purpose flour
2 tablespoons (24 grams) castor sugar
4 teaspoons (20 grams) baking powder
Pinch salt
6 tablespoons (84 grams) cold salted butter, grated
Jam, whipped cream, and butter, to serve

1. Preheat oven to 475°F (250°C).
2. In a small bowl, place demerara sugar; set aside.
3. In a 2-cup liquid-measuring cup, whisk together eggs. Add enough milk to measure 1¼ cups. Whisk well to combine. Reserve 2½ tablespoons (37 grams) egg mixture for egg wash.
4. In a large bowl, sift together flour, castor sugar, baking powder, and salt. Add cold

butter, and toss lightly to coat with flour. Using fingertips, rub butter into mixture until it resembles coarse crumbs. Make a well in center. Add remaining egg mixture. Using a fork, stir together until a soft dough forms.
5. Turn out dough onto a lightly floured surface. (Do not knead.) Shape dough into a round, and roll to 1-inch thickness. Using a 3-inch round cutter dipped in flour, cut dough, rerolling scraps once. Brush tops with reserved egg wash. Dip tops in demerara sugar. Place on a baking sheet.
6. Bake until tops are golden brown, 9 to 11 minutes. Remove from pan, and let cool completely on a wire rack. Serve with jam, whipped cream, and butter as desired.

Photo by Kylie Mazon-Chambersi

HERB SCONES WITH CHIVE CREAM AND SMOKED SALMON

Makes 14 scones

Recipe by Alice Choi

These scones are a lovely accompaniment to a cheese board. Serve them with strawberry jam, salami, Kerrygold Aged Cheddar Cheese with Irish Whiskey, and a light drizzle of honey!

3	cups (375 grams) all-purpose flour
2	tablespoons (30 grams) baking powder
2	teaspoons (6 grams) kosher salt
¾	cup (170 grams) cold unsalted butter, cubed
6	large eggs (300 grams), divided
½ to 1 cup (120 to 240 grams) whole milk
½	cup (16 grams) plus 1 to 1½ tablespoons (2 to 3 grams) finely diced fresh chives (see Note), divided
1	cup (240 grams) all-natural whole Greek yogurt
1	cup (240 grams) sour cream
2	teaspoons (10 grams) fresh lemon juice

Smoked salmon, to serve
Garnish: olive oil, fresh dill

1. Preheat oven to 400°F (200°C). Line 2 baking sheets with parchment paper.
2. In a large bowl, whisk together flour, baking powder, and salt. Using your fingers, rub cold butter into flour mixture until butter is pea-size. Make a well in center.
3. In a small bowl, whisk together 4 eggs (200 grams), ½ cup (120 grams) milk, and ½ cup (16 grams) chives; add egg mixture to flour mixture. Using one hand like a claw, mix together just until combined. Add up to remaining ½ cup (120 grams) milk, 1 tablespoon (15 grams) at a time, if needed. (Dough should be wet and sticky.)
4. Turn out dough onto a lightly floured surface. Lightly flour top of dough, and pat to ½-inch thickness. Using a 2½-inch round cutter, cut 14 scones from dough, rerolling scraps as needed. Place 1½ inches apart on prepared pans. (For alternative shaping method, see PRO TIP.)
5. In another small bowl, whisk remaining 2 eggs (100 grams). Brush tops of scones with egg wash.
6. Bake until golden brown, 14 to

15 minutes. Remove from pan, and let cool completely on wire racks.
7. In a medium bowl, whisk together yogurt, sour cream, lemon juice, and remaining 1 to 2 tablespoons (2 to 3 grams) chives. Serve scones with chive cream and salmon. Garnish with oil and dill, if desired. Scones are best served the same day.

Note: *A blend of chives and rosemary work well, too.*

Photo by Alice Choi

PRO TIP

For wedge scones, turn out dough onto a lightly floured surface, and divide in half. Lightly flour top of each dough half, and shape each into a 7½-inch disk. Cut each dough disk into 8 wedges. Brush tops of scones with egg wash, and place 1½ inches apart on prepared pans. Bake until golden brown, 14 to 15 minutes.

SODA BREAD PIZZA

Makes 6 to 8 servings

Recipe courtesy of Darina Allen

Like Darina Allen's ideal soda bread, this pizza comes together in a flash, making the most of wholesome ingredients and fresh herbs.

3⅔   cups (458 grams) all-purpose flour
1   teaspoon (5 grams) baking soda
1   teaspoon (6 grams) fine sea salt
1½ to 1¾ cups (360 to 420 grams) whole buttermilk
1   tablespoon (2 grams) chopped fresh rosemary
2   ounces (57 grams) sliced cured chorizo
⅔   cup (148 grams) pizza sauce
8   bocconcini* (306 grams), halved
3   tablespoons (15 grams) grated Parmesan cheese

Garnish: chopped fresh parsley, chopped green onion, flaked sea salt

1. Position oven rack in bottom third of oven. Preheat oven to 450°F (230°C).
2. In a large bowl, sift together flour, baking soda, and fine salt. Make a well in center. Add 1½ cups (360 grams) buttermilk. Using one hand like a claw, slowly fold flour mixture from sides of bowl into buttermilk until a softish, slack dough forms, adding up to remaining ¼ cup (60 grams) buttermilk if necessary. Turn out dough onto a lightly floured surface, and knead lightly for a few seconds; shape into a ¼-inch-thick rectangle. Turn dough over, and lightly roll into a 12x8-inch rectangle.
3. Brush a 13x9-inch baking pan with extra-virgin olive oil. Place dough in prepared pan. Press dough to fill pan, and sprinkle with rosemary. Scatter chorizo evenly onto dough. Spread pizza sauce over chorizo; place bocconcini on top. Sprinkle with Parmesan.
4. Bake for 15 minutes. Reduce heat to 400°F (200°C), and bake until cheese is browned and bubbly and an instant-read thermometer inserted in crust registers 200°F (93°C), 20 to 25 minutes more. Garnish with parsley, green onion, and flaked salt, if desired. Let cool for 5 minutes before serving.

*Bocconcini are a type of buffalo mozzarella formed into small balls. You can find them in your local grocery store.

Photo by Joann Pai

TOMATO IRISH SODA BREAD DINNER ROLLS WITH FRIED SHALLOT BUTTER

Makes 9 rolls

Recipe by Kylie Mazon-Chambers

These Irish soda bread dinner rolls are studded with chopped sun-dried tomato pieces and just enough ground red pepper for a bit of a kick and, finally, topped with Irish Cheddar.

3½ cups (438 grams) all-purpose flour
1   teaspoon (5 grams) baking soda
1   teaspoon (3 grams) kosher salt
1   teaspoon (2 grams) paprika
½   teaspoon (1 gram) ground red pepper
1½ cups (360 grams) whole buttermilk
¼   cup (40 grams) diced oil-packed
     sun-dried tomatoes
½   cup (52 grams) shredded sharp Irish
     Cheddar cheese
Vegetable oil, for frying
2   medium shallots (75 grams), thinly
     sliced

10   tablespoons (140 grams) unsalted
     butter, softened
1   teaspoon (3 grams) flaked sea salt

1. Preheat oven to 400°F (200°C).
2. In a large bowl, whisk together flour, baking soda, kosher salt, paprika, and red pepper until combined. Make a well in center.
3. In a medium bowl, stir together buttermilk and tomatoes. Add buttermilk mixture to flour mixture. Using one hand like a claw, slowly fold flour mixture from sides of bowl into buttermilk mixture until dough is soft but not too wet.
4. Line a baking sheet with parchment paper.
5. Turn out dough onto a lightly floured surface, and shape into an 8-inch square (1-inch thickness). Sprinkle with cheese. Using a sharp knife, cut into 9 squares, and place 1 inch apart on prepared pan.

6. Bake until golden brown, about 18 minutes. Remove from pan, and let cool on a wire rack.
7. In a 10-inch cast-iron skillet, pour oil to a depth of ½ inch, and heat over medium heat until an instant-read thermometer registers 350°F (180°C).
8. Fry shallots, in batches if necessary, stirring frequently, until deep golden brown and crispy, 8 to 10 minutes, adjusting heat as needed. Remove shallots using tongs, and let drain on a paper towel-lined plate for 5 minutes.
9. In the work bowl of a food processor, place shallots, butter, and sea salt; pulse just until combined, and transfer to a small bowl. Serve at room temperature with warm rolls.

Photo by Kylie Mazon-Chambers

SWEET POTATO-CHAI SCONES

Makes 6 scones

Warm with aromatic chai spice and made mouthwateringly tender with sweet potato, these scones are a fall breakfast dream complete with a final sprinkling of sparkling sugar.

2 cups (250 grams) all-purpose flour
¼ cup (55 grams) firmly packed light brown sugar
1¾ teaspoons (8.75 grams) baking powder
1½ teaspoons (3 grams) ground cardamom
1 teaspoon (2 grams) ground cinnamon
¾ teaspoon (2.25 grams) kosher salt
¼ teaspoon ground ginger
⅛ teaspoon ground cloves
⅛ teaspoon ground black pepper
½ cup (113 grams) cold unsalted butter, cubed
½ cup (118 grams) cold puréed cooked peeled sweet potato (see Note)
⅓ cup (80 grams) cold heavy whipping cream
1 teaspoon (4 grams) vanilla extract
¼ teaspoon (1 gram) tightly packed orange zest
1 large egg (50 grams), lightly beaten
Sparkling sugar, for sprinkling

1. Preheat oven to 375°F (190°C). Line a rimmed baking sheet with parchment paper.
2. In a large bowl, whisk together flour, brown sugar, baking powder, cardamom, cinnamon, salt, ginger, cloves, and black pepper, breaking up any clumps of brown sugar by hand as needed. Using a pastry blender or 2 forks, cut in cold butter until mixture resembles coarse crumbs.
3. In a medium bowl, stir together sweet potato, cold cream, vanilla, and orange zest. Gradually add sweet potato mixture to flour mixture, stirring with a fork until dry ingredients are moistened. (It's OK if dough is crumbly or shaggy in parts.)
4. Turn out dough onto a clean surface; gently knead 4 to 6 times to bring dough together. Roll or pat dough into a 1-inch-thick circle (about 6 inches wide), lightly flouring surface as needed to prevent sticking. Using a bench scraper or a thin-bladed knife, cut circle into 6 wedges, and place at least 2 inches apart on prepared pan. Brush tops with egg, and sprinkle with sparkling sugar.
5. Bake until golden brown, a wooden pick inserted in center comes out clean, and an instant-read thermometer inserted in center registers 200°F (93°C), 15 to 18 minutes. Let cool on pan for 5 minutes. Serve warm.

Note: *We like the bright color and convenience of using pre-cubed raw sweet potatoes, sold in 1-pound bags in the produce department of most grocery stores. Cook according to package direction. Purée in a food processor until mostly smooth.*

BANANA STREUSEL BREAD

Makes 1 (15-cup) loaf

Why yes, banana bread will Bundt. In this incarnation, our banana bread is an inverted Bundt beauty, boasting a crunchy cinnamon streusel topping that proves more addictive with each serving.

3½ cups (438 grams) plus 4 tablespoons (32 grams) all-purpose flour, divided
1½ cups (330 grams) plus 2 tablespoons (28 grams) firmly packed light brown sugar, divided
1⅓ cups (267 grams) plus 2 tablespoons (24 grams) granulated sugar, divided
1¾ teaspoons (3.5 grams) ground cinnamon, divided
4 teaspoons (20 grams) unsalted butter, cubed
2 cups (476 grams) mashed ripe banana
1 cup (214 grams) vegetable oil
4 large eggs (200 grams), room temperature
⅔ cup (160 grams) sour cream, room temperature
1 tablespoon (13 grams) vanilla extract
2 teaspoons (10 grams) baking powder
1¼ teaspoons (6.25 grams) baking soda
1¼ teaspoons (3.75 grams) kosher salt
½ teaspoon (1 gram) ground cloves
¼ teaspoon ground nutmeg

1. Preheat oven to 350°F (180°C).
2. In a medium bowl, stir together 4 tablespoons (32 grams) flour, 2 tablespoons (28 grams) brown sugar, 2 tablespoons (24 grams) granulated sugar, and ¾ teaspoon (1.5 grams) cinnamon. Add butter; using your fingers or 2 forks, work butter into flour mixture until mixture resembles coarse crumbs or slightly wet sand. Set aside.
3. In the bowl of a stand mixer fitted with the paddle attachment, beat banana, oil, eggs, sour cream, vanilla, remaining 1½ cups (330 grams) brown sugar, and remaining 1⅓ cups (267 grams) granulated sugar at medium-low speed until well combined, about 2 minutes, stopping to scrape sides of bowl.
4. In another medium bowl, whisk together baking powder, baking soda, salt, cloves, nutmeg, remaining 3½ cups (438 grams) flour, and remaining 1 teaspoon (2 grams) cinnamon. With mixer on low speed, gradually add baking powder mixture to banana mixture, beating until combined and stopping to scrape sides of bowl.
5. Spray a 15-cup Nordic Ware Anniversary Bundt Pan with baking spray with flour. Pour batter into prepared pan. Tap pan on a kitchen towel-lined counter a few times to settle batter and release any air bubbles.
6. Bake for 20 minutes. Sprinkle with streusel, and bake until golden brown and a wooden pick inserted near center comes out clean, 40 to 55 minutes, rotating pan halfway through baking and loosely covering with foil to prevent excess browning, if necessary. Let cool in pan on a wire rack for 20 minutes.
7. Using a small offset spatula, loosen bread from center of pan. Slowly invert bread onto a wire rack placed over a rimmed baking sheet. (Some streusel will fall off.) Using a large, flat plate or a cake lifter, turn bread streusel side up, and place on wire rack; let cool completely.

UPSIDE-DOWN HEIRLOOM TOMATO CORNBREAD

Makes 1 (10-inch) loaf

Featuring a caramelized tomato top, this crisp cornbread is made all the more delicious from cheese and fresh corn in the batter.

3 medium heirloom tomatoes (369 grams), sliced into ½-inch-thick rounds and seeded (about 11 slices)
2 cups (240 grams) plain fine yellow cornmeal
1 cup (125 grams) all-purpose flour
1 tablespoon (15 grams) baking powder
2 teaspoons (6 grams) kosher salt
2¼ cups (255 grams) shredded smoked white Cheddar cheese, divided
1 cup (154 grams) fresh yellow corn kernels (about 2 ears corn)
½ cup (14 grams) finely sliced fresh basil leaves

¼ cup (40 grams) diced seeded jalapeño
1¾ cups (420 grams) whole buttermilk
6 tablespoons (84 grams) unsalted butter, melted
2 large eggs (100 grams)
2 tablespoons (24 grams) granulated sugar
Garnish: fresh basil leaves

1. Preheat oven to 400°F (200°C). Line bottom of a 10-inch cast-iron skillet with parchment paper. Spray parchment and sides of skillet with cooking spray. Line a rimmed baking sheet with paper towels.
2. On prepared pan, place tomato slices.
3. In a large bowl, whisk together cornmeal, flour, baking powder, and salt. Stir in 1½ cups (170 grams) cheese, corn, basil, and jalapeño. Make a well in center.

4. In a medium bowl, whisk together buttermilk, melted butter, and eggs. Add buttermilk mixture to cornmeal mixture, stirring just until combined.
5. In bottom of prepared skillet, place tomato slices, overlapping if needed. Sprinkle with sugar, and top with ½ cup (57 grams) cheese. Spoon batter onto tomatoes, smoothing top.
6. Bake until golden brown and a wooden pick inserted in center comes out clean, 30 to 35 minutes, covering with foil to prevent excess browning, if necessary. Let cool in skillet for 10 minutes. Invert loaf onto a serving platter. Top with remaining ¼ cup (28 grams) cheese; garnish with basil, if desired. Serve warm.

BANANA MUFFIN TOPS

Makes 24 muffin tops

Let's be honest—the muffin top is the most coveted part of the breakfast quick bread, studded with crunchy streusel and glazed to perfection. These tender banana-packed rounds are all top, no filler, just the way you've always wanted them.

⅔ cup (150 grams) unsalted butter, softened
1⅓ cups (267 grams) granulated sugar
1 cup (220 grams) firmly packed light brown sugar
1 large egg (50 grams)
½ cup (114 grams) mashed ripe banana
1 tablespoon (13 grams) vanilla extract
4 cups (500 grams) all-purpose flour
4 teaspoons (20 grams) baking powder
1½ teaspoons (4.5 grams) kosher salt
1 cup (240 grams) sour cream
1 cup (113 grams) chopped pecans
¾ cup (150 grams) chopped banana
Pecan Streusel (recipe follows)
Glaze (recipe follows)

1. Preheat oven to 375°F (190°C). Line 3 baking sheets with parchment paper.
2. In the bowl of a stand mixer fitted with the paddle attachment, beat butter and sugars at medium speed until fluffy, 3 to 4 minutes, stopping to scrape sides of bowl. Add egg, beating well. Beat in mashed banana and vanilla.
3. In a medium bowl, whisk together flour, baking powder, and salt. With mixer on low speed, gradually add flour mixture to butter mixture in two additions alternately with sour cream, beginning and ending with flour mixture, beating just until combined after each addition. Stir in pecans and chopped banana. Using a ¼-cup spring-loaded scoop, scoop batter, and place at least 2 inches apart on prepared pans. Top with half (about 1 cup) of Pecan Streusel.
4. Bake for 6 minutes. Sprinkle with remaining Pecan Streusel, filling any empty spaces on top. Bake until a wooden pick inserted in center comes out clean, 6 to 8 minutes more. Let cool on pans for 5 minutes. Remove from pans, and place on wire racks. Drizzle with Glaze before serving. Serve warm.

PECAN STREUSEL
Makes about 2½ cups

⅔ cup (84 grams) all-purpose flour
6 tablespoons (72 grams) granulated sugar
4 tablespoons (55 grams) firmly packed light brown sugar
½ teaspoon (1.5 grams) kosher salt
½ teaspoon (1 gram) ground cinnamon
6 tablespoons (84 grams) cold unsalted butter, cubed
1 cup (113 grams) chopped pecans

1. In a medium bowl, stir together flour, sugars, salt, and cinnamon. Using fingers, cut in cold butter until mixture is crumbly and desired consistency is reached. Stir in pecans. Refrigerate until ready to use.

GLAZE
Makes about ½ cup

1½ cups (180 grams) confectioners' sugar
2½ tablespoons (37.5 grams) whole milk
⅛ teaspoon vanilla extract

1. In a medium bowl, whisk together all ingredients until smooth.

WHITE CHOCOLATE-PEPPERMINT SCONES

Makes 6 scones

Perhaps our easiest and most straight-forward make-ahead recipe, these peppermint-and-white chocolate scones offer a fabulously festive breakfast with minimal effort. On Christmas Eve, you can pull together the dough in a flash before popping it into the freezer. The morning of, it'll go from freezer directly to preheated oven, with only a brush of cream in between. Then, you're only a quick Vanilla Glaze drizzle away from your fastest, sweetest holiday breakfast.

2   cups (250 grams) all-purpose flour
¼   cup (50 grams) granulated sugar
2   teaspoons (10 grams) baking powder
1   teaspoon (3 grams) kosher salt
¼   cup (57 grams) cold unsalted butter, cubed
¾   cup (180 grams) cold heavy whipping cream, plus more for brushing
1   teaspoon (6 grams) vanilla bean paste
½   teaspoon (2 grams) peppermint extract*

3   ounces (85 grams) white chocolate*, finely chopped (about ½ cup)
½   cup (64 grams) crushed soft peppermint candies*
White sparkling sugar, for sprinkling
Vanilla Glaze (recipe follows)
Garnish: crushed soft peppermint candies

1. Line a baking sheet with parchment paper.
2. In a large bowl, whisk together flour, granulated sugar, baking powder, and salt. Using a pastry blender or 2 forks, cut in cold butter until mixture resembles coarse crumbs.
3. In a small bowl, stir together cold cream, vanilla bean paste, and peppermint extract. Gradually add cream mixture to flour mixture, stirring with a fork until dry ingredients are moistened. Gently stir in white chocolate and candies. (Dough will be quite crumbly or shaggy in parts.)
4. Turn out dough onto a clean surface; gently knead 8 to 10 times to bring dough together. Roll or pat dough into a 7-inch circle (about 1 inch thick), very lightly

flouring surface as needed to prevent sticking; press together any cracks that form, if necessary. Using a bench scraper or a thin-bladed knife, cut circle into 6 wedges; place wedges at least 2 inches apart on prepared pan. Wrap pan tightly with plastic wrap, and freeze overnight.
5. Preheat oven to 350°F (180°C).
6. Brush tops of scones with cream; sprinkle with sparkling sugar.
7. Bake until lightly golden and a wooden pick inserted in center comes out clean, 22 to 27 minutes.
8. Spoon Vanilla Glaze into a small pastry or resealable plastic bag; cut a ¼-inch opening in tip or corner. Drizzle glaze onto scones as desired. Garnish with candies, if desired. Serve warm or at room temperature.

*We used Nielsen-Massey Pure Peppermint Extract and Ghirardelli White Chocolate Baking Bars. Do not substitute hard peppermint candies.

VANILLA GLAZE
Makes about ⅓ cup

⅔   cup (80 grams) confectioners' sugar
2½   tablespoons (37.5 grams) heavy whipping cream
½   teaspoon (3 grams) vanilla bean paste
¼   teaspoon kosher salt

1. In a small bowl, stir together all ingredients until smooth and well combined. Use immediately.

GINGERBREAD LOAF WITH DARK CHOCOLATE AND SPICED CRUMBLE

Makes 2 (8½x4½-inch) loaves

Recipe by Maria Provenzano

This Gingerbread Loaf with Dark Chocolate and Spiced Crumble is a must this holiday season. This quick bread features all the flavors of a gingerbread cookie. The addition of dark chocolate and a spiced crumble topping pushes it right over the top.

Batter:
- 2 cups (250 grams) unbleached all-purpose flour
- 1 cup (220 grams) firmly packed light brown sugar
- 1 teaspoon (5 grams) baking powder
- 1 teaspoon (2 grams) pumpkin pie spice*
- ½ teaspoon (2.5 grams) baking soda
- ½ teaspoon (1.5 grams) kosher salt
- ¾ cup (180 grams) sour cream, room temperature
- 3 large eggs (150 grams), room temperature
- 2 tablespoons (42 grams) unsulphured molasses
- 2 teaspoons (8 grams) vanilla extract
- ½ cup (113 grams) unsalted butter, melted and cooled
- 1½ cups (255 grams) chopped 63% cacao dark chocolate*

Topping:
- ¾ cup (94 grams) unbleached all-purpose flour
- ½ cup (47 grams) old-fashioned oats
- ¼ cup (50 grams) granulated sugar
- ¼ cup (55 grams) firmly packed light brown sugar
- ½ teaspoon (1 gram) pumpkin pie spice
- ½ cup (113 grams) unsalted butter, melted and cooled

1. Preheat oven to 350°F (180°C). Generously spray 2 (8½x4½-inch) loaf pans with cooking spray.

2. For batter: In a large bowl, whisk together flour, brown sugar, baking powder, pie spice, baking soda, and salt.

3. In a medium bowl, stir together sour cream, eggs, molasses, and vanilla. Add sour cream mixture and melted butter to flour mixture, stirring just until combined. Fold in chocolate. Divide batter between prepared pans.

4. For topping: In a medium bowl, combine flour, oats, sugars, and pie spice. Using a fork, stir in melted butter in a slow, steady stream. Crumble topping evenly over each loaf.

5. Bake until center is set and a wooden pick inserted in center comes out clean, 35 to 40 minutes. Let cool in pans for 10 to 15 minutes. Remove from pans, and let cool completely on a wire rack.

*Cinnamon can be substituted for pumpkin pie spice, and chocolate chips can be used in place of chopped chocolate.

Photo by Bree McCool

CUCIDATI QUICK BREAD

Makes 2 (8½x4½-inch) loaves

Recipe by Maria Provenzano

The classic Italian fig-and-walnut Christmas cookies called cucidati *are a staple in many Italian American families, and each family has their own way of making them special. Traditionally, the classic flavors of dried fruit, nuts, and oranges are rolled inside of a buttery, soft cookie dough and then dipped in a simple frosting and topped with nonpareils after they are baked.*

3 cups (375 grams) all-purpose flour
1 tablespoon (15 grams) baking powder
2 teaspoons (2 grams) orange zest
1 teaspoon (2 grams) ground cinnamon
½ teaspoon (1.5 grams) kosher salt
1¼ cups (250 grams) granulated sugar
3 large eggs (150 grams), room temperature
¾ cup (168 grams) olive oil
¾ cup (180 grams) whole milk, room temperature
¼ cup (60 grams) sour cream, room temperature
¼ cup (60 grams) fresh orange juice
1 teaspoon (4 grams) vanilla extract
¾ cup (96 grams) dried figs, stemmed and chopped
¾ cup (96 grams) raisins
¼ cup (36 grams) toasted pine nuts
2 cups (240 grams) confectioners' sugar
2 to 3 tablespoons (30 to 45 grams) heavy whipping cream
Garnish: nonpareils

1. Preheat oven to 350°F (180°C). Spray 2 (8½x4½-inch) loaf pans with cooking spray.
2. In a large bowl, whisk together flour, baking powder, orange zest, cinnamon, and salt.
3. In the bowl of a stand mixer fitted with the paddle attachment, beat granulated sugar and eggs at low speed until light and fluffy and pale in color, 2 to 3 minutes.
4. In a medium bowl, whisk together oil, milk, sour cream, orange juice, and vanilla. With mixer on medium-low speed, add oil mixture to sugar mixture, beating until smooth and combined. Reduce mixer speed to low, and gradually add flour mixture, beating just until combined. (Do not overmix.) Fold in figs, raisins, and pine nuts. Divide batter between prepared pans.
5. Bake until a wooden pick inserted in center comes out clean, about 40 minutes. Let cool in pans for 15 minutes. Remove from pans, and let cool completely on a wire rack.
6. In another medium bowl, whisk together confectioners' sugar and 2 tablespoons (30 grams) cream until smooth; add up to remaining 1 tablespoon (15 grams) cream, 1 teaspoon (5 grams) at a time, until desired consistency is reached. (See Note.) Drizzle glaze onto cooled loaves. Garnish with nonpareils, if desired.

Note: *If the glaze becomes too runny, whisk in a little more confectioners' sugar. You want it to pour easily, but it should be thick enough to stick to the loaves.*

Photo by Bree McCool

YEAST
BREADS

Slow and steady wins the taste with these yeast-leavened doughs. Whether you start with ornately twisted babka or simple brioche buns, you're bound to make a luscious bread recipe that rises to the occasion.

HERBED PAIN D'ÉPI

Makes 2 loaves

This pain d'épi has all the rich texture and sourdough flavor without the need for a homemade starter.

1¼ cups (300 grams) warm water (110°F/43°C to 115°F/46°C), divided
1 (0.63-ounce) package (18 grams) instant sourdough yeast*
4 cups (508 grams) bread flour, divided
2¾ teaspoons (8.25 grams) kosher salt
1 teaspoon (2 grams) garlic powder
1 teaspoon chopped fresh rosemary
1 teaspoon chopped fresh sage
1 teaspoon chopped fresh thyme
½ teaspoon (1 gram) ground black pepper
1½ cups (360 grams) boiling water
Herbed olive oil, to serve

1. In the bowl of a stand mixer fitted with the paddle attachment, whisk together ¾ cup (180 grams) warm water and instant sourdough yeast by hand until dissolved. Add 1⅓ cups (169 grams) flour, and beat at low speed until combined, about 30 seconds. Cover and let rise in a warm, draft-free place (75°F/24°C) until doubled in size, 30 to 45 minutes.
2. Add salt, garlic powder, rosemary, sage, thyme, black pepper, remaining 2⅔ cups (339 grams) flour, and remaining ½ cup (120 grams) warm water to yeast mixture, and beat at low speed until dough comes together, about 30 seconds. Switch to the dough hook attachment. Beat at low speed for 2 minutes. (Dough will appear rough rather than smooth at this point.)
3. Lightly oil a large bowl. Place dough in bowl, turning to grease top. Cover and let stand in a warm, draft-free place (75°F/24°C) until smooth and elastic, 1½ hours, turning every 30 minutes. (To complete a turn, grab underside of dough, stretch it up, and fold it to center of dough. Do this four times around bowl.)
4. Turn out dough onto a very lightly floured surface, and divide in half. Gently pat one half into a 9x4-inch rectangle; fold one short side over center third, pinching to seal. Fold remaining third over folded portion, pinching to seal. Turn dough over so it is seam side down. Cover and let stand for 20 minutes. Repeat with remaining half of dough.

5. Line a rimmed baking sheet with parchment paper, letting excess extend slightly over sides of pan. Dust heavily with flour.
6. Gently pat each baguette into an 8x6-inch rectangle, one long side closest to you. Fold top third of dough to center, pressing to seal. Fold bottom third over folded portion, pressing to seal. Fold dough in half lengthwise so long edges meet. Using the heel of your hand, firmly press edges to seal. Roll into a 15- to 16-inch log of even thickness, tapering ends slightly. (Logs will shrink afterward.)
7. Place 1 log on prepared pan, seam side down, nestling it against one long side of pan. Pull up and fold parchment to create a wall on opposite side of log. Nestle remaining log on other side of parchment wall, seam side down. Repeat pulling and folding process with parchment to form a wall on opposite side of second log, and weigh down with a kitchen towel to prevent parchment from sliding. Cover and let rise in a warm, draft-free place (75°F/24°C) until slightly puffed, 45 to 50 minutes. (Alternatively, cover and refrigerate for 8 hours or overnight. Let rise in a warm, draft-free place (75°F/24°C) until slightly puffed, 45 to 50 minutes. Shape and bake as directed.)
8. Place a large cast-iron skillet on bottom rack of oven and a rimmed baking sheet on center rack. Preheat oven to 475°F (250°C).
9. Carefully transfer dough logs to a sheet of parchment paper; thoroughly dust tops with flour. Using kitchen scissors, make a quick, clean 45-degree cut about 1½ inches from end of 1 log, cutting about three-fourths of the way through. (Be careful not to cut all the way through dough.) Gently turn dough piece to one side. Make a second cut 1½ inches from first, and gently turn dough piece to opposite side. Repeat until you reach end of log, creating a wheat stalk shape. Repeat procedure with remaining log.
10. Remove preheated pan from oven. Carefully place parchment with dough on pan, and return to oven. Carefully pour 1½ cups (360 grams) boiling water into preheated skillet. (This will create a lot of steam, so wear oven mitts.) Immediately close oven door.
11. Bake until golden brown and an instant-read thermometer inserted in center registers 205°F (96°C), about 15 minutes. Let cool on pan on a wire rack. Serve with herbed olive oil.

We used Platinum® Instant Sourdough Yeast from Red Star®.

HERBED SOUR CREAM PULL-APART LOAF

Makes 1 (9x5-inch) loaf

Packed with fresh herbs, this buttery pull-apart loaf has an extra-fluffy texture thanks to the addition of sour cream in the dough.

3¼	cups (413 grams) bread flour, divided
2	tablespoons (24 grams) granulated sugar
2¼	teaspoons (7 grams) instant yeast
2	teaspoons (6 grams) kosher salt, divided
1	cup (240 grams) sour cream
¼	cup (57 grams) unsalted butter
¼	cup (60 grams) water
1	large egg (50 grams), room temperature
⅓	cup (76 grams) unsalted butter, melted
1	tablespoon (10 grams) minced garlic
1	tablespoon (2 grams) chopped fresh rosemary
1	tablespoon (2 grams) chopped fresh thyme
1	tablespoon (2 grams) chopped fresh parsley
½	teaspoon (2 grams) flaked sea salt

Garnish: chopped fresh rosemary, chopped fresh thyme, chopped fresh parsley

1. In the bowl of a stand mixer fitted with the paddle attachment, whisk together 1½ cups (191 grams) flour, sugar, yeast, and 1½ teaspoons (4.5 grams) kosher salt by hand.

2. In a medium saucepan, heat sour cream, butter, and ¼ cup (60 grams) water over medium heat until an instant-read thermometer registers 120°F (49°C) to 130°F (54°C).

3. With mixer on medium speed, pour warm sour cream mixture into flour mixture, beating until combined and cooled slightly, about 1 minute. Add egg, and beat at medium speed until combined. With mixer on low speed, gradually add remaining 1¾ cups (222 grams) flour, beating until well combined and stopping to scrape sides of bowl, about 1 minute.

4. Lightly spray a large bowl. Place dough in bowl, turning to grease top. Cover and let rise in a warm, draft-free place (75°F/24°C) until doubled in size, 45 minutes to 1 hour.

5. In a small bowl, stir together melted butter, garlic, rosemary, thyme, parsley, and remaining ½ teaspoon (1.5 grams) kosher salt.

6. Divide dough into 36 portions (22 grams each). With lightly floured hands, roll 1 portion into a smooth ball. (Keep remaining dough covered to prevent it from drying out.) Dip each ball into melted butter mixture, and place in a 9x5-inch loaf pan.

Repeat with remaining dough. Pour any remaining melted butter mixture over dough in pan. Cover and let rise in a warm, draft-free place (75°F/24°C) until doubled in size, 15 to 20 minutes.

7. Preheat oven to 350°F (180°C).

8. Sprinkle dough with flaked salt.

9. Bake until golden brown and an instant-read thermometer inserted in center registers 190°F (88°C), 35 to 40 minutes, covering with foil halfway through baking to prevent excess browning, if necessary. Let cool in pan for 10 minutes. Remove from pan, and garnish with rosemary, thyme, and parsley, if desired. Serve warm or at room temperature.

TAHINI BRIOCHE

Makes 2 (9x5-inch) loaves

Recipe by Justin Burke-Samson

One of Justin Burke-Samson's signature recipes, inspired by his time at Kindred in Davidson, North Carolina, this pillowy brioche gets rich and nutty notes from tahini swirled into the dough.

¼ cup (60 grams) warm whole milk (105°F/41°C to 110°F/43°C)

2¼ teaspoons (7 grams) active dry yeast

¼ cup (50 grams) plus ½ teaspoon (2 grams) granulated sugar, divided

6 large eggs (300 grams), divided

2⅔ cups (334 grams) all-purpose flour, divided

5 tablespoons (80 grams) tahini*

1 large egg yolk (19 grams)

1 tablespoon (9 grams) kosher salt

¾ cup plus 2 tablespoons (198 grams) cold unsalted butter, cubed

1 to 2 tablespoons (15 to 30 grams) whole milk

¼ cup (36 grams) benne seeds or sesame seeds

1. In the bowl of a stand mixer, whisk together warm milk, yeast, and ½ teaspoon (2 grams) sugar by hand until yeast is dissolved. Whisk in 2 eggs (100 grams). Slowly fold in 1 cup (125 grams) flour until almost combined; sprinkle ⅓ cup (42 grams) flour on top. Let stand until top is cracked and sponge is soft to the touch, about 30 minutes.

2. Add 3 eggs (150 grams), tahini, egg yolk, salt, remaining 1⅓ cups (167 grams) flour, and remaining ¼ cup (50 grams) sugar to yeast mixture. Using the dough hook attachment, beat at low speed until a dough starts to form. Increase mixer speed to medium, and beat until dough comes together around dough hook, 8 to 10 minutes. Scrape sides of bowl. Add half of cold butter, and beat at high speed until combined. Add remaining cold butter, and beat until dough is smooth, 10 to 15 minutes. Reduce mixer speed to medium-high, and beat until dough comes together and pulls away from sides of bowl. Check dough for proper gluten development using the windowpane test. (See Note.)

3. Lightly flour a medium bowl; scrape dough into bowl. Fold dough in half, and press down; turn dough over, fold again, and press down. Cover and refrigerate for 6 hours or overnight.

4. Butter 2 (9x5-inch) loaf pans.

5. Turn out dough onto a lightly floured surface, and divide in half. Roll one half into a 12x6-inch rectangle. Cut rectangle into 3 (12x2-inch) strips. Starting at top, braid strips together. Pinch ends of braid together, and place into a prepared pan, tucking ends under. Repeat with remaining dough. Cover and let rise in a warm, draft-free place (75°F/24°C) until doubled in size or until dough reaches top of pan, about 2 hours. To test if dough is ready, make a dent in dough about 1 inch deep. If dough springs back fully, it is not ready. If dent remains and springs back only a little bit, dough is properly proofed.

6. Preheat oven to 350°F (180°C).

7. In a small bowl, whisk together milk and remaining 1 egg (50 grams). Brush top of dough with egg wash, and sprinkle with seeds.

8. Bake until an instant-read thermometer inserted in center registers 200°F (93°C), 40 to 45 minutes, covering with foil after 35 minutes of baking to prevent excess browning. Let cool in pans on a wire rack.

*Benne butter can be substituted.

Note: *Test the dough for proper gluten development by using the windowpane test. Pinch off (don't tear) a small piece of dough. Slowly pull the dough out from the center. If the dough is ready, you will be able to stretch it until it's thin and translucent like a windowpane. If the dough tears, it's not quite ready. Beat for 1 minute, and test again.*

Photo by Bounjour Y'all Bakery

MEYER LEMON DANISH LOAVES

Makes 2 (8½x4½-inch) loaves

Inspired by Samantha Seneviratne's hybrid Danish bread recipe featured in her cookbook The Joys of Baking, this zesty recipe will brighten up even the chilliest winter morning. We packed the pillowy dough with Meyer lemon zest and topped it off with cream cheese and Meyer Lemon Curd for a cozy loaf that's sure to warm your soul.

- 3¼ to 3½ cups (406 to 438 grams) plus 1½ teaspoons (4.5 grams) all-purpose flour, divided
- ½ cup (100 grams) granulated sugar, divided
- 1 (0.25-ounce) package (7 grams) active dry yeast
- 1¼ teaspoons (3 grams) kosher salt, divided
- 1¾ teaspoons (3 grams) ground cinnamon, divided
- ¾ cup (180 grams) whole milk
- ½ cup (113 grams) unsalted butter, softened
- 2 large eggs (100 grams), room temperature
- 2 teaspoons (4 grams) packed Meyer lemon zest
- 1½ teaspoons (6 grams) vanilla extract, divided
- ½ teaspoon (1 gram) ground ginger
- 2 tablespoons (28 grams) unsalted butter, melted
- 8 ounces (226 grams) cream cheese, softened
- ¼ cup (30 grams) confectioners' sugar
- 1 large egg yolk (19 grams)
- 1 large egg white (30 grams), lightly beaten
- ½ cup (123 grams) Meyer Lemon Curd (recipe follows)
- Simple Vanilla Glaze (recipe follows)

1. In the bowl of a stand mixer fitted with the paddle attachment, beat 1 cup (125 grams) flour, ¼ cup (50 grams) granulated sugar, yeast, 1 teaspoon (3 grams) salt, and ¼ teaspoon cinnamon at medium-low speed until well combined.

2. In a medium saucepan, heat milk and softened butter over medium heat until an instant-read thermometer registers 120°F (49°C) to 130°F (54°C). Add warm milk

mixture to flour mixture; beat at medium speed for 2 minutes. Add eggs, lemon zest, and 1 teaspoon (4 grams) vanilla; beat at medium-high speed for 2 minutes. With mixer on low speed, gradually add 2¼ cups (281 grams) flour, beating just until combined and stopping to scrape sides of bowl.

3. Switch to the dough hook attachment. Beat at medium speed until a soft, tacky dough forms, 6 to 8 minutes, stopping to scrape sides of bowl and dough hook; add up to ¼ cup (31 grams) flour, 1 tablespoon (8 grams) at a time, if necessary. (Dough should pass the windowpane test [see Note] but may still stick slightly to sides of bowl.)

4. Spray a large bowl with cooking spray. Place dough in bowl, turning to grease top. Cover and let rise in a warm, draft-free place (75°F/24°C) until doubled in size, 40 minutes to 1 hour.

5. Line 2 (8½x4½-inch) loaf pans with parchment paper, letting excess extend over sides of pan.

6. In a small bowl, stir together ginger, remaining ¼ cup (50 grams) granulated sugar, remaining 1½ teaspoons (4.5 grams) flour, and remaining 1½ teaspoons (3 grams) cinnamon. Stir in melted butter until well combined.

7. Punch down dough; turn out dough, and divide in half. Pat each half into an 8-inch square. Divide ginger mixture between squares. Using an offset spatula, spread ginger mixture onto dough, leaving a 1-inch border. Roll up dough, jelly roll style, pinching seams to seal. Place, seam side down, in prepared pans, and gently press into an even layer. Cover with plastic wrap, and let rise in a warm, draft-free place (75°F/24°C) until doubled in size, 40 minutes to 1 hour.

8. Preheat oven to 375°F (190°C).

9. Clean bowl of stand mixer and paddle attachment. Beat cream cheese, confectioners' sugar, egg yolk, remaining ½ teaspoon (2 grams) vanilla, and remaining ¼ teaspoon salt at medium speed until smooth. Spoon cream cheese mixture into a large pastry bag; cut a ½-inch opening in tip. Set aside.

10. Using a small pastry brush, carefully brush tops of dough with egg white. Using

a tight zigzag motion, pipe half of cream cheese mixture on top of one loaf, leaving a ¾- to 1-inch border; repeat with second loaf. (Retrace pattern on both loaves as needed until cream cheese mixture is gone.) Using a small offset spatula, spread half of Meyer Lemon Curd on top of cream cheese mixture on one loaf; repeat with second loaf. (Cream cheese and lemon curd layer will be thick.)

11. Bake until golden brown and an instant-read thermometer inserted in center registers at least 190°F (88°C), 30 to 35 minutes, loosely covering with foil to prevent excess browning, if necessary. Let cool in pans for 20 minutes. (Center will fall slightly as it cools.) Using excess parchment as handles, remove from pans, and let cool completely on a wire rack.

12. Place Simple Vanilla Glaze in a small pastry bag; cut a ¼-inch opening in tip, and drizzle onto cooled loaves.

Note: *Test the dough for proper gluten development using the windowpane test. Pinch off (don't tear) a small piece of dough. Slowly pull the dough out from the center. If the dough is ready, you will be able to stretch it until it's thin and translucent like a windowpane. If the dough tears, it's not quite ready. Beat for 1 minute, and test again.*

MEYER LEMON CURD
Makes about 1 cup

- 2 large eggs (100 grams)
- 2 large egg yolks (37 grams)
- ½ cup (100 grams) granulated sugar
- 1 tablespoon (4 grams) packed Meyer lemon zest
- ½ cup (120 grams) fresh Meyer lemon juice
- ¼ teaspoon kosher salt
- ¼ cup (57 grams) unsalted butter, cubed

1. Place a fine-mesh sieve over a medium bowl; set aside. In another medium bowl, whisk together eggs and egg yolks until well combined; set aside.

2. In a medium saucepan, stir together sugar, lemon zest and juice, and salt. Cook over medium-low heat until sugar dissolves and mixture begins to steam. (Do not boil.)

Pour lemon mixture into egg mixture in a slow, steady stream, whisking constantly. Return mixture to saucepan. Cook, stirring slowly and constantly in a figure eight motion with a silicone spatula, until curd is thickened and can coat the back of a spoon and an instant-read thermometer registers 175°F (79°C) to 180°F (82°C), 10 to 12 minutes.

3. Press curd through prepared sieve, discarding solids. Add butter, 1 to 2 cubes at a time, stirring until melted after each addition. Cover with a piece of plastic wrap, pressing wrap directly onto surface of curd to prevent a skin from forming. Refrigerate until well chilled and set, at least 2 hours. Store in an airtight container in refrigerator for up to 2 weeks.

SIMPLE VANILLA GLAZE
Makes ½ cup

1½ cups (180 grams) confectioners' sugar
2½ tablespoons (37.5 grams) whole milk
½ teaspoon (2 grams) vanilla extract

1. In a small bowl, stir together all ingredients until smooth and well combined. Use immediately.

MEXICAN CHOCOLATE CINNAMON ROLLS

Makes 12 rolls

You won't ever go back to classic cinnamon rolls again. We filled these golden rolls with chocolate, but not just any chocolate— Mexican cinnamon chocolate. Stone-ground, Mexican-style dark chocolate is filled with warm cinnamon spice and has a subtle grittiness that gives these cinnamon rolls even more explosive flavor and complex texture. Once you smother the rolls in the luscious Cream Cheese Glaze, serve them straight from the skillet to keep them warm and gooey.

3½ to 3¾ cups (438 to 469 grams) all-purpose flour, divided
½   cup (100 grams) granulated sugar, divided
1   (0.25-ounce) package (7 grams) active dry yeast
2   teaspoons (6 grams) kosher salt, divided
½   cup (120 grams) whole milk
½   cup (120 grams) water
⅔   cup (152 grams) unsalted butter, softened and divided
1   large egg (50 grams)
2   tablespoons (10 grams) Dutch process cocoa powder
½   teaspoon (1 gram) ground cinnamon
⅔   cup (113 grams) chopped Mexican-style stone-ground cinnamon chocolate (3 disks) (see PRO TIP)
Cream Cheese Glaze (recipe follows)
Garnish: ground cinnamon

1. In the bowl of a stand mixer fitted with the paddle attachment, beat 1½ cups (188 grams) flour, ¼ cup (50 grams) sugar, yeast, and 1½ teaspoons (4.5 grams) salt at low speed until combined.
2. In a medium saucepan, heat milk, ½ cup (120 grams) water, and ⅓ cup (76 grams) butter over medium heat until an instant-read thermometer registers 120°F (49°C) to 130°F (54°C). Add warm milk mixture to flour mixture, and beat at medium speed until combined. Add egg, beating until combined. With mixer on low speed, gradually add 2 cups (250 grams) flour, beating just until combined and stopping to scrape sides of bowl.
3. Switch to the dough hook attachment. Beat at low speed until a soft, smooth, and somewhat sticky dough forms and pulls away from sides of bowl, 8 to 9 minutes; add up to remaining ¼ cup (31 grams) flour, if necessary. Turn out onto a lightly floured surface, and shape into a smooth round.
4. Lightly spray a large bowl. Place dough in bowl, turning to grease top. Cover and let rise in a warm, draft-free place (75°F/24°C) until doubled in size, 40 minutes to 1 hour.
5. Spray a 10-inch cast-iron skillet with cooking spray.

6. In a small bowl, stir together cocoa, cinnamon, remaining ⅓ cup (76 grams) butter, remaining ¼ cup (50 grams) sugar, and remaining ½ teaspoon (1.5 grams) salt.
7. Lightly punch down dough. Cover and let stand for 5 minutes. Turn out dough onto a lightly floured surface, and roll into an 18x12-inch rectangle. Spread cocoa mixture onto dough, leaving a ½-inch border on one long side. Sprinkle with chopped chocolate. Starting with long side opposite border, roll up dough, jelly roll style; pinch seam to seal. Gently shape log to 18 inches long and even thickness, if necessary. Using a serrated knife dipped in flour, cut log into 12 slices (about 1½ inches thick). Place slices, cut side down, in prepared skillet. Cover and let rise in a warm, draft-free place (75°F/24°C) until puffed, 20 to 30 minutes.
8. Preheat oven to 350°F (180°C).
9. Bake until lightly golden and an instant-read thermometer inserted in center registers 190°F (88°C), 35 to 40 minutes, loosely covering with foil to prevent excess browning, if necessary. Let cool in skillet for 10 minutes. Top with Cream Cheese Glaze; garnish with cinnamon, if desired. Serve warm or at room temperature.

CREAM CHEESE GLAZE
Makes about ¾ cup

4   ounces (113 grams) cream cheese, softened
1½ tablespoons (10.5 grams) confectioners' sugar
2 to 3 tablespoons (30 to 45 grams) whole milk

1. In a medium bowl, combine cream cheese and confectioners' sugar. Add milk, 1 tablespoon (15 grams) at a time, until fluid.

PRO TIP
We used Taza Chocolate Cinnamon Dark Chocolate Mexicano, available at Whole Foods, local Hispanic grocery stores, or online. Very minimally processed, Mexican chocolate has a grainier, chalkier texture than the chocolate you might normally get and offers more-complex, explosive flavor. Any type of Mexican cinnamon dark chocolate, available at most grocery stores, or 50% cacao dark chocolate will work in this recipe.

PINEAPPLE BUNS

Makes 10 buns

No pineapples were harmed to make these pillowy Pineapple Buns, which got their name due to their physical resemblance to the tropical fruit. Sweet, golden, and highly addictive, these tender buns have a Milk Roux base and crispy cookie-like cover. Be sure to make the Milk Roux and the topping before starting on the buns.

⅔ cup (160 grams) warm whole milk (100°F/38°C to 110°F/43°C)
5½ tablespoons (66 grams) granulated sugar, divided
2¼ teaspoons (7 grams) active dry yeast
Milk Roux (recipe follows), room temperature
3 cups (381 grams) bread flour
¼ cup (57 grams) unsalted butter, melted and cooled for 10 minutes
2 large eggs (100 grams), divided
1 teaspoon (3 grams) kosher salt
1 teaspoon (4 grams) vanilla extract
Pineapple Buns Topping (recipe follows)
1 tablespoon (15 grams) whole milk, room temperature

1. In the bowl of a stand mixer, whisk together warm milk, 1 tablespoon (12 grams) sugar, and yeast by hand. Let stand until foamy, about 10 minutes.
2. Add Milk Roux, flour, melted butter, 1 egg (50 grams), salt, vanilla, and remaining 4½ tablespoons (54 grams) sugar to yeast mixture; using the paddle attachment, beat at low speed just until combined, stopping to scrape sides of bowl. Switch to the dough hook attachment; beat at low speed for 3 minutes. Increase mixer speed to medium-low, and beat until a soft, smooth dough forms, 6 to 8 minutes, stopping to scrape sides of bowl. Check dough for proper gluten development using the windowpane test. (See Note.) Cover and let rise in a warm, draft-free place (75°F/24°C) until doubled in size, about 1 hour.
3. Line 2 baking sheets with parchment paper.
4. Punch down dough; let stand for 5 minutes. Divide dough into 10 portions (about 77 grams each). Roll each portion into a ball, and place on prepared pans.
5. Divide Pineapple Buns Topping into 10 portions (about 27 grams each); roll into balls. Place 1 ball between 2 sheets of plastic wrap; roll or pat into a 4-inch circle. Gently wrap circle over top of 1 bun, covering as much dough as possible. Repeat with remaining Pineapple Buns Topping and buns. Using a sharp knife, gently cut a crosshatch pattern into top of each bun through topping. Cover and let rise in a warm, draft-free place (75°F/24°C) until doubled in size, 40 minutes to 1 hour.
6. Preheat oven to 350°F (180°C).

7. In a small bowl, whisk together room temperature milk and remaining 1 egg (50 grams). Thoroughly brush top of buns with egg wash, being sure to get between rows of topping.
8. Bake until golden brown and an instant-read thermometer inserted in center registers at least 190°F (88°C), about 15 minutes. Let cool on pans for 10 minutes before serving.

Note: *Test the dough for proper gluten development using the windowpane test. Pinch off (don't tear) a small piece of dough. Slowly pull the dough out from the center. If the dough is ready, you will be able to stretch it until it's thin and translucent like a windowpane. If the dough tears, it's not quite ready. Beat for 1 minute, and test again.*

MILK ROUX

Makes about ⅓ cup

⅓ cup (80 grams) whole milk
2 tablespoons (16 grams) bread flour

1. In a small saucepan, whisk together milk and flour. Cook over medium-low heat, whisking constantly, until thickened, an instant-read thermometer registers 149°F (65°C), and whisk leaves lines on bottom of pan. Transfer to a small bowl, and let cool to room temperature before using.

PINEAPPLE BUNS TOPPING

Makes enough for 10 buns

¼ cup (57 grams) unsalted butter, softened
¼ cup (50 grams) granulated sugar
½ teaspoon (1.5 grams) kosher salt
1 large egg yolk (19 grams)
1 tablespoon (15 grams) whole milk, room temperature
¼ teaspoon (1 gram) vanilla extract
1 cup (125 grams) unbleached cake flour
2 tablespoons (10 grams) nonfat dry milk powder
½ teaspoon (2.5 grams) baking powder

1. In the bowl of a stand mixer fitted with the paddle attachment, beat butter, sugar, and salt at medium speed until creamy, 2 to 3 minutes, stopping to scrape sides of bowl. Beat in egg yolk, milk, and vanilla until well combined.
2. In a medium bowl, whisk together flour, milk powder, and baking powder. With mixer on low speed, gradually add flour mixture to butter mixture, beating just until combined. Turn out onto a sheet of plastic wrap, and shape into a 10-inch log (about 1½ inches thick). Wrap in plastic wrap, and refrigerate for at least 1 hour.

DO-IT-ALL DOUGH

Makes enough for 12 rolls

Created for our Better Baking Academy with Bob's Red Mill, this flexible enriched dough will become the most trusted recipe in your bread repertoire. Luxuriously rich with milk, butter, an egg, and just a dash of sugar, our Do-It-All Dough can become the tender base for both Almond Cream Rolls and Garlic Herb Clover Rolls.

3¾ cups (469 grams) all-purpose flour*, divided
2   tablespoons (24 grams) granulated sugar
1   tablespoon (9 grams) kosher salt
2¼   teaspoons (7 grams) active dry yeast
½   cup (120 grams) whole milk
½   cup (120 grams) water
⅓   cup (76 grams) unsalted butter
1   large egg (50 grams), room temperature

1. In the bowl of a stand mixer fitted with the paddle attachment, combine 1½ cups (188 grams) flour, sugar, salt, and yeast.
2. In a medium saucepan, heat milk, ½ cup (120 grams) water, and butter over medium heat until an instant-read thermometer registers 120°F (49°C) to 130°F (54°C). Add warm milk mixture to flour mixture, and beat at medium speed until combined. Add egg, beating until combined. With mixer on low speed, gradually add 2 cups (250 grams) flour, beating just until a shaggy dough comes together and stopping to scrape sides of bowl.

3. Switch to the dough hook attachment. Beat at low speed until a soft, somewhat sticky dough forms, 6 to 7 minutes, stopping to scrape sides of bowl and dough hook; add up to remaining ¼ cup (31 grams) flour, 1 tablespoon (8 grams) at a time, if dough is too sticky. Turn out dough onto a lightly floured surface, and shape into a smooth round.
4. Lightly oil a large bowl. Place dough in bowl, turning to grease top. Cover and let rise in a warm, draft-free place (75°F/24°C) until doubled in size, 40 minutes to 1 hour.

We used Bob's Red Mill Organic All-Purpose Flour.

GARLIC-HERB CLOVER ROLLS

Makes 12 rolls

We partnered up with Bob's Red Mill to create the ultimate versatile, tender base dough for the Better Baking Academy with Bob's Red Mill. This rendition of the Do-It-All Dough gets a generous brush of garlic herb butter before being popped into the oven. The result? Buttery, aromatic perfection.

Do-It-All Dough (recipe on page 154)
¼   cup (57 grams) unsalted butter, melted
¾   teaspoon (4.5 grams) garlic salt
½   tablespoon (1 gram) chopped fresh rosemary

½   tablespoon (1 gram) chopped fresh thyme
3   tablespoons (15 grams) grated Parmesan cheese, divided

1. Spray a 12-cup muffin pan with cooking spray.
2. Punch down Do-It-All Dough, and let stand for 5 minutes. Turn out dough onto a lightly floured surface, and divide into 12 portions (about 70 grams each). Divide 1 portion into 3 pieces (about 23 grams each). (Keep remaining dough covered to prevent it from drying out.) Roll each piece into a smooth ball. Place 3 dough balls, seam side down, in a prepared muffin cup. Repeat

with remaining dough. Cover and let rise in a warm, draft-free place (75°F/24°C) until doubled in size, 20 to 30 minutes.
3. Preheat oven to 350°F (180°C).
4. In a small bowl, stir together melted butter, garlic salt, rosemary, and thyme. Brush butter mixture onto rolls, and sprinkle with 1½ tablespoons (7.5 grams) cheese.
5. Bake until golden brown and an instant-read thermometer inserted in center registers 190°F (88°C), 8 to 12 minutes, rotating pan halfway through baking. Brush with butter mixture, and sprinkle with remaining 1½ tablespoons (7.5 grams) cheese. Serve warm or at room temperature. Store in an airtight container at room temperature for up to 4 days.

ALMOND CREAM ROLLS

Makes 12 rolls

With the Do-It-All Dough as its swirling base, these almond cream-filled delights show off the sweet versatility of the dough.

3	tablespoons (42 grams) unsalted butter, softened
¼	cup (50 grams) granulated sugar
⅔	cup (64 grams) almond flour*
1	large egg (50 grams), separated
⅛	teaspoon almond extract
¼	cup (31 grams) all-purpose flour*
1	tablespoon (6 grams) ground cinnamon
⅛	teaspoon kosher salt

Do-It-All Dough (recipe on page 154)
1   tablespoon (15 grams) whole milk
Almond Cream Cheese Glaze (recipe follows)

1. Preheat oven to 350°F (180°C). Line a 13x9-inch rimmed baking sheet with parchment paper. Spray sides of pan with cooking spray.

2. In a medium bowl, beat butter and sugar with a mixer at medium speed until fluffy, about 1 minute. Beat in almond flour until combined. With mixer on low speed, add egg white and almond extract, beating until combined. Beat in all-purpose flour, cinnamon, and salt. Refrigerate almond cream until ready to use.

3. Punch down Do-It-All Dough, and let stand for 5 minutes. Turn out dough onto a lightly floured surface, and roll into an 18x11-inch rectangle. Using a small offset spatula, spread almond cream onto dough, leaving a ½-inch border on one long side. Starting with opposite long side, roll up dough, jelly roll style. Gently shape log to 18 inches long and even thickness, if necessary. Using a serrated knife dipped in flour, cut log into 12 slices (about 1½ inches thick), trimming ends if needed. Tuck ends of rolls under, and place, tucked-end down, on prepared pan, leaving even space between rolls. Cover and let rise in a warm, draft-free place (75°F/24°C) until puffed, 20 to 30 minutes.

4. In a small bowl, whisk together egg yolk and milk. Brush tops and sides of rolls with egg wash.

5. Bake until golden brown and an instant-read thermometer inserted in center registers 190°F (88°C), 14 to 16 minutes. Let cool for 5 minutes. Spread Almond Cream Cheese Glaze onto warm rolls. Serve warm or at room temperature.

We used Bob's Red Mill Super-Fine Natural Almond Flour and Bob's Red Mill Organic All-Purpose Flour.

ALMOND CREAM CHEESE GLAZE
Makes ¾ cup

6	ounces (170 grams) cream cheese, softened
¼	cup (30 grams) confectioners' sugar
1	tablespoon (15 grams) whole milk
⅛	teaspoon kosher salt
⅛	teaspoon almond extract

1. In a medium bowl, beat cream cheese until smooth, about 1 minute. Add confectioners' sugar and all remaining ingredients, and beat until smooth.

Punch down the dough to remove excess air. Then let it stand for 5 minutes, allowing the gluten to relax. These steps make it easier to shape and roll out.

When rolling out the dough, preshape it into a rectangle and then roll out into a larger rectangle, rolling from the center to the corners to keep your corners sharp. Use your hands and eyes to look for even thickness throughout the dough. Use a ruler to check your dimensions.

When spreading the almond cream onto the dough, leave a ½-inch border on one long side. When you roll up the dough into a tight spiral, this border will allow the dough to form an airtight seal.

Once you roll up the dough, make sure you take the time to double-check that it is at least 18 inches long and even in thickness. If it is slightly longer than 18 inches or if the ends are not level or even, trim the dough to get it to the right size.

We use a ruler to score (or mark) the dough at 1½-inch intervals so we can make even cuts. We use a sharp serrated knife for cutting because its jagged edges more easily cut through the roll without pushing out the filling.

Always cut using a knife dipped in flour. Place your flour on the counter so you can easily place your knife in it as needed. As you cut, don't press down too hard. Instead, let the blade do the work so you don't smush the dough.

Once the dough is cut, take the end seam of each roll, tuck it in under the roll, and press the roll, tucked-end down, on the prepared pan. This adds height to the roll and can help the center pop up into a scroll.

When placing the rolls on the pan, leave enough space for them to proof. You don't want them to double in size here, only puff up about 66% to 75%. Conduct the finger dent test in an inconspicuous place to check for proper proofing.

FRENCH ONION BREAD

Makes 1 (9-inch) loaf

We're flipping the script on your favorite onion soup. This pillowy bread round combines sherry, thyme, and our Caramelized Onions to impart the traditional French onion flavor while Gruyère brings cheesy decadence to the formula.

4¼ cups (531 grams) all-purpose flour, divided
¼   cup (50 grams) granulated sugar
1   (0.25-ounce) package (7 grams) active dry yeast
1   teaspoon (3 grams) kosher salt
½   cup (120 grams) whole milk
½   cup (120 grams) water
⅓   cup (76 grams) unsalted butter
¼   cup (60 grams) sour cream
1   large egg (50 grams)
Caramelized Onions (recipe follows)
½   cup (113 grams) unsalted butter, softened
2   tablespoons (4 grams) chopped fresh thyme
8   ounces (226 grams) Gruyère cheese, shredded and divided

1. In the bowl of a stand mixer, whisk together 2 cups (250 grams) flour, sugar, yeast, and salt by hand.
2. In a medium saucepan, heat milk, ½ cup (120 grams) water, butter, and sour cream over medium heat until an instant-read thermometer registers 120°F (49°C) to 130°F (54°C). Add warm milk mixture to flour mixture; using the paddle attachment, beat at medium speed until combined. Add egg, beating until combined. With mixer on low speed, gradually add 2 cups (250 grams) flour, beating until combined.
3. Switch to the dough hook attachment. Beat at low speed until a soft, smooth, and somewhat sticky dough forms and pulls away from bowl, 9 to 10 minutes; add up to remaining ¼ cup (31 grams) flour if dough is too sticky. Turn out dough onto a lightly floured surface, and shape into a smooth round.
4. Lightly oil a large bowl. Place dough in bowl, turning to grease top. Cover and let rise in a warm, draft-free place (75°F/24°C) until doubled in size, 45 minutes to 1 hour.
5. Spray a 9-inch round cake pan with cooking spray.
6. Lightly punch down dough. Cover and let stand for 5 minutes. Turn out dough onto a lightly floured surface, and roll into a 21x12-inch rectangle. In a small bowl, combine softened butter and thyme. Spread thyme butter onto dough, leaving a ½-inch border on one long side. Sprinkle and spread Caramelized

Onions onto butter. Sprinkle 6 ounces (170 grams) cheese onto onions. Starting with long side opposite border, roll dough into a log, pinching seam to seal. Place log seam side down, and cut in half lengthwise, leaving 1½ inches at one end. Turn halves cut side up, and carefully twist dough pieces around each other; form into a circle. Place, cut side up, in prepared pan. Cover and let rise in a warm, draft-free place (75°F/24°C) until puffed, about 30 minutes.
7. Position one oven rack in center and one at top of oven. Preheat oven to 350°F (180°C).
8. Bake on center rack for 30 minutes. Sprinkle remaining 2 ounces (57 grams) cheese on top, and bake until cheese is melted and golden brown and an instant-read thermometer inserted in center registers 190°F (88°C), 15 to 20 minutes more, placing a piece of foil on top rack of oven to prevent excess browning, if necessary. Let cool in pan for 20 minutes. Remove from pan. Serve warm or at room temperature.

CARAMELIZED ONIONS
Makes 1 cup

¼   cup (57 grams) unsalted butter
2   pounds (908 grams) Vidalia onions, thinly sliced (about 8 cups)
1   teaspoon (3 grams) kosher salt
½   teaspoon (2 grams) granulated sugar
½   teaspoon (1 gram) ground black pepper
½   cup (120 grams) dry sherry

1. In a large Dutch oven, melt butter over medium heat. Add onion; cook, stirring occasionally, until softened, about 15 minutes. Add salt, sugar, and pepper; cook, stirring occasionally, until onion is deep golden brown, 30 to 40 minutes.
2. Increase heat to high. Add sherry to onion mixture; cook until most of liquid has evaporated. Transfer to a glass bowl, and let cool to room temperature.

GARLIC-HERB MONKEY BREAD

Makes 8 to 12 servings

Switching to the savory side of baking, our garlic- and herb-packed pull-apart bread is equally at home as part of the brunch spread or as an accompaniment to a fine dinner.

3¼ to 3½ cups (406 to 438 grams) all-purpose flour, divided
¼ cup (50 grams) granulated sugar
2½ teaspoons (7.5 grams) kosher salt, divided
1 (0.25-ounce) package (7 grams) instant yeast
¼ teaspoon ground nutmeg
1 cup (240 grams) whole milk
½ cup (113 grams) unsalted butter, softened
1 large egg (50 grams)
½ cup (113 grams) unsalted butter, melted
1½ tablespoons (7 grams) finely chopped fresh chives
1½ tablespoons (6 grams) finely chopped fresh tarragon
1½ tablespoons (6 grams) finely chopped fresh parsley
1 teaspoon (2 grams) garlic powder
¼ teaspoon crushed red pepper
Grated Parmesan cheese, for sprinkling

1. In the bowl of a stand mixer fitted with the paddle attachment, combine 1¼ cups (156 grams) flour, sugar, 2¼ teaspoons (6.75 grams) salt, yeast, and nutmeg; beat at low speed until combined.

2. In a medium saucepan, cook milk and softened butter over medium heat until butter is melted and an instant-read thermometer registers 120°F (49°C) to 130°F (54°C). Add warm milk mixture to flour mixture; beat at medium speed for 2 minutes, stopping to scrape sides of bowl. Add egg; beat at medium-high speed for 2 minutes. With mixer on low speed, gradually add 2 cups (250 grams) flour, beating until combined.

3. Switch to the dough hook attachment. Beat at medium-low speed until a soft, somewhat tacky dough forms, 6 to 8 minutes, stopping to scrape sides of bowl and dough hook; add up to remaining ¼ cup (31 grams) flour, 1 tablespoon (8 grams) at a time, if dough is too sticky. Check dough for proper gluten development using the windowpane test. (See Note.)

4. Spray a large bowl with cooking spray. Place dough in bowl, turning to grease top. Cover and let rise in a warm, draft-free place (75°F/24°C) until doubled in size, 40 minutes to 1 hour.

5. In a small bowl, stir together melted butter, chives, tarragon, parsley, garlic powder, red pepper, and remaining ¼ teaspoon salt.

6. Preheat oven to 350°F (180°C).

7. Punch down dough; let stand for 5 minutes. On a clean surface, divide dough into 36 portions (about 24 grams each); gently shape each portion into a ball, pinching closed any seams if needed. (Keep dough portions covered with a sheet of plastic wrap while working.)

8. Spray a 15-cup Nordic Ware Anniversary Bundt Pan with baking spray with flour.

9. Dip dough balls in butter mixture, turning until well coated; arrange evenly in prepared pan, pressing dough balls gently into each other and grooves of pan. Cover and let rise in a warm, draft-free place (75°F/24°C) until doubled in size and dough holds an indentation when pressed, 25 to 35 minutes. Reserve remaining butter mixture.

10. Bake until golden brown and an instant-read thermometer inserted near center registers at least 190°F (88°C), 25 to 30 minutes. Let cool in pan for 5 minutes; invert onto a serving plate.

11. Reheat reserved butter mixture, if necessary; brush all over warm bread. Sprinkle with Parmesan; serve immediately.

Note: *Test the dough for proper gluten development using the windowpane test. Pinch off (don't tear) a small piece of dough. Slowly pull the dough out from the center. If the dough is ready, you will be able to stretch it until it's thin and translucent like a windowpane. If the dough tears, it's not quite ready. Beat for 1 minute, and test again.*

CINNAMON-SUGAR PRETZELS

Makes 12 pretzels

A sugared and spiced take on the traditional pretzel, these sweet twists get a touch of brown sugar in the dough. A final dip in butter and cinnamon sugar sends them right over the edge into dessert bliss.

4½   cups (562 grams) all-purpose flour, divided
2   tablespoons (28 grams) firmly packed light brown sugar
1   tablespoon (9 grams) kosher salt
2¼   teaspoons (7 grams) instant yeast
1   cup (240 grams) whole milk
8½   cups (2,040 grams) plus 1 tablespoon (15 grams) water, divided
2   tablespoons (28 grams) unsalted butter
¼   cup (60 grams) baking soda
1   large egg yolk (19 grams)
2   cups (400 grams) granulated sugar
2   tablespoons (12 grams) ground cinnamon
2   tablespoons (28 grams) unsalted butter, melted

1. In the bowl of a stand mixer fitted with the paddle attachment, beat 2 cups (250 grams) flour, brown sugar, salt, and yeast at low speed until combined.

2. In a small saucepan, heat milk, ½ cup (120 grams) water, and butter over medium heat until an instant-read thermometer registers 120°F (49°C) to 130°F (54°C). Add warm milk mixture to flour mixture, and beat at medium speed until combined. Reduce mixer speed to low, and gradually add 2¼ cups (281 grams) flour, beating just until combined and stopping to scrape sides of bowl.

3. Switch to the dough hook attachment. Beat at low speed until a soft, somewhat sticky dough forms, 5 to 6 minutes, stopping to scrape sides of bowl and dough hook; add up to remaining ¼ cup (31 grams) flour, 1 tablespoon (8 grams) at a time, if dough is too sticky. Turn out onto a lightly floured surface, and shape into a smooth round.

4. Lightly oil a medium bowl. Place dough in bowl, turning to grease top. Cover and let rise in a warm, draft-free place (75°F/24°C) until doubled in size, 30 to 45 minutes.

5. Place a large piece of parchment paper on work surface; dust with flour. Set aside.

6. On a very lightly floured surface, divide dough into 12 portions (about 81 grams each). Shape each portion into a ball. Roll each ball into a 20-inch rope, tapering ends. Shape each rope into a "U" shape, and cross ends of rope about 3 inches down. Twist ends once; fold down, and place ends on dough, pinching to seal. (If there is too much flour for ends to stick, place a small amount of water on dough to help seal). Place on prepared parchment paper. Cover and let rise in a warm, draft-free place (75°F/24°C) for 20 minutes.

7. Preheat oven to 375°F (190°C). Line 2 baking sheets with parchment paper.

8. In a 4-quart stockpot, bring 8 cups (1,920 grams) water and baking soda to a gentle boil.

9. Carefully drop pretzels, 1 to 2 at a time, top side down, into boiling water mixture. Cook for 30 seconds; turn, and cook for 30 seconds. Using a spider strainer, lift, and let excess water drip off; place on prepared pans.

10. In a small bowl, whisk together egg yolk and remaining 1 tablespoon (15 grams) water. Brush dough with egg wash.

11. Bake until deep golden brown, 14 to 16 minutes. Let cool on pans for 5 minutes.

12. In a large bowl, combine granulated sugar and cinnamon.

13. Brush melted butter onto pretzels. Place 1 pretzel in cinnamon sugar, and toss until completely covered. Shake off excess, and place on serving platter. Repeat with remaining pretzels. Serve warm or at room temperature.

FETA CHEESE ROLLS

Makes 12 rolls

These savory, pillowy rolls are the perfect bed for the aromatic Feta Cheese Filling.

3¾ cups (469 grams) plus 1 tablespoon (8 grams) all-purpose flour, divided
2 tablespoons (24 grams) granulated sugar
1 (0.25-ounce) package (7 grams) instant yeast*
2 teaspoons (6 grams) kosher salt
½ cup (120 grams) plus 1 tablespoon (15 grams) water, divided
½ cup (120 grams) whole milk
⅓ cup (76 grams) unsalted butter, cubed
2 large eggs (100 grams), room temperature and divided
Feta Cheese Filling (recipe follows)
Garnish: chopped fresh tarragon, chopped fresh thyme

1. In the bowl of a stand mixer, whisk together 2 cups (250 grams) flour, sugar, yeast, and salt by hand.
2. In a medium saucepan, heat ½ cup (120 grams) water, milk, and butter over medium heat, stirring occasionally, until an instant-read thermometer registers 120°F (49°C) to 130°F (54°C).
3. With mixer on medium speed and using the paddle attachment, pour warm milk mixture into flour mixture, beating until combined and cooled slightly, about 1 minute. Add 1 egg (50 grams), and beat at medium speed until combined. Reduce mixer speed to low, and gradually add 1¾ cups (219 grams) flour, beating until a shaggy dough forms.
4. Switch to the dough hook attachment, and beat at low speed until dough is smooth and elastic, 12 to 14 minutes. Add remaining 1 tablespoon (8 grams) flour if dough is too sticky. Turn out dough onto a lightly floured surface, and shape into a smooth round.
5. Lightly oil a large bowl. Place dough in bowl, turning to grease top. Cover and let rise in a warm, draft-free place (75°F/24°C) until doubled in size, about 45 minutes.
6. Preheat oven to 375°F (190°C). Line 2 baking sheets with parchment paper.
7. Punch down dough, and let stand for

5 minutes. Turn out onto a lightly floured surface, and divided into 12 portions (about 70 grams each). Shape each portion into a smooth ball; press flat, and roll into a 3-inch circle. Place 6 circles 3 inches apart on each prepared pan. Cover and let rise in a warm, draft-free place (75°F/24°C) until puffed, 15 to 25 minutes. Press bottom of a 4-ounce glass Mason jar (2-inch diameter) dipped in flour into center of each circle. Press firmly to flatten center without tearing dough. Spoon 2 rounded tablespoons (about 36 grams) Feta Cheese Filling into center of each circle. (Do not overfill.)
8. In a small bowl, whisk together remaining 1 egg (50 grams) and remaining 1 tablespoon (15 grams) water. Lightly brush dough with egg wash.
9. Bake until light golden brown and an instant-read thermometer inserted in bread registers 190°F (88°C) to 200°F (190°C), 12 to 13 minutes. Let cool on pans for 5 minutes. Serve warm or at room temperature. Garnish with tarragon and thyme, if desired.

We used Platinum Yeast® from Red Star®.

FETA CHEESE FILLING
Makes about 2 cups

1½ cups (204 grams) creamy feta cheese crumbles
6 ounces (170 grams) cream cheese, softened
1 large egg (50 grams)
1½ tablespoons (21 grams) unsalted butter, softened
4 teaspoons (2.5 grams) chopped fresh tarragon
4 teaspoons (2.5 grams) chopped fresh thyme
½ teaspoon (1.5 grams) kosher salt
¼ teaspoon ground black pepper

1. In the bowl of a stand mixer fitted with the paddle attachment, beat all ingredients at medium-low speed until creamy and well combined, about 1 minute.

CHERRY-ALMOND SWEET ROLLS

Makes 16 rolls

Twisted and swirled with a cherry-almond filling, these sweet rolls get a boost in crunchiness from toasted, sliced almonds.

1¼ cups (360 grams) cherry spreadable fruit
2 tablespoons (26 grams) finely chopped dried tart cherries
1¼ teaspoons (4 grams) tapioca flour
¼ teaspoon ground cinnamon
⅛ teaspoon ground nutmeg
¼ teaspoon (1 gram) almond extract
4 cups plus 2 tablespoons (516 grams) all-purpose flour, divided
⅓ cup (67 grams) granulated sugar
1 (0.25-ounce) package (7 grams) instant yeast*
2 teaspoons (6 grams) kosher salt
1 cup (240 grams) whole milk
⅓ cup (76 grams) unsalted butter, softened
¼ cup (60 grams) sour cream, room temperature
2 large eggs (100 grams), divided
2 teaspoons (3 grams) packed lemon zest
1 teaspoon (6 grams) vanilla bean paste

2 tablespoons (14 grams) lightly toasted sliced almonds, finely chopped
Raw sliced almonds, for sprinkling

1. In a small saucepan, stir together spreadable fruit, dried cherries, tapioca flour, cinnamon, and nutmeg; cook over medium heat, stirring frequently, until mixture just starts to bubble, about 5 minutes. Immediately remove from heat; stir in almond extract. Transfer cherry mixture to a small bowl, and let cool completely; refrigerate until ready to use.
2. In the bowl of a stand mixer fitted with the paddle attachment, beat 1 cup (125 grams) all-purpose flour, sugar, yeast, and salt at medium-low speed until well combined.
3. In a medium saucepan, heat milk and butter over medium heat until an instant-read thermometer registers 120°F (49°C) to 130°F (54°C). Add warm milk mixture to flour mixture; beat at medium speed for 2 minutes. Add sour cream, 1 egg (50 grams), lemon zest, and vanilla bean paste; beat at medium-high speed for 2 minutes. With mixer on low speed, gradually add remaining 3 cups plus 2 tablespoons (391 grams) all-purpose flour, beating just until combined and stopping to scrape sides of bowl.

4. Switch to the dough hook attachment. Beat at medium speed until a soft, tacky dough forms, 6 to 8 minutes, stopping to scrape sides of bowl and dough hook. (Dough should pass the windowpane test [see Note] but may still stick slightly to sides of bowl.)
5. Spray a large bowl with cooking spray. Place dough in bowl, turning to grease top. Cover and let rise in a warm, draft-free place (75°F/24°C) until doubled in size, 45 minutes to 1 hour.
6. Preheat oven to 375°F (190°C). Line 2 rimmed baking sheets with parchment paper.
7. Lightly punch down dough; cover and let stand for 5 minutes. Turn out dough onto a very lightly floured surface, and roll into a 20x16-inch rectangle. Using a small offset spatula, spread cherry mixture onto dough, leaving a ½-inch border on short sides; sprinkle evenly with chopped almonds.
8. In a small bowl, whisk remaining 1 egg (50 grams). Brush one border with egg wash. Fold dough in half crosswise, trimming if needed, to create a 16x10-inch rectangle. Gently roll over dough to ensure filling is even. Cut dough into 16 (1-inch-wide) strips. Twist each strip 3 to 4 times; starting from one end, coil twisted dough strip into a spiral shape, tucking end under. Place rolls 1 to 1½ inches apart on prepared pans. Cover and let rise in a warm, draft-free place (75°F/24°C) until puffed, 30 minutes to 1 hour.
9. Brush rolls with remaining egg wash; sprinkle with sliced almonds.
10. Bake until lightly golden and an instant-read thermometer inserted in center registers 190°F (88°C), 12 to 14 minutes, rotating pans halfway through baking and loosely covering with foil to prevent excess browning, if necessary. Let cool on pans for 10 minutes. Serve warm.

We used Platinum® Yeast from Red Star®

Note: *Test the dough for proper gluten development using the windowpane test. Pinch off (don't tear) a small piece of dough. Slowly pull the dough out from the center. If the dough is ready, you will be able to stretch it until it's thin and translucent like a windowpane. If the dough tears, it's not quite ready. Beat for 1 minute, and test again.*

BLUEBERRY-LEMON CREAM CHEESE BREAD

Makes 8 to 10 servings

This elegant pull-apart star has a particularly elastic and forgiving dough, making this the ideal shareable recipe.

3¼ cups plus 2 tablespoons (422 grams) all-purpose flour, divided
¼ cup (50 grams) granulated sugar
2¼ teaspoons (7 grams) instant yeast
2 teaspoons (6 grams) kosher salt
1 cup (240 grams) whole milk
¼ cup (57 grams) unsalted butter, softened
2 large eggs (100 grams), room temperature and divided
2 teaspoons (12 grams) vanilla bean paste
4 ounces (113 grams) cream cheese, softened
¼ cup (30 grams) confectioners' sugar
¼ cup (9 grams) freeze-dried blueberries, finely crushed*
1 tablespoon (3 grams) lemon zest
1 tablespoon (15 grams) lightly beaten egg white
¼ teaspoon ground cardamom
1 tablespoon (15 grams) water
Sparkling sugar, for sprinkling
Cream Cheese Glaze (recipe follows)

1. In the bowl of a stand mixer fitted with the paddle attachment, beat 1 cup (125 grams) flour, granulated sugar, yeast, and salt at medium-low speed until well combined, stopping to scrape sides of bowl.
2. In a medium saucepan, heat milk and butter over medium heat until an instant-read thermometer registers 120°F (49°C) to 130°F (54°C). Add warm milk mixture to flour mixture; beat at medium speed for 2 minutes, stopping to scrape sides of bowl. Add 1 egg (50 grams) and vanilla bean paste; beat at medium-high speed for 2 minutes. With mixer on low speed, gradually add remaining 2¼ cups plus 2 tablespoons (297 grams) flour, beating just until combined and stopping to scrape sides of bowl.
3. Switch to the dough hook attachment. Beat at medium speed until a soft, somewhat sticky dough forms, 6 to 8 minutes, stopping to scrape sides of bowl and dough hook. (Dough should pass the windowpane test [see Note] but may still stick slightly to sides of bowl.)
4. Spray a large bowl with cooking spray. Place dough in bowl, turning to grease top. Cover and let rise in a warm, draft-free place (75°F/24°C) until doubled in size, 40 minutes to 1 hour.
5. Line a light-colored 17½x12½-inch rimmed baking sheet with parchment paper.
6. In a small bowl, stir together cream cheese, confectioners' sugar, blueberries, lemon zest, egg white, and cardamom until well combined.

7. Lightly punch down dough; cover and let stand for 5 minutes. Turn out dough, and divide into 4 portions (about 200 grams each); gently shape each into a ball. Cover with plastic wrap, and let stand for 15 minutes. Keeping other portions covered with plastic wrap, roll and pat 1 portion into an 11-inch circle; gently place on prepared pan. (Dough may shrink slightly.) Spread one-third of cream cheese mixture (about 3½ tablespoons [55 grams]) onto dough circle, leaving a ½-inch border. Repeat procedure twice, stacking circles on top of each other. Roll remaining dough portion into an 11-inch circle, and place on top of previous layers.
8. Preheat oven to 375°F (190°C).
9. Place a 1½-inch round cutter in center of dough; gently press down just to leave a mark. Using a sharp knife or a pizza cutter, make 16 evenly spaced cuts working from center mark to edge of dough. Grasping 1 cut piece in each hand, twist portions outward and away from each other twice; pinch ends firmly together to adhere. Repeat with remaining cut portions. Cover and let rise in a warm, draft-free place (75°F/24°C) until nearly doubled in size, 30 to 45 minutes. Pinch ends together again, if necessary.
10. In a small bowl, whisk together 1 tablespoon (15 grams) water and remaining 1 egg (50 grams). Brush top of dough with egg wash; sprinkle with sparkling sugar.
11. Bake until golden brown and an instant-read thermometer inserted in center registers at least 190°F (88°C), 16 to 22 minutes, loosely covering with foil to prevent excess browning, if necessary. Let cool completely on pan.
12. Just before serving, spoon Cream Cheese Glaze into a small pastry bag; cut a ¼-inch opening in tip. Pipe over bread as desired.

To finely crush whole freeze-dried blueberries, place in a large resealable plastic bag and pound with a rolling pin.

Note: *Test the dough for proper gluten development using the windowpane test. Pinch off (don't tear) a small piece of dough. Slowly pull the dough out from the center. If the dough is ready, you will be able to stretch it until it's thin and translucent like a windowpane. If the dough tears, it's not quite ready. Beat for 1 minute, and test again.*

CREAM CHEESE GLAZE
Makes ⅓ cup

¼ cup (30 grams) confectioners' sugar, sifted
2 ounces (57 grams) cream cheese, softened
1½ tablespoons (22.5 grams) whole milk
⅛ teaspoon kosher salt

1. In a small bowl, whisk together all ingredients until smooth. Use immediately.

FOR A BEAUTIFULLY SHAPED STAR

STEP 1: Turn out dough, and divide into 4 portions (about 200 grams each); gently shape each into a ball. Cover with plastic wrap, and let stand for 15 minutes.

STEP 2: Roll and pat 1 portion into an 11-inch circle; gently place on prepared pan.

STEP 3: Spread one-third of cream cheese mixture (about 3½ tablespoons [55 grams]) onto dough circle, leaving a ½-inch border. Repeat procedure twice, stacking circles on top of each other.

STEP 4: Roll remaining dough portion into an 11-inch circle, and place on top of previous layers.

STEP 5: Place a 1½-inch round cutter in the center of dough; gently press down just to leave a mark.

STEP 6: Using a sharp knife or a pizza cutter, make evenly spaced cuts from center mark to edge of dough.

STEP 7: Continue until you have 16 evenly spaced cuts around dough.

STEP 8: Grasping 1 cut piece in each hand, twist portions outward and away from each other twice; pinch ends firmly together to adhere.

STEP 9: Repeat with remaining cut portions.

PRETZEL BUNS

Makes 10 buns

With the saltiness and chewiness of your favorite ballpark snack, our Pretzel Buns bring brilliant texture and taste to the table.

4¼ to 4½ cups (540 to 572 grams) bread flour, divided
2 tablespoons (28 grams) firmly packed light brown sugar
2¼ teaspoons (7 grams) active dry yeast
1½ teaspoons (4.5 grams) kosher salt
9½ cups (2,280 grams) plus 1 tablespoon (15 grams) water, divided
2 tablespoons (28 grams) unsalted butter
¼ cup (60 grams) baking soda
1 large egg yolk (19 grams)
2 tablespoons (20 grams) flaked sea salt

1. In the bowl of a stand mixer fitted with the paddle attachment, beat 2 cups (254 grams) flour, brown sugar, yeast, and kosher salt at low speed until combined.
2. In a small saucepan, heat 1½ cups (360 grams) water and butter over medium heat until an instant-read thermometer registers 120°F (49°C) to 130°F (54°C). Add warm butter mixture to flour mixture, and beat at medium speed until combined. With mixer on low speed, gradually add 2¼ cups (286 grams) flour, beating just until combined and stopping to scrape sides of bowl.
3. Switch to the dough hook attachment. Beat at low speed until a soft, somewhat sticky dough forms, 7 to 8 minutes, stopping to scrape sides of bowl and dough hook; add up to remaining ¼ cup (32 grams) flour, 1 tablespoon (8 grams) at a time, if dough is too sticky. Turn out dough onto a lightly floured surface, and shape into a smooth round.
4. Lightly oil a large bowl. Place dough in bowl, turning to grease top. Cover and let rise in a warm, draft-free place (75°F/24°C) until doubled in size, 45 minutes to 1 hour.
5. Place a large sheet of parchment paper on work surface, and dust with flour.
6. In a 4-quart stockpot, bring 8 cups (1,920 grams) water and baking soda to a slow boil over low heat.

7. On a very lightly floured surface, divide dough into 10 portions (about 95 grams each). Shape each portion into a smooth ball. Press each ball flat into a 3-inch disk, and place on prepared parchment. Cover and let rise in a warm, draft-free place (75°F/24°C) for 20 minutes.
8. Preheat oven to 425°F (220°C). Line 2 baking sheets with parchment paper.
9. Carefully drop buns, 2 to 3 at a time, into boiling water mixture. Cook for 30 seconds; turn, and cook for 30 seconds. Using a spider strainer, lift, and let excess drip off; place at least 1½ inches apart on prepared pans.
10. In a small bowl, whisk together egg yolk and remaining 1 tablespoon (15 grams) water. Brush buns with egg wash. Using a lame or sharp paring knife, score a 1-inch "X" in top of each bun. Sprinkle with sea salt.
11. Bake until deep golden brown, 18 to 20 minutes. Let cool on pans for 15 minutes. Remove from pans, and let cool completely on wire racks before slicing.

 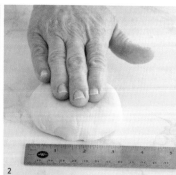  

Shape and Bake: Pretzel Buns

1. On a very lightly floured surface, divide dough into 10 portions (about 95 grams each). Use your palm to press down on dough to release any air bubbles. Rotate your hand until dough starts to form a ball; turn your hand, and make a "C" shape. Keep dough under your palm, and continue rotating your hand and applying pressure in same direction until dough becomes a smooth, tight ball.

2. Press each ball flat into a 3-inch disk, and place on floured parchment paper. Cover and let rise in a warm, draft-free place (75°F/24°C) for 20 minutes.

3. Carefully drop buns, 2 to 3 at a time, into boiling water mixture. Cook for 30 seconds; turn, and cook for 30 seconds. Using a spider strainer, lift, and let excess drip off; place at least 1½ inches apart on prepared pans.

4. In a small bowl, whisk together egg yolk and remaining 1 tablespoon (15 grams) water. Brush buns with egg wash. Using a lame or sharp paring knife, score a 1-inch "X" in top of each bun. Sprinkle with sea salt.

HOT DOG BUNS

Makes 8 buns

Fluffy and just a touch sweet, these buns have a milk bread base—the cotton-like white bread that hails from Japan.

3¼ cups (406 grams) all-purpose flour, divided
3   tablespoons (36 grams) granulated sugar
2½   teaspoons (7.5 grams) kosher salt
2¼   teaspoons (7 grams) active dry yeast
Flour Paste (recipe follows)
½   cup (120 grams) water
⅓   cup (80 grams) plus 1 tablespoon
     (15 grams) whole milk, divided
¼   cup (57 grams) unsalted butter
2   large eggs (100 grams), room temperature and divided

1. In the bowl of a stand mixer, whisk together 3 cups (375 grams) flour, sugar, salt, and yeast by hand. Add Flour Paste.
2. In a medium saucepan, heat ½ cup (120 grams) water, ⅓ cup (80 grams) milk, and butter over medium heat until an instant-read thermometer registers 120°F (49°C) to 130°F (54°C). Add warm warm milk mixture to flour mixture; using the paddle attachment, beat at low speed until combined. Beat in 1 egg (50 grams).
3. Switch to the dough hook attachment. Beat at low speed until a soft, somewhat sticky dough forms, 8 to 9 minutes, stopping to scrape sides of bowl and dough hook; add up to remaining ¼ cup (31 grams) flour, 1 tablespoon (8 grams) at a time, if dough is too sticky. Turn out dough onto a lightly floured surface, and shape into a smooth round.
4. Lightly oil a large bowl. Place dough in bowl, turning to grease top. Cover and let rise in a warm, draft-free place (75°F/24°C) until doubled in size, 45 minutes to 1 hour.
5. Line a baking sheet with parchment paper.
6. Punch down dough, and let stand for 5 minutes. Turn out onto a lightly floured surface. Divide dough into 8 portions (about 97 grams each). Press 1 portion into a 5x4-inch rectangle. (Keep remaining dough covered to prevent it from drying out.) Place rectangle widthwise in front of you. Starting with bottom 5-inch edge, fold dough, about ½ inch at a time, pressing to seal each time before folding again. Repeat until you have a tight cylinder. Place seam side up, and fold ends in. Place seam side down, and shape to 5 inches long and even thickness. Place on prepared pan, and press gently to flatten top. Repeat with a second portion of dough, and place about ¼ inch from first bun; press flat. Repeat with remaining dough, making 2 rows of 4 buns. Cover and let rise in a warm, draft-free place (75°F/24°C) until puffed, 30 to 45 minutes.
7. Preheat oven to 350°F (180°C).
8. In a small bowl, whisk together remaining 1 egg (50 grams) and remaining 1 tablespoon (15 grams) milk. Brush buns with egg wash.
9. Bake until golden brown and an instant-read thermometer inserted in center registers 190°F (88°C), 18 to 20 minutes. Let cool on pan for 10 minutes. Remove from pan, and let cool completely on a wire rack before slicing.

FLOUR PASTE
Makes about ⅓ cup

⅓   cup (80 grams) whole milk
2   tablespoons (16 grams) all-purpose flour

1. In a small saucepan, cook milk and flour over medium-low heat, whisking constantly, until thickened and whisk leaves lines on bottom of pan. Transfer to a small bowl, and let cool until an instant-read thermometer registers less than 130°F (54°C) before using.

Shape and Bake: Hot Dog Buns

1. Divide dough into 8 portions (about 97 grams each). Press 1 portion into a 5x4-inch rectangle. (Keep remaining dough covered to prevent it from drying out.)

2–4. Place rectangle widthwise in front of you. Starting with bottom 5-inch edge, fold dough, about ½ inch at a time, pressing to seal each time before folding again. Repeat until you have a tight cylinder.

5. Place seam side up, and fold ends in. Place seam side down, and shape to 5 inches long and even thickness.

6. Place on prepared pan, and press gently to flatten top. Repeat with a second portion of dough, and place about ¼ inch from first bun; press flat. Repeat with remaining dough, making 2 rows of 4 buns.

PULL-APART MILK BREAD WREATH

Makes 20 rolls

Our savory pull-apart bread wreath features the most versatile of doughs, Japanese milk bread—a tender enriched dough that receives a moist boost from tangzhong, or Milk Roux. Packed with dill, butter, and garlic powder, the bread dough is mixed, proofed, shaped, and assembled the day before. The day of, only a final proof and short bake remains!

⅔ cup (160 grams) plus 1 tablespoon (15 grams) whole milk, room temperature and divided
4 tablespoons (48 grams) granulated sugar, divided
1 (0.25-ounce) package (7 grams) active dry yeast
Milk Roux (recipe follows), room temperature
3 to 3¼ cups (381 to 413 grams) bread flour, divided
¼ cup (57 grams) plus 2 tablespoons (28 grams) unsalted butter, melted and divided
2 large eggs (100 grams), room temperature and divided
3 tablespoons (8 grams) lightly packed chopped fresh dill
2¼ teaspoons (6.75 grams) kosher salt
1 teaspoon (3 grams) garlic powder
Everything bagel seasoning, for sprinkling
Garnish: chopped fresh dill

1. In a small microwave-safe bowl, heat ⅔ cup (160 grams) milk on high in 10-second intervals until an instant-read thermometer registers 110°F (43°C) to 115°F (46°C).
2. In the bowl of a stand mixer, whisk together warm milk, 1 tablespoon (12 grams) sugar, and yeast by hand. Let stand until foamy, about 10 minutes.
3. Add Milk Roux, 3 cups (381 grams) flour, ¼ cup (57 grams) melted butter, 1 egg (50 grams), dill, salt, garlic powder, and remaining 3 tablespoons (36 grams) sugar to yeast mixture; using the paddle attachment, beat at low speed just until combined, stopping to scrape sides of bowl.
4. Switch to the dough hook attachment. Beat at low speed for 3 minutes. Increase mixer speed to medium-low, and beat until a soft, smooth dough forms, 6 to 8 minutes, stopping to scrape sides of bowl; add up to remaining ¼ cup (32 grams) flour, 1 tablespoon (8 grams) at a time, if dough is too sticky. Check dough for proper gluten development using the windowpane test. (See Note.) Cover and let rise in a warm, draft-free place (75°F/24°C) until doubled in size, 40 minutes to 1 hour.

5. Line a baking sheet with parchment paper. Place a 1¾-inch round metal cutter in center of prepared pan.
6. Punch down dough; let stand for 5 minutes. Divide dough into 20 portions (about 38 grams each). Roll each portion into a ball, pinching any seams closed if needed. Place 6 dough balls in a circle around cutter, leaving a ¼-inch gap between dough balls and cutter. Place remaining dough balls, evenly spaced and almost touching, outside first circle. Cover and refrigerate overnight.
7. Let rolls rise, covered, in a warm, draft-free place (75°F/24°C) until doubled in size and dough holds an indentation when poked, 1 to 2 hours.
8. Preheat oven to 350°F (180°C).
9. In a small bowl, whisk together remaining 1 egg (50 grams) and remaining 1 tablespoon (15 grams) milk.
10. Gently remove cutter from center of pan; brush top of dough with egg wash.
11. Bake until golden brown and an instant-read thermometer inserted in center registers at least 190°F (88°C), 15 to 18 minutes. Brush tops of warm rolls with remaining 2 tablespoons (28 grams) melted butter. Sprinkle with everything bagel seasoning. Garnish with dill, if desired. Serve immediately.

Note: *To use the windowpane test to check dough for proper gluten development, lightly flour hands and pinch off (don't tear) a small piece of dough. Slowly pull the dough out from the center. If the dough is ready, you will be able to stretch it until it's thin and translucent like a windowpane. If the dough tears, it's not quite ready. Beat for 1 minute, and test again.*

MILK ROUX
Makes about ⅓ cup

⅓ cup (80 grams) whole milk
2 tablespoons (16 grams) bread flour

1. In a small saucepan, whisk together milk and flour. Cook over medium-low heat, whisking constantly, until thickened, an instant-read thermometer registers 149°F (65°C), and whisk leaves lines on bottom of pan. Transfer to a small bowl, and let cool completely before using.

BRIOCHE BURGER BUNS

Makes 10 buns

Buttery and tender, our brioche buns are the luxurious accompaniment your cookouts need. We sprinkled them with sesame seeds and flaked sea salt for a touch of tradition.

2½   cups (313 grams) all-purpose flour, divided
2   cups (254 grams) bread flour, divided
3   tablespoons (36 grams) granulated sugar
1   tablespoon (9 grams) kosher salt
2¼   teaspoons (7 grams) active dry yeast
1   cup (240 grams) water
¼   cup (60 grams) plus 1 tablespoon (15 grams) whole milk, divided
¼   cup (57 grams) unsalted butter
2   large eggs (100 grams), room temperature and divided
1   large egg yolk (19 grams), room temperature
1   tablespoon (9 grams) sesame seeds
1½   teaspoons (5 grams) flaked sea salt

1. In the bowl of a stand mixer fitted with the paddle attachment, beat 1 cup (125 grams) all-purpose flour, 1 cup (127 grams) bread flour, sugar, kosher salt, and yeast at low speed until combined.

2. In a medium saucepan, heat 1 cup (240 grams) water, ¼ cup (60 grams) milk, and butter over medium heat until an instant-read thermometer registers 120°F (49°C) to 130°F (54°C). Add warm milk mixture to flour mixture, and beat at medium speed until combined. Add 1 egg (50 grams) and egg yolk, and beat until combined. With mixer on low speed, gradually add 1¼ cups (156 grams) all-purpose flour and remaining 1 cup (127 grams) bread flour, beating just until combined and stopping to scrape sides of bowl.

3. Switch to the dough hook attachment. Beat at low speed until a soft, somewhat sticky dough forms, 11 to 12 minutes, stopping to scrape sides of bowl and dough hook; add up to remaining ¼ cup (31 grams) all-purpose flour, 1 tablespoon (8 grams) at a time, if dough is too sticky. Turn out dough onto a lightly floured surface, and shape into a smooth round.

4. Lightly oil a large bowl. Place dough in bowl, turning to grease top. Cover and let rise in a warm, draft-free place (75°F/24°C) until doubled in size, 45 minutes to 1 hour.

5. Line a baking sheet with parchment paper.

6. Lightly punch down dough. Cover and let stand for 5 minutes. Turn out dough onto a lightly floured surface, and divide into 10 portions (about 101 grams each). Roll 1 portion into a smooth round. (Keep remaining dough covered to prevent it from drying out.) Press flat into a 3-inch disk. Repeat with remaining dough, and place at least 2 inches apart on prepared pan. Cover and let rise in a warm, draft-free place (75°F/24°C) until puffed, 30 to 45 minutes.

7. Preheat oven to 350°F (180°C).

8. In a small bowl, whisk together remaining 1 egg (50 grams) and remaining 1 tablespoon (15 grams) milk. Brush buns with egg wash. Top with sesame seeds and sea salt.

9. Bake until golden and an instant-read thermometer inserted in center registers 190°F (88°C), 12 to 15 minutes. Let cool on pan for 10 minutes. Remove from pan, and let cool completely on a wire rack.

Shape and Bake: Brioche Burger Buns

1. Turn out dough onto a lightly floured surface, and divide into 10 portions (about 101 grams each). Roll 1 portion into a smooth round, gently cupping and rolling dough between your palms to form a smooth ball. (Keep remaining dough covered to prevent it from drying out.)

2. Press flat into a 3-inch disk. Repeat with remaining dough, and place at least 2 inches apart on prepared pan.

3. Cover and let rise in a warm, draft-free place (75°F/24°C) until puffed, 30 to 45 minutes. Brush buns with egg wash. Top with sesame seeds and sea salt.

POTATO LOAF BREAD

Makes 1 (9x5-inch) loaf

Mashed potatoes are the miracle ingredient in this tall and tender loaf. The starchy addition creates a chewy, savory bread ready for any and all of your future sandwiches.

3½ cups (438 grams) all-purpose flour, divided
2 tablespoons (24 grams) granulated sugar
2¼ teaspoons (7 grams) active dry yeast
2 teaspoons (6 grams) kosher salt
½ cup (122 grams) mashed russet potatoes (see PRO TIPS)
½ cup (120 grams) plus 1 tablespoon
  (15 grams) whole milk, divided
¼ cup (57 grams) unsalted butter
¼ cup (60 grams) leftover potato water (see PRO TIPS) or water
2 large eggs (100 grams), divided

1. In the bowl of a stand mixer fitted with the paddle attachment, beat 1½ cups (188 grams) flour, sugar, yeast, and salt at low speed until combined.

2. In a medium saucepan, heat potatoes, ½ cup (120 grams) milk, butter, and ¼ cup (60 grams) potato water or water over medium heat until an instant-read thermometer registers 120°F (49°C) to 130°F (54°C). Add warm potato mixture to flour mixture, and beat at medium speed until combined. Beat in 1 egg (50 grams) until combined. With mixer on low speed, gradually add 1¾ cups (219 grams) flour, beating just until combined and stopping to scrape sides of bowl.

3. Switch to the dough hook attachment. Beat at low speed until a soft, somewhat sticky dough forms, 8 to 10 minutes, stopping to scrape sides of bowl and dough hook; add up to remaining ¼ cup (31 grams) flour, 1 tablespoon (8 grams) at a time, if dough is too sticky. Turn out dough onto a lightly floured surface, and shape into a smooth round.

4. Lightly oil a large bowl. Place dough in bowl, turning to grease top. Cover and let rise in a warm, draft-free place (75°F/24°C) until doubled in size, 45 minutes to 1 hour.

5. Spray a 9x5-inch loaf pan with cooking spray.

6. Turn out dough, and lightly pat into a 9x8-inch oval, with one 9-inch side closest to you. Fold top third of dough to center, pressing to seal. Fold bottom third over folded portion, pressing to seal. Fold dough in half lengthwise so long edges meet. Using the heel of your hand, firmly press edges to seal. Fold both ends in, and place seam side down; shape to 9 inches long and even thickness. Place, seam side down, in prepared pan. Cover and let rise in a warm, draft-free place (75°F/24°C) until doubled in size, 30 to 45 minutes.

7. Preheat oven to 350°F (180°C).

8. In a small bowl, whisk together remaining 1 egg (50 grams) and remaining 1 tablespoon (15 grams) milk. Gently brush top of dough with egg wash. Using a lame or sharp paring knife, score top with 2 diagonal cuts.

9. Bake until an instant-read thermometer inserted in center registers 190°F (88°C), 40 to 45 minutes. Let cool in pan for 15 minutes. Remove from pan, and let cool completely on a wire rack.

PRO TIPS

Peel and dice 2 medium russet potatoes (300 grams). In a large saucepan, bring potatoes and water to cover to a boil over medium-high heat; cook until tender, 10 to 12 minutes. Drain, reserving ¼ cup (60 grams) liquid. Mash potato with a potato masher.

The water left over from boiling your potatoes is full of starch and an excellent addition to this bread dough. In fact, your dough will probably rise faster if you use this potato water, because the potassium in the water will help activate your yeast.

Shape and Bake: Potato Loaf Bread

1. Turn out dough, and lightly pat into a 9x8-inch oval, with one 9-inch side closest to you.

2. Fold top third of dough to center, pressing to seal. Fold bottom third over folded portion, pressing to seal. Fold dough in half lengthwise so long edges meet. Using the heel of your hand, firmly press edges to seal.

3. Fold ends in, and place seam side down; shape to 9 inches long and even thickness. Place, seam side down, in prepared pan. Cover and let rise in a warm, draft-free place (75°F/24°C) until doubled in size, 30 to 45 minutes.

4. In a small bowl, whisk together remaining 1 egg (50 grams) and remaining 1 tablespoon (15 grams) milk. Gently brush top of dough with egg wash. Using a lame or razor blade, score top with 2 diagonal cuts.

CINNAMON ROLL LOAF

Makes 1 (9x5-inch) loaf

This recipe has all the foundation and familiarity of the original breakfast classic. We just rotated and stacked the dough spirals in a 9x5-inch loaf pan for a modern, compact version with double the visual appeal. The top layer takes on the traditional cinnamon roll look, while the rolls baked against the edges of the pan create sides covered in graphic swirls. Slice to reveal the gorgeous interior: a pillowy crumb filled with swirling tunnels and pockets of cinnamon.

4   cups (500 grams) all-purpose flour, divided
⅔   cup (133 grams) plus 3 tablespoons (36 grams) granulated sugar, divided
1   (0.25-ounce) packaged (7 grams) active dry yeast
2   teaspoons (6 grams) kosher salt, divided
⅔   cup (160 grams) water
½   cup (113 grams) unsalted butter
1   teaspoon (4 grams) vanilla extract
2   large eggs (100 grams), room temperature
2   teaspoons (4 grams) ground cinnamon
⅓   cup (76 grams) unsalted butter, room temperature
Cream Cheese Glaze (recipe follows)

1. In the bowl of a stand mixer fitted with the paddle attachment, beat 2 cups (250 grams) flour, 3 tablespoons (36 grams) sugar, yeast, and 1½ teaspoons (4.5 grams) salt at low speed until combined.
2. In a medium saucepan, heat ⅔ cup (160 grams) water, butter, and vanilla over medium heat until an instant-read thermometer registers 120°F (49°C) to 130°F (54°C). Add warm butter mixture to flour mixture, and beat at medium speed until combined. Beat in eggs. With mixer on low speed, gradually add remaining 2 cups (250 grams) flour, beating just until combined and stopping to scrape sides of bowl.
3. Switch to the dough hook attachment. Beat at low speed until a soft, somewhat sticky dough forms, 4 to 5 minutes, stopping to scrape sides of bowl and dough hook. Turn out dough onto a lightly floured surface, and shape into a smooth round.
4. Lightly oil a medium bowl. Place dough in bowl, turning to grease top. Cover and let rise in a warm, draft-free place (75°F/24°C) until doubled in size, 45 minutes to 1 hour.

5. Line a 9x5-inch loaf pan with parchment paper, letting excess extend over sides of pan.
6. In a small bowl, stir together cinnamon, remaining ⅔ cup (133 grams) sugar, and remaining ½ teaspoon (1.5 grams) salt.
7. Lightly punch down dough. Cover and let stand for 5 minutes. Turn out dough onto a lightly floured surface, and roll into a 26x7-inch rectangle. Using a small offset spatula, spread room temperature butter onto dough, leaving a ½-inch border on one long side. Sprinkle with cinnamon sugar. Starting with long side opposite border, roll up dough, jelly roll style; pinch seam to seal. Gently shape to 26 inches long and even thickness, if necessary. Using a serrated knife dipped in flour, cut into 26 (1-inch) slices. Place 5 slices, cut sides out, against 1 (9-inch) side of pan. Place 5 slices, cut sides out, against opposite 9-inch side of pan. Place 1 slice, cut side out, against each 5-inch side of pan. Place 3 slices, cut sides out, in center. (You should have 3 rows of 5 slices.) Place remaining slices, cut sides up, on top. Cover and let rise in a warm, draft-free place (75°F/24°C) until puffed, 30 to 40 minutes.
8. Preheat oven to 350°F (180°C).
9. Bake until lightly golden and an instant-read thermometer inserted in center registers 190°F (88°C), 55 minutes to 1 hour, loosely covering with foil to prevent excess browning, if necessary. Let cool in pan for 10 minutes. Using excess parchment as handles, remove from pan. Drizzle Cream Cheese Glaze onto warm loaf. Serve warm or at room temperature.

CREAM CHEESE GLAZE

Makes about ⅔ cup

4   ounces (113 grams) cream cheese, softened
¼   cup (30 grams) confectioners' sugar
2   tablespoons (30 grams) whole milk

1. Whisk together all ingredients until smooth and a pourable consistency is reached.

PEANUT BUTTER-BANANA BRAID

Makes 1 loaf

Elegant but packing the homey, nostalgic flavors of peanut butter and banana, this braided bread is the perfect way to enjoy something classic in a gorgeous new package.

3   cups (382 grams) bread flour, divided
3   tablespoons (36 grams) granulated sugar
2½   teaspoons (7.5 grams) kosher salt
2¼   teaspoons (7 grams) active dry yeast
½   cup (120 grams) whole milk
¼   cup plus 1 tablespoon (75 grams) water, divided
¼   cup (57 grams) unsalted butter
2   teaspoons (8 grams) vanilla extract
2   large eggs (100 grams), room temperature and divided
     Peanut Butter Filling (recipe follows)
½   cup (100 grams) chopped banana
     Garnish: confectioners' sugar

1. In the bowl of a stand mixer fitted with the paddle attachment, beat 1½ cups (191 grams) flour, granulated sugar, salt, and yeast at low speed until combined.
2. In a medium saucepan, heat milk, ¼ cup (60 grams) water, butter, and vanilla over medium heat until an instant-read thermometer registers 120°F (49°C) to 130°F (54°C). Add warm milk mixture to flour mixture, and beat at medium speed until combined. Beat in 1 egg (50 grams). With mixer on low speed, gradually add remaining 1½ cups (191 grams) flour, beating just until combined and stopping to scrape sides of bowl.
3. Switch to the dough hook attachment. Beat at low speed until a soft, somewhat sticky dough forms, 6 to 7 minutes, stopping to scrape sides of bowl and dough hook. (Dough will be elastic and pull away from sides of bowl but stick to bottom of bowl.) Turn out dough onto a lightly floured surface, and shape into a smooth round.
4. Lightly oil a large bowl. Place dough in bowl, turning to grease top. Cover and let rise in a warm, draft-free place (75°F/24°C) until almost doubled in size, 45 minutes to 1 hour.

5. Punch down dough, and let stand for 5 minutes. Turn out onto a lightly floured sheet of parchment paper. Roll into a 16x10-inch oval, one short side closest to you. Using a small knife or bench scraper, score (or mark) a 13x4-inch rectangle in center of dough, leaving a 1½-inch border on short sides and a 3-inch border on long sides. Spread Peanut Butter Filling in rectangle; sprinkle banana onto filling. Cut 1-inch-wide strips along long sides of filling. Trim short sides to width of filling, and fold over filling. Starting on left side, stretch, twist, and fold top strip over filling, ending just below opposite top strip. Repeat with top strip on right side. Continue pattern, alternating left and right, until you reach end of strips. Tuck and pinch last strip. (If dough is not sticking to itself, dab with a little water to help it seal.) Transfer dough, still on parchment, to a baking sheet. Cover and let rise in a warm, draft-free place (75°F/24°C) until puffed, 30 to 45 minutes.
6. Preheat oven to 350°F (180°C).
7. In a small bowl, whisk together remaining 1 egg (50 grams) and remaining 1 tablespoon (15 grams) water. Brush top and sides of dough with egg wash.
8. Bake until golden brown and an instant-read thermometer inserted in bread registers 190°F (88°C), 20 to 25 minutes. Garnish with confectioners' sugar, if desired. Serve warm or at room temperature.

PEANUT BUTTER FILLING

Makes about 1 cup

¼   cup (57 grams) unsalted butter, softened
⅓   cup (73 grams) firmly packed light brown sugar
⅓   cup (85 grams) creamy peanut butter

1. In a medium bowl, beat butter and brown sugar with a mixer at medium speed until fluffy, 1 to 2 minutes. Add peanut butter, and beat just until combined. Use immediately.

BRAID YOUR BREAD

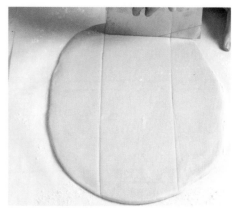

1. Roll dough into a 16x10-inch oval. Using a small knife or bench scraper, score (or mark) a 13x4-inch rectangle in center of dough, leaving a 1½-inch border on short sides and a 3-inch border on long sides.

2. Spread Peanut Butter Filling in rectangle; sprinkle banana onto filling.

3. Cut 1-inch-wide strips along long sides of filling. Trim short sides to width of filling, and fold over filling.

4. Starting on left side, stretch, twist, and fold top strip over filling, ending just below opposite top strip. Repeat with top strip on right side.

5. Continue pattern, alternating left and right, until you reach end of strips.

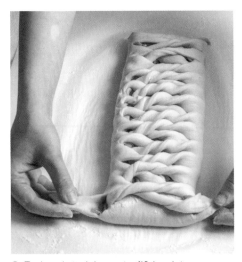

6. Tuck and pinch last strip. (If dough is not sticking to itself, dab with a little water to help it seal.)

SUMMER HERB DINNER ROLLS

Makes 12 rolls

Your summer get-togethers deserve dinner rolls that rise to the occasion. Enter these stunning sour cream knots. They have an unbelievably pillowy crumb that's loaded with dill and chives. With a quick rise and a shaping method that's a cinch, this recipe is one you'll keep on rotation all season long.

5 cups (625 grams) all-purpose flour, divided
¼ cup (50 grams) granulated sugar
4½ teaspoons (14 grams) instant yeast
1 tablespoon (9 grams) kosher salt
1 cup (240 grams) plus 1 tablespoon (15 grams) water
½ cup (120 grams) sour cream
¼ cup (57 grams) plus 2 tablespoons (28 grams) unsalted butter, melted and divided
2 large eggs (100 grams), room temperature and divided
¼ cup (12 grams) finely chopped fresh chives
2 teaspoons (1.5 grams) finely chopped fresh dill
¼ teaspoon (1.5 grams) garlic salt

1. In the bowl of a stand mixer fitted with the paddle attachment, beat 1½ cups (188 grams) flour, sugar, yeast, and kosher salt at low speed until combined.
2. In a medium saucepan, heat 1 cup (240 grams) water, sour cream, and ¼ cup (57 grams) melted butter over medium heat until an instant-read thermometer registers 120°F (49°C) to 130°F (54°C). Add warm sour cream mixture to flour mixture, and beat at medium speed until combined. Beat in 1 egg (50 grams) until combined. With mixer on low speed, gradually add 3¼ cups (406 grams) flour, chives, and dill, beating just until a shaggy dough forms.
3. Switch to the dough hook attachment. Beat at low speed until a soft, somewhat sticky dough forms, 7 to 8 minutes, stopping to scrape sides of bowl and dough hook; add up to remaining ¼ cup (31 grams) flour, 1 tablespoon (8 grams) at a time, if dough is too sticky. Cover and let stand in a warm, draft-free place (75°F/24°C) for 10 minutes. (Dough will puff slightly.)
4. Line a 13x9-inch rimmed baking sheet with parchment paper.

5. Divide dough into 12 portions (about 93 grams each). With lightly floured hands, roll 1 portion into a 12-inch-long rope. (Keep remaining dough covered to prevent it from drying out.) Tie a loose knot toward one end of rope, leaving about 1 inch on one end. Pinch together both ends of dough under knot, forming a knotted ball. Place, seam side down, on prepared pan. Cover and let rise in a warm, draft-free place (75°F/24°C) until doubled in size, 20 to 30 minutes.
6. Preheat oven to 375°F (190°C).
7. In a small bowl, whisk together remaining 1 egg (50 grams) and remaining 1 tablespoon (15 grams) water. Brush tops of dough with egg wash.
8. Bake until golden brown and an instant-read thermometer inserted in center registers 190°F (88°C), 20 to 25 minutes, covering with foil to prevent excess browning, if necessary.
9. In a small bowl, stir together garlic salt and remaining 2 tablespoons (28 grams) melted butter. Brush tops of warm rolls with garlic butter. Serve warm.

HUNGARIAN PULL-APART PECAN COFFEE CAKE

Makes 14 servings

This shareable masterpiece is inspired by arany galuska, a Hungarian dessert made up of yeasted dough balls rolled in butter and chopped nuts. We opted for browned butter to give our version extra richness.

¾ cup (170 grams) unsalted butter
2¾ cups (344 grams) all-purpose flour, divided
⅓ cup (67 grams) plus 2 tablespoons (24 grams) granulated sugar, divided
2¼ teaspoons (7 grams) instant yeast
2¼ teaspoons (6.75 grams) kosher salt, divided
⅓ cup (80 grams) whole milk
⅓ cup (80 grams) water
1 large egg (50 grams), room temperature
1½ cups (170 grams) ground pecans
Vanilla Dipping Sauce (recipe follows)

1. Line a 9-inch springform pan with parchment paper.
2. In a medium saucepan, melt butter over medium heat. Cook until butter turns a medium-brown color and has a nutty aroma, about 10 minutes. Remove from heat, and transfer to a small bowl.
3. In the bowl of a stand mixer fitted with the paddle attachment, combine 1½ cups (188 grams) flour, 2 tablespoons (24 grams) sugar, yeast, and 1½ teaspoons (4.5 grams) salt.

4. In a medium saucepan, heat milk, ⅓ cup (80 grams) water, and ¼ cup (60 grams) browned butter over medium heat until an instant-read thermometer registers 120°F (49°C) to 130°F (54°C). Add warm milk mixture to flour mixture, and beat at medium speed until combined. Add egg, beating until combined. With mixer on low speed, gradually add remaining 1¼ cups (156 grams) flour, beating just until a shaggy dough forms.
5. Switch to the dough hook attachment. Beat at low speed until a soft, somewhat sticky dough forms, 6 to 7 minutes, stopping to scrape sides of bowl and dough hook. Cover and let stand in a warm, draft-free place (75°F/24°C) for 10 minutes. (Dough will puff slightly.)
6. In a medium bowl, stir together pecans, remaining ⅓ cup (67 grams) sugar, and remaining ¾ teaspoon (2.25 grams) salt.
7. Turn out dough onto a lightly floured surface. (Do not punch down.) Gently divide dough into 14 portions (about 45 grams each). Dip each portion in remaining browned butter,

and roll in pecan mixture. Arrange evenly in prepared pan. Cover and let rise in a warm, draft-free place (75°F/24°C) until doubled in size, 30 to 40 minutes.
8. Preheat oven to 350°F (180°C).
9. Sprinkle top of dough with any remaining pecan mixture.
10. Bake until golden brown and an instant-read thermometer inserted in center registers 190°F (88°C), 25 to 30 minutes. Let cool in pan for 10 minutes. Remove from pan, and discard parchment paper. Serve warm or at room temperature with Vanilla Dipping Sauce.

VANILLA DIPPING SAUCE
Makes about ½ cup

1 cup (120 grams) confectioners' sugar
2 tablespoons (30 grams) whole milk
¼ teaspoon (1 gram) vanilla extract

1. In a small bowl, whisk together all ingredients until smooth.

SUMMER SQUASH FLATBREADS

Makes 2 flatbreads

Celebrate the summer harvest with these delectable savory flatbreads that pack a double dose of squash and zucchini.

3¾ cups (469 grams) all-purpose flour, divided
1 (0.63-ounce) package (18 grams) instant sourdough yeast*
2¼ teaspoons (6.75 grams) kosher salt
¾ cup (180 grams) water
½ cup (120 grams) whole milk
3½ tablespoons (49 grams) extra-virgin olive oil, divided
1 teaspoon (7 grams) honey
3 cloves garlic (15 grams), minced
½ teaspoon packed lemon zest
Cornmeal, for dusting
1½ cups (170 grams) shredded fontina cheese
⅔ cup (61 grams) finely shredded Parmesan cheese
½ cup (60 grams) ⅟₁₆-inch-sliced zucchini
½ cup (60 grams) ⅟₁₆-inch-sliced yellow squash
½ cup (65 grams) thinly sliced red onion
Garnish: shredded fontina cheese, flaked sea salt, fresh basil leaves, chopped fresh parsley

1. In the bowl of a stand mixer fitted with the paddle attachment, beat 2 cups (250 grams) flour, instant sourdough yeast, and kosher salt at low speed until well combined.
2. In a small saucepan, heat ¾ cup (180 grams) water, milk, 2 tablespoons (30 grams) oil, and honey over medium heat until an instant-read thermometer registers 120°F (49°C) to 130°F (54°C). Add warm milk mixture to flour mixture; beat at medium speed for 2 minutes. Reduce mixer speed to low; gradually beat in 1½ cups (188 grams) flour until a very soft, sticky dough is formed.
3. Switch to the dough hook attachment. Beat at medium-low speed for 13 minutes. (Dough should almost pull away from sides of bowl.) Add up to remaining ¼ cup (31 grams) flour, 1 tablespoon (8 grams) at a time, if needed. (Avoid adding too much flour; a slack dough is important for a light, airy crust.) Check dough for proper gluten development using the windowpane test. (See Note.) Using well-floured hands, shape dough into a ball.
4. Lightly oil a large bowl. Place dough in bowl, turning to grease top. Cover with plastic wrap, and let rise in a warm, draft-free place (75°F/24°C) until doubled in size, about 1½ hours.

5. Punch down dough. Divide dough in half (about 390 grams each). Using floured hands, shape each half into a smooth ball, and place each in a lightly oiled small bowl. Lightly brush tops with oil. Cover with a double layer of plastic wrap, and refrigerate overnight*.
6. About 1½ hours before baking, remove dough from refrigerator. Place a pizza stone on lowest oven rack. Preheat oven to 475°F (250°C). (Allow at least 1 hour for pizza stone to fully heat before baking.)
7. In a small microwave-safe bowl, combine garlic, lemon zest, and remaining 1½ tablespoons (21 grams) oil. Heat on high until mixture begins to bubble, about 20 seconds.
8. Generously dust a pizza peel or a rimless baking sheet with flour and cornmeal.
9. For each flatbread, drape each portion of dough over your knuckles. Using both hands, gently stretch dough with knuckles to form a ⅜-inch-thick oval, being careful not to press out any air bubbles. Place dough on prepared pizza peel, stretching to even out any thick areas. Shake pizza peel a few times to make sure dough always stays loose, dusting bottom with additional cornmeal if needed. (Continue to check dough a few times while topping. Dough must remain loose to slide easily onto pizza stone.)
10. Evenly spoon half of garlic mixture onto each flatbread. Top each with half of fontina and half of Parmesan; top each with half of zucchini, half of squash, and half of onion. Slide 1 flatbread onto hot pizza stone.
11. Bake until crust is deep golden brown, 10 to 12 minutes, using tongs to rotate flatbread halfway through baking. Immediately garnish with fontina, sea salt, basil, and parsley, if desired.
12. Repeat procedure with remaining flatbread. Immediately garnish with fontina, sea salt, basil, and parsley, if desired.

We used Platinum® Instant Sourdough Yeast from Red Star®.

Notes: *Test dough for proper gluten development using the windowpane test. Using floured fingers, pinch off (don't tear) a small piece of dough. Slowly pull the dough out from the center. If the dough is ready, you will be able to stretch it until it's thin and translucent like a windowpane. If the dough tears, it's not quite ready. Beat for 1 minute, and test again.*

Refrigerating this dough overnight allows it to develop better flavor and texture, but the flatbreads can be baked on the same day as well. Simply preheat pizza stone and oven while dough is rising and then shape flatbreads after punching down dough.

HONEY PEAR LOAF

Makes 1 (9-inch) loaf

The perfect sweet finish to any evening, this pear-packed honeyed loaf has a decadent, fluffy texture and warmly spiced filling. A final brushing of honey gives this loaf luxurious shine.

Dough:

2¾	cups (344 grams) all-purpose flour
1	(0.25-ounce) package (7 grams) instant yeast*
1¾	teaspoons (5.25 grams) kosher salt
⅓	cup plus 1 tablespoon (95 grams) warm whole milk (120°F/49°C to 130°F/54°C)
2	large eggs (100 grams), room temperature
2	tablespoons (42 grams) clover honey
1	teaspoon (5 grams) tightly packed orange zest
6	tablespoons (84 grams) unsalted butter, softened

Filling:

¼	cup (50 grams) granulated sugar
1	teaspoon (2 grams) ground cinnamon
½	teaspoon (1 gram) ground ginger
3	large firm ripe Bosc pears (726 grams)
⅓	cup (76 grams) unsalted butter, room temperature*
¼	cup (85 grams) clover honey
⅓	cup (38 grams) finely chopped toasted pecans
2	tablespoons (24 grams) packed finely chopped candied ginger

1	large egg (50 grams), lightly beaten

Turbinado sugar, for sprinkling

1. For dough: In the bowl of a stand mixer fitted with the paddle attachment, beat flour, yeast, and salt at low speed until combined, about 30 seconds. Add warm milk, and beat at low speed just until combined. (Mixture will be shaggy.) Add eggs, honey, and orange zest; beat until combined, about 1 minute, stopping to scrape sides of bowl.

2. Switch to the dough hook attachment. Beat at low speed until smooth and elastic, 6 to 8 minutes. Add softened butter, 1 tablespoon (14 grams) at a time, beating until combined after each addition, 6 to 8 minutes total, stopping to scrape sides of bowl and dough hook. (Dough may look slightly broken during this process but will come together later.) Increase mixer speed to medium-low; beat until a smooth, elastic dough forms, about 6 minutes, stopping to scrape dough hook. Turn out dough onto a clean surface, and knead 4 to 5 times. Shape dough into a smooth round.

3. Spray a large bowl with cooking spray. Place dough in bowl, turning to grease top. Cover and let rise in a warm, draft-free place (75°F/24°C) until doubled in size, 40 minutes to 1 hour.

4. Spray a 9-inch springform pan with baking spray with flour. Line bottom of pan with parchment paper.

5. Punch down dough; let stand for 5 minutes. On a lightly floured surface, roll dough into a 16x14-inch rectangle.

6. For filling: In a small bowl, stir together granulated sugar, cinnamon, and ground ginger.

7. Chop 1 to 2 pears into ⅛-inch pieces (½ cup [80 grams]). Chop remaining pears into ½- to ¾-inch pieces (⅓ cup [56 grams]).

8. In another small bowl, stir together room temperature butter and honey until well combined; reserve 3 tablespoons (46 grams) honey butter in a small microwave-safe bowl. Using a small offset spatula, spread remaining honey butter evenly onto dough, leaving a ½-inch border on one long side. Top with sugar mixture; sprinkle with ⅛-inch-chopped pears, pecans, and candied ginger. Starting with long side opposite border, roll dough into a log, pinching seam to seal. Gently shape log to 16 inches and even thickness, if necessary. Using a very sharp knife or a metal bench scraper, cut log in half lengthwise. Place halves, cut sides up, in an "X" shape. Twist dough halves together tightly, keeping cut sides up; pinch ends together. (This will be slightly messy but worth it.) Starting at one end, shape dough around itself to form a spiral, tucking end under; carefully place in prepared pan. Tuck ½- to ¾-inch-chopped pears into spiral as desired. Cover and let rise in a warm, draft-free place (75°F/24°C) until doubled in size and dough holds an indentation when poked, 25 to 35 minutes.

9. Preheat oven to 350°F (180°C).

10. Gently brush dough with beaten egg; sprinkle with turbinado sugar.

11. Bake until golden brown and an instant-read thermometer inserted in center registers 190°F (88°C), 35 to 40 minutes, rotating pan halfway through baking and loosely covering with foil to prevent excess browning, if necessary. Let cool in pan for 5 minutes; remove sides of pan.

12. Heat reserved honey butter on high in 10-second intervals, stirring between each, until melted; brush onto bread. Serve warm, or let cool completely on base of pan on a wire rack.

*We used Platinum® Yeast from Red Star®. Unlike softened butter, room temperature butter should provide no resistance when pressed with a finger. At this point, the butter is softened enough to easily mix with the honey in this recipe.

HAVARTI SAGE BABKA

Makes 1 (8½x4½-inch) loaf

Glorious Sage Butter and creamy Danish cheese join forces in this savory entry into babka. Havarti is celebrated for its buttery texture and taste, lending a decadently cheesy quality to the twisted loaf.

2½ cups (313 grams) plus 2 tablespoons (16 grams) all-purpose flour, divided
1 tablespoon (12 grams) granulated sugar
1½ teaspoons (4.5 grams) instant yeast
1¼ teaspoons (3.75 grams) kosher salt
¼ cup (60 grams) plus 1 tablespoon (15 grams) water, divided
¼ cup (57 grams) unsalted butter
¼ cup (60 grams) whole milk
2 large eggs (100 grams), room temperature and divided
Sage Butter (recipe follows)
⅔ cup (75 grams) grated aged Havarti cheese
1 teaspoon (3 grams) flaked sea salt

1. In the bowl of a stand mixer, whisk together 1 cup (125 grams) flour, sugar, yeast, and kosher salt by hand.
2. In a small saucepan, heat ¼ cup (60 grams) water, butter, and milk over medium-low heat until an instant-read thermometer registers 120°F (49°C) to 130°F (54°C). Add warm butter mixture to flour mixture. Using the paddle attachment, beat at medium-low speed until combined. Add 1 egg (50 grams), and beat until combined. With mixer on low speed, gradually add 1½ cups (188 grams) flour, beating just until combined and stopping to scrape sides of bowl.
3. Switch to the dough hook attachment. Beat at low speed until a soft, somewhat sticky dough forms, 5 to 7 minutes, stopping to scrape sides of bowl and dough hook; add up to remaining 2 tablespoons (16 grams) flour, 1 tablespoon (8 grams) at a time, if dough is too sticky. Turn out dough onto a very lightly floured surface, and shape into a smooth round.
4. Lightly oil a large bowl. Place dough in bowl, turning to grease top. Cover and let rise in a warm, draft-free place (75°F/24°C) until doubled in size, 30 to 45 minutes.
5. Turn out dough onto a very lightly floured surface, and gently press into an 8x6-inch rectangle. Loosely wrap in plastic wrap. Refrigerate for at least 1 hour or up to overnight.
6. On a lightly floured surface, roll dough into a 12x7-inch rectangle, one long side closest to you. Brush with Sage Butter. Fold into thirds, creating a 7x4-inch rectangle. Rotate 90 degrees, and repeat rolling, brushing, and folding into thirds. Wrap in plastic wrap, and refrigerate for 20 minutes. Place dough back on lightly floured surface, one long side closest to you. Repeat rolling into a 12x7-inch rectangle, brushing with butter, and folding into thirds. Wrap in plastic wrap, and refrigerate for 30 minutes.

7. Spray an 8½x4½-inch loaf pan with cooking spray. Line pan with parchment paper, letting excess extend over sides of pan.
8. On a lightly floured surface, roll dough into a 13x10-inch rectangle (about ¼ inch thick). Brush remaining Sage Butter onto dough, leaving a ½-inch border on both short sides and one long side. Sprinkle with cheese. Starting with long side opposite border, roll up dough, jelly roll style, and pinch seam to seal. Gently lift log at each end, and stretch to 14 inches long. Place seam side down, making sure seam is off to one side instead of in center. Using a sharp serrated knife, cut in half lengthwise. Turn halves cut side up, and place in an "X." Twist top half of "X" two times; pinch ends, and tuck under. Repeat with bottom half of "X." Place in prepared pan, making sure to keep cut sides up and ends tucked. Cover and let rise in a warm, draft-free place (75°F/24°C) until puffed, 30 minutes to 1 hour. (See Note.) Test dough for fermentation using the finger dent test. (See PRO TIP.)
9. Preheat oven to 350°F (180°C).
10. In a small bowl, whisk together remaining 1 egg (50 grams) and remaining 1 tablespoon (15 grams) water. Using a pastry brush, brush egg wash on top of dough. Sprinkle with sea salt.
11. Bake until golden brown and an instant-read thermometer inserted in center registers 190°F (88°C), 40 to 45 minutes, covering with foil to prevent excess browning, if necessary. Let cool in pan for 10 minutes. Using excess parchment as handles, remove from pan, and let cool completely on a wire rack.

Note: *Final rise time will depend on how long dough is chilled. The longer the dough is chilled, the longer it will take to rise.*

SAGE BUTTER
Makes about ¼ cup

¼ cup (57 grams) unsalted butter
1 clove garlic (5 grams), minced
1 teaspoon rubbed sage
¼ teaspoon kosher salt

1. In a small saucepan, melt butter over medium heat. Add garlic, and cook until fragrant, 30 seconds to 1 minute. Stir in sage and salt. Remove from heat. Let cool slightly before using.

> **PRO TIP**
> Once you think your dough has proofed, conduct the finger dent test. Gently press your finger about ½ inch into the surface. You should be able to watch the dough spring back slightly but still show an indentation. If the dent disappears, the dough is underproofed and needs more time. If the indentation stays completely, it has overproofed, but don't panic. Immediately pop it into the oven; the babka will still be great.

Light Lamination

Follow these steps to bring a touch of Sage Butter lamination to your savory babka

1. On a lightly floured surface, roll dough into a 12x7-inch rectangle, one long side closest to you. Brush with Sage Butter.
2. Fold into thirds, creating a 7x4-inch rectangle.
3. Repeat rolling into a 12x7-inch rectangle, brushing with butter, and folding into thirds. Wrap in plastic wrap, and refrigerate for 30 minutes.

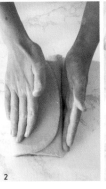

CHAI STREUSEL BABKA

Makes 1 (8½x4½-inch) loaf

Perfumed with warm chai spice, this crunchy and aromatic babka is a twist—pardon the pun—on the more common cinnamon babka, bringing all the comfort of your favorite tea latte to the enriched babka formula. You'll welcome this spicy changeup.

2½ cups (313 grams) plus 2 tablespoons (16 grams) all-purpose flour, divided
3 tablespoons (36 grams) granulated sugar
1½ teaspoons (4.5 grams) instant yeast
1¼ teaspoons (3.75 grams) kosher salt
¼ cup (60 grams) plus 1 tablespoon (15 grams) water, divided
¼ cup (57 grams) unsalted butter
¼ cup (60 grams) whole milk
½ teaspoon (2 grams) vanilla extract
2 large eggs (100 grams), room temperature and divided
Chai Filling (recipe follows)
Chai Streusel (recipe follows)

1. In the bowl of a stand mixer, whisk together 1 cup (125 grams) flour, sugar, yeast, and salt by hand.
2. In a small saucepan, heat ¼ cup (60 grams) water, butter, milk, and vanilla over medium-low heat until an instant-read thermometer registers 120°F (49°C) to 130°F (54°C). Add warm butter mixture to flour mixture. Using the paddle attachment, beat at medium-low speed until combined. Add 1 egg (50 grams), and beat until combined. With mixer on low speed, gradually add 1½ cups (188 grams) flour, beating just until combined and stopping to scrape sides of bowl.
3. Switch to the dough hook attachment. Beat at low speed until a soft, somewhat sticky dough forms, 5 to 7 minutes, stopping to scrape sides of bowl and dough hook; add up to remaining 2 tablespoons (16 grams) flour, 1 tablespoon (8 grams) at a time, if dough is too sticky. Turn out dough onto a very lightly floured surface, and shape into a smooth round.
4. Lightly oil a large bowl. Place dough in bowl, turning to grease top. Cover and let rise in a warm, draft-free place (75°F/24°C) until doubled in size, 30 to 45 minutes.

5. Turn out dough onto a very lightly floured surface, and gently press into an 8x6-inch rectangle. Loosely wrap with plastic wrap. Refrigerate for at least 1 hour or up to overnight.
6. Spray an 8½x4½-inch loaf pan with cooking spray. Line pan with parchment paper, letting excess extend over sides of pan.
7. On a lightly floured surface, roll dough into a 13x10-inch rectangle (about ¼ inch thick). Using a small offset spatula, spread Chai Filling on dough, leaving a ½-inch border on both short sides and one long side. Starting with opposite long side, roll up dough, jelly roll style, and pinch seam to seal. Gently lift log at each end, and stretch to 14 inches long. Place seam side down, making sure seam is off to one side instead of in center. Using a sharp serrated knife, cut in half lengthwise. Turn halves cut side up, and place in an "X." Twist top half of "X" two times; pinch ends, and tuck under. Repeat with bottom half of "X." Place in prepared pan, making sure to keep cut sides up and ends tucked. Cover and let rise in a warm, draft-free place (75°F/24°C) until puffed, 30 minutes to 1 hour. (See Note.) Test dough for fermentation using the finger dent test. (See PRO TIP on opposite page.)
8. Preheat oven to 350°F (180°C).
9. In a small bowl, whisk together remaining 1 egg (50 grams) and remaining 1 tablespoon (15 grams) water. Using a pastry brush, brush egg wash on top of dough. Sprinkle with half of Chai Streusel.
10. Bake for 20 minutes. Top with remaining Chai Streusel, and bake until golden brown and an instant-read thermometer inserted in center registers 190°F (88°C), 20 to 25 minutes more, covering with foil to prevent excess browning, if necessary. Let cool in pan for 10 minutes. Using excess parchment as handles, remove from pan, and let cool completely on a wire rack.

Note: *Final rise time will depend on how long the dough is chilled. The longer the dough is chilled, the longer it will take to rise.*

CHAI FILLING
Makes about ½ cup

⅓ cup (73 grams) firmly packed dark brown sugar
3 tablespoons (42 grams) unsalted butter, room temperature
2 teaspoons (4 grams) Chai Spice Mix (recipe follows)
¼ teaspoon kosher salt

1. In a medium bowl, combine brown sugar, butter, Chai Spice Mix, and salt. Using a silicone spatula, press and stir together until well combined.

CHAI SPICE MIX
Makes about ⅓ cup

For our all-purpose chai spice blend, we opted for a quintuplet of classic ground spices: cinnamon, ginger, cloves, cardamom, and black pepper.

3 tablespoons (18 grams) ground cinnamon
1½ tablespoons (9 grams) ground ginger
1 tablespoon (6 grams) ground cloves
½ tablespoon (3 grams) ground cardamom
½ tablespoon (3 grams) finely ground black pepper

1. In a small bowl, stir together all ingredients. Store in an airtight container for up to 2 months.

CHAI STREUSEL
Makes ⅓ cup

5 tablespoons (40 grams) all-purpose flour
4 teaspoons (16 grams) granulated sugar
¼ teaspoon kosher salt
¼ teaspoon Chai Spice Mix (recipe precedes)
1½ tablespoons (21 grams) cold unsalted butter, cubed

1. In a medium bowl, stir together flour, sugar, salt, and Chai Spice Mix. Using your fingers, cut in cold butter until mixture is crumbly. Crumble with your fingertips until desired consistency is reached. Refrigerate until ready to use.

PRO TIP

Once you think your dough has proofed, conduct the finger dent test. Gently press your finger about ½ inch into the surface. You should be able to watch the dough spring back slightly but still show an indentation. If the dent disappears, the dough is underproofed and needs more time. If the indentation stays completely, it has overproofed, but don't panic. Immediately pop it into the oven; the babka will still be great.

CHOCOLATE BABKA

Makes 1 (8½x4½-inch) loaf

The traditional take on babka is the quintessential chocolate-filled affair, brushed with Simple Syrup for sweet shine. When your nostalgic heart calls for babka, this is the recipe to turn to.

2½ cups (313 grams) plus 2 tablespoons (16 grams) all-purpose flour, divided
3 tablespoons (36 grams) granulated sugar
1½ teaspoons (4.5 grams) instant yeast
1¼ teaspoons (3.75 grams) kosher salt
¼ cup (60 grams) plus 1 tablespoon (15 grams) water, divided
¼ cup (57 grams) unsalted butter
¼ cup (60 grams) whole milk
½ teaspoon (2 grams) vanilla extract
2 large eggs (100 grams), room temperature and divided
Chocolate Filling (recipe follows)
⅓ cup (50 grams) finely chopped 66% cacao dark chocolate
Simple Syrup (recipe follows)

1. In the bowl of a stand mixer, whisk together 1 cup (125 grams) flour, sugar, yeast, and salt by hand.
2. In a small saucepan, heat ¼ cup (60 grams) water, butter, milk, and vanilla over medium-low heat until an instant-read thermometer registers 120°F (49°C) to 130°F (54°C). Add warm butter mixture to flour mixture. Using the paddle attachment, beat at medium-low speed until combined. Add 1 egg (50 grams), and beat until combined. With mixer on low speed, gradually add 1½ cups (188 grams) flour, beating just until combined and stopping to scrape sides of bowl.
3. Switch to the dough hook attachment. Beat at low speed until a soft, somewhat sticky dough forms, 5 to 7 minutes, stopping to scrape sides of bowl and dough hook; add up to remaining 2 tablespoons (16 grams) flour, 1 tablespoon (8 grams) at a time, if dough is too sticky. Turn out dough onto a very lightly floured surface, and shape into a smooth round.
4. Lightly oil a large bowl. Place dough in bowl, turning to grease top. Cover and let rise in a warm, draft-free place (75°F/24°C) until doubled in size, 30 to 45 minutes.
5. Turn out dough onto a very lightly floured surface, and gently press into an 8x6-inch rectangle. Loosely wrap with plastic wrap. Refrigerate for at least 1 hour or up to overnight.
6. Spray an 8½x4½-inch loaf pan with cooking spray. Line pan with parchment paper, letting excess extend over sides of pan.
7. On a lightly floured surface, roll dough into a 13x10-inch rectangle (about ¼ inch thick). Using a small offset spatula, spread Chocolate Filling on dough, leaving a ½-inch border on both short sides and one long side. Sprinkle with chopped chocolate. Starting with long side opposite border, roll up dough, jelly roll style, and pinch seam to seal. Gently lift log at

each end, and stretch to 14 inches long. Place seam side down, making sure seam is off to one side instead of in center. Using a sharp serrated knife, cut in half lengthwise. Turn halves cut side up, and place in an "X." Twist top half of "X" two times; pinch ends, and tuck under. Repeat with bottom half of "X." Place in prepared pan, making sure to keep cut sides up and ends tucked. Cover and let rise in a warm, draft-free place (75°F/24°C) until puffed, 30 minutes to 1 hour. (See Note.) Test dough for fermentation using the finger dent test. (See PRO TIP on opposite page.)
8. Preheat oven to 350°F (180°C).
9. In a small bowl, whisk together remaining 1 egg (50 grams) and remaining 1 tablespoon (15 grams) water. Using a pastry brush, brush egg wash on top of dough.
10. Bake until golden brown and an instant-read thermometer inserted in center registers 190°F (88°C), 45 to 50 minutes, covering with foil to prevent excess browning, if necessary. Brush with Simple Syrup. Let cool in pan for 10 minutes. Using excess parchment as handles, remove from pan, and let cool completely on a wire rack.

Note: *Final rise time will depend on how long dough is chilled. The longer the dough is chilled, the longer it will take to rise.*

CHOCOLATE FILLING
Makes ½ cup

⅓ cup (64 grams) chopped 66% cacao dark chocolate
3 tablespoons (42 grams) unsalted butter
¼ cup (30 grams) confectioners' sugar
3 tablespoons (15 grams) Dutch process cocoa powder
½ teaspoon (1.5 grams) kosher salt

1. In the top of a double boiler, combine chocolate and butter. Cook over simmering water, stirring occasionally, until smooth and combined. Remove from heat. Whisk in confectioners' sugar, cocoa, and salt until smooth. Let cool to room temperature before using.

SIMPLE SYRUP
Makes 1½ tablespoons

1½ tablespoons (18 grams) granulated sugar
1 tablespoon (15 grams) water

1. In a small microwave-safe bowl, stir together sugar and 1 tablespoon (15 grams) water. Heat on high in 15-second intervals, stirring between each, until sugar is completely melted. Let cool to room temperature before using

PRO TIP
Once you think your dough has proofed, conduct the finger dent test. Gently press your finger about ½ inch into the surface. You should be able to watch the dough spring back slightly but still show an indentation. If the dent disappears, the dough is underproofed and needs more time. If the indentation stays completely, it has overproofed, but don't panic. Immediately pop it into the oven; the babka will still be great.

Shipshape Babka A simple guide to perfectly shaped babka

1. On a lightly floured surface, roll dough into a 13x10-inch rectangle (about ¼ inch thick). Keep a ruler on hand to check your dimensions, as anything less or more than this 13x10-inch rectangle will keep your babka from fitting the pan.
2. Using a small offset spatula, spread Chocolate Filling on dough, leaving a ½-inch border on both short sides and one long side. Sprinkle with chopped chocolate. When you roll up the dough into a tight spiral, this border will allow the dough to form an airtight seal.
3. Starting with long side opposite border, roll up dough, jelly roll style, and pinch seam to seal. If you're having trouble closing the seam, simply wet the seam with some water and pinch

together with your fingers. The water will help create a stickier surface on the dough so the seam holds.
4. Gently lift log at each end, and stretch to 14 inches long. This will help make your internal spiral nice and tight. Place seam side down, making sure seam is off to one side instead of in center.
5. Using a sharp serrated knife, cut in half lengthwise. We used a sharp serrated knife for cutting because its jagged edges cut through the roll more easily without pushing out the filling.
6. Turn halves cut side up, and place in an "X." Creating the "X" shape will help you make even twists on both sides, yielding a symmetrical loaf.

7. Twist top half of "X" two times; pinch ends, and tuck under. Repeat with bottom half of "X." Twisting on one side and then the other keeps you from having to twist two long, heavy strands. Instead, you're working with manageable shorter strands of dough, which will help keep the filling from falling out and your dough from being overworked.
8. Place in prepared pan, making sure to keep cut sides up and ends tucked. If you fail to tuck the ends, they'll pop up during baking and mar your beautiful shape. Cover and let rise in a warm, draft-free place (75°F/24°C) until puffed, 30 minutes to 1 hour.

SWEET POTATO CINNAMON BUNS

Makes 10 buns

Our cinnamon buns boast an orange-gold swirl thanks to puréed sweet potato. Made epically tangy by a dose of buttermilk in the dough and in the glaze, this is the kind of baked good worth waking up for.

3 to 3⅓ cups (375 to 417 grams) all-purpose flour, divided
⅔   cup (146 grams) firmly packed light brown sugar, divided
1   (0.25-ounce) package (7 grams) instant yeast
1¾ teaspoons (5.25 grams) kosher salt
¼   teaspoon ground nutmeg
⅔   cup (160 grams) whole buttermilk
6   tablespoons (84 grams) plus ¼ cup (57 grams) unsalted butter, softened and divided
½   cup (118 grams) puréed cooked peeled sweet potato (see Notes)
1   large egg (50 grams)
2   tablespoons (12 grams) ground cinnamon
2   teaspoons (4 grams) ground ginger
1   cup (113 grams) chopped toasted pecans
Buttermilk Glaze (recipe follows)

1. In the bowl of a stand mixer fitted with the paddle attachment, beat 1 cup (125 grams) flour, ⅓ cup (73 grams) brown sugar, yeast, salt, and nutmeg at low speed just until combined.
2. In a medium saucepan, heat buttermilk and 6 tablespoons (84 grams) butter over medium heat, stirring frequently, until an instant-read thermometer registers 120°F (49°C) to 130°F (54°C). Add warm buttermilk mixture to flour mixture; beat at medium speed for 2 minutes. Add sweet potato and egg; beat at medium-high speed for 2 minutes. With mixer on low speed, gradually add 2 cups (250 grams) flour until combined.
3. Switch to the dough hook attachment. Beat at medium-low speed until a soft, somewhat sticky dough forms, 6 to 10 minutes, stopping to scrape sides of bowl and dough hook; add up to remaining ⅓ cup (42 grams) flour, 1 tablespoon (8 grams) at a time, if needed. (Dough should pass the windowpane test [see Notes] but may still stick slightly to sides of bowl.)
4. Spray a large bowl with cooking spray. Place dough in bowl, turning to grease top. Cover and let rise in a warm, draft-free place (75°F/24°C) until doubled in size, 40 minutes to 1 hour.
5. Preheat oven to 350°F (180°C). Spray a 12-inch cast-iron skillet with baking spray with flour.

6. In a small bowl, stir together cinnamon, ginger, and remaining ⅓ cup (73 grams) brown sugar.
7. Punch down dough; let stand for 5 minutes. On a lightly floured surface, roll dough into a 12x11-inch rectangle. Using a small offset spatula, spread remaining ¼ cup (57 grams) butter onto dough, leaving a ½-inch border on one long side. Generously sprinkle with cinnamon mixture and pecans. (Cinnamon-pecan layer will be quite thick.) Starting with long side opposite border, roll dough into a log, pinching seam to seal. Gently shape log to 12 inches long and even thickness, if necessary. Using a serrated knife dipped in flour, cut log into 10 slices (about 1¼ inches thick each). Place slices, cut side down, in prepared skillet. Cover and let rise in a warm, draft-free place (75°F/24°C) until doubled in size and dough holds an indentation when pressed with a finger, 25 to 35 minutes.
8. Bake until golden brown and an instant-read thermometer inserted in center registers 190°F (88°C), 20 to 25 minutes. Let cool in skillet for 15 minutes. Spread Buttermilk Glaze onto warm buns. Serve immediately.

Notes: *We like the bright color and convenience of using pre-cubed raw sweet potatoes, sold in 1-pound bags in the produce department of most grocery stores. Cook according to package directions. Purée in a food processor until mostly smooth.*

Test the dough for proper gluten development using the windowpane test. Pinch off (don't tear) a small piece of dough. Slowly pull the dough out from the center. If the dough is ready, you will be able to stretch it until it's thin and translucent like a windowpane. If the dough tears, it's not quite ready. Beat for 1 minute, and test again.

BUTTERMILK GLAZE
Makes about 1 cup

2½ cups (300 grams) confectioners' sugar
¼   cup (60 grams) whole buttermilk
2   tablespoons (28 grams) unsalted butter, melted
½   teaspoon (1.5 grams) kosher salt

1. In a medium bowl, stir together all ingredients until smooth and well combined. Use immediately.

MINI PRETZEL BATARDS (PRETZEL STICKS)

Makes 12 pretzel sticks

With a toothsome texture and shiny crust, these salt-flecked batards will become the shining star of your dinner breadbasket.

4½ cups (562 grams) all-purpose flour, divided
2   tablespoons (28 grams) firmly packed light brown sugar
1   tablespoon (9 grams) kosher salt
2¼ teaspoons (7 grams) instant yeast
1   cup (240 grams) whole milk
8½ cups (2,040 grams) plus 1 tablespoon (15 grams) water, divided
2   tablespoons (28 grams) unsalted butter
¼   cup (60 grams) baking soda
1   large egg yolk (19 grams)
2   tablespoons (20 grams) flaked sea salt

1. In the bowl of a stand mixer fitted with the paddle attachment, beat 2 cups (250 grams) flour, brown sugar, kosher salt, and yeast at low speed until combined.
2. In a small saucepan, heat milk, ½ cup (120 grams) water, and butter over medium heat until an instant-read thermometer registers 120°F (49°C) to 130°F (54°C). Add warm milk mixture to flour mixture, and beat at medium speed until combined. Reduce mixer speed to low, and gradually add 2¼ cups (281 grams) flour, beating just until combined and stopping to scrape sides of bowl.
3. Switch to the dough hook attachment. Beat at low speed until a soft, somewhat sticky dough forms, 5 to 6 minutes, stopping to scrape sides of bowl and dough hook; add up to remaining ¼ cup (31 grams) flour, 1 tablespoon (8 grams) at a time, if dough is too sticky. Turn out onto a lightly floured surface, and shape into a smooth round.
4. Lightly oil a medium bowl. Place dough in bowl, turning to grease top. Cover and let rise in a warm, draft-free place (75°F/24°C) until doubled in size, 30 to 45 minutes.
5. Place a large sheet of parchment paper on work surface; dust with flour. Set aside.
6. On a very lightly floured surface, divide dough into 12 portions (about 81 grams each). Shape each portion into a 4x3-inch rectangle, one long side closest to you. Starting with top edge, fold top third of dough to center, and press to seal. Fold bottom third over folded portion, and press to seal. Fold dough in half lengthwise so long edges meet. Using the heel of your hand, firmly press edges to seal. Roll into a 5-inch log, tapering ends slightly. Place logs, seam side down, on prepared parchment. Cover and let rise in a warm, draft-free place (75°F/24°C) for 20 minutes.
7. Preheat oven to 375°F (190°C). Line 2 baking sheets with parchment paper.
8. In a 4-quart stockpot, bring 8 cups (1,920 grams) water and baking soda to a gentle boil.
9. Carefully drop pretzels, 2 at a time, top side down, into boiling water mixture. Cook for 30 seconds; turn, and cook for 30 seconds. Using a spider strainer, lift, and let excess water drip off; place on prepared pans.
10. In a small bowl, whisk together egg yolk and remaining 1 tablespoon (15 grams) water. Brush dough with egg wash. Using a lame or sharp paring knife, score 3 lines on top of each log. Sprinkle with sea salt.
11. Bake until deep golden brown, 16 to 18 minutes. Let cool on pans for 10 minutes. Serve warm or at room temperature.

PEANUT BUTTER BABKA

Makes 1 (9x5-inch) loaf

A riff on Angela Garbacz's famous Fluffernutter buns at Goldenrod Pastries, this pillowy vegan dough is packed with creamy peanut butter.

Dough:
- ¾ cup (180 grams) milk, almond milk, or your favorite non-dairy milk
- 2½ cups (298 grams) all-purpose flour
- ¼ cup (54 grams) granulated sugar
- 1 tablespoon (9 grams) active dry yeast
- ¼ cup (56 grams) vegetable oil
- ½ teaspoon (3 grams) sea salt
- ¾ cup (190 grams) creamy peanut butter
- ¼ cup (45 grams) light brown sugar

Glaze:
- 1 recipe Classic Vanilla Glaze

Prepare the dough:

1. Heat the milk until it is warm to the touch, about 110°F (43°C). Remove from the heat and pour into a large bowl. Add the sugar and yeast. Whisk to combine. Let the yeast and sugar bloom together for about 5 to 10 minutes. The yeast is ready when the mixture looks foamy on top. Add the oil, salt, and flour. Use a wooden spoon to combine the ingredients. Once mostly combined, knead the dough by hand for about 10 minutes to develop the gluten and make a smooth, supple, soft ball of dough. Transfer the dough back to the mixing bowl and let it rise in a warm place for about 40 minutes, or until it is about double in size—but more important, feels softer, a little fluffier, and is very easily depressed when you press it gently with your finger.

2. Alternatively, you can use a stand mixer for this dough. Simply combine the dough ingredients with a stand mixer fitted with the dough hook and mix on medium speed for about 5 minutes. You will be looking for the same smooth, soft dough with this method as when you make the dough with your hands.

Assemble the babka:

1. Spray a 9x5-inch loaf pan well with nonstick cooking spray. Once your dough has risen and is super soft and impossibly fluffy, roll out to a 14x8-inch rectangle on a floured work surface. Spread the peanut butter gently over the rolled dough, then sprinkle with the brown sugar.

2. Roll the dough as though you were making cinnamon rolls, starting from one long side and rolling to the other long side, keeping the roll as tight as you can. Once rolled, use a sharp knife to cut directly down the middle length of the roll, keeping one end intact. Working with confidence, twist the two strands of swirled dough, one over the other. This may look messy at this point but I promise it will be great.

3. Lift the twisted dough by each end and transfer to your prepared loaf pan. You will have to greatly condense the long, twisted dough to fit in the loaf pan—it will make a tall, voluptuous-looking babka, which is, of course, what we want.

Bake the babka:

1. Preheat your oven to 350°F (180°C). Let the babka rise for about 30 minutes in a warm place. It should increase in volume and should feel very soft to the touch when gently pressed with your finger. Bake for approximately 30 minutes, or until the outside is dark golden brown and the middle of the babka does not give back at all when gently pressed. To be sure the dough is fully cooked, you can check to be sure the temperature reads 190°F (88°C) on a thermometer inserted into the center of the bread.

2. Remove from the oven and let cool at room temperature. Finish with the glaze. Store, covered, at room temperature to enjoy for up to 2 days.

CLASSIC VANILLA GLAZE
Makes 2 cups

- 5 cups (560 grams) confectioners' sugar
- ¼ cup plus 2 tablespoons (90 grams) milk, almond milk, or your favorite non-dairy milk
- 2 teaspoons (8 grams) vanilla extract

1. Whisk together the ingredients in a medium bowl until smooth.

Excerpted from Perfectly Golden: Inspired Recipes from Goldenrod Pastries. Copyright 2020 by Angela Garbacz, photographs by Daniel Muller. Reproduced by permission of The Countryman Press. All rights reserved.

PAN DE MUERTO

Makes 1 loaf

Made for Mexico's Day of the Dead celebrations, pan de muerto is shaped into a round loaf with strips of dough rolled out and arranged on top to resemble bones of the deceased.

3½   cups (438 grams) all-purpose flour, divided
⅓   cup (67 grams) plus 5 tablespoons (60 grams) granulated sugar, divided
2¼   teaspoons (7 grams) instant yeast
2   teaspoons (6 grams) kosher salt
2   teaspoons (5 grams) whole aniseed
½   cup (120 grams) water, plus more for brushing
⅓   cup (76 grams) unsalted butter
2   large eggs (100 grams), room temperature
1   tablespoon (15 grams) tightly packed orange zest
½   teaspoon (2 grams) orange extract
2   tablespoons (30 grams) fresh orange juice

1. In the bowl of a stand mixer, whisk together 1 cup (125 grams) flour, ⅓ cup (67 grams) sugar, yeast, salt, and aniseed by hand.

2. In a medium saucepan, heat ½ cup (120 grams) water and butter over medium heat until an instant-read thermometer registers 120°F (49°C) to 130°F (54°C). Add warm butter mixture to flour mixture; using the paddle attachment, beat at medium speed until combined. Add eggs, orange zest, and orange extract, and beat until combined. With mixer on low speed, gradually add 2¼ cups (281 grams) flour, beating just until combined and stopping to scrape sides of bowl.

3. Switch to the dough hook attachment. Beat at low speed until a soft, somewhat sticky dough forms, 15 to 16 minutes, stopping to scrape sides of bowl and dough hook; add up to remaining ¼ cup (31 grams) flour, 1 tablespoon (8 grams) at a time, if dough is too sticky. Turn out dough onto a lightly floured surface, and shape into a smooth round.

4. Lightly oil a large bowl. Place dough in bowl, turning to grease top. Cover and let rise in a warm, draft-free place (75°F/24°C) until doubled in size, 1 hour to 1 hour and 15 minutes.

5. Line a baking sheet with parchment paper.

6. Lightly punch down dough. Cover and let stand for 5 minutes. Turn out dough onto a lightly floured surface, and cut off one-fourth of dough (about 200 grams). Set aside, and cover to prevent it from drying out.

7. Press remaining dough into a ½-inch-thick disk. Lift bottom edge of dough, and gently stretch and fold bottom third over to center. Stretch right side out, and fold over to center; repeat with left side. Finish by folding top third over previous folds. Roll dough away from you, and using both hands, cup dough and pull it toward you to seal. Turn dough 90 degrees, and pull again, repeating until a tight, smooth boule forms. Place, seam side down, on prepared pan.

8. Divide reserved dough in half (about 100 grams each). Working with 1 portion at a time, roll into a 6½-inch log. In center of log (3¼ inches from either end), pinch dough, and roll with your fingers to form 2 smaller logs joined by a thin center. Measuring from center, in each direction, mark 1¾ inches. Pinch and roll at each mark to create 4 connected sections. Shape each section into a ball. Repeat with remaining reserved dough.

9. Lightly brush top of boule with water. Place a row of dough across top, pressing to adhere. Arrange second row over first row, crossing at center. Press gently to adhere. Cover and let rise in a warm, draft-free place (75°F/24°C) until almost doubled in size, 45 minutes to 1 hour.

10. Preheat oven to 350°F (180°C).

11. Bake until golden and an instant-read thermometer inserted in center registers 190°F (88°C), 40 to 45 minutes, covering with foil to prevent excess browning, if necessary. Remove from pan, and let cool on a wire rack for 30 minutes.

12. Meanwhile, in a small microwave-safe bowl, combine orange juice and 2 tablespoons (24 grams) sugar. Heat on high in 15-second intervals, stirring between each, until sugar dissolves. Let cool to room temperature.

13. Brush loaf with orange simple syrup. Sprinkle loaf with remaining 3 tablespoons (36 grams) sugar, shaking to remove excess. Serve immediately. (If preparing loaf ahead of time, wait to brush and sprinkle with sugar until ready to serve; sugar will dissolve when loaf is stored overnight).

---

1. Roll dough into a 6½-inch log. In center of log (3¼ inches from either end), pinch dough, and roll with your fingers to form 2 smaller logs joined by a thin center. Measuring from center, in each direction, mark 1¾ inches. Pinch and roll at each mark to create 4 sections still connected. Shape each section into a ball.

2. Place one row of dough across top, pressing to adhere.

3. Arrange second row over first row, crossing at center. Press gently to adhere.

1.   2.   3.

EGGNOG SWEET ROLLS

Makes 12 rolls

Regular sweet rolls will do for any day—for Christmas Day, take it up a notch with our Eggnog Sweet Rolls. You'll mix, proof, fill, and shape your sweet rolls the night before. Then, before you dig into your presents, pull the rolls out for a final proof. While the rolls bake, you can quickly whisk together your Eggnog-Rum Glaze. If tiny tots or alcohol-abstainers are expected at the table, you can replace the rum in the glaze with 1½ tablespoons (22.5 grams) water.

3½ to 4 cups (438 to 500 grams) all-purpose flour, divided
¼   cup (50 grams) granulated sugar
2¼ teaspoons (7 grams) instant yeast
2¼ teaspoons (6 grams) kosher salt, divided
¾   teaspoon (1 gram) ground nutmeg, divided
1¼ cups (300 grams) prepared eggnog
¾   cup (170 grams) unsalted butter, room temperature* and divided
1   large egg (50 grams), room temperature
¾   cup (165 grams) firmly packed light brown sugar
1½ tablespoons (9 grams) ground cinnamon
Eggnog-Rum Glaze (recipe follows)

1. In the bowl of a stand mixer fitted with the paddle attachment, beat 1½ cups (188 grams) flour, granulated sugar, yeast, 2 teaspoons (6 grams) salt, and ¼ teaspoon nutmeg at low speed just until combined.
2. In a medium saucepan, heat eggnog and ½ cup (113 grams) butter over medium heat until an instant-read thermometer registers 120°F (49°C) to 130°F (54°C). Add warm eggnog mixture to flour mixture; beat at medium-low speed for 2 minutes, stopping to scrape sides of bowl. Add egg; beat at medium speed for 2 minutes. With mixer on low speed, gradually add 2 cups (250 grams) flour, beating just until combined and stopping to scrape sides of bowl.
3. Switch to the dough hook attachment. Beat at medium-low speed until a soft, elastic dough forms, 6 to 10 minutes, stopping to scrape sides of bowl and dough hook; add up to remaining ½ cup (62 grams) flour, 1 tablespoon (8 grams) at a time, if dough is too sticky. Check dough for proper gluten development using the windowpane test. (See Note.)
4. Spray a large bowl with cooking spray. Place dough in bowl, turning to grease top. Cover and let rise in a warm, draft-free place (75°F/24°C) until doubled in size, 40 minutes to 1 hour.
5. Spray a 13x9-inch baking pan with cooking spray. Line pan with parchment paper, letting excess extend over sides of pan.
6. In a small bowl, stir together brown sugar, cinnamon, remaining ½ teaspoon (1 gram) nutmeg, and remaining ¼ teaspoon salt.
7. Lightly punch down dough. Cover and let stand for 5 minutes. Turn out dough onto a lightly floured surface, and roll into an 18x12-inch rectangle. Using a large offset spatula, spread remaining ¼ cup (57 grams) butter onto dough, leaving a ½-inch border on one long side. Sprinkle brown sugar mixture onto butter. Starting with long

side opposite border, roll up dough, jelly roll style, pinching seam to seal. Gently shape to 18 inches long and more even thickness, if necessary. Using a serrated knife, slice log into 12 rolls (about 1½ inches thick), trimming edges slightly if necessary. Place rolls, cut side down, in prepared pan. Cover and refrigerate overnight.
8. Let rolls rise, covered, in a warm, draft-free place (75°F/24°C) until nearly doubled in size and dough holds an indentation when poked, 3 to 4 hours. (See PRO TIP.)
9. Preheat oven to 375°F (190°C).
10. Bake until rolls are lightly golden and an instant-read thermometer inserted in center registers 190°F (88°C), 15 to 20 minutes, loosely covering with foil to prevent excess browning, if necessary. Let cool in pan for 10 minutes. Using excess parchment as handles, remove from pan. Spread Eggnog-Rum Glaze onto warm rolls. Serve warm.

Unlike softened butter, room temperature butter should provide no resistance when pressed with a finger. At this point, the butter is softened enough to easily melt as well as spread over dough.

Note: *To use the windowpane test to check dough for proper gluten development, lightly flour hands and pinch off (don't tear) a small piece of dough. Slowly pull the dough out from the center. If the dough is ready, you will be able to stretch it until it's thin and translucent like a windowpane. If the dough tears, it's not quite ready. Beat for 1 minute, and test again.*

EGGNOG-RUM GLAZE
Makes about 1 cup

2½ cups (300 grams) confectioners' sugar
3   tablespoons (45 grams) prepared eggnog
1½ tablespoons (22.5 grams) spiced rum
2   tablespoons (28 grams) unsalted butter, melted
¼   teaspoon kosher salt

1. In a medium bowl, stir together all ingredients until smooth and well combined. Use immediately.

PRO TIP
To help next-day rolls proof, especially if your house tends to be quite cool, uncover refrigerated rolls and place in a cold oven with a small saucepan of boiling water to create a warm, steamy environment. (Keep oven door closed.) Allow rolls to proof until nearly doubled in size and dough holds an indentation when poked. Rewarm hot water as needed.

SWEDISH CINNAMON BUNS

Makes about 18 buns

Twisted into adorable bows and sprinkled with crunchy Swedish pearl sugar, these pillow-soft buns are bursting with fragrant holiday spices, taking inspiration from the Swedish cinnamon bun, kanelbulle.

Dough:
3¼ to 3½ cups (406 to 437 grams) all-purpose flour, divided
¼ cup (50 grams) granulated sugar
2¼ teaspoons (7 grams) instant yeast
1½ teaspoons (4.5 grams) kosher salt
1½ teaspoons (3 grams) ground cardamom
1 cup (240 grams) whole milk
⅓ cup (76 grams) unsalted butter, softened
1 large egg (50 grams), room temperature

Filling:
½ cup (113 grams) unsalted butter, room temperature*
½ cup (110 grams) firmly packed light brown sugar
4 teaspoons (8 grams) ground cinnamon
2½ teaspoons (5 grams) ground cardamom
1¼ teaspoons (2.5 grams) ground ginger
½ teaspoon (1 gram) ground cloves
¼ teaspoon ground black pepper
⅛ teaspoon kosher salt

1 large egg (50 grams), lightly beaten
1 tablespoon (15 grams) water
Swedish pearl sugar, for sprinkling

1. For dough: In the bowl of a stand mixer fitted with the paddle attachment, beat 1 cup (125 grams) flour, granulated sugar, yeast, salt, and cardamom at low speed just until combined.
2. In a medium saucepan, heat milk and butter over medium heat, stirring occasionally, until an instant-read thermometer registers 120°F (49°C) to 130°F (54°C). Add warm milk mixture to flour mixture; beat at medium speed for 2 minutes. Add egg; beat at medium-high speed for 2 minutes. Gradually add 2¼ cups (281 grams) flour, beating just until combined and stopping to scrape sides of bowl.
3. Switch to the dough hook attachment. Beat at medium-low speed until a soft, smooth, elastic dough forms, 6 to 9 minutes, stopping to scrape sides of bowl and dough hook; add up to remaining ¼ cup (31 grams) flour, 1 tablespoon (8 grams) at a time, if needed. (Dough may still stick slightly to sides of bowl.) Check dough for proper gluten development using the windowpane test. (See Note.) Cover and let rise in a warm, draft-free place (75°F/24°C) until doubled in size, 30 to 45 minutes.

4. For filling: In a medium bowl, stir together butter, brown sugar, cinnamon, cardamom, ginger, cloves, pepper, and salt until well combined.
5. Punch down dough; cover and let stand for 5 minutes. On a lightly floured surface, roll dough into a 22x15-inch rectangle, one short side closest to you. Using a large offset spatula, dot filling onto dough, and spread in an even layer all the way to edges. Fold dough in thirds like a letter. Place on a parchment-lined baking sheet; cover with plastic wrap, and refrigerate for 10 minutes.
6. Line 2 rimmed baking sheets with parchment paper.
7. On a lightly floured surface, roll dough into a 15x8-inch rectangle, one long side closest to you. Using a pastry wheel or pizza cutter, cut into 18 strips (about 8x¾ inches each). Holding a strip with one end in each hand, twist strip 5 times, gently stretching until it is nearly double its original length. Grabbing one end of twisted strip between middle 2 or 3 fingers and thumb of same hand, loosely wrap dough around fingers twice, overlapping slightly. Place thumb of same hand over overlapped dough strands to secure; wrap remaining end of dough perpendicularly around overlapping dough strands to form a knot-like shape, tucking loose end under bottom of finished bun. Place buns 1½ to 2 inches apart on prepared pans. Cover and let rise in a warm, draft-free place (75°F/24°C) until doubled in size and dough holds an indentation when poked, 45 minutes to 1 hour.
8. Preheat oven to 350°F (180°C).
9. In a small bowl, whisk together egg and 1 tablespoon (15 grams) water. Brush top of buns with egg wash. Sprinkle with pearl sugar.
10. Bake until golden brown and an instant-read thermometer inserted in center registers at least 190°F (88°C), 12 to 14 minutes, rotating pans halfway through baking and loosely covering with foil to prevent excess browning, if necessary. Let cool on pans for 5 minutes. Serve warm.

Unlike softened butter, room temperature butter should provide no resistance when pressed with a finger. At this point, the butter is softened enough to easily spread over dough.

Note: *To use the windowpane test to check dough for proper gluten development, pinch off (don't tear) a small piece of dough. Slowly pull the dough out from the center. If the dough is ready, you will be able to stretch it until it's thin and translucent like a windowpane. If the dough tears, it's not quite ready. Beat for 1 minute, and test again.*

SUIKERBROOD

Makes 1 (8½x4½-inch) loaf

An ultra-sweet Dutch specialty hailing from Friesland, a Northern province of the Netherlands, suikerbrood, which translates to "sugar bread," is a spiced loaf with a surprise interior. Slice into the bread to unveil a hypnotizing amber swirl and glistening pockets of sugar courtesy of Belgian pearl sugar.

2½ to 2¾ cups (313 to 344 grams) all-purpose flour
1 tablespoon (12 grams) granulated sugar
1 (0.25-ounce) package (7 grams) instant yeast
1 teaspoon (3 grams) kosher salt
⅔ cup (160 grams) plus 1 tablespoon (15 grams) whole milk, divided
¼ cup (57 grams) unsalted butter, softened
2 large eggs (100 grams), room temperature and divided
2 tablespoons (40 grams) Honey-Ginger Syrup (recipe follows)
¾ cup (120 grams) plus 2 tablespoons (20 grams) Belgian pearl sugar, divided
1 teaspoon (2 grams) ground cinnamon
½ teaspoon (1 gram) ground ginger

1. In the bowl of a stand mixer fitted with the paddle attachment, beat 1 cup (125 grams) flour, granulated sugar, yeast, and salt at medium-low speed until combined.
2. In a medium saucepan, heat ⅔ cup (160 grams) milk and butter over medium heat until an instant-read thermometer registers 120°F (49°C) to 130°F (54°C). Add warm milk mixture to flour mixture; beat at medium speed for 2 minutes. Add 1 egg (50 grams) and Honey-Ginger Syrup; beat at medium-high speed for 2 minutes. Gradually add 1½ cups (188 grams) flour, beating just until combined and stopping to scrape sides of bowl.
3. Switch to the dough hook attachment. Beat at medium-low speed until a soft, smooth, elastic dough forms, 6 to 9 minutes, stopping to scrape sides of bowl and dough hook; add up to remaining ¼ cup (31 grams) flour, 1 tablespoon (8 grams) at a time, if needed. (Dough may still stick slightly to sides of bowl.) Check dough for proper gluten development using the windowpane test. (See Note on page 205.) Cover and let rise in a warm, draft-free place (75°F/24°C) until doubled in size, 30 to 45 minutes.
4. Spray an 8½x4½-inch loaf pan with cooking spray. Line pan with parchment paper, letting excess extend over sides of pan; lightly spray parchment.
5. Add ¾ cup (120 grams) pearl sugar to dough in mixer bowl; return bowl to stand mixer fitted with the dough hook attachment, and beat at medium-low speed just until pearl sugar is well combined, about 1 minute, kneading in sugar by hand toward end, if necessary.

Gently shape dough into a round; cover and let stand for 20 minutes.
6. Gently punch down dough. On a lightly floured surface, roll dough into a 14x6-inch rectangle, pushing any pearl sugar pieces that fall out back into dough.
7. In a small bowl, stir together cinnamon and ginger. Sprinkle cinnamon mixture evenly over dough, leaving a ¼-inch border around edges. Starting at one short side, roll up dough, jelly roll style; pinch seam to seal. Place, seam side down, in prepared pan. Cover and let rise in a warm, draft-free place (75°F/24°C) until doubled in size and dough holds an indentation when poked, 30 to 45 minutes.
8. Preheat oven to 350°F (180°C).
9. In a small bowl, whisk together remaining 1 egg (50 grams) and remaining 1 tablespoon (15 grams) milk. Brush egg wash on top of dough. Sprinkle with remaining 2 tablespoons (20 grams) pearl sugar.
10. Bake for 15 minutes. Loosely cover with foil, rotate pan, and bake until an instant-read thermometer inserted in center registers 190°F (88°C), 20 to 25 minutes more. Using excess parchment as handles, remove from pan, and let cool completely on a wire rack.

HONEY-GINGER SYRUP
Makes about 3 tablespoons

¼ cup (38 grams) ⅛-inch-sliced unpeeled fresh ginger
¼ cup (60 grams) water
3 tablespoons (63 grams) clover honey

1. In a small saucepan, combine ginger, ¼ cup (60 grams) water, and honey; using a wooden spoon, gently muddle ginger. Bring just to a boil over medium heat, stirring frequently. Reduce heat to medium-low, and simmer for 15 minutes. Remove from heat; cover and let stand for 30 minutes.
2. Strain syrup mixture through a fine-mesh sieve, discarding solids. Let cool to room temperature before using. Refrigerate in an airtight container for up to 1 week.

PRO TIP
Leftover Honey-Ginger Syrup is a great addition to tea, cocktails, sparkling water, and more. It can also be swirled into your favorite preserves, to taste, for a little flavor twist.

LE GIBASSIER

Makes 8 small loaves

A French bread from Provence, the gibassier is flavored with anise, candied orange peel, and orange blossom water. Cut and shaped to resemble a leaf, our baked Le Gibassier loaves get brushed with butter before a final roll in ginger- and cardamom-laced sugar.

2⅓ to 2⅔ cups (296 to 338 grams) bread flour, divided
1 cup (200 grams) granulated sugar, divided
2 (0.25-ounce) packages (14 grams) instant yeast*
2 teaspoons (6 grams) kosher salt
¾ teaspoon (1.5 grams) plus ⅛ teaspoon ground cardamom, divided
½ teaspoon ground ginger, divided
¼ cup (60 grams) whole milk
3 tablespoons (42 grams) olive oil
2 large eggs (100 grams), room temperature
2½ teaspoons (12.5 grams) orange blossom water
¾ cup (170 grams) unsalted butter, softened and divided
½ cup (72 grams) finely chopped candied orange
1½ teaspoons (4.5 grams) anise seeds

1. In the bowl of a stand mixer fitted with the paddle attachment, beat 1 cup (127 grams) flour, ⅓ cup (67 grams) sugar, yeast, salt, ¾ teaspoon (1.5 grams) cardamom, and ¼ teaspoon ginger at low speed until combined.
2. In a medium saucepan, heat milk and oil over medium heat until an instant-read thermometer registers 120°F (49°C) to 130°F (54°C). Add warm milk mixture to flour mixture; beat at low speed just until combined and yeast dissolves, stopping to scrape sides of bowl. Add eggs and orange blossom water; beat at medium-low speed just until combined, stopping to scrape sides of bowl. With mixer on low speed, gradually add 1⅓ cups (169 grams) flour, beating just until combined.
3. Switch to the dough hook attachment. Beat at medium-low speed until dough is smooth and elastic and pulls away from sides of bowl, 7 to 10 minutes, stopping to scrape sides of bowl; add up to remaining ⅓ cup (42 grams) flour, 1 tablespoon (8 grams) at a time, if dough is too sticky.
4. With mixer on low speed, add ¼ cup (57 grams) butter, 1 tablespoon (14 grams) at a time, beating until combined after each addition, 6 to 8 minutes total, stopping to scrape sides of bowl and dough hook. Increase mixer speed to medium-low, and beat until a smooth, elastic dough forms, 6 to 7 minutes, stopping to scrape dough hook. Check dough for proper gluten development using the windowpane test. (See Note.) Beat in candied orange and anise seeds

until combined. Turn out dough onto a clean surface; knead 6 to 10 times to help evenly disperse candied orange and anise seeds. Transfer dough to a medium bowl. Cover and let rise in a warm, draft-free place (75°F/24°C) until doubled in size, 1½ to 2½ hours.
5. Punch down dough; let stand for 5 minutes. Turn out dough onto a clean surface, and divide into 8 portions (about 92 grams each); shape into balls, pinching seams closed as needed. Cover with plastic wrap, and let stand for 25 minutes.
6. Preheat oven to 375°F (190°C). Line 2 baking sheets with parchment paper.
7. Roll each dough ball into a 3½-inch log; flatten and shape into about 4½x3-inch ovals (about ¼ inch thick). Place long side of dough ovals parallel to counter edge; using sharp kitchen shears or scissors, cut 3 slits crosswise and equally spaced within each oval, leaving about ½ to ¾ inch of dough intact on each side. Along one long side of each oval, cut ½- to ¾-inch-long slits, evenly spaced, to the side of each original center slit. Stretch dough gently just to open slits; place on prepared pans. Cover and let rise in a warm, draft-free place (75°F/24°C) until dough is puffed and holds an indentation when pressed with a finger, 45 minutes to 1 hour.
8. Bake, one batch at a time, until golden brown and an instant-read thermometer inserted in center registers 190°F (88°C), 6 to 10 minutes. Let cool for 3 to 5 minutes.
9. Meanwhile, in a small microwave-safe bowl, heat remaining ½ cup (113 grams) butter on high in 10-second intervals until melted.
10. Meanwhile, in a medium bowl, stir together remaining ⅔ cup (133 grams) sugar, remaining ¼ teaspoon ginger, and remaining ⅛ teaspoon cardamom.
11. Brush melted butter all over warm bread; immediately coat with sugar mixture. Serve warm, or let cool to room temperature on wire racks.

*We used Platinum® Yeast from Red Star®.

Note: *To use the windowpane test to check dough for proper gluten development, lightly flour hands and pinch off (don't tear) a small piece of dough. Slowly pull the dough out from the center. If the dough is ready, you will be able to stretch it until it's thin and translucent like a windowpane. If the dough tears, it's not quite ready. Beat for 1 minute, and test again.*

CUSTARD BRIOCHE TARTS

Makes 12 (4-inch) tarts

Recipe by Shane Smith

Shane's rich, fluffy brioche tarts are made all the better with fine Irish dairy and fresh local produce.

½ cup (120 grams) warm whole milk (110°F/43°C to 115°F/46°C)
3¼ teaspoons (10 grams) instant yeast
3¼ cups (406 grams) all-purpose flour
3 tablespoons (36 grams) castor/superfine sugar
2¼ teaspoons (6 grams) kosher salt, divided
5 medium eggs (235 grams), room temperature and divided
¾ cup plus 2 tablespoons (198 grams) unsalted butter, room temperature
1 teaspoon (5 grams) whole milk
Vanilla Custard (recipe follows)
Rhubarb Filling (recipe follows) (see Note)
⅔ cup (213 grams) warm orange marmalade
½ cup (100 grams) Swedish pearl sugar

1. In a small bowl, stir together warm milk and yeast. Let stand until foamy, about 10 minutes.
2. In the bowl of a stand mixer fitted with the dough hook attachment, combine flour, castor sugar, and 2 teaspoons (6 grams) salt. Add yeast mixture and 4 eggs (188 grams), and beat at medium speed until a dough forms, about 5 minutes. Gradually add butter, 1 tablespoon (14 grams) at a time, beating until smooth and combined after each addition, 10 to 15 minutes.
3. Spray a large bowl with cooking spray. Place dough in bowl, turning to grease top. Cover and refrigerate overnight.
4. Line 2 baking sheets with parchment paper.
5. Turn out dough onto a lightly floured surface, and divide into 12 portions (about 73 grams each). Shape each portion into a smooth ball, and place 2 inches apart on prepared pans. Using the palm of your hand, flatten dough balls into 4-inch disks. Using your index finger, press down in center of each disk to create a 1-inch indentation. Cover with a kitchen towel, and let rise in a warm, draft-free place (75°F/24°C) until doubled in size, 1½ to 2 hours.
6. Preheat oven to 350°F (180°C).
7. In a small bowl, whisk together milk, remaining 1 egg (47 grams), and remaining ¼ teaspoon salt. Brush egg wash onto dough. Spoon Vanilla Custard into center of each dough circle; top with 4 pieces of Rhubarb Filling.
8. Bake until brioche is golden brown, 15 to 20 minutes. Remove from pans, and let cool completely on wire racks. Before serving, brush with warm marmalade, and sprinkle with pearl sugar.

Note: *Rhubarb Filling can be substituted with 24 medium fresh strawberries (288 grams). Stem and halve each strawberry, and place 4 halves in center of each tart.*

Vanilla Custard
Makes about 2 cups

2 cups plus 1 tablespoon (495 grams) whole milk
1 teaspoon (4 grams) vanilla extract
6 medium egg yolks (102 grams)
⅓ cup plus 1 tablespoon (79 grams) castor/superfine sugar
2½ tablespoons (20 grams) cornstarch
2½ tablespoons (20 grams) all-purpose flour

1. In a medium saucepan, heat milk and vanilla over medium heat until steaming. (Do not boil.) Let stand to infuse, about 5 minutes.
2. In a medium bowl, whisk together egg yolks, castor sugar, cornstarch, and flour. Slowly add warm milk mixture to egg yolk mixture, whisking constantly. Strain through a fine-mesh sieve into another saucepan, and cook over medium-low heat until thickened, 2 to 3 minutes.
3. Transfer to another medium bowl, and cover with a piece of plastic wrap, pressing wrap directly onto surface of custard to prevent a skin from forming. Refrigerate until completely cool. Custard can be refrigerated for up to 3 days.

Rhubarb Filling
Makes 1½ cups

⅓ cup plus 1½ tablespoons (102.5 grams) water
1½ tablespoons (7.5 grams) packed orange zest (1 orange)
¼ cup (60 grams) fresh orange juice (1 orange)
1 tablespoon (12 grams) castor/superfine sugar
5 stalks rhubarb (255 grams), cut into 2-inch pieces

1. Preheat oven to 350°F (180°C).
2. In a medium bowl, stir together ⅓ cup plus 1½ tablespoons (102.5 grams) water, orange zest and juice, and castor sugar. Add rhubarb, tossing to combine. Pour onto a rimmed baking sheet, and cover with foil.
3. Bake for 8 minutes. Using a sharp paring knife, test rhubarb until it cuts easily but still holds its shape. If not ready, cover and bake for 3 to 4 minutes more, and test again. Let cool completely before using.

Note: *Be careful not to overcook the rhubarb. You want the pieces to retain their shape because they will be cooked again when baking the brioche.*

Photo by Joann Pai

BEER CHEESE PRETZEL TART

Makes 1 (9-inch) tart

Acting as a chewy edible bowl, a puffy pretzel tart base holds our decadent Beer Cheese Filling that packs a triple threat of Gouda, Cheddar, and cream cheese, offering all the wondrous flavors of Oktoberfest.

3   cups (375 grams) all-purpose flour, divided
2   tablespoons (28 grams) firmly packed light brown sugar
1½ teaspoons (4.5 grams) instant yeast
1½ teaspoons (4.5 grams) kosher salt
⅔   cup (160 grams) whole milk
⅓   cup (80 grams) water, plus more for brushing
2   tablespoons (28 grams) unsalted butter
1½ tablespoons (22.5 grams) hot water (200°F/93°C to 205°F/96°C)
⅛   teaspoon baking soda
1   large egg (50 grams), separated
Beer Cheese Filling (recipe follows)
1   tablespoon (20 grams) pretzel salt
Garnish: chopped fresh chives, ground red pepper

1. In the bowl of a stand mixer fitted with the paddle attachment, combine 1¼ cups (156 grams) flour, brown sugar, yeast, and kosher salt.
2. In a small saucepan, heat milk, ⅓ cup (80 grams) water, and butter over medium heat until an instant-read thermometer registers 120°F (49°C) to 130°F (54°C). Add warm milk mixture to flour mixture, and beat at medium speed until combined. Reduce mixer speed to low, and gradually add 1½ cups (188 grams) flour, beating just until combined and stopping to scrape sides of bowl.
3. Switch to the dough hook attachment. Beat at low speed until a soft, somewhat sticky dough forms, 4 to 5 minutes, stopping to scrape sides of bowl and dough hook; add up to remaining ¼ cup (31 grams) flour, 1 tablespoon (8 grams) at a time, if dough is too sticky. Turn out onto a lightly floured surface, and shape into a smooth round.
4. Lightly oil a medium bowl. Place dough in bowl, turning to grease top. Cover and let rise in a warm, draft-free place (75°F/24°C) until doubled in size, 30 to 40 minutes.
5. Preheat oven to 350°F (180°C). Spray a 9-inch square baking pan with cooking spray. Line pan with parchment paper, letting excess extend over sides of pan.
6. On a lightly floured surface, roll dough into an 11-inch square. Score a 9-inch square in center of dough. Brush water onto 9-inch square. Fold dough over at score mark. Using hands, lift dough, and place in prepared pan, making sure dough is even and fills corners of pan. Cover and let rise in a warm, draft-free place (75°F/24°C) until puffed, about 20 minutes.
7. Using your fingertips, dimple center square back down, leaving outside border as is. In a small bowl, stir together 1½ tablespoons (22.5 grams) hot water and baking soda. Gently brush hot water mixture onto outside border; brush egg yolk onto outside border. Pour warm Beer Cheese Filling in center.
8. Bake for 25 minutes. Brush crust with egg white, and sprinkle with pretzel salt. Bake until crust is golden brown and an instant-read thermometer inserted in filling registers at least 160°F (71°C) (but not over 175°F/79°C), about 5 minutes more. Let cool in pan for 10 minutes. Using excess parchment as handles, remove from pan, and let cool on a wire rack. Garnish with chives and red pepper, if desired.

BEER CHEESE FILLING
Makes 1⅔ cups

⅔   cup (150 grams) cream cheese, softened
⅓   cup (80 grams) amber beer, room temperature
2   teaspoons (10 grams) Dijon mustard
½   teaspoon (3 grams) garlic powder
⅛   teaspoon ground red pepper
⅔   cup (75 grams) shredded extra-sharp white Cheddar cheese
⅔   cup (75 grams) shredded Gouda cheese
1   large egg (50 grams), room temperature and lightly beaten
2   tablespoons (8 grams) chopped fresh chives

1. In a medium saucepan, cook cream cheese and half of beer over medium heat, stirring frequently, until cream cheese is melted and mixture is smooth. Add mustard, garlic powder, and red pepper. Slowly add remaining beer, whisking constantly, until combined.
2. In a small bowl, combine Cheddar and Gouda; slowly add to cream cheese mixture, about ¼ cup (28 grams) at a time, whisking until cheese is mostly melted after each addition. Whisk until completely smooth; remove from heat, and pour into a heatproof bowl. Let cool until an instant-read thermometer registers 140°F (60°C), about 5 minutes. Whisk in egg and chives. Use immediately. (See PRO TIP.)

PRO TIP
Timing is really important for this tart. You want the filling to be warm going into the oven, or it won't be hot enough when the bread is ready. The filling must be at least 160°F (71°C), but you do not want it to curdle, which will happen at about 182°F (83°C). We suggest making the filling during the dough's second rise, in step 6.

BIRTHDAY BRIOCHE BUNS

Makes 8 buns

Sprinkles and icing complete the celebratory look and taste of these delightful rolls.

2⅓ cups plus ¼ cup (323 grams) all-purpose flour, divided
3 tablespoons (36 grams) granulated sugar
2¼ teaspoons (7 grams) instant yeast
1½ teaspoons (4.5 grams) kosher salt
⅓ cup plus 1 tablespoon (95 grams) warm whole milk (120°F/49°C to 130°F/54°C)
2 large eggs (100 grams), lightly beaten
1 teaspoon (4 grams) vanilla extract
6 tablespoons (84 grams) unsalted butter, room temperature
Pastry Cream (recipe follows)
1 large egg yolk (19 grams)
1 tablespoon (15 grams) water
Sugar Icing (recipe follows)
Garnish: sprinkles

1. In the bowl of a stand mixer fitted with the paddle attachment, combine 1⅓ cups (167 grams) flour, sugar, yeast, and salt. With mixer on low speed, slowly add warm milk, beating until combined. Add eggs and vanilla, and beat until combined, about 1 minute. Add remaining 1¼ cup (156 grams) flour, beating just until a shaggy dough forms.
2. Switch to the dough hook attachment, and beat at low speed until elastic, about 8 minutes. Add butter, 1 tablespoon (14 grams) at a time, beating just until combined after each addition (about 6 minutes total). Beat until a smooth and elastic dough forms, about 8 minutes. Turn out dough onto a lightly floured surface, and knead 4 to 5 times; shape into a smooth round.
3. Lightly oil a medium bowl. Place dough in bowl, turning to grease top. Cover with plastic wrap, and let rise in a warm, draft-free place (75°F/24°C) until doubled in size, 30 to 45 minutes.
4. Lightly oil 2 (9-inch) round cake pans.
5. Lightly punch down dough. Cover and let stand for 5 minutes. Turn out dough onto a lightly floured surface, and divide into 8 pieces (76 grams each). Roll 1 piece into a smooth ball. Press flat, and roll into a 3-inch disk. (Keep remaining dough covered to prevent it from drying out.) Using a small rolling pin, roll edges thin, creating a 5-inch disk, keeping center thicker than edges.
6. Using a 1½-tablespoon spring-loaded scoop, scoop Pastry Cream, and place in center of disk. Fold disk in half over filling, pinching edges together. Gather and pinch edges toward center until well sealed. Place dough, seam side down, on work surface. Gently cup top of dough with your hand, and rotate 2 to 3 times to seal and create a smooth ball. (Check seam to make sure it is sealed.) Place in a prepared pan. Repeat procedure with remaining dough and filling, placing 4 buns (not touching) in each pan. Cover and let rise in a warm, draft-free place (75°F/24°C) until puffed, about 30 minutes.
7. Preheat oven to 350°F (180°C).
8. In a small bowl, whisk together egg yolk and 1 tablespoon (15 grams) water. Brush buns with egg wash.
9. Bake until golden and an instant-read thermometer inserted in side of bun registers 190°F (88°C), 14 to 18 minutes. Let cool in pans for 10 minutes. Remove from pans, and let cool completely on a wire rack.
10. Dip top of each cooled bun in Sugar Icing, letting excess drip off before setting back down. Garnish with sprinkles, if desired. Serve immediately, or refrigerate until ready to serve.

PASTRY CREAM
Makes 1½ cups

1½ cups (360 grams) whole milk
½ cup (100 grams) granulated sugar, divided
½ vanilla bean, split lengthwise, seeds scraped and reserved
4 large egg yolks (74 grams)
2 tablespoons (16 grams) cornstarch
¼ teaspoon kosher salt
2 tablespoons (28 grams) unsalted butter

1. In a large saucepan, whisk together milk, ¼ cup (50 grams) sugar, and vanilla bean and reserved seeds. Heat over medium heat until steaming. (Do not boil.) Discard vanilla bean.
2. In a large bowl, whisk together egg yolks, cornstarch, salt, and remaining ¼ cup (50 grams) sugar. Gradually add warm milk mixture to egg yolk mixture, whisking constantly. Return mixture to saucepan, and cook over medium heat, whisking constantly, until thickened and mixture starts to boil. Cook, whisking constantly, for 3 minutes. Strain through a fine-mesh sieve into a large bowl. Stir in butter. Cover with a piece of plastic wrap, pressing wrap directly onto surface of Pastry Cream to prevent a skin from forming. Refrigerate until completely cool. (This can be made ahead of time; for a quick chill, place bowl in an ice water bath.)

SUGAR ICING
Makes 1¼ cups

2 cups (240 grams) confectioners' sugar
3 tablespoons (45 grams) whole milk

1. In a medium bowl, whisk together confectioners' sugar and milk until smooth. Use immediately.

PASTRIES

GERMAN SOUR CREAM TWISTS

Makes 24 twists

Sour cream adds a hint of tanginess to these classic German pastries.

1½   cups (300 grams) granulated sugar
1   vanilla bean, halved lengthwise, seeds scraped and reserved
¼   cup (60 grams) warm water (105°F/41°C to 110°F/43°C)
2¼   teaspoons (7 grams) instant yeast
3¾   cups (469 grams) all-purpose flour
1   cup (227 grams) cold unsalted butter, cubed
¾   teaspoon (2.25 grams) kosher salt
¾   cup (180 grams) sour cream, room temperature
2   large eggs (100 grams), room temperature
1   teaspoon (4 grams) vanilla extract

1. In a medium bowl, place sugar and vanilla bean and reserved seeds. Using your fingers, rub vanilla into sugar until well combined. Cover and set aside.

2. In a small bowl, stir together ¼ cup (60 grams) warm water and yeast. Let stand until foamy, about 5 minutes.

3. In the bowl of a stand mixer fitted with paddle attachment, beat flour, cold butter, and salt at low speed until mixture resembles coarse crumbs, 3 to 5 minutes. Beat in yeast mixture, sour cream, eggs, and vanilla extract until well combined and a sticky dough forms. Cover and refrigerate for at least 2 hours or overnight.

4. Preheat oven to 375°F (190°C). Line 3 baking sheets with parchment paper.

5. Divide dough in half (about 513 grams each). Cover and return one half to refrigerator.

6. Sprinkle ¼ cup (50 grams) vanilla sugar on work surface. Roll one half of dough into a 12x8-inch rectangle. Sprinkle with 2 tablespoons (24 grams) vanilla sugar; fold into thirds, like a letter. Turn dough 90 degrees; repeat rolling, sprinkling, and folding twice. (If dough sticks in spots during rolling process, sprinkle vanilla sugar on those sticky spots as if it were flour.) Roll into a 12x8-inch rectangle, and cut into 12 (1-inch-wide) strips. Twist each strip into a coil. Place 6 twists on a prepared pan, and refrigerate; place 6 twists on another prepared pan.

7. Bake 6 twists until golden brown, 15 to 20 minutes. Let cool on pan for 5 minutes. Remove from pan, and let cool completely on wire racks. Bake remaining 6 twists.

8. Repeat procedure with remaining dough, refrigerating and baking in batches.

KLOBASNIKY (SAVORY KOLACHES)

Makes 12 klobasniky

Two cheeses, three meats, and a whole lot of our Homemade Everything Bagel Seasoning make these klobasniky your new brunch hero.

¾   cup (187 grams) ricotta cheese
¾   cup (92 grams) shredded mozzarella cheese
2   large eggs (100 grams), divided
1   tablespoon (14 grams) finely chopped oil-packed sun-dried tomatoes
1   tablespoon (4 grams) finely chopped fresh basil
¼   teaspoon ground black pepper
Kolache Dough (recipe follows)
24   slices (156 grams) thinly sliced 3-inch-wide sandwich pepperoni*
12   slices (132 grams) thinly sliced 4½-inch-wide Genoa salami*, cut in half
12   slices (192 grams) thinly sliced prosciutto*
Homemade Everything Bagel Seasoning (recipe follows), for sprinkling

1. In a medium bowl, stir together cheeses, 1 egg (50 grams), tomatoes, basil, and pepper until well combined.
2. Preheat oven to 375°F (190°C). Line 2 rimmed baking sheets with parchment paper.
3. Lightly punch down Kolache Dough; cover and let stand for 5 minutes. Turn out dough, and divide into 12 portions (about 81 grams each). Roll each portion into a 7½x5-inch oval; spoon about 5 teaspoons (about 27 grams) cheese mixture into center of each oval, spreading mixture into a 4x2½-inch oval. Layer pepperoni, salami, and prosciutto on top of cheese mixture. Stretch long sides of dough over filling, and pinch together; fold over short sides, pinching seams closed. Place, seam side down, on prepared pans. Cover and let rise in a warm, draft-free place (75°F/24°C) until puffed and dough holds an indentation when poked, 20 to 25 minutes. Pinch closed any seams, if needed.
4. In a small bowl, beat remaining 1 egg (50 grams). Brush dough with egg, and

sprinkle with Homemade Everything Bagel Seasoning.
5. Bake until golden brown and an instant-read thermometer inserted in center registers 190°F (88°C) to 200°F (93°C), 13 to 15 minutes. Let cool on pans for 5 minutes. Serve warm or at room temperature.

We used Boar's Head Sandwich Style Pepperoni, Boar's Head Genoa Salami Natural Casing, and Boar's Head Prosciutto di Parma, available in the grocery store deli.

KOLACHE DOUGH
Makes enough for 12 kolaches or klobasniky

This base dough will work for both your sweet and savory desires. You'll wonder what took you so long to try your hand at this easy and epically fluffy classic Czech-Texan pastry.

4 to 4¼ cups (500 to 531 grams) all-purpose flour, divided
⅓   cup (67 grams) granulated sugar
2½   teaspoons (7.5 grams) kosher salt
1   (0.25-ounce) package (7 grams) instant yeast
⅛   teaspoon ground nutmeg
¾   cup (180 grams) whole milk
⅓   cup (76 grams) unsalted butter, softened
¼   cup (60 grams) water
2   large eggs (100 grams)

1. In the bowl of a stand mixer fitted with the paddle attachment, beat 1¼ cups (156 grams) flour, sugar, salt, yeast, and nutmeg at medium-low speed until well combined.
2. In a medium saucepan, heat milk, butter, and ¼ cup (60 grams) water over medium heat until an instant-read thermometer registers 120°F (49°C) to 130°F (54°C). Add warm milk mixture to flour mixture; beat at medium speed for 2 minutes. Add eggs; beat at medium-high speed for 2 minutes. With mixer on low speed, gradually add 2¾ cups (344 grams) flour,

beating just until combined and stopping to scrape sides of bowl.
3. Switch to the dough hook attachment. Beat at medium speed until a soft, somewhat sticky dough forms, 6 to 8 minutes, stopping to scrape sides of bowl and dough hook; add up to remaining ¼ cup (31 grams) flour, 1 tablespoon (8 grams) at a time, if necessary. (Dough should pass the windowpane test [see Note] but may still stick slightly to sides of bowl.)
4. Spray a large bowl with cooking spray. Place dough in bowl, turning to grease top. Cover and let rise in a warm, draft-free place (75°F/24°C) until doubled in size, 40 minutes to 1 hour.

Note: *Test the dough for proper gluten development using the windowpane test. Pinch off (don't tear) a small piece of dough. Slowly pull the dough out from the center. If the dough is ready, you will be able to stretch it until it's thin and translucent like a windowpane. If the dough tears, it's not quite ready. Beat for 1 minute, and test again.*

HOMEMADE EVERYTHING BAGEL SEASONING
Makes ¼ cup

1   tablespoon (9 grams) white sesame seeds
1   tablespoon (9 grams) black sesame seeds
1½   teaspoons (4.5 grams) poppy seeds
1   teaspoon (4 grams) dried minced garlic
1   teaspoon (4 grams) dried minced onion

1. In a small bowl, stir together all ingredients. Use immediately, or store in an airtight container for up to 6 months.

Note: *We kept our everything bagel seasoning salt-free to balance out the meats in our Klobasniky (Savory Kolaches). This versatile seasoning goes great on anything from breads to bagels and beyond.*

1. Roll each portion into a 7½x5-inch oval.

2. Spread cheese mixture into a 4x2½-inch oval.

3. Layer pepperoni, salami, and prosciutto on top of cheese mixture.

4. Stretch long sides of dough over filling, and pinch together.

5. Fold over short sides, pinching seams closed.

6. Brush dough with egg, and sprinkle with Homemade Everything Bagel Seasoning.

SWEET POTATO HAND PIES

Makes 9 hand pies

The perfect pastry package, these hand pies hide the welcome surprise of a spiced brown sugar-laden sweet potato filling. Drizzled with a warm glaze, each one is the buttery celebration of autumn's sweetest tuber.

1¼ cups (284 grams) unsalted butter
2¼ cups (281 grams) all-purpose flour
2¼ teaspoons (6.75 grams) plus ⅛ teaspoon kosher salt, divided
½ cup (120 grams) ice water
½ cup (118 grams) puréed cooked peeled sweet potato (see Note)
3 tablespoons (42 grams) firmly packed light brown sugar
½ teaspoon (2 grams) vanilla extract
¼ teaspoon ground cinnamon
¼ teaspoon ground ginger
⅛ teaspoon ground nutmeg
1 large egg (50 grams), lightly beaten
Cinnamon-Brown Sugar Glaze (recipe follows)
Garnish: turbinado sugar

1. Cube butter, and freeze for 30 minutes.
2. In the work bowl of a food processor, place flour and 2¼ teaspoons (6.75 grams) salt; pulse until combined. Add frozen butter; pulse until butter is dime-size. With processor running, add ½ cup (120 grams) ice water in a slow, steady stream just until dough comes together and forms a ball. Turn out dough onto a lightly floured surface; shape into a 6-inch square. Wrap in plastic wrap, and refrigerate for at least 30 minutes.
3. On a lightly floured surface, roll dough into a 15x7½-inch rectangle, lightly flouring surface as needed to prevent sticking. Fold dough in thirds, like a letter, and turn 90 degrees. Repeat procedure twice. Wrap in plastic wrap, and refrigerate for at least 20 minutes.
4. Line 2 baking sheets with parchment paper.
5. Divide dough in half. On a lightly floured surface, roll 1 portion into a 12x9-inch rectangle, lightly flouring surface and dough as needed to prevent sticking. Using a pastry wheel, cut dough into 9 rectangles (about 4x3 inches each). Place evenly spaced on a prepared pan, and refrigerate; repeat procedure with remaining dough.

6. Preheat oven to 350°F (180°C).
7. In a small bowl, stir together sweet potato, brown sugar, vanilla, cinnamon, ginger, nutmeg, and remaining ⅛ teaspoon salt; divide sweet potato mixture among 9 dough rectangles (about 2½ teaspoons [16 grams] each); using a small offset spatula, spread sweet potato mixture evenly within each rectangle, leaving a ¼- to ½-inch border around edges. Brush egg onto border of each rectangle; top each with a second dough rectangle. Using the tines of a fork, crimp edges to seal each pastry pocket; brush egg onto dough, and poke tops 3 to 4 times with tines of fork. Using a small sharp knife, trim rectangles to create cleaner edges, if desired.
8. Bake until puffed and golden brown, 20 to 25 minutes. Let cool on pans for at least 10 minutes. Just before serving, spoon and spread Cinnamon-Brown Sugar Glaze onto hand pies, working quickly. Garnish immediately with turbinado sugar, if desired. Serve warm or at room temperature.

Note: *We like the bright color and convenience of using pre-cubed raw sweet potatoes, sold in 1-pound bags in the produce department of most grocery stores. Cook according to package direction. Purée in a food processor until mostly smooth.*

CINNAMON-BROWN SUGAR GLAZE
Makes about ¾ cup

¼ cup (57 grams) unsalted butter
¼ cup (55 grams) firmly packed light brown sugar
¼ teaspoon kosher salt
¼ cup (60 grams) heavy whipping cream
1 cup (120 grams) confectioners' sugar
1 teaspoon (4 grams) vanilla extract
¾ teaspoon (1.5 grams) ground cinnamon

1. In a medium saucepan, combine butter, brown sugar, and salt; cook over medium-low heat, stirring frequently, until melted and well combined. Stir in cream; bring to a boil over medium heat, stirring frequently. Immediately remove from heat; stir in confectioners' sugar, vanilla, and cinnamon until well combined. Use immediately.

SWEET KOLACHES

KOLACHE DOUGH

Makes enough for 12 kolaches or klobasniky

This base dough will work for both your sweet and savory desires. You'll wonder what took you so long to try your hand at this easy and epically fluffy classic Czech-Texan pastry.

4 to 4¼ cups (500 to 531 grams)
 all-purpose flour, divided
⅓ cup (67 grams) granulated sugar
2½ teaspoons (7.5 grams) kosher salt
1 (0.25-ounce) package (7 grams)
 instant yeast
⅛ teaspoon ground nutmeg
¾ cup (180 grams) whole milk
⅓ cup (76 grams) unsalted butter,
 softened
¼ cup (60 grams) water
2 large eggs (100 grams)

1. In the bowl of a stand mixer fitted with the paddle attachment, beat 1¼ cups (156 grams) flour, sugar, salt, yeast, and nutmeg at medium-low speed until well combined.
2. In a medium saucepan, heat milk, butter, and ¼ cup (60 grams) water over medium heat until an instant-read thermometer registers 120°F (49°C) to 130°F (54°C). Add warm milk mixture to flour mixture; beat at medium speed for 2 minutes. Add eggs; beat at medium-high speed for 2 minutes. With mixer on low speed, gradually add 2¾ cups (344 grams) flour, beating just until combined and stopping to scrape sides of bowl.
3. Switch to the dough hook attachment. Beat at medium speed until a soft, somewhat sticky dough forms, 6 to 8 minutes, stopping to scrape sides of bowl and dough hook; add up to remaining ¼ cup (31 grams) flour, 1 tablespoon (8 grams) at a time, if necessary. (Dough should pass the windowpane test [see Note] but may still stick slightly to sides of bowl.)
4. Spray a large bowl with cooking spray. Place dough in bowl, turning to grease top. Cover and let rise in a warm, draft-free place (75°F/24°C) until doubled in size, 40 minutes to 1 hour.

Note: *Test the dough for proper gluten development using the windowpane test. Pinch off (don't tear) a small piece of dough. Slowly pull the dough out from the center. If the dough is ready, you will be able to stretch it until it's thin and translucent like a windowpane. If the dough tears, it's not quite ready. Beat for 1 minute, and test again.*

APRICOT-FILLED KOLACHES WITH LEMON GLAZE

Makes 12 kolaches

A favorite filling for kolaches, dried apricots pack a sweet-tart flavor delicately complemented by a bright lemon glaze.

1 cup (240 grams) water
¾ cup (147 grams) packed finely chopped
 dried apricots
1 cup (200 grams) granulated sugar
¼ cup (60 grams) fresh orange juice
¾ teaspoon (4 grams) fresh lemon juice
¼ teaspoon ground cardamom
1¼ teaspoons (5 grams) vanilla extract,
 divided
Kolache Dough (recipe precedes)
1 large egg (50 grams), lightly beaten
1⅓ cups (160 grams) confectioners' sugar
5 tablespoons (75 grams) heavy whipping
 cream
1 teaspoon (4 grams) tightly packed
 lemon zest
½ teaspoon (1.5 grams) kosher salt

1. In a medium saucepan, bring 1 cup (240 grams) water and apricots to a boil over medium-high heat; cook, stirring constantly, until water is absorbed and apricots are plump, 3 to 4 minutes. Stir in granulated sugar, orange juice, lemon juice, and cardamom; return to a boil, and cook until thickened, 7 to 8 minutes. (Mixture will continue to thicken as it cools.) Remove from heat; stir in ¼ teaspoon (1 gram) vanilla. Transfer to a medium bowl; let cool to room temperature.
2. Preheat oven to 375°F (190°C). Line 2 rimmed baking sheets with parchment paper.

3. Lightly punch down Kolache Dough; cover and let stand for 5 minutes. Turn out dough, and divide into 12 portions (about 81 grams each). Shape each portion into a smooth round; press flat, and roll into a 3-inch circle. Place 6 circles on each prepared pan. Cover and let rise in a warm, draft-free place (75°F/24°C) until puffed and dough holds an indentation when pressed, 20 to 25 minutes.
4. Using a 4-ounce glass Mason jar or 1-cup measuring cup (2-inch diameter) dipped in flour, press down center of each dough circle to create a ½-inch-deep well. Divide apricot mixture among wells (about 30 grams each). Lightly brush dough with egg.
5. Bake until golden brown and an instant-read thermometer inserted in center registers 190°F (88°C) to 200°F (93°C), 13 to 15 minutes. Let cool on pans for 5 minutes.
6. In a small bowl, stir together confectioners' sugar, cream, lemon zest, salt, and remaining 1 teaspoon (4 grams) vanilla until smooth and well combined. Spoon into a small pastry bag or resealable plastic bag, and cut a ¼-inch opening in tip or corner. Drizzle onto kolaches before serving. Serve warm or at room temperature.

RED PLUM JAM & CREAM CHEESE KOLACHES

Makes 12 kolaches

With a nod toward the original kolaches that made use of cottage cheese and povidla, or plum butter, this kolache recipe has a flavor of both the New and Old Worlds.

5 ounces (142 grams) cream cheese,
 softened
4½ tablespoons (54 grams) granulated
 sugar, divided
1 large egg yolk (19 grams)
⅓ cup (42 grams) plus 2 teaspoons
 (6 grams) all-purpose flour, divided
½ teaspoon (3 grams) vanilla bean paste
Kolache Dough (recipe precedes)
½ cup (160 grams) red plum (damson)
 jam

1   large egg (50 grams), lightly beaten
⅛   teaspoon kosher salt
⅛   teaspoon ground cinnamon (optional)
2   tablespoons (28 grams) unsalted butter, melted

1. In a medium bowl, beat cream cheese with a mixer at medium speed until smooth, 30 seconds to 1 minute. Add 2 tablespoons (24 grams) sugar, egg yolk, 2 teaspoons (6 grams) flour, and vanilla bean paste; beat at medium speed until smooth and well combined, stopping to scrape sides of bowl.

2. Preheat oven to 375°F (190°C). Line 2 rimmed baking sheets with parchment paper.

3. Lightly punch down Kolache Dough; cover and let stand for 5 minutes. Turn out dough, and divide into 12 portions (about 81 grams each). Shape each portion into a smooth round; press flat, and roll into a 3-inch circle. Place 6 circles on each prepared pan. Cover and let rise in a warm, draft-free place (75°F/24°C) until puffed and dough holds an indentation when pressed, 20 to 25 minutes.

4. Using a 4-ounce glass Mason jar or 1-cup measuring cup (2-inch diameter) dipped in flour, press down center of each dough circle to create a ½-inch-deep well. Divide cream cheese mixture among wells (about 13 grams each). Top with jam (about 12 grams each). Lightly brush dough with egg.

5. In another medium bowl, whisk together salt, cinnamon (if using), and remaining 2½ tablespoons (30 grams) sugar. Stir in melted butter; fold in remaining ⅓ cup (42 grams) flour just until combined. Crumble mixture over kolaches.

6. Bake until golden brown and an instant-read thermometer inserted in center registers 190°F (88°C) to 200°F (93°C), 13 to 15 minutes. Let cool on pans for 5 minutes. Serve warm or at room temperature.

1. Make a ½-inch-deep well.

2. Divide apricot mixture among wells.

PIES AND TARTS

PIES

Filled to the brim and baked to buttery perfection, our pie collection will take you down memory lane with a sweet-and-sour lemon Shaker classic all the way to the modern marvel of a dark chocolate Black Forest masterpiece piled high with whipped cream

MEYER LEMON SHAKER PIE

Makes 1 (9-inch) pie

Originally thought up by the Shaker community in the Midwest, Shaker pie is made up of whole slices of macerated lemons and a rustic, flaky crust. We twirled up the traditional recipe by using Meyer lemons for our filling. The maceration process releases the Meyers' subtle floral quality while our Ginger Pie Dough balances out the filling's tart flavor with a sweet and spicy kick.

2   large Meyer lemons (349 grams)
1¾   cups (350 grams) granulated sugar
¼   cup (55 grams) firmly packed light brown sugar
½   teaspoon (1.5 grams) kosher salt
Ginger Pie Dough (recipe follows)
3   tablespoons (24 grams) all-purpose flour
¼   teaspoon ground cinnamon
⅛   teaspoon ground nutmeg
4   large eggs (200 grams), lightly beaten
¼   cup (57 grams) unsalted butter, melted
1   large egg white (30 grams), lightly beaten
1   tablespoon (15 grams) water
Sparkling sugar, for sprinkling

1. Using a serrated knife, cut lemons crosswise into ⅛- to 1⁄16-inch-thick slices, discarding ends and seeds. Coarsely chop lemon slices into ½- to ¾-inch pieces, and place in a large bowl with any juices. Stir in granulated sugar, brown sugar, and salt; cover and let stand at room temperature, stirring occasionally, for 4 hours or up to overnight.
2. Preheat oven to 425°F (220°C).
3. Let Ginger Pie Dough stand at room temperature until slightly softened, 15 to 20 minutes. On a lightly floured surface, roll half of dough into a 12-inch circle (about ⅛ inch thick). Press into bottom and up sides of a 9-inch pie plate.
4. In a medium bowl, whisk together flour, cinnamon, and nutmeg. Add eggs and melted butter, whisking until well combined. Add flour mixture to lemon mixture, stirring until well combined; pour into prepared crust.
5. In a small bowl, whisk together egg white and 1 tablespoon (15 grams) water. Brush dough edges with egg wash.
6. On a lightly floured surface, roll remaining dough into a 12-inch circle. Carefully place over filling; trim dough to ½- to 1-inch overhang. Fold edges under, and crimp, if desired. Brush dough with egg wash; sprinkle with sparkling sugar. Using a sharp knife, cut 8 slits in top to vent.
7. Bake for 25 minutes, covering edges with foil to prevent excess browning and re-cutting slits in top, if necessary. Reduce oven temperature to 350°F (180°C). Bake until crust is golden brown, 20 to 25 minutes more. Let cool completely before serving.

GINGER PIE DOUGH
Makes 1 (9-inch) double crust

3   cups (375 grams) all-purpose flour
3   tablespoons (36 grams) granulated sugar
2   teaspoons (4 grams) ground ginger
1¾   teaspoons (5.25 grams) kosher salt
1   cup (227 grams) cold unsalted butter, cubed
6   tablespoons (90 grams) ice water

1. In the work bowl of a food processor, place flour, sugar, ginger, and salt; pulse until combined, about 4 times. Add cold butter; pulse until butter is pea-size. Add 6 tablespoons (90 grams) ice water; pulse until dough forms large clumps.
2. Turn out dough onto a lightly floured surface. Divide in half, and shape into disks. Wrap tightly in plastic wrap, and refrigerate for at least 1 hour.

SPICED HONEY-OAT PIE

Makes 1 (9-inch) pie

This richly spiced oat pie is a nut-free take on the classic pecan pie, inspired by a brilliant recipe by Southern Baked Pie Company founder Amanda Wilbanks. A gooey oat-packed filling is poured into an aromatic cinnamon piecrust and baked to golden perfection.

Cinnamon Pie Dough (recipe follows)
1⅓   cups (125 grams) old-fashioned oats
⅔   cup (147 grams) firmly packed light brown sugar
1¼   teaspoons (3.75 grams) kosher salt
¼   teaspoon ground ginger
⅛   teaspoon ground nutmeg
½   cup (170 grams) light corn syrup
6   tablespoons (84 grams) unsalted butter, melted
⅓   cup (113 grams) clover honey
1½   tablespoons (19.5 grams) Irish whiskey
2   teaspoons (8 grams) vanilla extract
4   large eggs (200 grams), room temperature
Whiskey Whipped Cream (recipe follows), to serve

1. Preheat oven to 400°F (200°C).
2. Let Cinnamon Pie Dough stand at room temperature until softened, 10 to 15 minutes. On a lightly floured surface, roll dough into a 12-inch circle. Transfer to a 9-inch pie plate, pressing into bottom and up sides. Fold edges under, and crimp, if desired; freeze until firm, about 15 minutes.
3. Top Cinnamon Pie Dough with a piece of parchment paper, letting ends extend over edges of plate. Add pie weights.
4. Bake until edges are lightly golden, 10 to 15 minutes. Carefully remove parchment and weights. Bake until dry and set, about 10 minutes more, lightly covering edges with foil to prevent excess browning, if necessary. Let cool completely on a wire rack. Reduce oven temperature to 350°F (180°C).
5. Line a rimmed baking sheet with parchment paper. Place oats on prepared pan.
6. Bake until lightly toasted, about 10 minutes, stirring occasionally. Let cool completely on pan on a wire rack. Position

oven rack in lower third of oven. Reduce oven temperature to 325°F (170°C).
7. In a large bowl, whisk together brown sugar, salt, ginger, and nutmeg. Add corn syrup, melted butter, honey, whiskey, and vanilla; whisk until well combined. Add eggs, one at a time, whisking well after each addition. Stir in toasted oats; pour filling into prepared crust.
8. Bake until filling is set and slightly puffed and an instant-read thermometer inserted in center registers 200°F (93°C), 40 to 45 minutes, loosely covering crust with foil to prevent excess browning, if necessary. Let cool completely on a wire rack. Serve with Whiskey Whipped Cream.

CINNAMON PIE DOUGH

Makes 1 (9-inch) crust

1½   cups (188 grams) all-purpose flour
1½   tablespoons (18 grams) granulated sugar
1   teaspoon (3 grams) kosher salt
¾   teaspoon (1.5 grams) ground cinnamon
½   cup (113 grams) cold unsalted butter, cubed
3   tablespoons (45 grams) ice water

1. In the work bowl of a food processor, place flour, sugar, salt, and cinnamon; pulse until combined, about 4 times. Add cold butter; pulse until butter is almond-size. Pour 3 tablespoons (45 grams) ice water through food chute in a slow, steady stream. Pulse until dough just forms a ball.
2. Turn out dough onto a lightly floured surface. Shape into a disk; wrap tightly with plastic wrap. Refrigerate for at least 1 hour.

WHISKEY WHIPPED CREAM

Makes about 2½ cups

1   cup (240 grams) cold heavy whipping cream
1½   tablespoons (19.5 grams) Irish whiskey
1   tablespoon (21 grams) clover honey

1. In the bowl of a stand mixer fitted with the whisk attachment, beat all ingredients at medium-high speed until medium-stiff peaks form. Use immediately, or cover and refrigerate until ready to serve.

BLACK FOREST PIE

Makes 1 (9-inch) pie

Recipe by Erin Jeanne McDowell

It's impossible not to love this pie: a thick layer of super-creamy chocolate pudding topped with a thin layer of juicy cherries and plenty of whipped cream. Use black cocoa in a chocolate crust for an especially beautiful result.

Dark Chocolate Black-Bottom Base (recipe follows), still warm
Chocolate All Buttah Pie Dough (recipe follows), blind-baked and cooled completely

Chocolate Filling:
1   cup (228 grams) whole milk
½   cup (118 grams) heavy whipping cream
3   ounces (85 grams) bittersweet chocolate, finely chopped
2   ounces (57 grams) unsweetened chocolate, finely chopped
½   cup (99 grams) granulated sugar
3   tablespoons (21 grams) cornstarch
½   teaspoon (2 grams) fine sea salt
3   large egg yolks (64 grams)
1   tablespoon (14 grams) unsalted butter, room temperature
1   teaspoon (5 grams) vanilla extract

Cherry Topping:
1¼   pounds (567 grams) fresh cherries, pitted and halved
1   tablespoon (15 grams) fresh lemon juice
⅓   cup (66 grams) granulated sugar
2   tablespoons (14 grams) cornstarch
1   teaspoon (5 grams) vanilla extract
¼   teaspoon (2 grams) almond extract

Classic Whipped Cream (recipe follows)
Garnish: whole or halved pitted fresh cherries

1. Pour the warm black-bottom base into the cooled piecrust and spread into an even layer over the bottom.
2. Make the Chocolate Filling: In a medium pot, heat the milk and cream over medium-low heat until the mixture begins to simmer. Turn off the heat, add both chocolates, and stir until fully combined. Turn the heat back on to medium-low and heat, stirring

constantly, until the chocolate is fully melted. Keep warm over low heat.
3. In a medium bowl, whisk the sugar, cornstarch, and salt together to combine. Add the egg yolks and whisk until well combined. Pour about one-quarter of the hot chocolate mixture into the bowl to temper the yolk mixture, whisking constantly. Return this mixture to the pot, whisking, and cook over medium-low heat, stirring constantly with a silicone spatula, until the mixture is very thick and large bubbles break the surface, 2 to 3 minutes.
4. Remove the pot from the heat and stir in the butter and vanilla extract. Strain the pudding into the prepared piecrust and spread into an even layer. Place a piece of plastic wrap directly against the surface and chill until set, 35 to 45 minutes.
5. While the pie sets, make the topping: In a medium pot, toss the cherries and lemon juice to combine. In a small bowl, stir the sugar and cornstarch together to combine. Add this mixture to the cherries and cook over medium heat, stirring constantly, until the cherries are softened but not broken down and the mixture has thickened, about 5 minutes. Stir in the vanilla and almond extracts. Transfer the topping to a shallow baking dish (or rimmed baking sheet) to help it cool quickly to room temperature.
6. Once the Cherry Topping is cool, remove the plastic wrap from the chocolate filling and spoon the cherry mixture over it in an even layer. Return the pie to the refrigerator until ready to serve.
7. When ready to serve, spread or pipe the whipped cream evenly over the pie and garnish with cherries.

CHOCOLATE ALL BUTTAH PIE DOUGH
Makes 1 (9-inch) crust

1   cup (125 grams) all-purpose flour
⅓   cup (28 grams) unsweetened cocoa powder
¼   teaspoon (1 gram) fine sea salt
8   tablespoons (113 grams) cold unsalted butter, cut into ½-inch cubes
¼   cup (57 grams) ice water, plus more as needed

1. In a large bowl, whisk together the flour, cocoa, and salt. Add the cubed butter, tossing the cubes through the flour until each individual piece is well coated. "Cut" the butter into the flour by pressing the pieces between your fingers, flattening the cubes into big shards. As you work, continue to toss the butter through the flour, recoating the shingled pieces.
2. Continue cutting the butter into the flour just until the pieces of butter are about the size of walnut halves.
3. Make a well in the center of the flour mixture. Add the amount of ice water listed in the recipe to the well, but have more on hand. Use a tossing motion with your hands to start to mix the two together (this begins to combine them without creating too much gluten). As it begins to become hydrated, you can start to use more of a kneading motion, but don't overdo it, as this will make the dough tough. Add more water, about 1 tablespoon (14 grams) at a time, until the dough is properly hydrated. It should be uniformly combined and hold together easily, but it won't look totally smooth. Dough that is too dry may have sort of a "dusty" appearance or pockets of un-hydrated flour. It will not hold together and will appear crumbly. Dough that is too wet will feel sticky or tacky to the touch and is often smoother and/or lighter in color.
4. Form the dough into an even disk (or if you are multiplying the recipe to make multiple crusts, divide the dough appropriately). Wrap tightly in plastic wrap and refrigerate for at least 30 minutes or up to 2 days. (We suggest chilling overnight.)
5. To Roll Out the Dough: Lightly dust a work surface with flour, and lightly dust a rolling pin, if desired. Roll out the dough to about ¼ inch thick, rotating it as you work to help prevent it from sticking. To transfer the dough to the pan, gently roll it up, wrapping it around the pin and then unfurl it into the pie plate.
6. To Prepare the Edge for Crimping: On a single-crust pie, use scissors to trim away the excess dough, leaving about ½ inch excess all the way around the outside edge of the pie plate. Tuck this excess dough under, pressing gently to make it flush with

the edge of the pie plate. On a double-crust pie, gently press the top and bottom crusts together to flatten the dough slightly and then trim the excess and tuck under as directed for a single-crust pie.

7. To Par-Bake the Dough: Dock the crimped single-crust pie dough with a fork and chill well (at least 30 minutes). Cut a square of parchment paper slightly larger than the diameter of a pie plate, and press it into the base of the pie plate. Fill with pie weights to the top inner rim of the pie plate. Bake in a 425°F (220°C) oven until the edges begin to lightly brown, 15 to 17 minutes. Remove the parchment paper and pie weights, and return to the oven until the lower portion of the crust appears dry and set, 2 to 3 minutes more. Cool completely before filling.

8. To Blind-Bake the Dough: Follow the instructions for par-baking, but bake until it is fully golden brown. After removing the pie weights, bake for 5 to 7 minutes. Cool completely before filling.

DARK CHOCOLATE BLACK-BOTTOM BASE
Makes 1½ cups (185 grams)

Black-bottom bases, which are just a simple ganache, not only add a punch of chocolaty flavor, but they also help protect the crust from moisture from a wet filling (like custard or a cream filling).

¾ cup (113 grams) finely chopped 72% cacao dark chocolate
⅓ cup (78 grams) heavy whipping cream

1. Place the chocolate in a medium heatproof bowl. In a small saucepan, bring the cream to a boil over medium heat. Pour the hot cream over the chocolate and let sit for 15 seconds undisturbed; stir gently until the ganache is thick and smooth.
2. To use, pour the ganache into the bottom of a cooled par-baked piecrust and spread into an even layer. Let set for 15 to 20 minutes before adding the filling.

CLASSIC WHIPPED CREAM
Makes 3 cups (283 grams)

1 cup (235 grams) heavy whipping cream
¼ cup (50 grams) granulated sugar
1 teaspoon (5 grams) vanilla extract

1. In the bowl of a stand mixer fitted with the whip attachment, whip the cream on medium-low speed until it begins to thicken, 1 to 2 minutes. Increase the speed to medium and add the sugar in a slow, steady stream, then continue to whip to medium peaks. Add the vanilla, if using, and mix to combine.

Photo by Mark Weinberg

MAKE AHEAD AND STORAGE
The crust can be blind-baked up to 1 day ahead. The pie can be made up to 1 day ahead; cover pie in plastic wrap, and store in refrigerator. Keep in mind that it's best to add the Classic Whipped Cream just before serving. Refrigerate leftovers in an airtight container for up to 2 days.

BLUEBERRY LEMON MERINGUE PIE

Makes 1 (9-inch) pie

Recipe by Erin Jeanne McDowell

Why decide between sweet, juicy blueberry pie and tart, toasty lemon meringue when you can have both?

Blueberry Filling:
3½ cups (595 grams) fresh blueberries, divided
1 tablespoon (15 grams) fresh lemon juice
½ cup (100 grams) granulated sugar, divided
¼ cup (30 grams) all-purpose flour
¼ teaspoon (1 gram) fine sea salt
1 tablespoon (14 grams) unsalted butter
1 teaspoon (5 grams) vanilla extract

All Buttah Pie Dough (recipe follows), par-baked and cooled

Lemon Curd Filling:
¾ cup (150 grams) granulated sugar
¼ cup (28 grams) cornstarch
6 tablespoons (85 grams) unsalted butter
1 cup (226 grams) fresh lemon juice (about 5 to 6 lemons)
6 large egg yolks (128 grams)
¼ teaspoon (1 gram) fine sea salt

Mile-High Meringue Topping:
4 large egg whites (142 grams)
1 cup (198 grams) granulated sugar
2 teaspoons (10 grams) vanilla extract (optional)
½ teaspoon (2 grams) cream of tartar
Large pinch fine sea salt

1. For blueberry filling: In a medium saucepan, toss together 2½ cups (495 grams) blueberries, ¼ cup (50 grams) sugar, and lemon juice. Cook over medium-low heat, stirring occasionally, until berries start to break down and become juicy, 8 to 10 minutes. Using a potato masher, coarsely mash berries a few times.
2. In a small bowl, whisk together flour, salt, and remaining ¼ cup (50 grams) sugar. Sprinkle flour mixture onto blueberry mixture, and stir until well combined. Bring to a boil, stirring constantly, and cook for 1 minute. Turn off heat, and stir in butter and vanilla.

3. Using an immersion blender, purée blueberry mixture until relatively smooth. (Alternatively, transfer to a blender or food processor, and process until relatively smooth.) Stir in remaining 1 cup (170 grams) blueberries. Let cool completely. (To cool quickly, pour blueberry filling onto a rimmed baking sheet.)
4. Preheat oven to 400°F (200°C).
5. On a parchment paper-lined baking sheet, place par-baked All Buttah Pie Dough crust. Pour cooled blueberry filling into prepared crust, and spread into an even layer.
6. Bake until crust is deeply golden and filling is bubbly and has a matte surface, 30 to 35 minutes. Let cool completely.
7. For lemon curd filling: In a small bowl, whisk together sugar and cornstarch until combined.
8. In a medium saucepan, melt butter over medium heat. Reduce heat to medium-low, and add sugar mixture, lemon juice, egg yolks, and salt. Cook, whisking constantly, until mixture begins to thicken, 15 to 18 minutes. Cook, stirring constantly with a silicone spatula (be sure to get into edges and corners of pot), until thickened and large bubbles begin to break surface in center of pan, 2 to 3 minutes.
9. Strain lemon curd filling through a fine-mesh sieve into cooled prepared crust, and spread into an even layer on top of blueberry filling. Cover with a piece of plastic wrap, pressing wrap directly onto surface of lemon curd filling to prevent a skin from forming. Refrigerate until completely cool, at least 4 hours or up to 24 hours.
10. For mile-high meringue topping: In the heatproof bowl of a stand mixer, whisk together egg whites, sugar, vanilla (if using), cream of tartar, and salt. Place bowl over a saucepan of simmering water, and cook, whisking constantly, until an instant-read thermometer registers 160°F (71°C).
11. Return bowl to stand mixer. Using the whisk attachment, beat at medium-high speed until stiff peaks form, 4 to 5 minutes.
12. Pile meringue on top of cooled pie. Spread meringue to edges, but keep it piled a bit higher in center. Using a handheld kitchen torch, carefully brown meringue before serving, if desired.

All Buttah Pie Dough
Makes 1 (9-inch) crust

This is my go-to pie dough. I learned to make pie dough using butter and shortening or lard, but when it came time to choose my one and only fat, it's all buttah, all the time. The flavor and flakiness butter gives piecrust just can't be beat. This recipe doubles (and even triples or quadruples) well if you're making a double crust pie or want additional dough for decorative effects.

1¼ cups (151 grams) all-purpose flour
¼ teaspoon (1 gram) fine sea salt
8 tablespoons (113 grams) cold unsalted butter, cut into ½-inch cubes
¼ cup (57 grams) ice water, plus more as needed

1. In a large bowl, whisk together the flour and salt. Add the cubed butter, tossing the cubes through the flour until each individual piece is well coated. "Cut" the butter into the flour by pressing the pieces between your fingers, flattening the cubes into big shards. As you work, continue to toss the butter through the flour, recoating the shingled pieces.
2. Continue cutting the butter into the flour just until the pieces of butter are about the size of walnut halves.
3. Make a well in the center of the flour mixture. Add the amount of ice water listed in the recipe to the well, but have more on hand. Use a tossing motion with your hands to start to mix the two together (this begins to combine them without creating too much gluten). As it begins to become hydrated, you can start to use more of a kneading motion, but don't overdo it, as this will make the dough tough. Add more water, about 1 tablespoon (14 grams) at a time, until the dough is properly hydrated. It should be uniformly combined and hold together easily, but it won't look totally smooth. Dough that is too dry may have sort of a "dusty" appearance or pockets of un-hydrated flour. It will not hold together and will appear crumbly. Dough that is too wet will feel sticky or tacky to the touch and is often smoother and/or lighter in color.
4. Form the dough into an even disk (or if you are multiplying the recipe to make multiple

crusts, divide the dough appropriately). Wrap tightly in plastic wrap and refrigerate for at least 30 minutes or up to 2 days. (We suggest chilling overnight.)

5. To Roll Out the Dough: Lightly dust a work surface with flour, and lightly dust a rolling pin, if desired. Roll out the dough to about ¼ inch thick, rotating it as you work to help prevent it from sticking. To transfer the dough to the pan, gently roll it up, wrapping it around the pin and then unfurl it into the pie plate.

6. To Prepare the Edge for Crimping: On a single-crust pie, use scissors to trim away the excess dough, leaving about ½ inch excess all the way around the outside edge of the pie plate. Tuck this excess dough under, pressing gently to make it flush with the edge of the pie plate. On a double-crust pie, gently press the top and bottom crusts together to flatten the dough slightly and then trim the excess and tuck under as directed for a single-crust pie.

7. To Par-Bake the Dough: Dock the crimped single-crust pie dough with a fork and chill well (at least 30 minutes). Cut a square of parchment paper slightly larger than the diameter of a pie plate, and press it into the base of the pie plate. Fill with pie weights to the top inner rim of the pie plate. Bake in a 425°F (220°C) oven until the edges begin to lightly brown, 15 to 17 minutes. Remove the parchment paper and pie weights, and return to the oven until the lower portion of the crust appears dry and set, 2 to 3 minutes more. Cool completely before filling.

8. To Blind-Bake the Dough: Follow the instructions for par-baking, but bake until it is fully golden brown. After removing the pie weights, bake for 5 to 7 minutes. Cool completely before filling.

Photo by Mark Weinberg

MAKE AHEAD AND STORAGE
The crust can be par-baked up to 1 day ahead. The blueberry filling can be made up to 2 days ahead; refrigerate in an airtight container. The pie can be made up to 1 day ahead; cover pie in plastic wrap, and store in refrigerator. Keep in mind that it's best to add the meringue just before serving. Refrigerate leftovers in an airtight container for up to 2 days.

BANANA COCONUT CREAM PIE

Makes 1 (9-inch) pie

Recipe by Erin Jeanne McDowell

Coconut cream pie meets banana pudding in one glorious whipped cream-topped beauty. Half the coconut custard is poured into the toasted coconut piecrust and topped with a layer of vanilla wafers before being covered with even more custard filling. After chilling, bananas and plenty of whipped cream round out this ultimate cream pie.

1 **(13.5-ounce) can (383 grams) coconut milk**
1 **cup (226 grams) whole milk**
2 **cups (468 grams) heavy whipping cream, divided**
¾ **cup (149 grams) plus ⅓ cup (66 grams) granulated sugar, divided**
1 **vanilla bean, split lengthwise, seeds scraped and reserved**
⅓ **cup (37 grams) cornstarch**
½ **teaspoon (2 grams) fine sea salt**
3 **large egg yolks (64 grams)**
1 **large egg (56 grams)**
2 **tablespoons (28 grams) unsalted butter**
1¼ **cups (88 grams) toasted unsweetened flaked coconut, divided**
2 **teaspoons (10 grams) vanilla extract, divided**
Toasted Coconut Pie Dough (recipe follows), blind-baked and cooled completely
25 **vanilla wafers (100 grams), divided**
2 to 3 **medium bananas (310 grams), very thinly sliced and divided**

1. In a medium stockpot, heat coconut milk, whole milk, ½ cup (115 grams) cream, ¼ cup (50 grams) sugar, and reserved vanilla bean seeds over medium heat just until bubbles form around edges of pot. (Do not boil.)
2. In a medium bowl, whisk together ½ cup (99 grams) sugar, cornstarch, and salt until combined. Whisk in egg yolks and egg until well combined.
3. Pour about one-fourth of hot coconut milk mixture into sugar mixture, whisking constantly. Pour sugar mixture into remaining hot coconut milk mixture in pot, whisking

constantly. Reduce heat to medium-low, and cook, stirring constantly with a silicone spatula, until thickened and large bubbles begin to break surface in center of pot. Remove from heat, and stir in butter until melted and mixture is smooth. Stir in 1 cup (70 grams) flaked coconut and 1 teaspoon (5 grams) vanilla. Pour about half of mixture into cooled blind-baked Toasted Coconut Pie Dough, and spread into an even layer. Arrange about 20 vanilla wafers on top of filling in a single layer. Pour remaining filling on top of vanilla wafers, and spread into an even layer. Cover with a piece of plastic wrap, pressing wrap directly onto surface of filling to prevent a skin from forming, and refrigerate until completely cool and set, at least 4 hours or up to 24 hours.
4. Arrange about two-thirds of banana slices in an even layer on top of pie, overlapping each slice. Crumble remaining vanilla wafers, and sprinkle on top of banana slices in an even layer.
5. In the bowl of a stand mixer fitted with the whisk attachment, beat remaining 1½ cups (353 grams) cream, remaining ⅓ cup (66 grams) sugar, and remaining 1 teaspoon (5 grams) vanilla at medium speed until medium peaks form, 2 to 3 minutes. Spread, spoon, or pipe whipped cream on top of pie. Top with remaining ¼ cup (18 grams) flaked coconut and remaining banana slices. Refrigerate until ready to serve.

Toasted Coconut Pie Dough

Makes 1 (9-inch) crust

1¼ **cups (151 grams) all-purpose flour**
¼ **teaspoon (1 gram) fine sea salt**
8 **tablespoons (113 grams) cold unsalted butter, cut into ½-inch cubes**
⅓ **cup (38 grams) toasted unsweeted flaked coconut**
¼ **cup (57 grams) ice water, plus more as needed**

1. In a large bowl, whisk together the flour and salt. Add the cubed butter, tossing the cubes through the flour until each individual piece is well coated. 'Cut' the butter into the flour by pressing the pieces between your fingers,

flattening the cubes into big shards. As you work, continue to toss the butter through the flour, recoating the shingled pieces.
2. Continue cutting the butter into the flour just until the pieces of butter are about the size of walnut halves. Stir in coconut.
3. Make a well in the center of the flour mixture. Add the amount of ice water listed in the recipe to the well, but have more on hand. Use a tossing motion with your hands to start to mix the two together (this begins to combine them without creating too much gluten). As it begins to become hydrated, you can start to use more of a kneading motion, but don't overdo it, as this will make the dough tough. Add more water, about 1 tablespoon (14 grams) at a time, until the dough is properly hydrated. It should be uniformly combined and hold together easily, but it won't look totally smooth. Dough that is too dry may have sort of a "dusty" appearance or pockets of un-hydrated flour. It will not hold together and will appear crumbly. Dough that is too wet will feel sticky or tacky to the touch and is often smoother and/or lighter in color.
4. Form the dough into an even disk (or if you are multiplying the recipe to make multiple crusts, divide the dough appropriately). Wrap tightly in plastic wrap and refrigerate for at least 30 minutes or up to 2 days. (We suggest chilling overnight.)
5. To Roll Out the Dough: Lightly dust a work surface with flour, and lightly dust a rolling pin, if desired. Roll out the dough to about ¼ inch thick, rotating it as you work to help prevent it from sticking. To transfer the dough to the pan, gently roll it up, wrapping it around the pin and then unfurl it into the pie plate.
6. To Prepare the Edge for Crimping: On a single-crust pie, use scissors to trim away the excess dough, leaving about ½ inch excess all the way around the outside edge of the pie plate. Tuck this excess dough under, pressing gently to make it flush with the edge of the pie plate. On a double-crust pie, gently press the top and bottom crusts together to flatten the dough slightly and then trim the excess and tuck under as directed for a single-crust pie.

7. To Par-Bake the Dough: Dock the crimped single-crust pie dough with a fork and chill well (at least 30 minutes). Cut a square of parchment paper slightly larger than the diameter of a pie plate, and press it into the base of the pie plate. Fill with pie weights to the top inner rim of the pie plate. Bake in a 425°F (220°C) oven until the edges begin to lightly brown, 15 to 17 minutes. Remove the parchment paper and pie weights, and return to the oven until the lower portion of the crust appears dry and set, 2 to 3 minutes more. Cool completely before filling.

8. To Blind-Bake the Dough: Follow the instructions for par-baking, but bake until it is fully golden brown. After removing the pie weights, bake for 5 to 7 minutes. Cool completely before filling.

Photo by Mark Weinberg

PRO TIP

Butter can be harder for beginners to work with, because it has a lower melting point than fats such as shortening. Once you know how to handle the dough, it's easy. The key? Colder is always better when pie dough is involved. When in doubt, toss everything (the ingredients, the bowl, and maybe even the half-mixed dough) into the fridge before proceeding.

MAKE AHEAD AND STORAGE

The crust can be blind-baked up to 1 day ahead. The pie can be made up to 1 day ahead; cover pie in plastic wrap, and store in refrigerator. Keep in mind that it's best to add the whipped cream just before serving. Refrigerate leftovers in an airtight container for up to 2 days.

MILE-HIGH CREAMY APPLE PIE

Makes 1 (9-inch) pie

Recipe by Erin Jeanne McDowell

Pre-cooking is the key to this rich, caramelly apple pie filling. It starts with browned butter and dark brown sugar, but the stovetop time does more than meld the flavors together—it also pulls moisture from the apples to ensure the filling is ultimately thick enough when sliced. But the really special element doesn't happen until the pie is nearly done baking, when a super simple custard is slowly poured into the pie through the vents in the top crust, melding with the apple filling inside to create a deliciously creamy combo.

Apple Filling:

6	tablespoons (85 grams) unsalted butter
18	cups (2,137 grams) diced peeled apples (about 16 medium apples, such as Honeycrisp)
1	cup (212 grams) firmly packed dark muscovado or dark brown sugar
2	tablespoons (30 grams) fresh lemon juice
1½	tablespoons (5 grams) ground cinnamon
2	teaspoons (10 grams) vanilla extract
1	teaspoon (4 grams) fine sea salt
½	teaspoon (1 gram) freshly grated nutmeg
⅔	cup (80 grams) all-purpose flour
⅔	cup (132 grams) granulated sugar
2	recipes Cinnamon Pie Dough (recipe follows), prepared, shaped into 2 disks, wrapped well, and chilled
1	large egg (56 grams)
1	tablespoon (15 grams) water

Turbinado sugar, for sprinkling

Custard Filling:

1	cup (235 grams) heavy whipping cream
3	tablespoons (37 grams) granulated sugar
1	large egg (56 grams)
1	large egg yolk (21 grams)
1	teaspoon (5 grams) vanilla extract

Sweetened whipped cream, to serve

1. For apple filling: In a large stockpot, melt butter over medium heat. Reduce heat to low, and cook, stirring occasionally, until butter solids are golden and nutty in aroma, 4 to 5 minutes. Add apples, muscovado or brown sugar, lemon juice, cinnamon, vanilla, salt, and nutmeg, and toss well to combine. Cook, stirring frequently, until smooth and glossy, 4 to 5 minutes.

2. In a medium bowl, whisk together flour and granulated sugar. Sprinkle flour mixture onto apple mixture, and stir well to combine. Increase heat to medium, and cook, stirring constantly, until mixture is thickened and begins to boil. Transfer to a large bowl, cover, and let cool completely. (The apple filling can be prepared and refrigerated for up to 2 days. We suggest chilling overnight).

3. On a lightly floured surface, roll half of Cinnamon Pie Dough to about ¼-inch thickness. Transfer to a 9-inch pie plate, pressing into bottom and up sides. Trim dough to ½ inch beyond edge of plate. Spoon cooled apple filling into prepared crust, mounding it slightly higher in center. Refrigerate.

4. On a lightly floured surface, roll remaining Cinnamon Pie Dough to about ¼-inch thickness. Place on top of apple filling. Using your fingers, press top and bottom crusts together all the way around pie; trim dough to ½ inch beyond edge of plate. Fold edges under, and crimp, if desired. Refrigerate for at least 30 minutes or up to 1 hour.

5. Place a baking steel or baking stone on bottom rack of oven. Preheat oven to 400°F (200°C).

6. Line a baking sheet with foil. Place pie on prepared pan (to catch any spillage), and place on middle rack in oven.

7. In a small bowl, whisk together egg and 1 tablespoon (15 grams) water. Brush egg wash onto center of pie, and generously sprinkle with turbinado sugar. Using a sharp paring knife, cut 4 to 5 vents (about 1½ inches long) across center of pie.

8. Bake for 25 minutes. Reduce oven temperature to 375°F (190°C), and bake until crust is deeply golden brown and filling bubbles up through vents, 40 to 45 minutes more.

9. Meanwhile, for custard filling: In a 2-cup liquid-measuring cup, whisk together cream, granulated sugar, egg, egg yolk, and vanilla.

10. Gradually pour custard filling into pie through vents. (It will take a bit of time to "soak" into pie, so add a little into one vent and then move on to another. Continue pouring, bit by bit, until all custard filling has been added.) Bake for 15 to 17 minutes more, covering with foil to prevent excess browning, if necessary. Let cool completely before serving.

CINNAMON PIE DOUGH
Makes 1 (9-inch) crust

1¼	cups (151 grams) all-purpose flour
2	teaspoons (4 grams) ground cinnamon
¼	teaspoon (1 gram) fine sea salt
8	tablespoons (113 grams) cold unsalted butter, cut into ½-inch cubes
¼	cup (57 grams) ice water, plus more as needed

1. In a large bowl, whisk together the flour, cinnamon, and salt. Add the cubed butter, tossing the cubes through the flour until each individual piece is well coated. 'Cut' the butter into the flour by pressing the pieces between your fingers, flattening the cubes into big shards. As you work, continue to toss the butter through the flour, recoating the shingled pieces.

2. Continue cutting the butter into the flour just until the pieces of butter are about the size of walnut halves.

3. Make a well in the center of the flour mixture. Add the amount of ice water listed in the recipe to the well, but have more on hand. Use a tossing motion with your hands to start to mix the two together (this begins to combine them without creating too much gluten). As it begins to become hydrated, you can start to use more of a kneading motion, but don't overdo it, as this will make the dough tough. Add more water, about 1 tablespoon (14 grams) at a time, until the dough is properly hydrated. It should be uniformly combined and hold together easily, but it won't look totally smooth. Dough that is too dry may have sort of a "dusty" appearance or pockets of un-hydrated flour. It will not hold together and will appear crumbly. Dough that is too wet will feel sticky or tacky to the touch and is often smoother and/or lighter in color.

4. Form the dough into an even disk (or if you are multiplying the recipe to make multiple crusts, divide the dough appropriately). Wrap tightly in plastic wrap and refrigerate for at least 30 minutes or up to 2 days. (We suggest chilling overnight.)

5. To Roll Out the Dough: Lightly dust a work surface with flour, and lightly dust a rolling pin, if desired. Roll out the dough to about ¼ inch thick, rotating it as you work to help prevent it from sticking. To transfer the dough to the pan, gently roll it up, wrapping it around the pin and then unfurl it into the pie plate.

6. To Prepare the Edge for Crimping: On a single-crust pie, use scissors to trim away the excess dough, leaving about ½ inch excess all the way around the outside edge of the pie plate. Tuck this excess dough under, pressing gently to make it flush with the edge of the pie plate. On a double-crust pie, gently press the top and bottom crusts together to flatten the dough slightly and then trim the excess and tuck under as directed for a single-crust pie.

7. To Par-Bake the Dough: Dock the crimped single-crust pie dough with a fork and chill well (at least 30 minutes). Cut a square of parchment paper slightly larger than the diameter of a pie plate, and press it into the base of the pie plate. Fill with pie weights to the top inner rim of the pie plate. Bake in a 425°F (220°C) oven until the edges begin to lightly brown, 15 to 17 minutes. Remove the parchment paper and pie weights, and return to the oven until the lower portion of the crust appears dry and set, 2 to 3 minutes more. Cool completely before filling.

8. To Blind-Bake the Dough: Follow the instructions for par-baking, but bake until it is fully golden brown. After removing the pie weights, bake for 5 to 7 minutes. Cool completely before filling.

Photo by Mark Weinberg

PRO TIP

The pie is best eaten the same day it's made. If there are leftovers, though, wrap them in plastic wrap, and store at room temperature for up to 2 days.

STRAWBERRIES & CREAM PIE

Makes 1 (9-inch) pie

Double-crusted and jam-packed with strawberries, this pie is delicious with a generous scoop of freshly whipped cream.

Pie Dough (recipe follows), divided
6   cups (882 grams) ½-inch-diced fresh strawberries
½   cup (100 grams) granulated sugar
½   cup (60 grams) tapioca flour
2   teaspoons (2 grams) lemon zest
1   tablespoon (15 grams) lemon juice
2   teaspoons (12 grams) vanilla bean paste
1   large egg (50 grams)
1   tablespoon (15 grams) water
Sparkling sugar, for sprinkling
Vanilla Whipped Cream (recipe follows)
Garnish: halved fresh strawberries

1. Preheat oven to 425°F (220°C). Spray a 9-inch pie plate with baking spray with flour.
2. On a lightly floured surface, roll half of Pie Dough into a 12-inch circle. Transfer to prepared plate, pressing into bottom and up sides. Trim edges to ¼ inch past rim of plate, if necessary.
3. In a large bowl, toss together strawberries, granulated sugar, flour, lemon zest and juice, and vanilla bean paste. Let stand for 10 minutes, stirring occasionally. Pour into prepared crust.
4. On a lightly floured surface, roll remaining Pie Dough into a 12-inch circle. Cut into 1-inch-wide strips. Place 6 dough strips horizontally on pie, spacing evenly apart. Fold back alternating strips, and place 1 dough strip vertically across horizontal strips; unfold folded strips. Fold back alternating horizontal strips, and place another vertical strip across first strips, spacing evenly. Unfold horizontal folded strips and then fold back alternating horizontal strips. Place another vertical strip across first strips, spacing evenly. Unfold horizontal folded strips. Repeat with remaining vertical strips. Press strips into bottom crust, and trim strips even with bottom crust. Fold edges under, and crimp, if desired. Freeze for 10 minutes.
5. In a small bowl, whisk together egg and 1 tablespoon (15 grams) water until smooth. Brush onto prepared crust. Sprinkle with sparkling sugar. Place pie on a parchment-lined baking sheet.

6. Bake for 15 minutes. Reduce oven temperature to 350°F (180°C), and bake until filling is bubbly in center, 1 hour and 30 minutes to 1 hour and 35 minutes, covering with foil after 30 minutes of baking to prevent excess browning. Let cool completely before serving. Serve with Vanilla Whipped Cream. Garnish with halved strawberries, if desired.

PIE DOUGH
Makes 1 (9-inch) double crust

3   cups (375 grams) all-purpose flour
2   tablespoons (24 grams) granulated sugar
1½ teaspoons (4.5 grams) kosher salt
1   cup (227 grams) cold unsalted butter, cubed
8 to 9 tablespoons (120 to 135 grams) ice water

1. In the work bowl of a food processor, pulse together flour, sugar, and salt until combined. Add cold butter, and pulse until mixture is crumbly. With processor running, add 8 tablespoons (120 grams) ice water in a slow, steady stream just until dough comes together. (Mixture may appear crumbly. It should be moist and hold together when pinched. Add remaining 1 tablespoon [15 grams] ice water, if needed.)
2. Turn out dough; divide in half (about 386 grams each), and shape into disks. Wrap tightly in plastic wrap, and refrigerate for at least 30 minutes. Dough can be refrigerated for up to 3 days or frozen for up to 2 months.

VANILLA WHIPPED CREAM
Makes about 1 cup

½   cup (120 grams) cold heavy whipping cream
1   tablespoon (12 grams) granulated sugar
½   teaspoon (3 grams) vanilla bean paste

1. In a medium bowl, whisk together all ingredients until soft to medium peaks form. Refrigerate until ready to use.

TARTS

From a classically round sweet potato tart mounded with clouds of toasted meringue to a square savory pretzel tart brimming with beer cheese, these tarts come in all shapes and sizes to satisfy every craving

CHOCOLATE-PECAN TART

Makes 1 (9-inch) tart

In this sophisticated take on classic pecan pie, pecans add nuttiness to the shortbread crust and make the chocolate-studded filling all the more indulgent.

1¼ cups (156 grams) plus 3 tablespoons (24 grams) all-purpose flour, divided
½ cup (113 grams) cold unsalted butter, cubed
⅓ cup (40 grams) confectioners' sugar
¼ cup (28 grams) chopped pecans*
1¾ teaspoons (5.25 grams) kosher salt, divided
1 cup (220 grams) firmly packed dark brown sugar
½ cup (170 grams) light corn syrup
⅓ cup (113 grams) clover honey
2 large eggs (100 grams), room temperature
1 large egg white (30 grams), room temperature
2 tablespoons (26 grams) vanilla extract
1 tablespoon (14 grams) unsalted butter, melted

1¼ cups (141 grams) pecan halves*
¼ cup (43 grams) plus 1 tablespoon (11 grams) 46% cacao semisweet chocolate chips, divided
Whipped cream, to serve
Garnish: flaked sea salt

1. Position oven rack in center of oven. Preheat oven to 350°F (180°C). Spray a 9-inch fluted round removable-bottom tart pan with baking spray with flour.
2. In the work bowl of a food processor, combine 1¼ cups (156 grams) flour, cold butter, confectioners' sugar, chopped pecans, and ½ teaspoon (1.5 grams) kosher salt. Pulse until mixture forms large clumps and holds together when pinched between fingers. Press mixture into bottom and up sides of prepared pan. Freeze for 15 minutes.
3. Top crust with a piece of parchment paper, letting ends extend over edges of pan. Add pie weights.
4. Bake until edges are lightly golden, 15 to 18 minutes. Let cool on a wire rack for 10 minutes. Carefully remove parchment

and weights; bake until bottom of crust is dry and set, 5 to 8 minutes more. Let cool completely on a wire rack. Leave oven on.
5. In a medium bowl, whisk together brown sugar, remaining 3 tablespoons (24 grams) flour, and remaining 1¼ teaspoons (3.75 grams) kosher salt until well combined. Beat in corn syrup, honey, eggs, egg white, vanilla, and melted butter. Scatter pecan halves and ¼ cup (43 grams) chocolate chips in prepared crust; pour sugar mixture over pecans and chocolate. Sprinkle with remaining 1 tablespoon (11 grams) chocolate chips, gently patting into filling.
6. Bake until crust is golden brown, filling is set, and an instant-read thermometer inserted in center registers 200°F (93°C), about 45 minutes, loosely covering with foil to prevent excess browning, if necessary. Let cool completely on a wire rack. Serve with whipped cream. Garnish with sea salt, if desired.

We used Sunnyland Farms Raw Georgia Pecan Halves.

SWEET EGG TARTS

Makes 8 (2½-inch) tarts

We kept our egg tarts simple and classic to the Hong Kong formula, with a tender pâte sucrée crust holding a glistening custard filling.

⅓   cup (76 grams) unsalted butter, softened

¼   cup (30 grams) confectioners' sugar

½   teaspoon kosher salt, divided

4   large egg yolks (75 grams), room temperature and divided

¾   teaspoon (3 grams) vanilla extract, divided

1   cup (125 grams) all-purpose flour

¼   cup (31 grams) unbleached cake flour

¼   cup (60 grams) water

2½   tablespoons (30 grams) granulated sugar

2½   tablespoons (37.5 grams) evaporated milk

1. In the bowl of a stand mixer fitted with the paddle attachment, beat butter, confectioners' sugar, and ¼ teaspoon salt at medium speed until creamy, 1 to 2 minutes, stopping to scrape sides of bowl. Add 1 egg yolk (19 grams); beat until well combined. Beat in ¼ teaspoon (1 gram) vanilla.

2. In a medium bowl, whisk together flours. With mixer on low speed, gradually add flour mixture to butter mixture, beating just until a dough forms.

3. Spray 8 (2½-inch) fluted round tart pans with baking spray with flour; place on a rimmed baking sheet.

4. Divide dough into 8 portions (about 35 grams each), and shape into balls. Press 1 dough ball into bottom and up sides of 1 prepared tart pan; trim any excess dough. Repeat with remaining dough and remaining prepared tart pans.

5. In a medium bowl, whisk together remaining 3 egg yolks (56 grams).

6. In a small saucepan, combine ¼ cup (60 grams) water, granulated sugar, evaporated milk, remaining ½ teaspoon (2 grams) vanilla, and remaining ¼ teaspoon salt. Cook over medium heat until mixture is steaming and sugar dissolves. Gradually whisk sugar mixture into egg yolks until well combined.

7. Position oven rack in lower third of oven. Preheat oven to 400°F (200°C).

8. Place a fine-mesh sieve over a large liquid-measuring cup or widemouthed pitcher. Strain egg yolk mixture through prepared sieve; discard any solids. Divide strained mixture among prepared crusts (about 18 grams each).

9. Bake until crust is lightly browned, 10 to 12 minutes, rotating pans halfway through baking. Reduce oven temperature to 350°F (180°C). Bake just until edges of filling start to puff, about 5 minutes more. Open oven door about 2 inches; bake until filling is set, a wooden pick inserted in center stands up straight, and an instant-read thermometer inserted in center registers at least 175°F (79°C), 5 to 7 minutes more. Let cool in pans for 15 minutes. Serve warm or at room temperature.

SILKY CHOCOLATE TART

Makes 1 (9-inch) tart

Inspired by French silk pie, this tangy tart receives a triple boost of cream cheese in its crust, filling, and whipped topping.

Crust:
½   cup (113 grams) unsalted butter, softened
⅓   cup plus 2 teaspoons (85 grams) cream cheese, softened
1   cup (125 grams) all-purpose flour
½   teaspoon (1.5 grams) kosher salt

Filling:
¼   cup (50 grams) granulated sugar
¼   cup (55 grams) firmly packed light brown sugar
2   large eggs (100 grams)
2.5 ounces (71 grams) 64% cacao semisweet chocolate baking bars, finely chopped
1   teaspoon (2 grams) instant espresso powder
¼   teaspoon kosher salt
¼   cup (57 grams) unsalted butter, softened
¼   cup (56 grams) cream cheese, softened
1¼   cups (300 grams) cold heavy whipping cream
1   tablespoon (20 grams) coffee liqueur*

Topping:
3   ounces (86 grams) cream cheese, softened
⅓   cup (67 grams) granulated sugar
1   cup (240 grams) cold heavy whipping cream

Garnish: chocolate shavings

1. For crust: In the bowl of a stand mixer fitted with the paddle attachment, beat butter and cream cheese at medium speed until smooth. With mixer on low speed, gradually add flour and salt, beating until combined. Turn out dough onto a lightly floured surface, and shape into a disk. Wrap in plastic wrap, and refrigerate for at least 1 hour.

2. Preheat oven to 350°F (180°C). Lightly spray a 1-inch-tall 9½-inch fluted round removable-bottom tart pan with cooking spray.

3. Let dough stand at room temperature until slightly softened, about 10 minutes. On a lightly floured surface, roll dough into a 12- to 13-inch circle (about ⅛ inch thick). Transfer to prepared pan, pressing into bottom and up sides. Trim excess dough.

Using a fork, prick bottom and sides of dough. Freeze until firm, about 15 minutes.

4. Lightly spray a piece of parchment paper with cooking spray; top dough with parchment, spray side down, letting ends extend over edges of pan. Add pie weights.

5. Bake until edges are lightly golden and set, about 20 minutes. Carefully remove parchment and weights. Bake until crust is golden brown, 10 to 15 minutes more, pricking bottom and sides with a fork again and gently pressing down center of crust if needed. (It's OK if crust shrinks slightly in pan.) Let cool completely in pan on a wire rack.

6. For filling: In the top of a double boiler, whisk together sugars and eggs. Cook over simmering water, stirring frequently, until mixture is thick enough to coat the back of a spoon and an instant-read thermometer registers 160°F (71°C), 5 to 10 minutes. Add chocolate, espresso powder, and salt, stirring until smooth and well combined. Remove from heat; let cool for 10 minutes.

7. Meanwhile, in the bowl of a stand mixer fitted with the paddle attachment, beat butter at medium speed until creamy, 30 seconds to 1 minute, stopping to scrape sides of bowl. Add cream cheese; beat until smooth and well combined, about 30 seconds, stopping to scrape sides of bowl. Beat in cooled chocolate mixture until well combined, stopping to scrape sides of bowl. Transfer mixture to a large bowl.

8. Clean bowl of stand mixer. Using the whisk attachment, beat cream and liqueur at medium-high speed until stiff peaks form, 2 to 3 minutes. Fold cream mixture into chocolate mixture in three additions until smooth and well combined; spoon into prepared crust, piling high; spread and swirl with an offset spatula or the back of a spoon as desired.

9. For topping: Clean bowl of stand mixer and whisk attachment. Beat cream cheese and sugar at medium speed until smooth and well combined, about 1 minute, stopping to scrape sides of bowl. Reduce mixer speed to medium-low; slowly beat in one-third of cold cream until smooth, stopping frequently to scrape sides of bowl. Increase mixer speed to medium, and gradually add remaining cold cream, beating until stiff peaks form, 2 to 4 minutes. (Do not overprocess.) Spread and swirl topping on tart as desired. Refrigerate for at least 4 hours or overnight. Just before serving, garnish with chocolate shavings, if desired.

*We used Kahlúa.

BANANAS FOSTER TART

Makes 1 (10-inch) tart

Adorned with halved bananas doused in a luxurious rum sauce, this tart celebrates the simple, mellow sweetness of ripe bananas when paired with cream and dark spiced rum.

Pâte Sablée (recipe follows)
3   cups (720 grams) heavy whipping cream
1   vanilla bean, split lengthwise, seeds scraped and reserved
½   teaspoon (1.5 grams) kosher salt
¾   cup (150 grams) granulated sugar
5   large egg yolks (93 grams), room temperature
2   large eggs (100 grams), room temperature
6   tablespoons (90 grams) dark spiced rum, divided
⅓   cup (73 grams) firmly packed light brown sugar
⅓   cup (76 grams) unsalted butter, cubed
½   teaspoon (3.5 grams) light corn syrup
4   small bananas (400 grams), halved lengthwise

1. Preheat oven to 325°F (170°C).
2. On a lightly floured sheet of parchment paper, roll Pâte Sablée into a 13-inch circle (¼ inch thick). Transfer dough, still on parchment, to a baking sheet. Refrigerate until slightly firm, about 15 minutes.
3. Spray a 10-inch fluted round removable-bottom tart pan with cooking spray. Transfer dough to prepared pan, lightly pressing into bottom and up sides. Trim any excess dough, if necessary, and discard scraps. (See Note.) Freeze until hard, about 10 minutes.
4. Prick bottom of dough with a fork. Place on a rimmed baking sheet. Top with a piece of parchment paper, letting ends extend over edges of pan. Add pie weights.
5. Bake until edges look dry, about 15 minutes. Carefully remove parchment and weights. Bake until crust is dry, 10 to 12 minutes more. Let cool completely on baking sheet. Reduce oven temperature to 300°F (150°C).
6. In a medium saucepan, heat cream, vanilla bean and reserved seeds, and salt over medium heat just until bubbles form around edges of pan. (Do not boil.) Remove from heat, and let stand for 15 minutes.
7. In a medium bowl, whisk together granulated sugar, egg yolks, and eggs. Add to cream mixture, whisking until smooth. Strain through a fine-mesh sieve into a liquid-measuring cup, discarding solids. Stir in 3 tablespoons (45 grams) rum.

8. Place baking sheet with tart pan on oven rack; pour filling into prepared crust.
9. Bake until filling is set around edges but still jiggles slightly in center and an instant-read thermometer inserted in center registers 170°F (77°C) to 175°F (79°C), 50 to 55 minutes. Remove from baking sheet, and let cool completely in tart pan on a wire rack. Cover and refrigerate overnight.
10. In a 12-inch skillet, combine brown sugar, butter, and corn syrup. Cook over medium heat, whisking occasionally, until mixture has a caramel consistency and begins to gently boil, 3 to 5 minutes. (Mixture may look granulated but will smooth out.) Add remaining 3 tablespoons (45 grams) rum, whisking until smooth. Bring to a gentle boil over medium heat, and add bananas; reduce heat to medium-low, and cook until bananas are softened, about 3 minutes, gently turning halfway through cooking.
11. Gently pat top of tart with a paper towel to remove any moisture, if necessary. Serve tart with bananas and sauce.

Note: *You can also press the Pâte Sablée into the tart pan after refrigerating for 1 hour if you don't want to roll it out. It should be ¼ inch thick in pan.*

Pâte Sablée
Makes 1 (10-inch) crust

1   cup (227 grams) unsalted butter, softened
⅔   cup (80 grams) confectioners' sugar
1   teaspoon (3 grams) kosher salt
2   large egg yolks (37 grams)
½   teaspoon (2 grams) vanilla extract
3   cups (375 grams) pastry flour

1. In the bowl of a stand mixer fitted with the paddle attachment, beat butter at medium-low speed until smooth, about 1 minute. Add confectioners' sugar and salt, and beat until smooth, about 1 minute. Add egg yolks and vanilla, and beat until combined, about 1 minute. Add flour in two additions, beating just until combined after each addition. Turn out dough, and gently knead 3 to 4 times. Shape into a disk, and wrap in plastic wrap. Refrigerate for 1 hour.

GIN-LEMON TART WITH STRAWBERRIES

Makes 1 (13¾x4½-inch) tart

A decent dose of crisp, dry Irish gin helps balance out the sweetness and heighten the zest of this lemon tart with a crumbly gingersnap crust.

- 1¾ cups (254 grams) finely crushed gingersnap cookies (36 to 37 cookies)
- 3 tablespoons (42 grams) unsalted butter, melted
- 3 large eggs (150 grams)
- 3 large egg yolks (56 grams)
- ½ cup (100 grams) granulated sugar
- 2 tablespoons (16 grams) cornstarch
- ¼ teaspoon kosher salt
- 1½ tablespoons (7 grams) packed lemon zest
- ¾ cup (180 grams) fresh lemon juice
- ¼ cup (57 grams) unsalted butter, cubed and softened
- 3 tablespoons (36 grams) Irish gin, divided
- 2 tablespoons (40 grams) strawberry preserves
- 1½ cups (225 grams) sliced fresh strawberries

1. Preheat oven to 350°F (180°C). Spray a 13¾x4½-inch fluted removable-bottom tart pan* with baking spray with flour.

2. In the work bowl of a food processor, combine crushed cookies and melted butter; pulse until well combined and mixture holds together when pinched between fingers. Press crumb mixture into bottom and up sides of prepared pan.

3. Bake until lightly toasted and fragrant, 5 to 7 minutes. (If crust bubbles slightly, carefully press down where necessary while warm.) Let cool completely in pan on a wire rack.

4. Place a fine-mesh sieve over a medium bowl. In another medium bowl, whisk together eggs and egg yolks until well combined.

5. In a medium saucepan, whisk together sugar, cornstarch, and salt; add lemon zest and juice, whisking until well combined. Cook over medium-low heat until sugar dissolves and mixture begins to steam. (Do not boil.) Pour lemon mixture into egg mixture in a slow, steady stream, whisking constantly. Return mixture to saucepan. Bring to a boil over medium-high heat, whisking constantly; cook, whisking constantly, until thickened and mixture no longer tastes like cornstarch, 2 to 3 minutes. Press mixture through prepared sieve, discarding solids. Add softened butter, 1 to 2 cubes at a time, stirring until melted and combined after each addition. Stir in 2 tablespoons (24 grams) gin until well combined.

6. Pour curd into prepared crust; using the back of a small spoon, spread curd into an even layer. Cover with a piece of plastic wrap, pressing wrap directly onto surface of curd to prevent a skin from forming. Refrigerate until well chilled and set, 2 to 4 hours or overnight.

7. Carefully remove tart from pan, and place on a serving platter; let stand at room temperature for 30 minutes.

8. In a medium microwave-safe bowl, heat preserves on high in 10-second intervals, stirring between each, until melted. Stir in strawberries and remaining 1 tablespoon (12 grams) gin. Using the back of a small spoon, swoop lemon curd in tart as desired, and spoon strawberry mixture on top.

We used Williams Sonoma Rectangular Tart Pan.

SWEET POTATO TART

Makes 1 (9½-inch) tart

A twist on the classic sweet potato pie, our tart has a speculoos cookie crust filled with vanilla bean seed-speckled sweet potato filling and garnished with a billowy meringue that'll inspire only the fluffiest of marshmallow fantasies.

1⅓ cups (202 grams) firmly packed finely crushed speculoos cookies* (about 26 cookies)
¼   cup (57 grams) unsalted butter, melted
1¼   teaspoons (2.5 grams) ground cinnamon, divided
½   teaspoon kosher salt, divided
5   ounces (142 grams) cream cheese, room temperature
1¼   cups (295 grams) puréed cooked peeled sweet potato (see Note on page 222)
½   cup (110 grams) firmly packed light brown sugar
2   teaspoons (6 grams) all-purpose flour
¾   teaspoon (4.5 grams) vanilla bean paste
½   teaspoon (1 gram) ground ginger
⅛   teaspoon ground cloves

2   large eggs (100 grams), room temperature
Vanilla Bean Meringue (recipe follows)

1. Preheat oven to 350°F (180°C). Spray a 9½-inch fluted round removable-bottom tart pan with baking spray with flour.
2. In a large bowl, stir together crushed cookies, melted butter, ½ teaspoon (1 gram) cinnamon, and ¼ teaspoon salt until well combined; using a small straight-sided measuring cup, press mixture into bottom and up sides of prepared pan.
3. Bake until set and fragrant, 8 to 10 minutes. Let cool completely on a wire rack. Reduce oven temperature to 325°F (170°C).
4. In the bowl of a stand mixer fitted with the paddle attachment, beat cream cheese at medium speed until smooth and creamy, about 2 minutes, stopping to scrape sides of bowl. Add sweet potato, brown sugar, flour, vanilla bean paste, ginger, cloves, remaining ¾ teaspoon (1.5 grams) cinnamon, and remaining ¼ teaspoon salt; beat at medium-low speed just until combined. Increase mixer speed to medium, and beat

until well combined, about 2 minutes, stopping to scrape sides of bowl. Add eggs, one at a time, beating until well combined after each addition and stopping to scrape sides of bowl. (Mixture will be on the thicker side.) Spoon into prepared crust; using a small offset spatula, spread into an even layer.
5. Bake until top is set and an instant-read thermometer inserted in center registers 155°F (68°C), 22 to 28 minutes. Let cool completely in pan on a wire rack; cover and refrigerate for at least 8 hours or overnight.
6. Carefully remove tart from pan; transfer to a serving plate. Spoon and spread Vanilla Bean Meringue onto tart as desired. Using a handheld kitchen torch, carefully brown meringue as desired. Serve immediately.

*We used Biscoff Cookies.

Vanilla Bean Meringue
Makes about 5 cups

1¼   cups (250 grams) granulated sugar
6   large egg whites (180 grams), room temperature
¼   teaspoon (1 gram) cream of tartar
¼   teaspoon kosher salt
2   teaspoons (12 grams) vanilla bean paste

1. In the heatproof bowl of a stand mixer, whisk together sugar, egg whites, cream of tartar, and salt. Place over a saucepan of simmering water, and cook, stirring frequently, until an instant-read thermometer registers 160°F (71°C), 15 to 20 minutes.
2. Return bowl to stand mixer. Using the whisk attachment, beat sugar mixture at medium-high speed until bowl is room temperature and meringue forms glossy stiff peaks, about 10 minutes. Beat in vanilla bean paste. Use immediately.

WARM APPLE GALETTE WITH SPICED TOFFEE DRIZZLE

Makes 8 servings

A gorgeous ode to fall, this galette features a buttery crust and a sweet apple filling while a Spiced Toffee Drizzle imparts a note of caramel.

1½ cups (188 grams) all-purpose flour
⅓ cup (67 grams) plus 2 tablespoons (24 grams) granulated sugar, divided
1 teaspoon (2 grams) ground ginger
1 teaspoon (2.25 grams) kosher salt, divided
10 tablespoons (140 grams) cold unsalted butter*, cubed
3 tablespoons (45 grams) ice water
½ teaspoon (1 gram) ground cinnamon
¼ teaspoon ground nutmeg
¼ teaspoon ground allspice
6 cups (534 grams) thinly sliced Honeycrisp apples (about 1½ pounds)
1 teaspoon (5 grams) apple cider vinegar
½ teaspoon orange zest
½ teaspoon (2 grams) vanilla extract
1 large egg white (30 grams), lightly beaten
Sparkling sugar, for sprinkling
Spiced Toffee Drizzle (recipe follows)

1. In the work bowl of a food processor, combine flour, 2 tablespoons (24 grams) granulated sugar, ginger, and ¾ teaspoon (2.25 grams) salt; pulse until combined, about 3 times. Add cold butter; pulse until mixture is crumbly. Add 3 tablespoons (45 grams) ice water; pulse until mixture forms large clumps. Turn out dough onto a lightly floured surface, and shape into a disk. Wrap in plastic wrap; refrigerate for 1 hour.
2. Preheat oven to 400°F (200°C). Line a light-colored rimmed baking sheet with parchment paper.
3. In a large bowl, whisk together cinnamon, nutmeg, allspice, remaining ⅓ cup (67 grams) granulated sugar, and remaining ¼ teaspoon salt. Add apples, vinegar, orange zest, and vanilla; stir until well combined.
4. Let dough stand at room temperature until slightly softened, 10 to 15 minutes. On a lightly floured surface, roll dough into a 12-inch circle (about ⅛ inch thick); transfer to prepared pan. Arrange apples in center of dough as desired, leaving a 1½- to 2-inch border; drizzle with any liquid left in bowl. Gently fold and pleat dough edges over filling, leaving apples exposed in center. Brush dough with egg white; sprinkle with sparkling sugar.

5. Bake until crust is golden brown, filling is bubbly, and apples are tender, 35 to 40 minutes, loosely covering apples with foil to prevent excess browning, if necessary. Let cool on pan for 20 minutes. Top with Spiced Toffee Drizzle, and serve warm.

*We used Président® Butter.

SPICED TOFFEE DRIZZLE
Makes ¾ cup

½ cup (110 grams) firmly packed dark brown sugar
⅓ cup (113 grams) dark corn syrup
2½ tablespoons (37.5 grams) heavy whipping cream
2 tablespoons (28 grams) unsalted butter, cubed
½ teaspoon (1.5 grams) kosher salt
¼ teaspoon ground cinnamon
¼ teaspoon ground nutmeg
¼ teaspoon ground allspice
½ teaspoon (2 grams) vanilla extract

1. In a medium saucepan, combine brown sugar, corn syrup, cream, butter, salt, cinnamon, nutmeg, and allspice. Bring to a boil over medium-high heat; cook, stirring constantly, for 2 minutes. Remove from heat, and whisk in vanilla. Transfer to a medium heatproof bowl; let cool for at least 20 minutes before using.

Note: *If Spiced Toffee Drizzle begins to harden, microwave on high in 10-second intervals, stirring between each, until melted and smooth.*

AUTHENTIC IRISH APPLE TARTS

Makes 6 (4- to 4½-inch) tarts

Recipe by Allie Roomberg

This recipe embodies the Irish classic in every way, from the buttery crust to the nutty filling to the crumbly streusel topping. And, of course, tender apples play the starring role!

Tart Dough (recipe follows)
1½   cups (144 grams) almond meal
⅔   cup (133 grams) granulated sugar
¼   cup (60 grams) apple brandy
2   large eggs (100 grams)
2   tablespoons (28 grams) unsalted
     butter, melted
1   tablespoon (3 grams) lemon zest (about
     1 lemon)
1   teaspoon (4 grams) vanilla extract
¼   teaspoon kosher salt
4   medium Granny Smith apples
     (560 grams)
2   tablespoons (40 grams) warm apple
     jelly
Crumb Topping (recipe follows)
Custard Sauce (recipe follows)
Vanilla ice cream, to serve (see Note)
Garnish: confectioners' sugar

1. Preheat oven to 375°F (190°C).
2. Turn out Tart Dough onto a lightly floured surface, and divide into 6 portions (about 62 grams each). Roll each portion into a 7-inch circle, and transfer each to a 4- to 4½-inch fluted round removable-bottom tart pan, lightly pressing into bottom and up sides. Trim off excess. Using a fork, prick bottoms a few times.
3. Bake for 10 minutes. (If crust puffs up in middle, press down gently while still warm.) Leave oven on.
4. In a large bowl, stir together almond meal, granulated sugar, brandy, eggs, melted butter, lemon zest, vanilla extract, and salt. Divide among prepared crusts.
5. Peel apples, and cut in half; core each half, and cut into ⅛-inch-thick slices, making sure to keep slices grouped together. Fan apple slices on top of filling. Brush

apples with jelly, and top with Crumb Topping.
6. Bake until crust is just golden around edges and apples are tender, 20 to 25 minutes for 4-inch tarts or about 35 minutes for 4½-inch tarts. Remove from pans. Serve warm with Custard Sauce and ice cream. Garnish with confectioners' sugar, if desired. Refrigerate in an airtight container for up to 5 days.

Note: *We recommend using Tillamook Vanilla Ice Cream, or you can make your own vanilla ice cream from scratch. Find Allie's recipe at bakingamoment.com.*

TART DOUGH
Makes 6 (4- to 4½-inch) crusts

1½   cups (188 grams) all-purpose flour
⅓   cup (40 grams) confectioners' sugar
¼   teaspoon kosher salt
½   cup (113 grams) cold unsalted butter,
     cubed
1   large egg yolk (19 grams)
1½   tablespoons (22.5 grams) heavy
     whipping cream
½   teaspoon (2 grams) vanilla extract

1. In the work bowl of a food processor, place flour, confectioners' sugar, and salt; pulse until combined. Add cold butter, and pulse until mixture resembles coarse bread crumbs. Add egg yolk, cream, and vanilla, and process until dough forms a ball and pulls away cleanly from sides of bowl.

Note: *It is not necessary to chill this dough.*

CRUMB TOPPING
Makes about 1½ cups

6   tablespoons (84 grams) unsalted butter
1½   cups (188 grams) all-purpose flour
½   cup (100 grams) granulated sugar
1   tablespoon (3 grams) lemon zest (about
     1 lemon)
¼   teaspoon kosher salt

1. In a small saucepan, melt butter over medium-low heat. Remove from heat; using a fork, stir in flour, sugar, lemon zest, and salt until combined and mixture is crumbly. Let cool completely before using.

Note: *Crumb Topping can be made a few days ahead; refrigerate in an airtight container until ready to use. Extra topping can be stored in the freezer for other uses.*

CUSTARD SAUCE
Makes about 2 cups

1   cup (240 grams) whole milk
¾   cup (180 grams) heavy whipping cream
1   medium vanilla bean, split lengthwise,
     seeds scraped and reserved
4   large egg yolks (74 grams)
⅓   cup (67 grams) granulated sugar

1. In a small saucepan, combine milk, cream, and vanilla bean and reserved seeds. Heat over medium-low heat just until bubbles form around edges of pan. (Do not boil.) Discard vanilla bean.
2. In a medium bowl, whisk together egg yolks and sugar. Gradually add warm milk mixture to egg yolk mixture, whisking constantly. Return mixture to saucepan, and cook over low heat, whisking constantly, until slightly thickened and mixture can coat the back of a wooden spoon, about 5 minutes. (Mixture will continue to thicken as it cools.) Strain through a fine-mesh sieve into a heatproof bowl. Place bowl in an ice water bath until sauce is chilled. Remove bowl from ice water bath, cover sauce with plastic wrap, and refrigerate until ready to use.

Note: *Custard Sauce can be made 1 day ahead; refrigerate in an airtight container until ready to use.*

Photo by Allie Roomberg

APPELTAART

Makes 1 (9-inch) pie

Inspired by the world-famous appeltaart at Amsterdam's Winkel 43, this recipe is everything an appeltaart should be: a buttery, tender crust brimming with sizeable pieces of aromatic spiced apple. Baking the apple chunks before assembling ensures a hefty filling with height while preventing a soggy bottom.

1½ cups (340 grams) unsalted butter, softened
1¾ cups (350 grams) plus 1 teaspoon (4 grams) granulated sugar, divided
¼ cup (55 grams) firmly packed light brown sugar
2 large eggs (100 grams), room temperature
1 large egg (50 grams), room temperature and divided
1 tablespoon (14 grams) vanilla bean paste
3¾ cups (469 grams) all-purpose flour
1½ teaspoons (7.5 grams) baking powder
1¼ teaspoons (3 grams) kosher salt, divided
½ teaspoon (2.5 grams) baking soda
6 large Honeycrisp apples (1,377 grams)
2 large Pink Lady apples (484 grams)
⅓ cup (43 grams) cornstarch
2 tablespoons (12 grams) ground cinnamon
2 tablespoons (6 grams) lemon zest
1 tablespoon (15 grams) fresh lemon juice
Whipped cream, to serve

1. In the bowl of a stand mixer fitted with the paddle attachment, beat butter, 1¼ cups (250 grams) granulated sugar, and brown sugar at low speed just until combined. Increase mixer speed to medium, and beat until fluffy, about 3 minutes, stopping to scrape sides of bowl. Add eggs and egg yolk, one at a time, beating until well combined after each addition. Beat in vanilla bean paste.
2. In a large bowl, whisk together flour, baking powder, 1 teaspoon (3 grams) salt, and baking soda. With mixer on low speed, gradually add flour mixture to butter mixture, beating just until combined. Shape about two-thirds of dough (about 763 grams) into a 7-inch disk; wrap in plastic wrap. Divide remaining dough in half; shape each into a 4-inch disk. Wrap

each disk in plastic wrap, and refrigerate for at least 2 hours.
3. Preheat oven to 350°F (180°C). Line 2 rimmed baking sheets with parchment paper.
4. Core apples; cut into 1- to 1½-inch chunks.
5. In a very large bowl, whisk together ½ cup (100 grams) granulated sugar, cornstarch, cinnamon, lemon zest, and remaining ¼ teaspoon salt; add apples and lemon juice, tossing to coat thoroughly. Divide apples evenly between prepared pans.
6. Bake until apples appear slightly dried, golden, and tender, 25 to 30 minutes, stirring apples and rotating pans halfway through baking. Let apples cool completely on pans, about 30 minutes. Transfer to a large bowl. Leave oven on.
7. Let dough stand at room temperature until slightly softened, 15 to 20 minutes. On a heavily floured surface, roll large dough disk into a 13-inch circle (about ¼ inch thick).
8. Spray a light-colored 9-inch springform pan with baking spray with flour. Line bottom of pan with parchment paper.
9. Using a 9-inch round cake pan or plate as a guide, cut a circle in center of rolled dough; gently transfer to prepared pan, pressing into bottom. (It's OK if dough tears while transferring; gently move to pan, and press together.) Cut remaining rolled dough into 4 pieces; gently transfer to prepared pan, overlapping if needed, pressing all the way up sides, and sealing any seams with bottom. Trim dough flush with top edge of pan; fill with cooled apple mixture.
10. On a heavily floured surface, roll remaining dough disks into 2 (9-inch) circles. Using a pastry wheel or pizza cutter, cut 1 circle into 3 (3-inch-wide) strips. Gently place strips parallel and spaced ¼ inch apart on apple mixture. Repeat with remaining dough circle, arranging strips on and perpendicular to first set of strips. Trim dough flush with edge of pan. Brush dough with egg white; sprinkle with remaining 1 teaspoon (4 grams) granulated sugar.
11. Bake until top is golden brown and slightly puffed, about 1 hour, rotating pan halfway through baking and loosely covering with foil to prevent excess browning, if

necessary. Let cool in pan for 10 minutes. Carefully remove sides of pan, and let cool completely on base of pan on a wire rack. Serve with whipped cream.

Transfer dough pieces to pan. Press overlapping seams together to seal and create an even surface. It's OK if dough tears while transferring. You can press together once it's in pan.

After you've filled crust with cooled apple mixture, place dough strips parallel and spaced ¼ inch apart on apple mixture. Repeat with remaining strips, arranging on and perpendicular to first set of strips.

Trim dough flush with edge of pan. Brush dough with egg white; sprinkle with remaining granulated sugar.

ALMOND PLUM TART

Makes 1 (10-inch) tart

Recipe by Zoë François

Perfect for summer, this simple tart features a creamy almond filling studded with fresh plums and topped with an almond cream topping that bakes to golden perfection.

1½ cups (188 grams) plus 2 tablespoons (16 grams) unbleached all-purpose flour, divided
10 tablespoons (140 grams) unsalted butter, softened
½ cup (60 grams) confectioners' sugar
¼ cup (24 grams) almond meal
1 large egg yolk (19 grams)
1 teaspoon (4 grams) vanilla extract
Pinch salt
8 ounces (226 grams) almond paste
½ cup (113 grams) unsalted butter, room temperature

¼ cup (50 grams) plus 3 tablespoons (36 grams) granulated sugar, divided
2 large eggs (100 grams)
2 tablespoons (30 grams) heavy whipping cream
1 teaspoon (4 grams) almond extract
4 to 5 plums (496 grams), pitted and cut into 8 wedges
½ cup (57 grams) sliced almonds
½ teaspoon orange zest
¼ teaspoon (1 gram) orange blossom water

1. Preheat oven to 350°F (180°C).
2. In the work bowl of a food processor, place 1½ cups (188 grams) flour, softened butter, confectioners' sugar, almond meal, egg yolk, and vanilla; process until dough just comes together and forms a uniform ball, about 1 minute. Press into bottom and up sides of a 10-inch fluted round removable-bottom tart pan; trim excess dough. Freeze for about 15 minutes.

3. In the clean work bowl of a food processor, place almond paste, room temperature butter, 3 tablespoons (36 grams) granulated sugar, and remaining 2 tablespoons (16 grams) flour; process until smooth, stopping to scrape sides of bowl. Add eggs, cream, and almond extract; process until smooth. Spread in frozen tart shell. Arrange plums, cut side up, in filling.
4. In a small bowl, combine almonds, orange zest, orange blossom water, and remaining ¼ cup (50 grams) granulated sugar. (Mixture should resemble lightly wet sand.) Sprinkle onto tart.
5. Bake until filling is set and golden, about 50 minutes, covering with foil after 40 minutes of baking to prevent excess browning. Let cool completely in pan. Remove from pan, and serve.

Photo by Eliesa Johnson

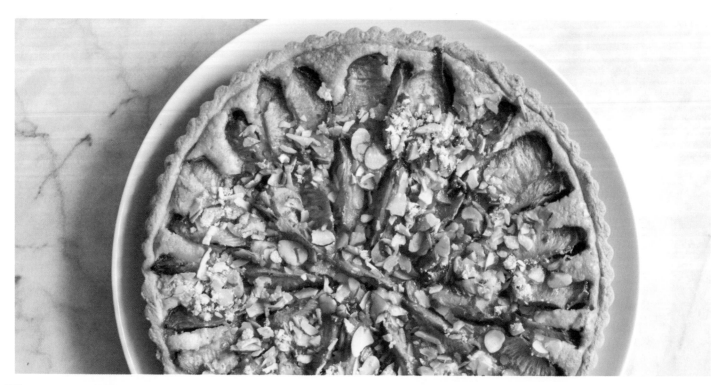

SPICED PLUM LINZER TORTE

Makes 1 (9½-inch) tart

Named after the city of Linz, Austria, the Linzer torte is a classic European pastry usually served during Christmas. Traditionally made with a buttery shortcrust dough accented by ground nuts, the Linzer torte often hides a jewel-toned jam filling beneath an elaborate lattice crust. We followed sweet tradition to a T, gently arranging a hazelnut flour and almond flour crust over a beautiful plum preserves filling.

1½   cups (188 grams) all-purpose flour
1¼   cups (120 grams) finely ground hazelnut flour
1   cup (96 grams) super-fine blanched almond flour
⅓   cup (67 grams) granulated sugar
⅓   cup (73 grams) firmly packed light brown sugar
1   teaspoon (3 grams) tightly packed orange zest
¾   teaspoon (2.25 grams) kosher salt
¾   teaspoon (1.5 grams) ground cinnamon
½   teaspoon (2.5 grams) baking powder
¼   teaspoon ground ginger
⅛   teaspoon ground nutmeg
⅛   teaspoon ground cloves
¾   cup plus 2 tablespoons (198 grams) cold unsalted butter, cubed
1   large egg (50 grams)
1   teaspoon (6 grams) vanilla bean paste
2   cups (600 grams) damson plum preserves
Confectioners' sugar, for dusting

1. In the work bowl of a food processor, combine flours, granulated sugar, brown sugar, orange zest, salt, cinnamon, baking powder, ginger, nutmeg, and cloves; pulse until well combined, stopping to scrape sides of bowl. Add cold butter, and pulse until mixture resembles coarse crumbs. Add egg and vanilla bean paste; pulse just until dough comes together, stopping to scrape sides of bowl. (Mixture should be moist but not sticky and should hold together when pinched.) Turn out dough onto a clean surface; reserve one-third of dough (about 264 grams), and cover with plastic wrap.
2. Spray a 9½-inch fluted round removable-bottom tart pan with baking spray with flour. Press remaining dough into bottom and up sides of prepared pan, trimming any excess with a small sharp knife; add any dough trimmings to reserved one-third of dough. Cover with plastic wrap.
3. Lightly flour a sheet of wax paper; place reserved dough on prepared wax paper, and lightly flour top of dough. Place another sheet of wax paper on dough, and roll dough into a 12-inch circle (about ⅛ inch thick); place on a baking sheet. Refrigerate rolled dough and dough in pan for 1 hour.
4. Preheat oven to 350°F (180°C).
5. Using a small offset spatula, spread preserves evenly onto dough in pan.
6. Remove top wax paper from rolled dough; using a pastry wheel or pizza cutter, cut dough into 1-inch-wide strips; cover and refrigerate until firm, about 15 minutes.
7. Gently arrange strips about ½ inch apart in a lattice pattern on preserves; press strips into edges of dough in pan, trimming off excess to create a clean edge. (If dough becomes too soft, refrigerate in 15-minute intervals as needed; a lightly floured large offset spatula can help move strips.) Create additional strips as needed by rerolling excess dough to ⅛-inch thickness between lightly floured sheets of wax paper. (This is a delicate dough. If it tears while moving, simply press it back together; alternatively, reroll, cut, and refrigerate dough, and try again.) Refrigerate assembled tart for 20 minutes.
8. Bake until crust is golden brown and set and filling is starting to bubble, 30 to 35 minutes. Let cool completely in pan on a wire rack. Remove from pan. Dust with confectioners' sugar just before serving.

POACHED PEAR BUTTERMILK TART

Makes 1 (9½-inch) tart

A sophisticated twist on buttermilk chess pie, this stunning tart combines a tangy, creamy buttermilk filling with a wine-poached pear topping. Our ginger-scented shortcrust pastry dough and poached pears can be made a day ahead of time, offering a streamlined process for the busy baker.

1   (750-ml) bottle (750 grams) fruity white wine, such as pinot grigio
2½   cups (500 grams) granulated sugar, divided
2   cups (480 grams) water
3   tablespoons (45 grams) fresh lemon juice
2   (2½- to 3-inch) cinnamon sticks
6   whole cloves
2   medium firm ripe Bartlett pears (404 grams), peeled, halved, stemmed, and cored
Ginger Shortcrust Pastry (recipe follows)
2   tablespoons (16 grams) all-purpose flour
¼   teaspoon kosher salt
⅔   cup (160 grams) whole buttermilk, room temperature
⅓   cup (80 grams) heavy whipping cream, room temperature
¼   cup (57 grams) unsalted butter, melted and cooled for 5 minutes
1   large egg (50 grams), room temperature
1   large egg yolk (19 grams), room temperature
2   teaspoons (12 grams) vanilla bean paste
Garnish: finely chopped lightly toasted pistachios, sliced lightly toasted almonds, confectioners' sugar

1. In a large saucepan, combine wine, 2 cups (400 grams) granulated sugar, 2 cups (480 grams) water, lemon juice, cinnamon sticks, and cloves. Bring to a boil over medium-high heat; reduce heat to medium-low, and simmer for 5 minutes. Add pears; place a round of parchment paper on surface of wine mixture, pressing down slightly to help keep pears submerged. Simmer, turning pears occasionally, until pears are fork-tender, 25 to 40 minutes. Using a slotted spoon, transfer pears to a medium heatproof bowl.
2. Discard cinnamon sticks and cloves. Increase heat to medium-high; cook wine mixture until reduced to 3 cups, 15 to 18 minutes. Pour wine mixture over pears in bowl; place a sheet of plastic wrap directly on surface to keep pears submerged, and refrigerate for at least 1 hour.
3. Preheat oven to 350°F (180°C). Spray a 9½-inch fluted round removable-bottom tart pan with baking spray with flour.
4. Let pears in wine mixture stand at room temperature until ready to use.
5. Let Ginger Shortcrust Pastry stand at room temperature until softened, about 15 minutes. On a lightly floured surface, roll dough into a 12-inch circle (about ⅛ inch thick), flouring rolling pin and work surface as needed; trim dough slightly so circle has clean edges. Transfer dough to prepared pan, pressing into bottom and

up sides; fold any overhanging dough inside, and press to create a double thickness. (It's OK if dough tears in spots; just press back together.) Using a small sharp knife, trim dough flush with edges of tart pan. Pinch sides lightly so dough sits about ⅛ inch above top edge of pan; use any extra dough to patch thinner spots in crust. Cover and freeze for 15 minutes.
6. Place tart pan on a parchment-lined rimmed baking sheet. Top frozen dough with a sheet of parchment paper, letting ends extend over edges of tart pan. Add pie weights.
7. Bake until edges are lightly golden, 15 to 20 minutes, rotating pan halfway through baking. Carefully remove parchment and weights. Bake until crust is dry and set, about 5 minutes more. Let cool completely on baking sheet on a wire rack. Leave oven on.
8. In the bowl of a stand mixer, whisk together flour, salt, and remaining ½ cup (100 grams) granulated sugar by hand. Add buttermilk, cream, melted butter, egg, egg yolk, and vanilla bean paste; using the whisk attachment, beat at medium speed until smooth and well combined, stopping to scrape sides of bowl.
9. Using a slotted spoon, remove pear halves from wine mixture. Pat pears dry, and slice each half lengthwise into 8 wedges. Arrange wedges in a tight overlapping circular pattern along edge of prepared crust. Pour buttermilk mixture in center of crust, shaking pan gently to evenly distribute between pears. (Pan will be quite full but will not overflow during baking.)
10. Bake until filling is just set (it may still jiggle in center) and an instant-read thermometer inserted in center registers 170°F (76°C) to 175°F (79°C), 25 to 28 minutes. Let cool completely on baking sheet on a wire rack. Remove from tart pan. Before serving, garnish with pistachios, almonds, and confectioners' sugar, if desired.

GINGER SHORTCRUST PASTRY

Makes 1 (9½-inch) crust

1¾   cups (219 grams) all-purpose flour
⅓   cup (67 grams) granulated sugar
1½   teaspoons (3 grams) ground ginger
½   teaspoon (1.5 grams) kosher salt
½   cup (113 grams) cold unsalted butter, cubed
1   large egg (50 grams), lightly beaten

1. In the work bowl of a food processor, place flour, sugar, ginger, and salt; pulse until combined. Add cold butter, and pulse until mixture resembles coarse crumbs. Add egg, and pulse just until dough comes together, stopping to scrape sides of bowl. (Mixture should be moist but not sticky and should hold together when pinched.)
2. Turn out dough, and shape into a 7-inch disk. Wrap in plastic wrap, and refrigerate for at least 25 minutes.

SPARKLING WINE CHOCOLATE GANACHE TART

Makes 1 (9½-inch) tart

Sparkling wine and chocolate are a winning combination, creating a celebratory tart ideal for the holiday season. With a graham cracker crumb base, a semisweet ganache filling, and a sparkling wine-spiked white chocolate cream topping, this tart is chilled perfection.

1½ cups (176 grams) chocolate graham cracker crumbs (about 12 sheets)
2   tablespoons (24 grams) granulated sugar
6   tablespoons (84 grams) unsalted butter, melted
10 ounces (284 grams) 64% cacao semisweet chocolate*, finely chopped (about 1⅔ cups)
2   cups (480 grams) cold heavy whipping cream, divided
¼   teaspoon kosher salt
⅓   cup (80 grams) plus 2 tablespoons (30 grams) brut sparkling white wine, divided
6   ounces (170 grams) white chocolate*, finely chopped (about 1 cup)
Garnish: dark chocolate crunchy pearls, semisweet chocolate shavings

1. Preheat oven to 350°F (180°C). Spray a 9½-inch fluted round removable-bottom tart pan with baking spray with flour.
2. In the work bowl of a food processor, combine graham cracker crumbs and sugar; pulse until well combined. Add melted butter; pulse until well combined and mixture holds together when pinched. Press graham cracker mixture into bottom and up sides of prepared pan.
3. Bake until crust is set and fragrant, 8 to 10 minutes. Let cool completely on a wire rack.
4. In the top of a double boiler, combine semisweet chocolate, 1 cup (240 grams) cold cream, and salt. Cook over simmering water, stirring frequently, until chocolate is melted and mixture is smooth. Remove from heat; gradually whisk in ⅓ cup (80 grams) wine until smooth and well

combined. Pour mixture into prepared crust. Refrigerate until filling is set, at least 3 hours or up to overnight.
5. In the clean top of a double boiler, combine white chocolate and ⅓ cup (80 grams) cold cream. Cook over simmering water, stirring frequently, until chocolate is melted and mixture is smooth. Transfer white chocolate mixture to the bowl of a stand mixer, and let cool to room temperature (70°F/21°C).
6. Using the whisk attachment, beat cooled white chocolate mixture at medium speed; gradually add remaining 2 tablespoons (30 grams) wine, beating until well combined. Reduce mixer speed to medium-low; slowly add ⅓ cup (80 grams) cold cream, beating until smooth and stopping frequently to scrape sides of bowl. Increase mixer speed to medium; gradually add remaining

⅓ cup (80 grams) cold cream, beating until medium-stiff peaks form. (Whisk by hand toward end if needed; do not overmix.) Spread and swirl topping on tart as desired, being careful not to overhandle topping. Garnish with chocolate pearls and chocolate shavings, if desired. Refrigerate until topping is set, about 30 minutes. Remove from pan, and serve immediately.

We used Guittard 64% Cacao Semisweet Chocolate Baking Bars and Ghirardelli White Chocolate Baking Bars.

PEAR AND CRANBERRY KUCHEN

Makes 1 (9-inch) tart

Kuchen, the German word for "cake," can mean a number of things, depending on where you live. In North and South Dakota, the kuchen you can expect is a cross between a pie and a tart, with a pastry crust filled with a blend of seasonal fruit and, of course, custard. This historic baked good was brought over by Germanic homesteaders who settled in the Dakotas, and it has since become the state dessert of South Dakota. Our version honors its forebearers with a simple spiced shortcrust filled with a generous pour of custard and an artful arrangement of pears and cranberries.

Spiced Shortcrust Pastry (recipe follows)
2   medium Anjou pears (314 grams), peeled, halved, stemmed, and cored
2   teaspoons (10 grams) fresh lemon juice
⅔   cup (160 grams) heavy whipping cream
¼   cup (50 grams) granulated sugar
2   large egg yolks (37 grams)
⅛   teaspoon kosher salt
⅛   teaspoon ground cinnamon
⅛   teaspoon ground ginger
⅛   teaspoon ground cloves
¾   cup (83 grams) fresh or frozen cranberries
Garnish: confectioners' sugar, apricot preserves

1. Preheat oven to 400°F (200°C).
2. Top prepared Spiced Shortcrust Pastry with a piece of parchment paper, letting ends extend over edges of pan. Add pie weights.
3. Bake until edges look dry, about 15 minutes. Carefully remove parchment and weights. Bake until bottom crust looks dry, about 5 minutes more. Reduce oven temperature to 300°F (150°C).
4. Slice each pear half lengthwise into ¼-inch-thick slices. Working with one half at a time, slide pieces into a line, and place, evenly spaced, in a line in prepared crust. Brush lemon juice all over pears.
5. In a small bowl, whisk together cream, granulated sugar, egg yolks, salt, cinnamon, ginger, and cloves. Pour mixture between pears in crust; sprinkle cranberries on top.
6. Bake until edges are set, center jiggles

slightly, and an instant-read thermometer inserted in center registers 170°F (77°C) to 175°F (79°C), 40 to 50 minutes. Let cool completely in pan on a wire rack. Serve immediately, or refrigerate until ready to serve. Just before serving, place an 8-inch circle of parchment paper in center of tart, and dust confectioners' sugar onto outside edge, if desired. Brush pears with apricot preserves, if desired. Serve chilled or at room temperature.

SPICED SHORTCRUST PASTRY
Makes 1 (9-inch) crust

1¾   cups (219 grams) all-purpose flour
⅓   cup (67 grams) granulated sugar
½   teaspoon (1.5 grams) kosher salt
½   teaspoon (1 gram) ground cinnamon
½   teaspoon (1 gram) ground ginger
¼   teaspoon (1.25 grams) baking powder
¼   teaspoon ground cloves
½   cup (113 grams) cold unsalted butter, cubed

1   large egg (50 grams), lightly beaten
1   tablespoon (15 grams) heavy whipping cream

1. Spray a 9-inch fluted round removable-bottom tart pan with cooking spray.
2. In the bowl of a stand mixer fitted with the paddle attachment, beat flour, sugar, salt, cinnamon, ginger, baking powder, and cloves at low speed until combined. Add cold butter, and beat until mixture is crumbly and resembles fine bread crumbs and no large pieces of butter remain, 2 to 3 minutes. Add egg and cream, and beat at low speed until a dough forms. Press dough into bottom and up sides of prepared pan. (Alternatively, on a lightly floured surface, roll dough into an 11-inch circle [about ¼ inch thick]; transfer to prepared pan, pressing into bottom and up sides.) Trim excess dough, and discard. Using a fork, prick bottom of dough all over. Freeze until firm, 10 to 15 minutes.

COOKIES AND BARS

COOKIES

Swirl up some rich molasses marvels, take a spin with Pecan Pinwheels, or sink your teeth into a handheld favorite: the sandwich cookie. These cookies will take you from sweet summer sensations to holiday highs.

CARROT CAKE SANDWICH COOKIES

Makes 22 sandwich cookies

We kept the base flavors of these tender cookies faithful to the original, with a carrot-rich dough brimming with pecans. A thick layer of Sour Cream Buttercream rounds out every bite with just the right amount of tang.

1   cup (227 grams) unsalted butter, softened
1¼   cups (275 grams) firmly packed dark brown sugar
½   cup (100 grams) granulated sugar
2   large eggs (100 grams), room temperature
2   teaspoons (8 grams) vanilla extract
2¾   cups (344 grams) all-purpose flour
1½   teaspoons (3 grams) ground cinnamon
1   teaspoon (3 grams) kosher salt
¾   teaspoon (3.75 grams) baking soda
½   teaspoon (1 gram) ground allspice
½   teaspoon (1 gram) ground ginger
1½   cups (120 grams) old-fashioned oats
1   cup (107 grams) lightly packed grated carrot
½   cup (57 grams) finely chopped pecans*
       Sour Cream Buttercream (recipe follows)

1. Preheat oven to 350°F (180°C). Line several baking sheets with parchment paper.
2. In the bowl of a stand mixer fitted with the paddle attachment, beat butter and sugars at medium speed until fluffy, 3 to 4 minutes, stopping to scrape sides of bowl. Add eggs, one at a time, beating well after each addition. Beat in vanilla.
3. In a medium bowl, whisk together flour, cinnamon, salt, baking soda, allspice, and ginger. With mixer on low speed, gradually add flour mixture to butter mixture, beating just until combined. Beat in oats, carrot, and pecans. Using a 1½-tablespoon scoop, scoop dough (about 28 grams each). Using floured hands, roll each scoop into a smooth ball; press into a 2-inch disk (⅝ inch thick). Place 2 inches apart on prepared pans.
4. Bake until edges are golden brown, 11 to 14 minutes. Let cool on pans for 5 minutes. Remove from pans, and let cool completely on wire racks.
5. Place Sour Cream Buttercream in a pastry bag fitted with ½-inch round piping tip (Wilton 1A). Pipe a large dollop of buttercream onto flat side of half of cookies, leaving a ¼-inch border around edges. Place remaining cookies, flat side down, on top of buttercream, pressing lightly to push buttercream to edges of cookies. Cover and refrigerate until ready to serve. Let stand at room temperature for 10 to 15 minutes to soften slightly before serving.

SOUR CREAM BUTTERCREAM
Makes about 2½ cups

½   cup (113 grams) unsalted butter, softened
½   cup (120 grams) sour cream, divided
½   teaspoon (2 grams) vanilla extract
¼   teaspoon kosher salt
3   cups (360 grams) confectioners' sugar, divided

1. In the bowl of a stand mixer fitted with the paddle attachment, beat butter at medium speed until smooth, about 1 minute. Add ¼ cup (60 grams) sour cream, vanilla, and salt, beating just until combined. Add 1½ cups (180 grams) confectioners' sugar, beating until combined. Beat in remaining ¼ cup (60 grams) sour cream. Add remaining 1½ cups (180 grams) confectioners' sugar, beating until smooth and fluffy. Use immediately.

PEANUT BUTTER COOKIES

Makes about 12 cookies

Chewy, cakey, and full of addictive nuttiness, this fuss-free recipe checks off all the boxes for the ultimate peanut butter cookie. Plus, it's the supersized bakery style you know and love. You'll turn to these again and again when the late-night cravings call.

½   cup (113 grams) unsalted butter, softened
1   cup (220 grams) firmly packed light brown sugar
1   large egg (50 grams)
2   large egg yolks (37 grams)
¾   cup (192 grams) creamy peanut butter
1   tablespoon (21 grams) honey
1   teaspoon (4 grams) vanilla extract
1¾ cups (219 grams) all-purpose flour
¾   teaspoon (3.75 grams) baking powder
¼   teaspoon (1.5 grams) kosher salt
¼   teaspoon (1.25 grams) baking soda
½   cup (100 grams) granulated sugar

1. In the bowl of a stand mixer fitted with the paddle attachment, beat butter and brown sugar at medium speed until fluffy, 3 to 4 minutes, stopping to scrape sides of bowl. Add egg and egg yolks, beating well. Add peanut butter, honey, and vanilla, beating until combined.

2. In a medium bowl, stir together flour, baking powder, salt, and baking soda. With mixer on low speed, gradually add flour mixture to butter mixture, beating just until combined. Cover and refrigerate for 1 hour.

3. Preheat oven to 325°F (170°C). Line 2 baking sheets with parchment paper.

4. Using a ¼-cup spring-loaded scoop, scoop dough (67 grams each), and toss in granulated sugar. Place 3 inches apart on prepared pans. Press tines of a fork into surface of dough, making a crosshatch design.

5. Bake until light golden brown, 18 to 20 minutes, rotating pans halfway through baking. Let cool on pans for 5 minutes. Remove from pans, and let cool completely on wire racks.

SPICED LEMON CRINKLE SANDWICH COOKIES

Makes about 16 sandwich cookies

Boasting a double dose of Meyer lemon zest and juice, these chewy sandwich cookies are the ultimate citrusy indulgence. A touch of cardamom and ginger rounds out this recipe with sweet heat, and a tangy Cream Cheese Frosting plays up the Meyer lemon's sweetness.

1⅓ cups (267 grams) granulated sugar, divided
½ cup (113 grams) unsalted butter, melted and cooled
½ teaspoon (2 grams) vanilla extract
1 large egg (50 grams), room temperature
1 large egg yolk (19 grams), room temperature
2 tablespoons (9 grams) packed Meyer lemon zest
2 tablespoons (30 grams) fresh Meyer lemon juice
2 cups (250 grams) all-purpose flour
¾ teaspoon (2.25 grams) kosher salt
½ teaspoon (2.5 grams) baking soda
½ teaspoon (1 gram) ground cardamom
¼ teaspoon ground ginger
½ cup (60 grams) confectioners' sugar, sifted
Cream Cheese Frosting (recipe follows)

1. In a large bowl, whisk together 1 cup (200 grams) granulated sugar, melted butter, and vanilla until well combined. Add egg and egg yolk, whisking until well combined. Whisk in lemon zest and juice.
2. In a medium bowl, whisk together flour, salt, baking soda, cardamom, and ginger. Add flour mixture to sugar mixture in two additions, folding until well combined after each addition. Cover and refrigerate for at least 2 hours.
3. Preheat oven to 325°F (170°C). Line 2 rimmed baking sheets with parchment paper.
4. In a small bowl, place confectioners' sugar. In another small bowl, place remaining ⅓ cup (67 grams) granulated sugar.
5. Working in batches and using a 1-tablesoon spring-loaded scoop, scoop dough, and shape into balls. Roll in granulated sugar; roll in confectioners' sugar. Place 1½ to 2 inches apart on prepared pans.
6. Bake until edges are set and cracks have formed, 8 to 10 minutes. Let cool completely on pans.
7. Place Cream Cheese Frosting in a pastry bag fitted with a medium open star piping tip (Wilton 1M). Pipe Cream Cheese Frosting onto flat sides of half of cookies. Place remaining cookies, flat side down, on top of frosting. Serve immediately.

Note: *If dough begins to get too soft, refrigerate until firm, 10 to 15 minutes.*

CREAM CHEESE FROSTING
Makes about 1½ cups

4 ounces (113 grams) cream cheese, softened
¼ cup (57 grams) unsalted butter, softened
½ teaspoon (1.5 grams) kosher salt
½ teaspoon (2 grams) vanilla extract
2½ cups (300 grams) confectioners' sugar, sifted

1. In the bowl of a stand mixer fitted with the paddle attachment, beat cream cheese and butter at medium speed until smooth and well combined, 1 to 2 minutes, stopping to scrape sides of bowl. Beat in salt and vanilla. With mixer on low speed, gradually add confectioners' sugar, beating just until combined. Increase mixer speed to medium; beat until fluffy, 1 to 2 minutes, stopping to scrape sides of bowl. Use immediately.

WALNUT COOKIES

Makes 23 cookies

A common treat found in pastry shops in China year-round, during Chinese New Year, home bakers often make hup toh soh *as a crunchy treat to welcome visitors and family to their home. Our Walnut Cookies have more walnuts in the dough than the traditional cookie, but the center walnut and speckle of sesame seeds instantly marks these as a classic example of* hup toh soh.

⅓ cup (76 grams) unsalted butter, melted and cooled
¼ cup (50 grams) granulated sugar
1 large egg (50 grams), room temperature
2 tablespoons (28 grams) firmly packed light brown sugar
2 tablespoons (28 grams) canola oil
1 teaspoon (4 grams) vanilla extract
¾ teaspoon (2.25 grams) kosher salt
1¾ cups (219 grams) unbleached cake flour
½ teaspoon (2.5 grams) baking powder
½ teaspoon (1 gram) ground ginger
¼ teaspoon (1.25 grams) baking soda
½ cup (57 grams) finely chopped toasted walnuts
¼ cup (44 grams) finely chopped candied ginger
Walnut halves, for topping
1 large egg white (30 grams), lightly beaten
Black sesame seeds, for sprinkling

1. Preheat oven to 350°F (180°C). Line 2 baking sheets with parchment paper.
2. In the bowl of a stand mixer fitted with the paddle attachment, beat melted butter, granulated sugar, egg, brown sugar, oil, vanilla, and salt at medium speed until well combined, 1 to 2 minutes, stopping to scrape sides of bowl.
3. In a medium bowl, whisk together flour, baking powder, ground ginger, and baking soda. Add flour mixture to butter mixture all at once; beat at low speed just until combined. Fold in chopped walnuts and candied ginger. Using a 1½-tablespoon spring-loaded scoop, scoop dough (about 25 grams each), and roll into balls; place at least 1 inch apart on prepared pans. Flatten into 2-inch disks (½ inch thick); press a walnut half into center of each disk. Brush tops with egg white; sprinkle with sesame seeds.
4. Bake until golden brown, 10 to 12 minutes. Remove from pans, and let cool completely on a wire rack.

SNICKERDOODLE BROOKIE

Makes 1 (9-inch) cookie

The brookie: a heavenly hybrid of brownie and cookie. But the Snickerdoodle Brookie? It's a whole new level of epic dessert mash-up. Cinnamon-scented cookie dough is blended with fudgy brownie batter to create a treat you never knew you wanted—until that first fantastic bite.

Brownie batter:
6   ounces (170 grams) 60% cacao bittersweet chocolate baking bars, finely chopped
½   cup (113 grams) unsalted butter, cubed
1   cup (200 grams) granulated sugar
2   large eggs (100 grams), lightly beaten
1   teaspoon (4 grams) vanilla extract
¾   cup (94 grams) all-purpose flour
¼   cup (21 grams) Dutch process cocoa powder
½   teaspoon (1.5 grams) kosher salt

Snickerdoodle dough:
⅓   cup (76 grams) unsalted butter, softened
½   cup (100 grams) granulated sugar
1   large egg (50 grams)
½   teaspoon (2 grams) vanilla extract
1   cup (125 grams) all-purpose flour
½   teaspoon (1.5 grams) kosher salt
½   teaspoon (1 gram) ground cinnamon
¼   teaspoon (1.25 grams) baking powder

Cinnamon sugar:
1   tablespoon (12 grams) granulated sugar
⅛   teaspoon ground cinnamon

1. Preheat oven to 350°F (180°C).
2. For brownie batter: In the top of a double boiler, combine chocolate and butter. Cook over simmering water, stirring occasionally, until smooth. Turn off heat, and whisk in sugar. Remove from heat, and let cool slightly. Whisk in eggs and vanilla.
3. In a medium bowl, whisk together flour, cocoa, and salt. Fold flour mixture into chocolate mixture just until combined. Set aside.
4. For snickerdoodle dough: In the bowl of a stand mixer fitted with the paddle attachment, beat butter and sugar at medium speed until fluffy, 3 to 4 minutes, stopping to scrape sides of bowl. Add egg, beating well. Beat in vanilla.
5. In a medium bowl, whisk together flour, salt, cinnamon, and baking powder. Gradually add flour mixture to butter mixture, beating just until combined.
6. Spray a 9-inch round cake pan with baking spray with flour. Spoon large dollops (about 3 tablespoons each) of brownie batter into prepared pan, leaving space between each. Crumble and sprinkle snickerdoodle dough between brownie batter. Top with any remaining brownie batter and snickerdoodle dough. Tap pan on a kitchen towel-lined counter to level top.
7. Bake until a wooden pick inserted in center comes out with a few crumbs, 30 to 35 minutes.
8. Meanwhile, for cinnamon sugar: In a small bowl, stir together sugar and cinnamon.
9. Immediately sprinkle cinnamon sugar on top of hot brookie. Serve warm in pan, or let cool completely, and remove from pan.

CREAM CHEESE-FILLED CHOCOLATE CHIP COOKIES

Makes 24 cookies

We added cream cheese to our classic chocolate chip cookie dough formula to make it chewy and puffy. Why add the cream cheese filling, too? Because we could. It turns a great cookie into something transcendentally extravagant—emphasis on the "extra."

½   cup (113 grams) unsalted butter, softened

10   ounces (284 grams) cream cheese, softened and divided

⅔   cup (147 grams) firmly packed dark brown sugar

⅓   cup (67 grams) plus 3½ tablespoons (42 grams) granulated sugar, divided

1   large egg (50 grams), room temperature

1   tablespoon (13 grams) vanilla extract

2   cups (250 grams) all-purpose flour

1½   teaspoons (4.5 grams) cornstarch

1   teaspoon (5 grams) baking soda

1   teaspoon (2.25 grams) kosher salt, divided

4.5 ounces (128 grams) milk chocolate, chopped (about ¾ cup)

3   ounces (85 grams) 66% cacao semisweet chocolate, chopped (about ½ cup)

1. In the bowl of a stand mixer fitted with the paddle attachment, beat butter at medium speed until smooth and creamy, about 1 minute, stopping halfway to scrape sides of bowl. Add 2 ounces (57 grams) cream cheese; beat until smooth and well combined, about 30 seconds. Scrape sides of bowl. Add brown sugar and ⅓ cup (67 grams) granulated sugar; beat until fluffy, about 2 minutes, stopping to scrape sides of bowl. Beat in egg and vanilla until combined.

2. In a large bowl, whisk together flour, cornstarch, baking soda, and ¾ teaspoon (2.25 grams) salt. Add flour mixture to butter mixture all at once; beat at low speed just until combined. Fold in chocolates. Cover and refrigerate for 30 minutes.

3. Preheat oven to 350°F (180°C). Line 2 rimmed baking sheets with parchment paper.

4. In a medium bowl, stir together remaining 8 ounces (227 grams) cream cheese, remaining 3½ tablespoons (42 grams) granulated sugar, and remaining ¼ teaspoon salt. Cover and freeze for 15 minutes.

5. Divide dough into 48 portions (about 18 grams each); shape each portion into a ball, and flatten into 1½- to 2-inch disks. Spoon about 1½ teaspoons (9 grams) cream cheese mixture in center of 1 dough disk, and cover with a second disk. Crimp edges to seal, and gently shape into a ball. (See technique images below.) Repeat with remaining dough disks and remaining cream cheese mixture. Place dough balls 1½ to 2 inches apart on prepared pans. Gently flatten balls to ¾-inch thickness, crimping any cracks to seal, if necessary.

6. Bake until edges are set and lightly golden, 8 to 10 minutes. Let cool on pans on wire racks for 2 minutes. Serve warm, or remove from pans, and let cool completely on wire racks.

PRO TIPS

Cookie dough and cream cheese filling can be made 1 day ahead, covered, and refrigerated separately overnight. Let stand at room temperature until softened, about 30 minutes. Shape as directed. Bake until edges are set and lightly golden, 10 to 15 minutes. Serve as directed.

To get photo-worthy cookies like the ones shown, press a few pieces of semisweet chocolate onto the exterior of each dough ball before flattening them.

CHOCOLATE-DIPPED MACAROONS

Makes about 32 macaroons

With just a touch of aromatic orange zest mixed in with the creamy condensed milk and flaked coconut base, these classic macaroons pair notes of chocolate and citrus within their sweet snowball packages.

1   (14-ounce) can (397 grams) sweetened condensed milk

2   teaspoons (8 grams) vanilla extract

½   teaspoon (2 grams) tightly packed orange zest

2½   cups (258 grams) sweetened flaked coconut

2   cups (146 grams) unsweetened flaked coconut

2   large egg whites (60 grams)

¼   teaspoon kosher salt

4   ounces (113 grams) 60% cacao bittersweet chocolate baking bar, finely chopped

½   teaspoon (2 grams) coconut oil

Garnish: flaked sea salt

1. Preheat oven to 325°F (170°C). Line 2 rimmed baking sheets with parchment paper.

2. In a large bowl, stir together condensed milk, vanilla, and orange zest; add flaked coconuts, and stir until well combined.

3. In the bowl of a stand mixer fitted with the whisk attachment, beat egg whites and kosher salt at medium-high speed until stiff peaks form, 3 to 4 minutes. Gently fold egg white mixture into coconut mixture until well combined. Using a 1½-tablespoon spring-loaded scoop, scoop mixture, and place at least 1 inch apart on prepared pans.

4. Bake until golden brown, about 15 minutes. Let cool completely on pans on wire racks.

5. Place a large wire rack over a parchment paper-lined large rimmed baking sheet; spray with cooking spray.

6. In a small microwave-safe bowl, heat chocolate and oil on high in 10-second intervals, stirring between each, until chocolate is melted and mixture is smooth.

7. Dip bottoms of macaroons in chocolate mixture, letting excess drip off. Place on prepared rack. (Alternately, spoon chocolate mixture into a small pastry bag or resealable plastic bag; cut a ¼-inch opening in tip or corner. Place cooled macaroons on prepared rack; drizzle with chocolate mixture as desired.) Refrigerate until chocolate is set, about 20 minutes. Using a large offset spatula, loosen dipped macaroons from wire rack, if necessary. Just before serving, garnish with sea salt, if desired.

VANILLA-STRAWBERRY SANDWICH COOKIES

Makes about 12 sandwich cookies

To accentuate the sweetness of our strawberry frosting-filled sandwich cookies, we relied on a triple dose of vanilla. Vanilla extract and vanilla bean paste pump up the flavor of the cookies and frosting while a final roll in vanilla sugar gives the cookies a satisfying, vanilla-forward crunch.

½ cup (100 grams) granulated sugar
½ cup (113 grams) unsalted butter, melted and cooled for 10 minutes
¼ cup (55 grams) firmly packed light brown sugar
2 teaspoons (8 grams) vanilla extract
1 large egg (50 grams), room temperature
1⅔ cups (208 grams) all-purpose flour
1 teaspoon (3 grams) cornstarch
½ teaspoon (2.5 grams) baking powder
½ teaspoon (2.5 grams) baking soda
½ teaspoon (1.5 grams) kosher salt
⅓ cup (76 grams) vanilla sugar*
Strawberry Jam Frosting (recipe follows)

1. In the bowl of a stand mixer fitted with the paddle attachment, beat granulated sugar, melted butter, brown sugar, and vanilla extract at medium-low speed until well combined, 1 to 2 minutes, stopping to scrape sides of bowl. Add egg, beating until well combined.
2. In a medium bowl, whisk together flour, cornstarch, baking powder, baking soda, and salt. Add flour mixture to sugar mixture all at once; beat at low speed just until combined, stopping to scrape sides of bowl.
3. Preheat oven to 350°F (180°C). Line 2 rimmed baking sheets with parchment paper.
4. In a small shallow bowl, place vanilla sugar.
5. Divide dough into 24 portions (about 22 grams each), and shape into balls. Roll dough balls in vanilla sugar, and place at least 2 inches apart on prepared pans.
6. Bake until edges are lightly golden and set, 8 to 10 minutes. (Centers may still seem slightly underdone.) Let cool completely on pan on a wire rack.

7. Place Strawberry Jam Frosting in a large pastry bag fitted with a medium open star piping tip (Wilton 1M); pipe frosting onto flat side of half of cookies. Place remaining cookies, flat side down, on top of frosting. Serve immediately.

We used Heilala Vanilla Sugar.

STRAWBERRY JAM FROSTING
Makes about 2 cups

½ cup (113 grams) unsalted butter, softened
2 teaspoons (12 grams) vanilla bean paste
½ teaspoon (1.5 grams) kosher salt
3½ cups (420 grams) confectioners' sugar, sifted
½ cup (10 grams) freeze-dried strawberries, very finely crushed (see Note)
6 tablespoons (106 grams) seedless strawberry jam
2 tablespoons (30 grams) heavy whipping cream

1. In the bowl of a stand mixer fitted with the paddle attachment, beat butter, vanilla bean paste, and salt at medium speed until smooth and well combined, about 1 minute, stopping to scrape sides of bowl. With mixer on low speed, gradually add confectioners' sugar and freeze-dried strawberries, beating until combined. Add jam and cream; increase mixer speed to medium, and beat until fluffy, about 2 minutes. Use immediately.

Note: *To finely crush whole freeze-dried strawberries, place in a small resealable plastic bag and pound with a rolling pin.*

CORNMEAL MA'AMOUL WITH APRICOT & PISTACHIO

Makes 28 cookies

Recipe by Majed Ali

Cornmeal gives these cookies an extra-crumbly texture while apricot and pistachio are a bright, modern twist on ma'amoul's classic date filling. Using a traditional wooden ma'amoul mold to render a unique design on top of the cookie is truly what sets this treat apart. If you don't own a mold, don't fret. You can shape the dough by hand, and use a fork to create your own pattern on top.

3¼	cups (488 grams) semolina flour
1¼	cups (173 grams) plain yellow cornmeal
2½	teaspoons (5 grams) ground cinnamon
2	teaspoons (4 grams) mahlab*
1	teaspoon (3 grams) kosher salt
1⅓	cups (303 grams) unsalted butter, melted
¼	cup (60 grams) rose water
¼	cup (60 grams) warm water (105°F/41°C to 110°F/43°C)
1	tablespoon (12 grams) granulated sugar
½	teaspoon (1.5 grams) active dry yeast
14	ounces (397 grams) finely chopped dried apricots (about 2¾ cups)
½	cup (75 grams) very finely chopped pistachios
¼	cup (80 grams) apricot preserves
¼	cup (60 grams) room temperature water, plus more if needed

Confectioners' sugar, for dusting

1. In a large bowl, combine semolina, cornmeal, cinnamon, mahlab, and salt. Add melted butter; using your fingers, rub mixture together until it resembles wet sand. Add rose water, and rub mixture together. Cover with plastic wrap, and let stand overnight to soften.

2. In a small bowl, combine ¼ cup (60 grams) warm water, granulated sugar, and yeast. Let stand until foamy, 5 to 10 minutes.

3. Add yeast mixture to semolina mixture; using your fingers, rub mixture together. Cover with plastic wrap, and let stand for 1 hour.

4. Line a baking sheet with parchment paper.

5. In a medium bowl, combine apricots, pistachios, and preserves. Using a 2-teaspoon spring-loaded scoop, scoop 28 mounds of apricot mixture (about 18 grams each), and place on prepared pan. Set aside.

6. Preheat oven to 400°F (200°C). Line 2 large baking sheets with parchment paper.

7. Add ¼ cup (60 grams) room temperature water to semolina mixture until well combined. (Mixture should feel like soft cookie dough that can be flattened and shaped into a ball without significant cracking. Add more room temperature water, 1 Tablespoon [15 grams] at a time, if needed, until desired consistency is reached.)

8. Divide dough into 28 portions (about 40 grams each). Place 1 portion in palm of one hand; using fingertips of your other hand, flatten dough into a 3¼-inch circle, pressing edges slightly thinner than center. Place 1 mound of apricot mixture in center of dough circle. Shape dough into a ball around apricot mixture. Repeat procedure with remaining dough and remaining apricot mixture mounds. Dust a 2½-inch-wide, ½-inch-deep ma'amoul mold (see Note) with flour. Press 1 dough ball into mold, and flatten using your hand. Tap mold on a clean surface to release. (Alternatively, gently press dough balls to ½-inch thickness, and use the tines of a fork to make a pattern on top.) Repeat with remaining dough balls, reflouring mold as needed. Place 1 inch apart on prepared pans.

9. Bake until dry, set, and lightly golden, 18 to 20 minutes. Let cool completely on pans on wire racks. Dust with confectioners' sugar before serving.

*Mahlab is a powder made from the seeds of the St. Lucy's cherry, found in different parts of the Mediterranean. You can find this baking spice at local specialty grocery stores or online.

Note: *We used Ma'amoul Carved Round Wooden Mould Press, Middle Eastern Cookie & Cake Mold, available at amazon.com. Using a 2½-inch fluted round tart pan is another option; line pan with plastic wrap before pressing in dough to remove shaped cookie with ease.*

CHOCOLATE-COCONUT MACARONS

Makes 20 to 24 macarons

With coconut-accented shells and a bittersweet chocolate filling, this traditional recipe for macarons plays subtle homage to their American cookie cousin.

1⅓	cups (128 grams) superfine blanched almond flour
1	cup (120 grams) confectioners' sugar
⅛	teaspoon kosher salt
3	large egg whites (90 grams), room temperature
½	cup (100 grams) granulated sugar
½	teaspoon (2 grams) coconut extract
¼	teaspoon (1 gram) vanilla extract

Bittersweet Chocolate Buttercream (recipe follows)

2	ounces (57 grams) 60% cacao bittersweet chocolate baking bar*, finely chopped
½	teaspoon (2 grams) coconut oil

1. Using a permanent marker, draw 1½-inch circles 1 inch apart on 2 sheets of parchment paper. Place parchment on 2 rimmed baking sheets; top with nonstick baking mats.

2. In the work bowl of a food processor, place flour, confectioners' sugar, and salt; process until well combined and mixture is a uniform, fine texture, stopping to scrape sides of bowl. Sift flour mixture through a fine-mesh sieve twice.

3. In the bowl of a stand mixer fitted with the whisk attachment, beat egg whites at medium-high speed until foamy. Gradually add granulated sugar, and beat at medium-high speed until stiff peaks form. Gently fold flour mixture into egg white mixture in three additions, adding extracts with final addition; fold until well combined and batter runs together smoothly when a spatula is dragged through center. (Batter should fall off spatula in a continuous ribbon while making a figure 8 pattern.)

4. Transfer batter to a pastry bag fitted with a ½-inch round piping tip (Wilton No. 2A). Holding tip ½ inch above and perpendicular to pan, pipe batter onto drawn circles underneath mats; apply even pressure to bag, leaving tip stationary, until batter reaches drawn circle. Release pressure, and move tip in a quick circular motion to finish piping each macaron shell. (It's OK if some drawn circles remain unfilled.) Slam pans vigorously on counter several times to smooth batter and release air bubbles; use a wooden pick to release and fill any large air bubbles, slamming pans again to smooth. Let stand at room temperature until a skin forms on top of macaron shells, about 1 hour. (Batter should feel dry to the touch and should not stick to your finger.)

5. Preheat oven to 275°F (140°C).

6. Bake, one pan at a time, until firm to the touch, about 15 minutes, rotating pan every 5 minutes. (To test for doneness, place a fingertip on top of a macaron shell, and try to gently move it from side to side; if it slides, bake for 1 minute more, and check again. If it doesn't move, macaron shells are done.) Let cool completely on pans. (If you have trouble removing macaron shells from pans, place pans in freezer for about 15 minutes.)

7. Place Bittersweet Chocolate Buttercream in a pastry bag fitted with a ½-inch round piping tip (Wilton No. 2A). Pipe buttercream onto flat side of half of macaron shells. Place remaining macaron shells, flat side down, on top of buttercream. Place macarons on a parchment paper-lined baking sheet.

8. In a small microwave-safe bowl, heat chocolate and oil on high in 10-second intervals, stirring between each, until chocolate is melted and mixture is smooth. Spoon chocolate mixture into a small pastry bag or resealable plastic bag; cut a ¼-inch opening in tip or corner, and drizzle onto macarons as desired. Refrigerate until chocolate is set, about 20 minutes.

*We used Ghirardelli 60% Cacao Bittersweet Chocolate Baking Bar.

BITTERSWEET CHOCOLATE BUTTERCREAM
Makes about 1¼ cups

4	ounces (113 grams) 60% cacao bittersweet chocolate baking bar, finely chopped
¾	teaspoon (1 gram) instant espresso powder
⅛	teaspoon kosher salt
⅓	cup (76 grams) unsalted butter, softened
⅔	cup (80 grams) confectioners' sugar
½	teaspoon (2 grams) vanilla extract

1. In the top of a double boiler, combine chocolate, espresso powder, and salt. Cook over simmering water, stirring frequently, until chocolate is melted and mixture is smooth. Remove from heat; let cool for 5 minutes.

2. In the bowl of a stand mixer fitted with the paddle attachment, beat butter at medium speed until smooth, 1 to 2 minutes. Add cooled chocolate mixture; beat until well combined, 1 to 2 minutes, stopping to scrape sides of bowl. Gradually add confectioners' sugar, beating at low speed just until combined. Add vanilla; increase mixer speed to medium, and beat until light and fluffy, about 2 minutes, stopping to scrape sides of bowl. Use immediately.

PECAN PINWHEELS

Makes about 24 cookies

Uniting the rich flavor of smooth butter and nutty pecans in one mesmerizing swirl, these cakey cookies are coated in sugar and finely chopped pecans for irresistible crunch. This slice-and-bake dough needs some time to chill before slicing, so it's the ultimate make-ahead treat.

1⅔ cups (208 grams) plus 1½ cups (188 grams) all-purpose flour, divided
2 teaspoons (4 grams) ground cinnamon
1½ teaspoons (4.5 grams) kosher salt, divided
1 teaspoon (5 grams) baking powder, divided
½ cup (57 grams) pecan pieces, toasted (see PRO TIPS)
1 cup (226 grams) unsalted butter, softened and divided
½ cup (110 grams) firmly packed light brown sugar
3 large eggs (150 grams), divided
2½ teaspoons (10 grams) vanilla extract, divided
½ cup (100 grams) granulated sugar
½ cup (57 grams) finely chopped pecans
¼ cup (50 grams) turbinado sugar

1. In a medium bowl, whisk together 1½ cups (188 grams) flour, cinnamon, 1 teaspoon (3 grams) salt, and ½ teaspoon (2.5 grams) baking powder. Set aside.

2. In the work bowl of a food processor, place pecan pieces and 2 tablespoons flour mixture; pulse until pecans are finely ground. (See PRO TIPS.) Add pecan mixture to remaining flour mixture, whisking to combine.

3. In the bowl of a stand mixer fitted with the paddle attachment, beat ½ cup (113 grams) butter and brown sugar at medium speed until creamy, 2 to 3 minutes, stopping to scrape sides of bowl. Add 1 egg (50 grams) and 1 teaspoon (4 grams) vanilla, beating until combined. With mixer on low speed, gradually add flour-pecan mixture to butter mixture, beating until combined. Turn out dough onto a lightly floured surface, and shape into a disk. Wrap in plastic wrap, and refrigerate for at least 1 hour.

4. Clean bowl of stand mixer and paddle attachment. Using the paddle attachment, beat granulated sugar and remaining ½ cup (113 grams) butter at medium speed until creamy, 2 to 3 minutes, stopping to scrape sides of bowl. Add 1 egg (50 grams) and remaining 1½ teaspoons (6 grams) vanilla, beating until combined.

5. In a medium bowl, whisk together remaining 1⅔ cups (208 grams) flour, remaining ½ teaspoon (1.5 grams) salt, and remaining ½ teaspoon (2.5 grams) baking powder. With mixer on low speed, gradually add flour mixture to butter mixture, beating until combined. Turn out dough onto a lightly floured surface, and shape into a disk. Wrap in plastic wrap, and refrigerate for at least 1 hour.

6. Let doughs stand at room temperature until slightly softened, about 5 minutes. On a lightly floured sheet of parchment paper, roll vanilla dough into a 14x10-inch rectangle (⅛ inch thick). Transfer dough on parchment to a baking sheet. Refrigerate for 15 minutes. Repeat procedure with pecan dough.

7. Transfer vanilla dough on parchment to a flat surface. Carefully invert pecan dough on top of vanilla dough. Between sheets of parchment, gently roll over doughs a few times to press together. Peel away top sheet of parchment. Starting at one long side, roll dough into a log, using bottom sheet of parchment to help lift and roll. (If dough cracks, stop rolling, and let stand for a few minutes until pliable.) Be sure to roll doughs together as tightly as possible to avoid gaps. Trim any pecan dough if uneven after rolling. Tightly wrap in parchment paper, twisting ends of parchment to seal. Transfer to a baking sheet, seam side down. Refrigerate for at least 2 hours, or freeze until ready to use.

8. Preheat oven to 325°F (170°C). Line 2 baking sheets with parchment paper.

9. In a small bowl, whisk remaining 1 egg (50 grams). In another small bowl, stir together chopped pecans and turbinado sugar. Pour onto a piece of parchment paper. Brush log with egg wash, and roll in pecan sugar. Roll back and forth a few times so sugar sticks to log. Using a sharp knife, cut log into ½-inch-thick slices. Place about 1 inch apart on prepared pans.

10. Bake until edges are just beginning to turn golden, 12 to 14 minutes, rotating pans halfway through baking. Let cool completely on pans. Store in airtight containers for up to 2 weeks.

PRO TIPS

To toast pecans in the oven, preheat your oven to 350°F (180°C) and spread your pecans in a single layer on a parchment paper–lined rimmed baking sheet. When the oven is ready, bake the nuts until lightly browned and fragrant, 5 to 10 minutes. Remember that nuts continue to cook even after they have been removed from the oven, so don't hesitate to pull them from the oven once they begin to change color. Once the nuts are warm but not too hot to handle, chop as desired. Nuts are still slightly soft when they're still warm, so this will make cleaner cuts than if you wait to chop them when the nuts are cool and brittle.

We like to add a little bit of flour to absorb the oils from the nuts and prevent a nut butter from forming in the food processor.

CHOCOLATE-PEANUT BUTTER-PISTACHIO BISCOTTI

Makes about 36 biscotti

For bakers looking to send loved ones homemade comfort, crisp biscotti is a shipping dream, with a long shelf life and a rigid shape that can handle the long, bumpy road ahead. Our chocolate-peanut butter combo is made all the more decadent by the addition of yuletide-green pistachios.

- 6 ounces (170 grams) 64% cacao semisweet chocolate*, finely chopped and divided
- ½ cup (113 grams) unsalted butter, softened
- 1 cup (200 grams) granulated sugar
- ¼ cup (55 grams) firmly packed light brown sugar
- 2 large eggs (100 grams), room temperature
- 2 teaspoons (8 grams) vanilla extract
- 1¾ cups (219 grams) all-purpose flour
- ¾ cup (70 grams) Dutch process cocoa powder, sifted
- 1 teaspoon (5 grams) baking powder
- 1 teaspoon (1 gram) instant espresso powder*
- ¾ teaspoon (2.25 grams) kosher salt
- ½ cup (82 grams) peanut butter chips
- ½ cup (66 grams) roasted pistachios, roughly chopped

1. Preheat oven to 325°F (170°C). Line a rimmed baking sheet with parchment paper.
2. In the top of a double boiler, place 4 ounces (113 grams) chocolate. Cook over simmering water, stirring frequently, until melted and smooth. Remove from heat; set aside.

3. In the bowl of a stand mixer fitted with the paddle attachment, beat butter and sugars at medium speed until fluffy, 2 to 3 minutes, stopping to scrape sides of bowl. Add eggs and vanilla; beat until well combined, stopping to scrape sides of bowl. Add melted chocolate, beating until well combined.
4. In a medium bowl, whisk together flour, cocoa, baking powder, espresso powder, and salt. With mixer on low speed, gradually add flour mixture to butter mixture, beating just until combined and stopping to scrape sides of bowl. Fold in peanut butter chips, pistachios, and remaining 2 ounces (57 grams) chocolate.
5. Turn out dough onto a lightly floured surface, and divide in half. Shape each half into a 9x3-inch loaf, and place 2 to 2½ inches apart on prepared pan.
6. Bake until set and loaves spring back when touched, 35 to 40 minutes. Let cool on pan on a wire rack for 15 minutes.

Reduce oven temperature to 300°F (150°C).
7. Line 2 rimmed baking sheets with parchment paper.
8. Place 1 cooled loaf on a cutting board. Using a serrated knife, cut crosswise into ½-inch-thick slices. Gently place, cut side down, ½ to ¾ inch apart on prepared pans. Repeat with remaining loaf.
9. Bake, one batch at a time, until cut sides feel toasted and mostly dry, about 25 minutes, turning slices halfway through baking. Let cool on pan for 2 minutes. Carefully remove from pan, and let cool completely on wire racks. (Biscotti will continue to crisp as they cool.) Store in an airtight container for up to 2 weeks.

We used Guittard 64% Cacao Semisweet Chocolate Baking Bars and Williams Sonoma Espresso Powder.

GLAZED OAT COOKIES

Makes about 26 cookies

Called "biscuits" in Ireland, these chewy, golden cookies pack a caramelized sweetness supercharged by a crème fraîche drizzle. Oats give this recipe an essential boost in texture, lending a crispy exterior and a chewy interior.

1 cup (227 grams) unsalted butter, softened
½ cup (100 grams) granulated sugar
¼ cup (55 grams) firmly packed light brown sugar
1 teaspoon (3 grams) tightly packed orange zest
1 teaspoon (6 grams) vanilla bean paste
2¼ cups (212 grams) old-fashioned oats
1¾ cups (219 grams) unbleached self-rising flour
¼ cup (44 grams) steel-cut oats
¼ teaspoon kosher salt
Crème Fraîche Glaze (recipe follows)

1. Preheat oven to 350°F (180°C). Line 2 rimmed baking sheets with parchment paper.

2. In the bowl of a stand mixer fitted with the paddle attachment, beat butter, sugars, orange zest, and vanilla bean paste at medium speed until creamy, 2 to 3 minutes, stopping to scrape sides of bowl.

3. In a medium bowl, stir together old-fashioned oats, flour, steel-cut oats, and salt. Add oats mixture to butter mixture all at once; beat at medium-low speed just until combined, stopping to scrape sides of bowl. Using a 2-tablespoon spring-loaded scoop, scoop dough (about 32 grams each), and roll into balls. Place at least 2 inches apart on prepared pans; press to about ¾-inch thickness, pinching closed any cracks and smoothing edges, if needed.

4. Bake in batches until edges are golden, 12 to 16 minutes. Let cool on pans for 2 minutes. Remove from pans, and let cool completely on a wire rack placed over a parchment paper-lined baking sheet.

5. Place Crème Fraîche Glaze in a small pastry bag or resealable plastic bag; cut a ¼-inch opening in tip or corner. Drizzle glaze onto cooled cookies as desired; let stand until set, about 15 minutes.

PRO TIP
For softer, chewier cookies, bake for 10 to 12 minutes. The cookies' edges should be set. The centers may seem underdone but will continue to set as cookies cool.

CRÈME FRAÎCHE GLAZE
Makes ¾ cup

1½ cups (180 grams) confectioners' sugar
3 tablespoons (45 grams) crème fraîche
1½ tablespoons (22.5 grams) fresh orange juice

1. In a small bowl, stir together all ingredients until smooth and well combined. Use immediately.

CHOCOLATE-CHERRY BROWNED BUTTER SANDWICH COOKIES WITH WHISKEY BUTTERCREAM

Makes 16 sandwich cookies

These browned butter cookies are jam-packed with chocolate as well as dried tart cherries cooked in Irish whiskey, but we didn't stop there—there's also Irish whiskey and browned butter in the frosting. We could eat this buttercream by the spoonful.

1¼ cups (283 grams) unsalted butter, cubed
½ cup (115 grams) packed dried tart cherries, chopped
¼ cup (52 grams) plus 1½ teaspoons (6.5 grams) Irish whiskey, divided
⅔ cup (133 grams) granulated sugar
⅔ cup (147 grams) firmly packed light brown sugar
1 large egg (50 grams), room temperature
½ teaspoon (2 grams) vanilla extract
1¾ cups (219 grams) all-purpose flour
2 tablespoons (16 grams) cornstarch
1 teaspoon (3 grams) kosher salt
½ teaspoon (2.5 grams) baking powder
½ teaspoon (2.5 grams) baking soda
½ cup (85 grams) chopped 66% cacao dark chocolate*
Whiskey Buttercream (recipe follows)

1. In a medium saucepan, melt butter over medium heat. Cook, stirring frequently, until butter solids are golden and nutty in aroma, 7 to 12 minutes. Pour ¾ cup (139 grams) browned butter into a medium shallow baking dish or bowl. Pour remaining ½ cup (94 grams) browned butter into another medium shallow baking dish or bowl, reserving for Whiskey Buttercream. (See Note.) Refrigerate both until browned butter is solid, 2 to 3 hours. Let stand at room temperature until softened before using, about 30 minutes.
2. In a small microwave-safe bowl, combine cherries and ¼ cup (52 grams) whiskey; heat on high until hot, about 2 minutes. Let stand for at least 30 minutes, stirring occasionally. Drain cherries.
3. In the bowl of a stand mixer fitted with the paddle attachment, beat ¾ cup (139 grams) browned butter at medium speed until creamy, 30 seconds to 1 minute; scrape sides of bowl. Add sugars, and beat until fluffy, about 2 minutes, stopping to scrape sides of bowl. Beat in egg, vanilla, and remaining 1½ teaspoons (6.5 grams) whiskey until well combined.
4. In a medium bowl, whisk together flour, cornstarch, salt, baking powder, and baking soda. Add flour mixture to butter mixture all at once, and beat at low speed just until combined. Fold in cherries and chocolate. Cover and refrigerate for 1 hour.

5. Preheat oven to 350°F (180°C). Line 2 large rimmed baking sheets with parchment paper.
6. Using a 1½-tablespoon spring-loaded scoop, scoop dough (about 28 grams each), and roll into balls. Place 1½ to 2 inches apart on prepared pans.
7. Bake until light golden brown, about 10 minutes. (Cookies may still seem slightly underdone in centers but will set up as they cool; any warm cookies can be formed right out of the oven into a more circular shape, if desired. Using an offset spatula, gently press and curve uneven edges of still-warm cookies.) Let cool on pans for 5 minutes. Remove from pans, and let cool completely on wire racks.
8. Spoon Whiskey Buttercream into a large pastry bag fitted with a medium open star piping tip (Wilton 1M). Pipe buttercream onto flat side of half of cookies. Place remaining cookies, flat side down, on top of buttercream. Serve immediately.

We used Valrhona Caraïbe 66% Cacao Dark Chocolate Fèves. Valrhona Caraïbe 66% Cacao Baking Bars would work as well.

Note: *Gram weights of browned butter may vary slightly depending on the brand of butter used.*

WHISKEY BUTTERCREAM
Makes 2 cups

½ cup (94 grams) browned butter, reserved from Chocolate-Cherry Browned Butter Sandwich Cookies with Whiskey Buttercream (recipe precedes), softened
¼ teaspoon kosher salt
3½ tablespoons (45.5 grams) Irish whiskey
2 tablespoons (30 grams) heavy whipping cream
4 cups (480 grams) confectioners' sugar, sifted

1. In the bowl of a stand mixer fitted with the paddle attachment, beat browned butter and salt at medium speed until creamy, 30 seconds to 1 minute; scrape sides of bowl.
2. In a small bowl, whisk together whiskey and cream.
3. With mixer on low speed, gradually add confectioners' sugar to butter mixture alternately with whiskey mixture, beginning and ending with confectioners' sugar, beating just until combined after each addition and stopping to scrape sides of bowl. Increase mixer speed to medium, and beat until fluffy, about 2 minutes, stopping to scrape sides of bowl. Use immediately.

CHAI GREEK WEDDING COOKIES

Makes about 25 cookies

We remixed the classic kourabiedes *recipe by adding a touch of aromatic chai spice.*

1 cup (227 grams) unsalted butter, softened
1¾ cups (210 grams) confectioners' sugar, divided
1 large egg yolk (19 grams)
1 tablespoon (15 grams) bourbon
½ teaspoon (2 grams) almond extract
2¾ cups (344 grams) all-purpose flour
2 teaspoons (4 grams) Chai Spice Mix (recipe follows)
½ teaspoon (2.5 grams) baking powder
½ teaspoon (1.5 grams) kosher salt

1. Preheat oven to 350°F (180°C). Line 2 baking sheets with parchment paper.
2. In the bowl of a stand mixer fitted with the paddle attachment, beat butter at medium speed until smooth and creamy, 2 to 3 minutes, stopping to scrape sides of bowl. Add ¼ cup (30 grams) confectioners' sugar, and beat until well combined, about 1 minute. Beat in egg yolk. Slowly add bourbon and almond extract, beating until combined.
3. In a medium bowl, whisk together flour, Chai Spice Mix, baking powder, and salt. With mixer on low speed, gradually add flour mixture to butter mixture, beating just until combined. (Dough should be firm enough to shape but still soft.) Divide dough into 25 portions (about 25 grams each). Roll each portion into a smooth ball; roll each ball into a 3½-inch log. Shape each log into a "U," and place on prepared pans.
4. Bake until tops are light tan and bottoms are lightly golden, 15 to 20 minutes. Let cool on pans for 5 minutes.
5. Place a sheet of parchment paper on work surface, and top with a wire rack. Place another sheet of parchment paper on work surface, and evenly dust with ½ cup (60 grams) confectioners' sugar.
6. Place half of cookies on confectioners' sugar-dusted parchment; sift ½ cup (60 grams) confectioners' sugar on top of cookies. Using a fork, push confectioners' sugar around cookies to cover any bare spots. Lift cookies with fork, tapping on work surface to remove excess confectioners' sugar. Place on prepared rack, and let cool completely. Repeat procedure with remaining cookies and remaining ½ cup (60 grams) confectioners' sugar. Store in an airtight container for up to 4 days.

CHAI SPICE MIX
Makes about ⅓ cup

3 tablespoons (18 grams) ground cinnamon
1½ tablespoons (9 grams) ground ginger
1 tablespoon (6 grams) ground cloves
½ tablespoon (3 grams) ground cardamom
½ tablespoon (3 grams) finely ground black pepper

1. In a small bowl, stir together all ingredients. Store in an airtight container for up to 2 months.

PAN-BANGING SNICKERDOODLES

Makes 12 cookies

Recipe by Sarah Kieffer

Bakers love snickerdoodles. Bakers also love Sarah Kieffer's pan-banging cookies. Merging the two sweet concepts leads to an epic cookie.

2   cups (284 grams) all-purpose flour
1   teaspoon (5 grams) baking soda
¾   teaspoon (2.5 grams) kosher salt
½   teaspoon (1.5 grams) cream of tartar
¼   teaspoon freshly grated nutmeg
1   cup (2 sticks or 227 grams) unsalted
     butter, at room temperature
1¾   cups (350 grams) granulated sugar
1   large egg (50 grams)
1   teaspoon (4 grams) pure vanilla extract
1   tablespoon (6 grams) ground cinnamon

1. Adjust an oven rack to the middle of the oven. Preheat the oven to 350°F (180°C). Line three sheet pans with aluminum foil, dull-side up.
2. In a small bowl, whisk together the flour, baking soda, salt, cream of tartar, and nutmeg.

3. In the bowl of a stand mixer fitted with a paddle, beat the butter on medium speed until creamy, about 1 minute. Add 1½ cups (300 grams) of the sugar and beat on medium speed until light and fluffy, 2 to 3 minutes. Add the egg and vanilla and mix on low speed to combine. Add the flour mixture and mix on low speed until combined.
4. In a small bowl, combine the remaining ¼ cup (50 grams) of sugar and the cinnamon.
5. Form the dough into 3-ounce [85-gram] balls (¼ cup). Roll each ball in the cinnamon-sugar mixture. Place 3 or 4 cookies an equal distance apart on the sheet pans. Bake the cookies one pan at a time. Bake until the dough balls have flattened but are puffed slightly in the center, 8 minutes. Lift one side of the sheet pan up about 4 inches (10 centimeters) and gently let it drop down against the oven rack, so the edges of the cookies set and the center falls back down. After the cookies puff up again in 2 minutes, repeat lifting and dropping the pan. Repeat a few more times to create ridges around the edge of the cookie. Bake for 14 to 15 minutes total, until

the cookies have spread out and the edges are golden brown but the centers are much lighter and not fully cooked.
6. Transfer the pan to a wire rack. Let the cookies cool for 10 minutes, then move them to a wire rack to finish cooling. Store cookies in an airtight container at room temperature for 2 days (or refrigerate for up to 3 days).

Reprinted from *100 Cookies* by Sarah Kieffer with permission from Chronicle Books, 2020.

PAN-BANGING PRO TIPS

Some wisdom from Sarah Kieffer on the art of (pan) slam dunk cookies:

Cookie dough can be refrigerated overnight before using. Shape the dough into balls, and cover with plastic wrap before refrigerating; bring the dough balls to room temperature before baking. (When the cookies are chilled solid, they won't ripple as well.)

These cookies are delicious warm, but I've found I love them chilled even more. I usually store them in the refrigerator for a day or two and sneak pieces of them cold.

I find that foil helps the cookies spread a bit more and creates a slightly crisper bottom, but parchment paper will work well, too.

MOLASSES-SWIRLED SUGAR COOKIES

Makes about 32 cookies

Molasses cookie dough is folded with sugar cookie dough to create a slice-and-bake log.

Sugar dough:
1   cup (227 grams) unsalted butter, softened
1   cup (200 grams) granulated sugar
1   large egg (50 grams), room temperature
1½ teaspoons (6 grams) vanilla extract
3¼ cups (406 grams) all-purpose flour
1½ teaspoons (7.5 grams) baking powder
1   teaspoon (3 grams) kosher salt

Molasses dough:
⅔   cup (150 grams) unsalted butter, softened
½   cup (110 grams) firmly packed dark brown sugar
3   tablespoons (63 grams) unsulphured molasses
1   large egg yolk (19 grams), room temperature
1   teaspoon (4 grams) vanilla extract
2   cups plus 1 tablespoon (258 grams) all-purpose flour
1   teaspoon (5 grams) baking powder
½   teaspoon (1.5 grams) kosher salt

1. For sugar dough: In the bowl of a stand mixer fitted with the paddle attachment, beat butter and granulated sugar at medium speed until creamy, 3 to 4 minutes, stopping to scrape sides of bowl. Add egg and vanilla, beating until combined.
2. In a medium bowl, whisk together flour, baking powder, and salt. With mixer on low speed, gradually add flour mixture to butter mixture, beating until a dough forms. Turn out onto a large piece of parchment paper, and knead dough if any flour bits remain. Shape into a 13x3-inch rectangle.
3. For molasses dough: Clean bowl of stand mixer and paddle attachment. Using the paddle attachment, beat butter and brown sugar at medium speed until creamy, 3 to 4 minutes, stopping to scrape sides of bowl. Beat in molasses. Add egg yolk and vanilla, beating until combined.
4. In a medium bowl, whisk together flour, baking powder, and salt. With mixer on low speed, gradually add flour mixture to butter mixture, beating until a dough forms. Turn out onto parchment paper, and knead dough if any flour bits remain. Shape into a 13x3-inch rectangle, and place next to sugar dough.

5. Turn parchment so short side of dough is closest to you. Starting in top corner, fold molasses dough down diagonally over sugar dough. Fold sugar dough diagonally over molasses dough. Alternate folding doughs until you reach other end. Keep folding until doughs overlap. Press dough out until 1 inch thick; cut dough in half, and stack one half of dough on top of other half. Press dough out to 1 inch thick. Cut dough in half, and stack one half of dough on top of other half. On a lightly floured surface, roll dough into a log until 2¼ inches thick (about 16 inches long). Wrap in plastic wrap, and place in 2 cardboard paper towel tubes split lengthwise. Refrigerate until firm, 3 to 4 hours or up to overnight.
6. Preheat oven to 400°F (200°C). Line 3 baking sheets with parchment paper.
7. Using a chef's knife, cut dough into ½-inch-thick slices. Place at least 1½ inches apart on prepared pans. (If baking in batches, refrigerate remaining dough, and let pan cool completely before reusing.)
8. Bake until bottoms are just beginning to brown and tops are dry, 10 to 12 minutes. Let cool on pans for 5 minutes. Remove from pans, and let cool completely on wire racks.

MARBLE YOUR DOUGH

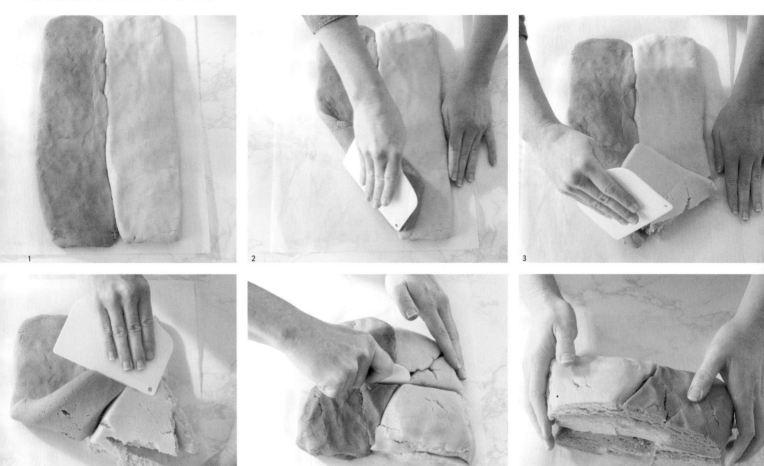

1. Shape sugar dough into a 13x3-inch rectangle. Shape molasses dough into a 13x3-inch rectangle, and place next to sugar dough.

2. Turn parchment so short side of dough is closest to you. Starting in top corner, fold molasses dough down diagonally over sugar dough.

3. Fold sugar dough down diagonally over folded molasses dough.

4. Continue folding alternating sides until you reach the end and doughs overlap.

5. Press dough out until 1 inch thick, and cut dough in half.

6. Stack one half of dough on top of other half.

7. Press dough out again to 1 inch thick.

8. Cut in half, and stack one half of dough on top of other half.

9. On a lightly floured surface, roll dough into a log until 2¼ inches thick (about 16 inches long).

10. To help dough log maintain its shape, wrap dough in plastic wrap, and place in two cardboard paper towel tubes split lengthwise before chilling.

CREAM CHEESE-STUFFED VANILLA-PEPPERMINT COOKIES

Makes about 14 cookies

These holiday cookies pack a cream cheese surprise. We rounded out the festive look by rolling our cream cheese-stuffed cookie dough balls in crushed soft peppermint candies, creating a very merry cookie.

- ½ cup (113 grams) unsalted butter, softened
- ¾ cup (150 grams) plus 2 tablespoons (24 grams) granulated sugar, divided
- 1 large egg (50 grams), room temperature
- 1½ teaspoons (6 grams) peppermint vanilla extract*
- 1⅔ cups (208 grams) all-purpose flour
- 1½ teaspoons (7.5 grams) baking powder
- ¾ teaspoon (2.25 grams) kosher salt
- 4 ounces (113 grams) cream cheese, softened
- ½ cup (64 grams) crushed soft peppermint candies*

Garnish: crushed soft peppermint candies

1. In the bowl of a stand mixer fitted with the paddle attachment, beat butter and ¾ cup (150 grams) sugar at medium speed until fluffy, 2 to 3 minutes, stopping to scrape sides of bowl. Beat in egg and peppermint vanilla extract until well combined, stopping to scrape sides of bowl.

2. In a large bowl, whisk together flour, baking powder, and salt. Add flour mixture to butter mixture all at once; beat at low speed just until combined, stopping to scrape sides of bowl.

3. In a small bowl, stir together cream cheese and remaining 2 tablespoons (24 grams) sugar until well combined. Cover cream cheese mixture and dough with plastic wrap; freeze for 25 minutes.

4. Preheat oven to 350°F (180°C). Line 2 rimmed baking sheets with parchment paper.

5. In a small shallow bowl, place candies.

6. Using a 1-tablespoon spring-loaded scoop, scoop dough (about 18 grams each); flatten into 2-inch disks. Place 1½ teaspoons (about 9 grams) cream cheese mixture in center of 1 dough disk; cover with a second disk, and crimp edges to seal. Gently shape into a ball; roll in candies. (See Note.) Repeat with remaining dough and remaining cream cheese mixture. Place dough balls 1½ inches apart on prepared pans, and gently flatten to ¾-inch thickness, pressing together any cracks in edges, if necessary.

7. Bake, one batch a time, until edges are set and bottoms are golden brown, 12 to 15 minutes. Carefully garnish warm cookies with candies, if desired. Let cool on pans for 3 minutes. Remove from pans, and let cool completely on wire racks.

We used Heilala Peppermint Vanilla Extract. Do not substitute hard peppermint candies.

Note: *If crushed soft peppermint candies aren't sticking well, lightly dampen hands with water as needed before rolling dough into balls and coating in candies.*

SLICE-AND-BAKE HOLIDAY CONFETTI COOKIES

Makes about 50 cookies

Slice-and-bake cookies are easy to make and easier to ship. Packed with holiday nonpareils and glistening with sparkling sugar, this recipe makes enough to fill several care packages.

1   cup (227 grams) unsalted butter, softened
⅔   cup (133 grams) granulated sugar
2   teaspoons (8 grams) vanilla extract
½   teaspoon (2 grams) almond extract
2   cups (250 grams) all-purpose flour
½   teaspoon (1.5 grams) kosher salt
⅓   cup (70 grams) holiday nonpareils
½   cup (112 grams) white sparkling sugar, plus more for sprinkling
1   large egg (50 grams), lightly beaten

1. In the bowl of a stand mixer fitted with the paddle attachment, beat butter and granulated sugar at medium speed until creamy, 2 to 3 minutes, stopping to scrape sides of bowl. Beat in extracts.

2. In a medium bowl, whisk together flour and salt. With mixer on low speed, gradually add flour mixture to butter mixture, beating until combined. Fold in nonpareils. (Dough will be rather soft at this point.) Divide dough in half. Shape each half into a 7-inch log (about 2 inches thick). Wrap each log in plastic wrap; holding ends of plastic wrap, roll log over work surface, creating a more rounded shape. Refrigerate until firm, about 2 hours. (See Note.)

3. Preheat oven to 325°F (170°C). Line 2 to 3 rimmed baking sheets with parchment paper.

4. In a large rimmed baking dish or plate, place sparkling sugar.

5. Working with one dough log at a time, unwrap log, and brush outside with egg; roll in sparkling sugar. Working in batches and using a serrated knife, cut logs crosswise into ¼-inch-thick rounds, and place 1 to 1¼ inches apart on prepared pans; flatten rounds slightly so they lay flat on baking sheet. (If dough rounds crack when flattening, simply press and smooth back together.) Sprinkle tops with sparkling sugar.

6. Bake, one batch at a time, until edges are lightly golden, about 15 minutes. Let cool on pan for 5 minutes. Using a large offset or flat metal spatula, remove from pan, and let cool completely on wire racks. Store in an airtight container for up to 1 week.

Note: *Let dough that has been refrigerated for longer time spans stand at room temperature until slightly softened and easier to slice, 15 to 30 minutes.*

PEARL SUGAR GINGER COOKIES

Makes about 24 cookies

Pearl sugar saves the day again with these beautiful, polka-dotted ginger cookies. Acting as gorgeous decoration and a protective crunchy layer, pearl sugar helps make sure the cookies arrive to your far-flung loved ones in serious style. The molasses also helps the cookies stay fresher for longer, as the hygroscopic sugar keeps them moist.

- ½ cup (113 grams) unsalted butter, softened
- ¾ cup (150 grams) granulated sugar
- ¼ cup (55 grams) firmly packed light brown sugar
- 1 teaspoon (3 grams) lemon zest
- ⅓ cup (113 grams) molasses (not blackstrap)
- 1 large egg (50 grams), room temperature
- 2¼ cups (281 grams) all-purpose flour
- 2 teaspoons (4 grams) ground ginger
- 1 teaspoon (5 grams) baking soda
- 1 teaspoon (3 grams) kosher salt
- ¾ teaspoon (1.5 grams) ground cinnamon
- ½ teaspoon (1 gram) ground cardamom
- ½ teaspoon (1 gram) ground cloves
- ½ cup (104 grams) Swedish pearl sugar

1. Preheat oven to 350°F (180°C). Line 2 rimmed baking sheets with parchment paper.
2. In the bowl of a stand mixer fitted with the paddle attachment, beat butter, granulated sugar, brown sugar, and lemon zest at medium speed until fluffy, 2 to 3 minutes, stopping to scrape sides of bowl. Add molasses and egg; beat until well combined, stopping to scrape sides of bowl.
3. In a medium bowl, whisk together flour, ginger, baking soda, salt, cinnamon, cardamom, and cloves. Add flour mixture to butter mixture all at once; beat at low speed until combined, stopping to scrape sides of bowl.
4. In a small shallow bowl, place pearl sugar.
5. Using a 1½-tablespoon spring-loaded scoop, scoop dough (about 30 grams each), and roll into balls. Roll dough balls in pearl sugar (see Note), and place 1¾ to 2 inches apart on prepared pans.
6. Bake, one batch at a time, until cookies appear cracked and edges are just set but centers look slightly underdone, about 10 minutes. Let cool on pan for 4 minutes. Remove from pan, and let cool completely on wire racks. Store in an airtight container for up to 1 week.

Note: *If the pearl sugar isn't sticking as well, lightly dampen hands with water before rolling dough into balls and coating in sugar.*

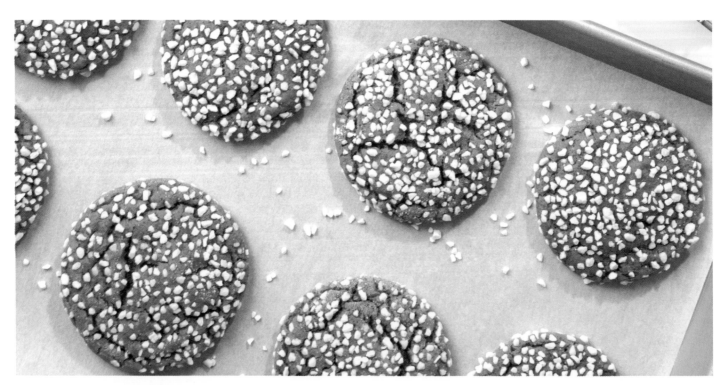

PEPPERMINT CUSTARD-STUFFED CHOCOLATE COOKIES

Makes about 27 cookies

Cookies get all kinds of delicious fillings these days, but our peppermint custard-filled cookies take it to the next level. These peppermint candy-topped chocolate cookies hide a wintry pastry cream flavored with both peppermint extract and soft peppermint candies. To streamline this process, feel free to make both the pastry cream and the cookie dough a day before baking.

1½ cups (340 grams) unsalted butter, softened
2¼ cups (450 grams) granulated sugar
3 large eggs (150 grams), room temperature
1½ teaspoons (6 grams) peppermint extract
4 cups (500 grams) all-purpose flour
1 cup (85 grams) Dutch process cocoa powder, sifted
4½ teaspoons (22.5 grams) baking powder
1 teaspoon (3 grams) kosher salt
Peppermint Pastry Cream (recipe follows)
2 tablespoons (30 grams) water
1½ cups (270 grams) crushed soft peppermint candies

1. In the bowl of a stand mixer fitted with the paddle attachment, beat butter and sugar at medium speed until fluffy, 3 to 4 minutes, stopping to scrape sides of bowl. Add eggs, one at a time, beating well after each addition. Beat in peppermint extract.
2. In a medium bowl, whisk together flour, cocoa, baking powder, and salt. With mixer on low speed, gradually add flour mixture to butter mixture, beating just until combined and stopping to scrape sides of bowl. Cover and refrigerate until dough doesn't stick to your fingers when pinched, 30 to 45 minutes.
3. Preheat oven to 350°F (180°C). Line 4 rimmed baking sheets with parchment paper.
4. Using a 1½-tablespoon spring-loaded scoop, scoop dough (about 26 grams each), and roll into balls. Press balls into 2½-inch disks. Place 2 teaspoons (12 grams) Peppermint Pastry Cream in center of half of disks; cover with remaining disks, and

crimp edges closed. Gently shape into balls, and place on prepared pans; gently press into 2¼-inch disks, pressing together any cracks in edges, if necessary. Brush tops of cookies with 2 tablespoons (30 grams) water; top with candies.
5. Bake until edges are set and tops look dry, 12 to 14 minutes. (See Note.) Carefully top with any remaining candies. Let cool completely on pans.

Note: *If you need to bake the cookies in batches, refrigerate any disks that are waiting to be baked.*

PEPPERMINT PASTRY CREAM
Makes about 1¾ cups

1½ cups (360 grams) whole milk
6 tablespoons (72 grams) granulated sugar, divided
3 large egg yolks (56 grams)
3½ tablespoons (28 grams) cornstarch
¼ teaspoon kosher salt
2 tablespoons (16 grams) finely crushed soft peppermint candies

1 tablespoon (14 grams) unsalted butter, softened
½ teaspoon (2 grams) vanilla extract
¼ teaspoon (1 gram) peppermint extract

1. In a medium saucepan, heat milk and 3 tablespoons (36 grams) sugar over medium heat, stirring occasionally, until steaming. (Do not boil.)
2. In a medium bowl, whisk together egg yolks, cornstarch, salt, and remaining 3 tablespoons (36 grams) sugar. Whisk hot milk mixture into egg yolk mixture. Return mixture to saucepan, and bring to a boil, whisking constantly. Cook, whisking constantly, until cornstarch flavor has cooked out, 2 to 3 minutes. (Mixture will be thick.) Remove from heat, and strain through a fine-mesh sieve into a medium heatproof bowl. Stir in candies, butter, and extracts until completely combined. Cover with plastic wrap, pressing wrap directly onto surface of pastry cream to prevent a skin from forming. Refrigerate until completely cooled, 2 to 3 hours or up to overnight. Whisk smooth before using.

CHRISTMAS SUGAR COOKIES

Makes about 36 cookies

Our base cookie dough yields tender, buttery sugar cookies prime for our Royal Icing decoration. The best part about these cookies? No chilling or freezing required! Whether you're making ornaments, trees, or snowflakes, simply roll out your dough, cut into desired shapes, and bake.

1   cup (227 grams) unsalted butter, softened
2   cups (240 grams) confectioners' sugar
1   large egg (50 grams), room temperature
2   teaspoons (8 grams) vanilla extract
3¼   cups (406 grams) all-purpose flour
1½   teaspoons (7.5 grams) baking powder
1   teaspoon (3 grams) kosher salt
Royal Icing (recipe follows)

1. Preheat oven to 400°F (200°C). Line 3 baking sheets with parchment paper.
2. In the bowl of a stand mixer fitted with the paddle attachment, beat butter and confectioners' sugar, slowly increasing mixer speed to medium, until fluffy, 3 to 4 minutes, stopping to scrape sides of bowl. Add egg and vanilla, beating until combined.
3. In a medium bowl, whisk together flour, baking powder, and salt. With mixer on low speed, gradually add flour mixture to butter mixture, beating until a dough forms. Scrape sides of bowl, and knead dough 3 to 4 times in bowl to make sure everything is well combined.
4. Divide dough in half; cover one half with plastic wrap. On a heavily floured surface, roll remaining half to ¼-inch thickness. (Lightly flour top of dough if it sticks to rolling pin.) Using desired holiday cutters, cut dough, rerolling scraps as necessary. Using a small offset spatula, place cookies at least 1 inch apart on prepared pans.
5. Bake, one batch at a time, until lightly browned, 7 to 8 minutes. Let cool on pan for 5 minutes. Using a large offset or flat metal spatula, remove from pan, and let cool completely on wire racks. Decorate cooled cookies as desired with Royal Icing.

ROYAL ICING
Makes about 6 cups

Confectioners' sugar, meringue powder, water, and extract are the only ingredients needed to make royal icing, a baker's number one tool for making edible art. For food safety and east, we used meringue powder—a blend of dried, pasteurized egg whites, sugar, cornstarch, and citric acid—rather than the traditional raw egg whites. Whipped into a stiff mixture, this icing will appear dense and thick, not light and fluffy like your typical meringue—that's good! The meringue powder isn't needed for creating volume. Instead, it's the secret ingredient to creating a structured, pipable icing that will harden into a resilient edible adornment.

1   (2-pound) package (907 grams) confectioners' sugar
5   tablespoons (50 grams) meringue powder
¾   cup (180 grams) warm water (105°F/41°C to 110°F/43°C)
1   teaspoon (4 grams) almond extract

1. In the bowl of a stand mixer fitted with the paddle attachment, beat confectioners' sugar and meringue powder at low speed until combined. Slowly add ¾ cup (180 grams) warm water and almond extract, beating until fluid, about 1 minute. Increase mixer speed to medium, and beat until stiff, 4 to 5 minutes. Store in an airtight container for up to 3 days.

PRO TIP
It's the nature of this icing to harden and dry out—so if you get busy with other projects in the kitchen, be sure to cover the top of your Royal Icing with a damp paper towel to keep it fluid and fresh, for up to 1 hour. For longer periods of time, store in an airtight container.

ORNAMENT COOKIES

Like the vintage ornaments you were never allowed to touch as a kid, these marvelously marbled cookies are extraordinarily ornate and brilliantly colored.

MATERIALS NEEDED:

Royal Icing (recipe on page 295)

Water, as needed

Wilton Gel Food Coloring in Kelly Green, Juniper Green, Christmas Red, Golden Yellow, and Black

3 to 6 pastry bags

3 piping bottles (optional)

3 Wilton No. 1 piping tips

3 Wilton No. 3 piping tips

36 (3½-inch) ornament-shaped Christmas Sugar Cookies (recipe on page 295)

Wooden picks

1. Divide Royal Icing among 3 bowls: 3 cups (540 grams) in the first, 1½ cups (270 grams) in the second, and 1½ cups (270 grams) in the third. Cover bowls with a damp paper towel or kitchen towel to keep icing from drying out.

2. To the first bowl (3 cups [540 grams]), add water, 1 teaspoon (5 grams) at a time, until border consistency is reached. Place 1 cup (180 grams) in a pastry bag fitted with a very small round piping tip (Wilton No. 1). To the remaining 2 cups (360 grams), add water, 1 teaspoon (5 grams) at a time, until flood consistency is reached. Place in a pastry bag or a small piping bottle (if using) fitted with small round piping tip (Wilton No. 3). To the second bowl (1½ cups [270 grams]), slowly add Kelly green food coloring until a bright green is reached; slowly add juniper green until the desired color is reached. Add water, 1 teaspoon (5 grams) at a time, until border consistency is reached. Place ½ cup (90 grams) in a separate bowl, cover airtight, and set aside. To the remaining 1 cup (180 grams), add water, 1 teaspoon (5 grams) at a time, until flood consistency is reached. Place in a pastry bag or a small piping bottle (if using) with small round piping tip (Wilton No. 3).

3. To the third bowl (1½ cups [270 grams]), add Christmas red food coloring until desired color is reached; add golden yellow and a touch of black to keep it from going pink. Add water, 1 teaspoon (5 grams) at a time, until border consistency is reached. Place ½ cup (90 grams) in a separate bowl, cover airtight, and set aside. To the remaining 1 cup (180 grams), add water, 1 teaspoon (5 grams) at a time, until flood consistency is reached. Place in a pastry bag or a small piping bottle fitted with small round piping tip (Wilton No. 3).

4. Using white border icing, pipe an outline along edges of a cookie. Using the white flood icing, fill in the top quarter of the round part of the ornament cookie; pipe a line each of red flood icing, green flood icing, white flood icing, green flood icing, and red flood icing. Fill in the remaining area with white flood icing. Using a wooden pick, remove any air bubbles and make sure there are no gaps in the icing. Using a clean wooden pick, drag down through the centr of the colored band of icing, wipe pick clean, and repeat 2 more times, to the left and right of the center, spacing evenly and wiping pick clean after each drag. Then drag up 2 times, between the down drags, wiping pick clean after each drag. Repeat with remaining cookies. Let dry for 2 to 3 hours.

5. Uncover the red and green border icings, and place each in a pastry bag fitted with a very small round piping tip (Wilton No. 1). Above the marble design, pipe a red line and then a green line. Below design, pipe a green line and then a red line. Pipe 2 more red lines, between each level down the point of the ornament shape on the lower part of the cookie. Pipe a horizontal row of green dots between bottom red lines (4 dots and then 3 dots); pipe a vertical row of 2 green dots on the bottom tip of the ornament. Let dry until hardened, about 30 minutes. Store in an airtight container for up to 1 week.

Decoration Details: Ornament Cookies

1. Using the white flood icing, fill in the top quarter of the round part of the ornament cookie; pipe a line each of red flood icing, green flood icing, white flood icing, green flood icing, and red flood icing. Keep a steady hand as you pipe your alternating flood icings, as any wiggling will lead to uneven icing bleed. Try to keep the lines an even thickness as well, as one heavier line can overwhelm a thinner line. You don't need to touch the border icing as you pipe; if it doesn't naturally settle into the edges, you can use a wooden pick to gently nudge it to the edge.

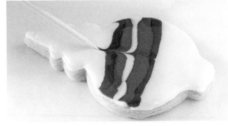

2. Using a clean wooden pick, drag a line down through the center of the colored band of icing. Wipe pick clean, and repeat 2 more times, to the left and right of the center, spacing evenly and wiping pick clean after each drag (any residual icing left on the pick will muddy the colors). Then drag up 2 times, between the down drags, wiping pick clean after each drag. Let dry for 2 to 3 hours.

3. Above the marble design, pipe a red line and then a green line. Below design, pipe a green line and then a red line. Pipe 2 more red lines, between each level down the point of the ornament shape on the lower part of the cookie. Pipe a horizontal row of green dots between bottom red lines (4 dots and then 3 dots); pipe a vertical row of 2 green dots on the bottom tip of the ornament. Let dry until hardened, about 30 minutes. Store in an airtight container for up to 1 week.

WINTER TREE COOKIES

With a paintbrush and bit of icing, our verdant green trees get a romantic dappling of winter snow.

MATERIALS NEEDED:
Royal Icing (recipe on page 295)
Wilton Gel Food Coloring in Kelly Green,
        Juniper Green, and Brown
Water, as needed
3 pastry bags
2 Wilton No. 1 piping tips
Squeeze bottle
1 Wilton No. 2 piping tip
36 (3½-inch) tree-shaped Christmas Sugar
        Cookies (recipe on page 295)
Wooden picks
Paintbrush

1. Divide Royal Icing among 3 bowls: 4 cups (720 grams) in the first, 1¾ cups (315 grams) in the second, and ¼ cup (45 grams) in the third. Cover bowls with a damp paper towel or kitchen towel to keep from drying out.
2. To the first bowl (4 cups [720 grams]), slowly add Kelly green food coloring until a bright green is reached; slowly add juniper green until the desired color is reached. Add water, 1 teaspoon (5 grams) at a time, until border consistency is reached. Place 1 cup (180 grams) in a pastry bag fitted with a very small round tip (Wilton No. 1). To the remaining 3 cups (540 grams), add water, 1 teaspoon (5 grams) at a time, until flood consistency is reached. Place in a large squeeze bottle.
3. To the second bowl (1¾ cups [315 grams]), add water, 1 teaspoon (5 grams) at a time, until border consistency is reached; cover airtight, and set aside.
4. To the third bowl (¼ cup [45 grams]), add brown food coloring until desired color is reached. Add water, 1 teaspoon (5 grams) at a time, until border consistency is reached. Place in a pastry bag fitted with a very small round piping tip (Wilton No. 1).
5. Using green border icing, pipe an outline along edges of tree part of a cookie. Using green flood icing, fill in center. Using a wooden pick, remove any air bubbles and make sure there are no gaps in the icing.

Using the brown icing, pipe border of trunk (including next to green icing). Fill in using the same consistency, and use a wooden pick to remove any air bubbles and make sure there are no gaps in the icing. Repeat with remaining cookies. Let dry for 2 to 3 hours.
6. Place white border icing in a pastry bag fitted with small round tip (Wilton No. 2). Place paintbrush in water. Starting at the base of the tree, pipe a row of dots, keeping in mind they will be grouped in 2 or 3. Remove brush from water, and wipe off excess water. Place brush tip in the center of each dot and brush away from you, creating groups of 2 or 3 that meet. (Wipe off any excess icing as needed that the brush picks up.) Place brush back in water and then pipe another row of dots. Remove any excess water from the brush, and repeat procedure until you reach the top of the tree. Repeat with remaining cookies. Let dry until hardened, about 30 minutes. Store in an airtight container for up to 1 week.

Decoration Details: Winter Tree Cookies

1. Once your green and brown base icing has dried, you can begin creating snowy details. Place white border icing in a pastry bag fitted with a small round tip (Wilton No. 2). Place paintbrush in water. Starting at the base of the tree, pipe a row of dots, keeping in mind they will be grouped in 2 or 3. These should be generous dots of icing, not tiny pinpoints, so you can brush them into snowy sweeps.

2. Remove brush from water, and wipe off excess water. Too much water on the brush will dilute your icing and make you lose definition. Place brush tip in the center of each dot and brush away from you, creating groups of 2 or 3 that meet. It should look like dimpled teardrops that join thinly at the top.
3. A fine-tipped paintbrush like the one we used tends to spring into a narrow cone shape. We

want a more fanned-out broom shape, leaving dramatic swept trails in the icing. If you start losing the detailed sweep look, flatten your brush tip between your fingers to fan it out again.
4. Continue to dot and sweep your way to the top of your cookie. Use 2-dot clusters in narrow spaces at the top and edges. Let dry until hardened, about 30 minutes.

SNOWFLAKE COOKIES

Complete with two icy designs, these cookies look like the intricate inner workings of a snowflake. In reality, a simple series of lines, dots, and "V" shapes make up its pattern, offering the gold standard of royal iced cookies: easy execution, dazzling results.

MATERIALS NEEDED:

Royal Icing (recipe on page 295)
Wilton Gel Food Coloring in Cornflower Blue
Water, as needed
3 pastry bags
2 Wilton No. 1 piping tips
Squeeze bottle
36 (3⅛-inch) snowflake-shaped Christmas Sugar Cookies (recipe on page 295)
Wooden picks
Wilton No. 2 piping tip
White pearls
Tweezers

1. Divide Royal Icing into 3 bowls: 4 cups (720 grams) in the first, 1½ cups (270 grams) in the second, and ½ cup (90 grams) in the third. Cover bowls with a damp paper towel or kitchen towel to keep from drying out.

2. To the first bowl (4 cups [720 grams]), add cornflower blue food coloring, until a soft blue or desired color is reached. Add water, 1 teaspoon (5 grams) at a time, until border consistency is reached. Place 1 cup (180 grams) in a pastry bag fitted with a very small round tip (Wilton No. 1). To the remaining 3 cups (540 grams), add water, 1 teaspoon (5 grams) at a time, until flood consistency is reached. Place in a large squeeze bottle.

3. To the second bowl (1½ cups [270 grams]), add water, 1 teaspoon (5 grams) at a time, until border consistency is reached; cover airtight, and set aside.

4. To the third bowl (½ cup [90 grams]), add cornflower blue food coloring until dark blue or desired color is reached. Add water, 1 teaspoon (5 grams) at a time, until border consistency is reached; cover airtight, and set aside.

5. Using the light blue border icing, pipe an outline along edges of a cookie. Using light blue flood icing, fill in center. Using a wooden pick, remove any air bubbles and make sure there are no gaps in the icing. Repeat with remaining cookies. Let dry for 2 to 3 hours.

6. Place white border icing in a pastry bag fitted with very small round tip (Wilton No. 1). Place dark blue border icing in a pastry bag fitted with a small round tip (Wilton No. 2).

7. For design 1: Starting at one tip of snowflake, pipe a thin white line to the opposite tip, leaving a rounded end at each tip. Repeat with the remaining tips, making sure each line (there will be 3 total) meets the others in the center. On each line going from the center, pipe 3 "V" shapes with the points going toward the center. Using the dark blue, pipe a small dot between each line (there will be 6) and 1 larger dot in the center, where the white lines meet.

8. For design 2: Starting at one tip of snowflake, pipe a thin white line to the opposite tip, leaving a rounded end at each tip and making sure to leave space for a dot at each tip. Repeat with the remaining tips, making sure each line (there will be 3 total) meets the others in the center. Pipe smaller lines over the center, between the larger lines (3 total). On each larger line going from the center, pipe 2 "V" shapes with the points going toward the center. Using the dark blue, pipe small dots at each tip of the snowflake; pipe dots between the "V" shapes on each line (1 on each side of the line), and pipe a small dot at the end of the smaller lines coming from the center. Place a white pearl in the center. (Use tweezers for easier placement.) Repeat with remaining cookies. Let dry until hardened, about 30 minutes. Store in an airtight container for up to 1 week.

Decoration Details: Snowflake Cookies Design #1

1

2

3

1. Starting at one tip of the snowflake, pipe a thin white line to the opposite tip, leaving a rounded end at each tip. Repeat with the remaining tips, making sure each line (there will be 3 total) meets the others in the center. Like when piping a border, you'll make a thread of icing that'll span the expanse of the cookie, only touching down on the cookie with your tip to create the rounded ends.

2. On each line going from the center, pipe 3 "V" shapes with the points going toward the center. Try to keep the "V" shapes tucked to the main line so that as you pipe more "V" shapes on the other lines, they won't overlap and touch.

3. Using the dark blue, pipe a small dot between each line (there will be 6) and 1 larger dot in the center, where the white lines meet. Let dry until hardened, about 30 minutes. Store in an airtight container for up to 1 week

Design #2

Design 1 is slightly simpler than design 2, but have similar steps. After making the long bisecting lines mentioned in step 1, you'll pipe smaller lines over the center, between the larger lines (3 total). Then you'll pipe 2 "V" shapes at the top of each of the longer lines. A smattering of blue dots fills the empty space, and a pearl sprinkle is placed in the center as a crowning jewel. Use tweezers for exact pearl placement so you keep from accidentally smudging the icing.

CHOCOLATE CINNAMON CRINKLE COOKIES

Makes 28 cookies

Recipe by Rebecca Firth

These chocolate crinkle cookies are loaded with a whopping 1½ tablespoons (9 grams) ground cinnamon that perfectly complements the rich chocolate flavor of the cookies. They are delightfully chewy but with the perfect amount of crunch from the sugary exterior. You can roll these cookies in either granulated sugar or sparkling sugar—both work wonderfully!

1 cup (227 grams) unsalted butter, softened
1½ cups (300 grams) granulated sugar
½ cup (110 grams) firmly packed dark brown sugar
1½ tablespoons (9 grams) ground cinnamon
2 large eggs (100 grams), room temperature
1 tablespoon (13 grams) vanilla extract
2¾ cups (344 grams) all-purpose flour
½ cup (43 grams) unsweetened cocoa powder, sifted
1 tablespoon (15 grams) baking soda
1 teaspoon (3 grams) sea salt
½ cup (100 grams) sparkling sugar

1. Position oven rack in center of oven. Preheat oven to 350°F (180°C). Line several baking sheets with parchment paper.
2. In the bowl of a stand mixer fitted with the paddle attachment, beat butter, 1½ cups (300 grams) granulated sugar, brown sugar, and cinnamon at medium speed until light and fluffy, about 5 minutes, stopping to scrape sides of bowl. With mixer on low speed, add eggs, one at a time, beating until combined after each addition. Beat in vanilla until well combined, about 1 minute.
3. In a medium bowl, whisk together flour, cocoa, baking soda, and salt. With mixer on low speed, add flour mixture to butter mixture, beating just until combined.

4. In a small shallow bowl, place sparkling sugar.
5. Using a 2-tablespoon spring-loaded scoop, scoop dough, and roll into balls. Roll dough balls in sparkling sugar to coat. Place 3 inches apart on prepared pans.
6. Bake, one batch at a time, until edges are set and centers are puffed, about 9 minutes. Let cool on pans for 10 minutes. Remove from pans, and let cool completely on wire racks. Store in an airtight container for up to 3 days.

Photo by Rebecca Firth

FIVE-SPICE CRANBERRY JAM THUMPRINT COOKIES

Makes 21 cookies

Recipe by Rebecca Firth

These little thumbprint cookies are a cinch to throw together and require zero fridge time. The Five-Spice Cranberry Jam is a holiday favorite—consider making extra to serve with your next cocktail hour cheese board!

½ cup (113 grams) unsalted butter, softened and cut into 8 pieces
½ cup (100 grams) granulated sugar
1 large egg yolk (19 grams), room temperature
2 tablespoons (30 grams) whole milk, room temperature
1 teaspoon (4 grams) almond extract
1 cup (125 grams) all-purpose flour
½ cup (64 grams) bread flour
½ teaspoon (2.5 grams) baking powder
½ teaspoon (1.5 grams) sea salt
½ cup (60 grams) confectioners' sugar
Five-Spice Cranberry Jam (recipe follows)

1. Position oven rack in center of oven. Preheat oven to 350°F (180°C). Line several baking sheets with parchment paper.
2. In the bowl of a stand mixer fitted with the paddle attachment, beat butter and granulated sugar at medium speed until light and fluffy, 4 to 5 minutes, stopping to scrape sides of bowl. Add egg yolk, milk, and almond extract, and beat at low speed for 1 minute.
3. In a medium bowl, whisk together flours, baking powder, and salt. Add flour mixture to butter mixture, and beat at low speed until dough comes together, stopping to scrape sides and bottom of bowl. Using a 1-tablespoon spring-loaded scoop, scoop dough, and roll into balls; place 2 inches apart on prepared pans. Using your thumb, press down center of each dough ball. Freeze or refrigerate for 10 minutes.
4. Bake, one batch at a time, until tops are dry to the touch, about 11 minutes. Using the curved end of a wooden spoon, immediately press down centers. Let cool on pan for 5 minutes. Remove from pan, and let cool completely on wire racks.
5. Sift confectioners' sugar over cooled cookies. Spoon 1 teaspoon (7 grams) Five-Spice Cranberry Jam into center of each cookie.

Note: *These are best served the same day they are made. If you want to prepare them ahead of time, wait to sift with confectioners' sugar and fill with the Five-Space Cranberry Jam until just before serving.*

FIVE-SPICE CRANBERRY JAM
Makes about 1 cup

1½ cups (165 grams) fresh or thawed frozen cranberries
⅓ cup (67 grams) granulated sugar
2 tablespoons (12 grams) tightly packed orange zest
¼ cup (60 grams) fresh orange juice
1 teaspoon (2 grams) Chinese five-spice powder

1. In a medium saucepan, bring cranberries, sugar, and orange zest and juice to a boil over medium-high heat. Reduce heat, and simmer until liquid is reduced, about 15 minutes. Using the edge of a spatula, mash cranberries. Stir in five-spice powder. Transfer to a heatproof bowl, and let cool completely before using. Refrigerate in an airtight container for up to 1 week.

Photo by Rebecca Firth

BITTERSWEET ORANGE COOKIES WITH CAMPARI BUTTERCREAM

Makes 36 cookies

Recipe by Rebecca Firth

This is a cookie that celebrates all that is delicious in a Negroni. Lots of bittersweet citrus notes come from the combination of grapefruit, orange, and lime, with a splash of orange blossom water added to the mix. Olive oil is used for half of the fat to infuse the cookie with some herbaceous notes; pick a delicious olive oil that you wouldn't mind drinking straight from the bottle. If you're lucky enough to come across actual bitter or Seville oranges, you can use the zest of two of those in place of the citrus listed.

½   cup (113 grams) unsalted butter, softened
3   cups (600 grams) granulated sugar, divided
3   tablespoons (18 grams) tightly packed grapefruit zest
2   tablespoons (12 grams) tightly packed orange zest
1½ tablespoons (9 grams) tightly packed lime zest
¾   cup (168 grams) olive oil
2   large eggs (100 grams), room temperature
1½ teaspoons (6 grams) orange blossom water
1¾ cups (219 grams) all-purpose flour
1   cup (127 grams) bread flour
1¼ teaspoons (3 grams) sea salt, divided
1   teaspoon (5 grams) baking powder
1   teaspoon (5 grams) baking soda
4   large egg whites (120 grams)
1   cup (227 grams) slightly chilled unsalted butter, cubed
2   tablespoons (30 grams) Campari

1. Position oven rack in center of oven. Preheat oven to 350°F (180°C). Line several baking sheets with parchment paper.
2. In the bowl of a stand mixer fitted with the paddle attachment, beat softened butter, 1¾ cups (350 grams) sugar, and zests at medium speed until light and fluffy, 4 to 5 minutes, stopping to scrape sides of bowl. Reduce mixer speed to low; add oil in a slow, steady stream, beating until combined. Add eggs, one at a time, beating until combined after each addition. Add orange blossom water, and beat for 1 minute.
3. In a medium bowl, whisk together flours, 1 teaspoon (3 grams) salt, baking powder, and baking soda. Add flour mixture to butter mixture, and beat at low speed for several seconds. Using a silicone spatula, stir until completely combined, stopping to scrape bottom of bowl. (Dough will be on the wet side.) Cover tightly with plastic wrap, and refrigerate for at least 4 hours or up to 4 days.
4. Using a 1½-tablespoon spring-loaded scoop, scoop dough, and roll into balls. Freeze for 10 minutes.
5. In a small shallow bowl, place ½ cup (100 grams) sugar. Roll dough balls in sugar, and place 2 inches apart on prepared pans.
6. Bake in batches until edges are set and centers are puffed, about 9 minutes. Let cool on pans for 10 minutes. Remove from pans, and let cool completely on wire racks.
7. In the heatproof bowl of a stand mixer, combine egg whites, remaining ¾ cup (150 grams) sugar, and remaining ¼ teaspoon salt. Place bowl over a saucepan of simmering water. Cook, whisking constantly, until mixture is thick and opaque and no longer feels gritty when rubbed between 2 fingers and an instant-read thermometer registers 160°F (71°C), about 10 minutes.
8. Return bowl to stand mixer. Using the whisk attachment, beat at high speed until stiff peaks form and meringue and bowl are cool to the touch, about 15 minutes.
9. Switch to the paddle attachment. With mixer on medium speed, add chilled butter, one cube at a time, beating until combined after each addition. (If mixture curdles, your butter may be too cold. If mixture is soupy, you may need to refrigerate your buttercream.) Beat until smooth, glossy, and voluminous, about 2 minutes. Add Campari, beating until combined.
10. Place buttercream in a pastry bag fitted with a star piping tip (Ateco #843). Holding tip perpendicular to cookie, squeeze out a small bit of buttercream and then lift up tip. Repeat pattern across tops of all of cookies.

Photo by Rebecca Firth

TOASTED MACADAMIA NUT AND CRANBERRY CHOCOLATE CHIP COOKIES

Makes 29 cookies

Recipe by Rebecca Firth

These cookies are everything you want in a holiday cookie: cozy from the mega brown sugar-caramel flavors, ample at 3 tablespoons of dough per cookie, and completely loaded with flavor and texture from the crunchy toasted macadamia nuts, the chewy and bright cranberries, and the rich white and earthy dark chocolate bits. If you're feeling frisky, soak the dried cranberries overnight in 3 to 4 tablespoons (45 to 60 grams) bourbon before baking. The flavor is subtle but delicious!

1   cup (128 grams) dried cranberries
½   cup (113 grams) unsalted butter, softened
1½   cups (330 grams) firmly packed light brown sugar
½   cup (100 grams) granulated sugar
½   cup (112 grams) olive oil
1   tablespoon (13 grams) vanilla extract
2   large eggs (100 grams), room temperature
2¾   cups (344 grams) all-purpose flour
1   teaspoon (5 grams) baking soda
1   teaspoon (5 grams) baking powder
1   teaspoon (3 grams) sea salt
½   cup (57 grams) coarsely chopped toasted macadamia nuts
½   cup (85 grams) coarsely chopped white chocolate
½   cup (85 grams) coarsely chopped 56% cacao dark chocolate

1. Position oven rack in center of oven. Preheat oven to 350°F (180°C). Line several baking sheets with parchment paper.
2. In a small heatproof bowl, combine cranberries and boiling water to cover; set aside.
3. In the bowl of a stand mixer fitted with the paddle attachment, beat butter and sugars at medium speed until light and fluffy, about 5 minutes, stopping to scrape sides and bottom of bowl. Reduce mixer speed to low; add oil in a slow, steady stream, beating just until combined. Beat in vanilla until combined. Add eggs, one at a time, beating until combined after each addition.
4. In a medium bowl, whisk together flour, baking soda, baking powder, and salt. Add flour mixture to butter mixture, and beat at low speed until barely combined and a few streaks of flour remain.
5. Drain cranberries; add cranberries, nuts, white chocolate, and dark chocolate to dough, and beat at low speed just until combined, about 10 seconds. (Do not overmix.) Using a 3-tablespoon spring-loaded scoop, scoop dough, and place 2 inches apart on prepared pans.
6. Bake, one batch at a time, until lightly bronzed, about 9 minutes. Let cool on pans for 5 to 10 minutes. Remove from pans, and let cool completely on wire racks. Store in an airtight container for up to 3 days.

Photo by Rebecca Firth

STRAWBERRY CARDAMOM LINZER COOKIES

Makes about 24 sandwich cookies

Recipe by Mike Johnson

Linzers are popular Austrian cookies often made during the holiday season. The cardamom in this cookie dough makes for a deliciously warm taste that pairs exceedingly well with the strawberry preserves.

1 cup (227 grams) unsalted butter, softened
1½ cups (180 grams) confectioners' sugar
1 large egg (50 grams)
1 teaspoon (2 grams) ground cardamom
1 teaspoon (6 grams) vanilla bean paste
½ teaspoon (1.5 grams) kosher salt
½ teaspoon (1 gram) ground cinnamon
2½ cups (313 grams) all-purpose flour
1 cup (96 grams) almond flour
½ cup (160 grams) strawberry preserves
Garnish: confectioners' sugar

1. In the bowl of a stand mixer fitted with the paddle attachment, beat butter and confectioners' sugar at medium speed until pale and fluffy, about 2 minutes, stopping to scrape sides of bowl. Beat in egg, cardamom, vanilla bean paste, salt, and cinnamon.
2. In a medium bowl, whisk together flours. With mixer on low speed, gradually add flour mixture to butter mixture, beating just until combined. Using lightly floured hands, divide dough in half. Shape each half into a ½-inch-thick disk, and wrap in plastic wrap. Refrigerate until firm, at least 2 hours.
3. Preheat oven to 350°F (180°C). Line baking sheets with parchment paper.
4. On a lightly floured surface, roll half of dough into a ¼-inch-thick circle. (If dough becomes too soft, rewrap in plastic wrap, and refrigerate until firm again.) Using a 2-inch fluted round cutter, cut dough, and place about 1 inch apart on prepared pans. Using desired 1-inch holiday cutter,

cut centers from half of cookies. Reserve centers, and reroll with scraps once.
5. Bake until edges are lightly golden, 10 to 12 minutes. Let cool on pans for 5 minutes. Remove from pans, and let cool completely on wire racks. Repeat procedure with remaining dough.
6. Spread about 1 teaspoon (7 grams) preserves onto flat side of solid cookies. Garnish cookies with cutouts with confectioners' sugar, if desired. Place cookies with cutouts, flat side down, on top of preserves. Store in an airtight container for up to 3 days.

Photo by Mike Johnson

BROWNED BUTTER SUGAR COOKIES

Makes about 24 cookies

Recipe by Mike Johnson

Infused with browned butter and rolled in festive nonpareils, these Browned Butter Sugar Cookies are the perfect treat for the holidays.

1   cup (227 grams) unsalted butter, cubed
1   cup (200 grams) granulated sugar
½   cup (110 grams) firmly packed light brown sugar
1   large egg (50 grams), room temperature
1   large egg yolk (19 grams), room temperature
1   teaspoon (6 grams) vanilla bean paste
2   cups (250 grams) all-purpose flour
1   teaspoon (5 grams) baking soda
½   teaspoon (2.5 grams) baking powder
½   teaspoon (1.5 grams) kosher salt
Garnish: holiday nonpareils

1. In a light-colored medium saucepan, melt butter over medium heat, stirring constantly. Cook, stirring constantly, until butter turns a medium-brown color and has a nutty aroma, 5 to 8 minutes. Remove from heat, and pour into the bowl of a stand mixer. Let cool slightly, about 5 minutes.
2. Add sugars to browned butter. Using the paddle attachment, beat at medium-high speed until combined, about 1 minute. With mixer on low speed, beat in egg, egg yolk, and vanilla bean paste.
3. In a medium bowl, whisk together flour, baking soda, baking powder, and salt. With mixer on low speed, add flour mixture to butter mixture; slowly increase mixer speed to high, beating until well combined. (Dough will be thick and a little greasy.)
4. Line a baking sheet with parchment paper.

5. Using a 1½-tablespoon spring-loaded scoop, scoop dough (about 30 grams each), and roll into balls. Roll in nonpareils, if desired, and place on prepared pan. Loosely cover with plastic wrap, and refrigerate for 45 minutes.
6. Preheat oven to 350°F (180°C). Line baking sheets with parchment paper.
7. Place dough balls 3 inches apart on prepared pans.
8. Bake in batches until lightly browned on edges, 12 to 13 minutes. Let cool on pans for 5 minutes. Remove from pans, and let cool completely on wire racks. Store in an airtight container for up to 3 days.

Photo by Mike Johnson

CHOCOLATE-COVERED PEANUT BUTTER COOKIES

Makes about 24 cookies

Recipe by Mike Johnson

This easy recipe starts with a sweet, buttery peanut butter slice-and-bake cookie, which is then covered in peanut butter and then completely dipped in chocolate.

½ cup (113 grams) unsalted butter, softened
½ cup (110 grams) firmly packed dark brown sugar
1 teaspoon (6 grams) vanilla bean paste
1¾ cups (448 grams) creamy peanut butter, divided
2 cups (250 grams) all-purpose flour
1 tablespoon (15 grams) water, plus more if needed
½ teaspoon (1.5 grams) kosher salt
16 ounces (454 grams) milk chocolate, melted
1 tablespoon (15 grams) canola oil
2 ounces (57 grams) 60% cacao semisweet chocolate, melted

1. In the bowl of a stand mixer fitted with the paddle attachment, beat butter, brown sugar, and vanilla bean paste until light and fluffy, about 3 minutes. Beat in ¾ cup (192 grams) peanut butter until combined. Add flour, 1 tablespoon (15 grams) water, and salt, and beat until combined and dough forms a ball. (If dough seems too crumbly, add water, 1 teaspoon [5 grams] at a time, until it comes together. Dough should not be overly sticky.)
2. Divide dough in half. Place each half on a large piece of plastic wrap. Using your hands, shape each half into a 6x2-inch rectangle. Wrap in plastic wrap, and refrigerate for at least 3 hours or overnight. (Alternatively, shape each dough half into a 6-inch log, about 2 inches thick, to make round cookies.)
3. Preheat oven to 350°F (180°C). Line 2 baking sheets with parchment paper.
4. Cut dough rectangle into ½-inch-thick slices, and place 1 inch apart on prepared pans. (Alternatively, cut dough log into ½-inch-thick slices, and place 1 inch apart on prepared pans.)
5. Bake until edges are golden brown, 13 to 15 minutes. Let cool on pans for 10 minutes. Remove from pans, and let cool completely on wire racks.
6. Spread remaining 1 cup (256 grams) peanut butter on top of cookies (about a heaping ½ tablespoon [8 grams] each), and place on a parchment paper-lined baking sheet. Freeze until set, about 20 minutes. (This makes coating in chocolate easier.)
7. Stir oil into melted milk chocolate. Place each cookie in melted milk chocolate; using a fork, lift cookies out of chocolate, and gently tap on side of bowl to remove excess. Return to pan. Refrigerate until chocolate is set, about 15 minutes. Drizzle with melted semisweet chocolate. Refrigerate until chocolate is set, about 15 minutes. Store in an airtight container for up to 5 days.

Photo by Mike Johnson

PEANUT BUTTER-CHAI MACARONS

Makes about 32 macarons

Recipe by Mike Johnson

These macarons are filled with a delicious, lightly spiced Peanut Butter-Chai Buttercream, perfect for enjoying with a cup of tea!

4   large egg whites (120 grams), room temperature
½   cup (100 grams) granulated sugar
5   drops brown gel food coloring (optional)
1⅓   cups (200 grams) confectioners' sugar
1⅓   cups (128 grams) almond flour
Peanut Butter-Chai Buttercream (recipe follows)
Garnish: granulated sugar

1. Line baking sheets with silicone baking mats or parchment paper. Using a pencil, draw 1½-inch circles 2 inches apart on parchment paper; turn parchment over. (If using silicone baking mats, place parchment templates underneath baking mats.)
2. In the bowl of a stand mixer fitted with the whisk attachment, beat egg whites at medium speed until foamy and whisk begins leaving visible trails. Gradually add granulated sugar; increase mixer speed to high, and beat until stiff peaks form. Beat in food coloring (if using). (Do not overwhip, or you risk drying out your egg whites.)
3. In a medium bowl, sift together confectioners' sugar and flour. Using a rubber spatula, fold confectioners' sugar mixture into egg white mixture from bottom of bowl upward; press flat side of spatula through middle and against side of bowl. (Batter will look very thick at first, but it will get thinner as you fold.) Fold until batter reaches a lavalike consistency. (See PRO TIP.)
4. Transfer batter to a large pastry bag fitted with a ⅜-inch round piping tip (Wilton No. 2A). Holding piping tip at a 90-degree angle to a prepared pan, pipe batter onto drawn circles of template underneath mat, or pipe batter onto drawn circles if using parchment. Lift pans 6 inches above counter, and drop to release any air bubbles; repeat 3 to 4 times. (If you don't release air bubbles, they will expand during baking and crack your macaron shells.) Garnish with granulated sugar, if desired. Let stand at room temperature until a skin develops, about 30 minutes. (You should be able to lightly touch a shell without batter getting stuck to your finger; on a humid day, it might take 1 hour or more.)
5. Preheat oven to 300°F (150°C).
6. Bake, one batch at a time, for 18 to 20 minutes, rotating pan halfway through baking. Let cool on pan for 10 minutes. Remove from pan, and let cool completely on a wire rack. (If bottoms are a tiny bit sticky, let cool on pan for 10 to 15 minutes more. If, however, bottoms are already browned, they peel off cleanly, or they appear overbaked, immediately remove from pan to let cool completely on a wire rack.)
7. Place Peanut Butter-Chai Buttercream in a pastry bag; cut a ¼-inch opening in tip. Pair each macaron shell with another of a similar size; pipe buttercream onto flat side of half of macaron shells. Place remaining macaron shells, flat side down, on top of buttercream, gently sandwiching them together. Refrigerate macarons in an airtight container for up to 5 days; let come to room temperature before serving.

Note: *Macarons are best enjoyed the next day, after they have matured in the refrigerator (since the flavors will be absorbed into the shell). If your shells are hard, crunchy, or overbaked, letting them mature will also cause the shells to absorb the moisture from the filling, softening them up and giving them their signature chewy texture. It's always better to overbake rather than underbake your macarons because the maturation process can typically salvage ones that are overbaked.*

PEANUT BUTTER-CHAI BUTTERCREAM

Makes about 1½ cups

1½   cups (180 grams) confectioners' sugar
¼   teaspoon ground cinnamon
¼   teaspoon ground ginger
⅛   teaspoon ground cardamom
⅛   teaspoon ground allspice
Dash ground cloves
¼   cup (57 grams) unsalted butter, softened
¼   cup (65 grams) creamy peanut butter
3   tablespoons (45 grams) heavy whipping cream

1. In a medium bowl, sift together confectioners' sugar, cinnamon, ginger, cardamom, allspice, and cloves.
2. In the bowl of a stand mixer fitted with the paddle attachment, beat sugar mixture, butter, peanut butter, and cream at low speed for about 30 seconds; increase mixer speed to medium-high, and beat until light and fluffy, about 3 minutes. Use immediately, or refrigerate in an airtight container for up to 3 days. If refrigerating, let come to room temperature and rewhip before using.

Photo by Mike Johnson

PRO TIP
The figure eight test is a great way to check your batter's consistency. Pick up the batter with your spatula, and let it flow down into the bowl while drawing the figure "8." If you can do that without the batter breaking, immediately stop folding.

EGGNOG SAMMIES WITH SPICED RUM BUTTERCREAM

Makes 24 sandwich cookies

Recipe by Rebecca Firth

Nothing says the holidays to me more than eggnog. These get a little crisp from the sparkling sugar they're generously rolled in but are still incredibly tender to the bite . . . and don't even get me started on this buttercream! The base is a Swiss meringue made with brown sugar, which pairs perfectly with the spices, vanilla, and rum added at the end. Consider this the holiday sandwich cookie of your dreams.

1   cup (227 grams) unsalted butter, softened
1¾ cups (350 grams) granulated sugar
1   tablespoon (14 grams) oil, such as sunflower seed oil or olive oil
2   large eggs (100 grams), room temperature
1½ teaspoons (6 grams) rum extract
1¾ cups (219 grams) all-purpose flour
1¼ cups (159 grams) bread flour
1   teaspoon (5 grams) baking powder
1   teaspoon (5 grams) baking soda
1   teaspoon (3 grams) sea salt
1   teaspoon grated fresh nutmeg
¾   teaspoon (1.5 grams) ground cinnamon
½   cup (100 grams) sparkling sugar
Spiced Rum Buttercream (recipe follows)

1. In the bowl of a stand mixer fitted with the paddle attachment, beat butter and granulated sugar at medium speed until light and fluffy, 4 to 5 minutes, stopping to scrape sides of bowl. Reduce mixer speed to low; add oil in a slow, steady stream, beating until well combined. Add eggs, one at a time, beating until combined after each addition. Add rum extract, and beat for 1 minute.
2. In a medium bowl, whisk together flours, baking powder, baking soda, salt, nutmeg, and cinnamon. Add flour mixture to butter mixture, and beat at low speed just until combined and no streaks of flour remain. Cover tightly with plastic wrap, and refrigerate for 2 hours.
3. Position oven rack in center of oven. Preheat oven to 350°F (180°C). Line several baking sheets with parchment paper.
4. In a small shallow bowl, place sparkling sugar.
5. Using a 1-tablespoon spring-loaded scoop, scoop dough, and roll into balls. Roll in sparkling sugar, and place 2 inches apart on prepared pans.

6. Bake, one batch at a time, until edges are slightly bronzed and centers are puffed, 10 to 12 minutes. Let cool on pan for 10 minutes. Remove from pan, and let cool completely on wire racks.
7. Place Spiced Rum Buttercream in a pastry bag fitted with a small round piping tip. Pipe buttercream onto flat side of half of cookies. Place remaining cookies, flat side down, on top of buttercream, pressing down slightly. Refrigerate in an airtight container for up to 3 days.

SPICED RUM BUTTERCREAM
Makes about 3 cups

¾ cup (165 grams) firmly packed light brown sugar
4 large egg whites (120 grams)
¼ teaspoon sea salt
1 cup (227 grams) slightly chilled unsalted butter, cubed
½ vanilla bean, split lengthwise, seeds scraped and reserved (optional)
2 tablespoons (30 grams) rum
½ teaspoon (1 gram) ground cinnamon
½ teaspoon grated fresh nutmeg

1. In the heatproof bowl of a stand mixer, combine brown sugar, egg whites, and salt. Place over a saucepan of simmering water. Cook, whisking constantly, until mixture is thick and frothy and no longer feels gritty when rubbed between 2 fingers and an instant-read thermometer registers 160°F (71°C).
2. Return bowl to stand mixer. Using the whisk attachment, beat at medium-high speed until meringue and bowl are cool to the touch, about 15 minutes.
3. Switch to the paddle attachment. With mixer on medium speed, add butter, 1 cube at a time, beating until combined after each addition. (If mixture curdles, your butter may be too cold. If mixture is soupy, you may need to refrigerate the buttercream.) Beat until light and fluffy, about 2 minutes. Beat in reserved vanilla bean seeds (if using), rum, cinnamon, and nutmeg. Use immediately.

Photo by Rebecca Firth

ORANGE-VANILLA JAM RIBBONS

Makes about 36 cookies

Taking a cue from the traditional Finnish raspberry ribbons, this dough is formed into a log that receives a sweet channel of jam; then it's baked and sliced to form crunchy, jam-filled cookies. In a departure from the original recipe, we added orange zest to the dough and have both apricot preserves and raspberry jam represented.

¾   cup (170 grams) unsalted butter, softened
½   cup (100 grams) granulated sugar
¼   cup (30 grams) confectioners' sugar
¼   teaspoon packed orange zest
1   large egg (50 grams), room temperature
1½   teaspoons (9 grams) vanilla bean paste
2   cups (250 grams) all-purpose flour
½   teaspoon (2.5 grams) baking powder
¼   teaspoon kosher salt
4   tablespoons (64 grams) seedless raspberry jam or apricot preserves*
Orange Glaze (recipe follows)

1. Preheat oven to 350°F (180°C).
2. In the bowl of a stand mixer fitted with the paddle attachment, beat butter, sugars, and orange zest at medium speed until creamy, about 2 minutes, stopping to scrape sides of bowl. Beat in egg and vanilla bean paste until combined.
3. In a medium bowl, whisk together flour, baking powder, and salt. Add flour mixture to butter mixture all at once; beat at low speed just until combined.
4. Turn out dough onto a clean surface, and divide into 4 portions (about 148 grams each). Roll each portion into a 10-inch log (about 1 inch thick). Place logs 1½ to 2 inches apart on a sheet of parchment paper; flatten each log until about 1¼ inches wide. Using a thin rounded spoon handle or a finger, make a ¾-inch-wide, ¼-inch-deep channel lengthwise down center of each log. (Dough logs will now be about 1½ inches wide.) Transfer dough logs, still on parchment, to a baking sheet.
5. In a small bowl, whisk jam or preserves until smooth; spoon into a small pastry bag or resealable plastic bag, and cut a ½-inch opening in tip or corner. Pipe jam or preserves into channels (about 1 tablespoon [16 grams] each), spreading into an even layer as needed.
6. Bake until edges are lightly golden, 10 to 15 minutes. Let cool on pans for 5 minutes. Using a serrated knife, cut logs diagonally crosswise into 1-inch-thick strips, wiping knife clean between cuts. Transfer to a wire rack set over a parchment paper-lined baking sheet; let cool completely.
7. Spoon Orange Glaze into a small pastry bag or resealable plastic bag; cut a ¼-inch opening in tip or corner. Drizzle glaze onto cooled cookies; let stand until set, about 15 minutes.

We used Smucker's Seedless Red Raspberry Jam and Apricot Preserves.

ORANGE GLAZE
Makes about ⅓ cup

1   cup (120 grams) confectioners' sugar
1½   tablespoons (22.5 grams) fresh orange juice

1. In a small bowl, stir together confectioners' sugar and orange juice until smooth and well combined. Use immediately.

PEPPERMINT MOCHA RED VELVET MARBLE COOKIES

Makes about 54 cookies

Red velvet gets a magically marbled look in these slice-and-bake cookies. Two doughs— one creamy peppermint and one crimson mocha—get folded and swirled together before being rolled in festive nonpareils.

1 cup (227 grams) unsalted butter, softened
1¼ cups (250 grams) granulated sugar
2 large eggs (100 grams), room temperature and divided
3 cups (375 grams) all-purpose flour
¾ teaspoon (2.25 grams) kosher salt
½ teaspoon (2.5 grams) baking powder
½ teaspoon (2 grams) peppermint extract
4 teaspoons (8 grams) dark-roast instant coffee granules
1 teaspoon (5 grams) water
1 tablespoon (5 grams) unsweetened cocoa powder
Red gel food coloring*
½ cup (100 grams) holiday nonpareils*

1. In the bowl of a stand mixer fitted with the paddle attachment, beat butter and sugar at medium-low speed just until combined.

Increase mixer speed to medium, and beat until fluffy, 2 to 3 minutes, stopping to scrape sides of bowl. Beat in 1 egg (50 grams) until well combined.

2. In a large bowl, whisk together flour, salt, and baking powder. With mixer on low speed, gradually add flour mixture to butter mixture, beating just until combined. Transfer half of dough (about 447 grams) to a medium bowl; gently knead in peppermint extract. Cover and set aside.

3. In a small bowl, stir together instant coffee and 1 teaspoon (5 grams) water until granules dissolve. Add coffee mixture and cocoa to dough in stand mixer bowl; beat at low speed until combined. Add food coloring until desired color is reached, kneading together by hand as needed.

4. Divide each dough into 10 portions (about 44 grams each). Layer pieces, in a random, alternating fashion, into 1 large dough log. Cut log in half, and shape each half into a 7-inch log (about 2 inches thick). Wrap each log in plastic wrap; while holding ends of plastic wrap, roll log over work surface, creating a more rounded shape. Refrigerate until firm, about 2 hours. (See Note.)

5. Preheat oven to 350°F (180°C).

6. In a large rimmed baking dish or plate, place nonpareils.

7. In a small bowl, whisk remaining 1 egg (50 grams). Working with 1 dough log at a time, unwrap log, and brush outside with egg; roll in nonpareils.

8. Working in batches, cut each log crosswise into ¼-inch-thick slices; round edges, if necessary, and roll in nonpareils, if desired. Place, cut side down, 1 to 1¼ inches apart on prepared pans, flattening slightly with your hand so dough rounds are flush with pan. (If dough rounds crack when flattening, simply press and smooth back together.)

9. Bake until set and bottoms are lightly golden, about 10 minutes. Let cool on pans for 2 minutes. Remove from pans, and let cool completely on wire racks.

*We used Wilton Color Right Performance Food Coloring and Wilton Holiday Nonpareils.

Note: *Let dough that has been refrigerated for longer time spans stand at room temperature until slightly softened and easier to slice, 15 to 30 minutes.*

FRANGIPANE-STUFFED GINGER COOKIES

Makes 18 cookies

Stuffed cookies are just better. In this recipe, an aromatic ginger cookie dough gets a soft and chewy Frangipane Filling, pairing nutty decadence with warm spice.

⅓ cup (76 grams) unsalted butter, softened
⅓ cup (73 grams) firmly packed light brown sugar
¼ cup (50 grams) granulated sugar
¼ cup (85 grams) molasses (not blackstrap)
1 large egg (50 grams), room temperature
1¾ cups (219 grams) all-purpose flour
1 tablespoon (8 grams) cornstarch
1½ teaspoons (3 grams) ground ginger
¾ teaspoon (2.25 grams) kosher salt
½ teaspoon (2.5 grams) baking soda
½ teaspoon (1 gram) ground cinnamon
¼ teaspoon (1.25 grams) baking powder
¼ teaspoon ground cloves
¼ teaspoon ground cardamom
Frangipane Filling (recipe follows)
¾ cup (85 grams) sliced almonds, roughly crushed
½ cup (100 grams) sanding sugar or sparkling sugar

1. In the bowl of a stand mixer fitted with the paddle attachment, beat butter, brown sugar, and granulated sugar at medium speed until fluffy, 2 to 3 minutes, stopping to scrape sides of bowl. Add molasses and egg; beat until well combined, stopping to scrape sides of bowl.
2. In a medium bowl, whisk together flour, cornstarch, ginger, salt, baking soda, cinnamon, baking powder, cloves, and cardamom. Add flour mixture to butter mixture all at once; beat at low speed just until combined. Cover and freeze for 40 minutes.
3. Line a rimmed baking sheet with parchment paper.
4. Divide Frangipane Filling into 18 portions (about 7 grams each), and place on prepared pan. Shape each portion into a 1½-inch disk. Cover and set aside.
5. Preheat oven to 350°F (180°C). Line 2 baking sheets with parchment paper.
6. In a small shallow bowl, place almonds. In another small shallow bowl, place sanding sugar or sparkling sugar.

7. Divide dough into 36 portions (about 15 grams each); flatten portions into 2-inch disks. Place 1 Frangipane Filling disk in center of 1 dough disk; cover with a second dough disk, and crimp edges closed. Gently shape into a ball. Roll in almonds; roll in sanding sugar or sparkling sugar. (See Note.) Repeat with remaining dough and remaining Frangipane Filling. Place dough balls 1½ to 2 inches apart on prepared pans; gently flatten to ¾-inch thickness, pressing together any cracks in edges, if necessary. Sprinkle tops with sanding sugar or sparkling sugar.
8. Bake, one batch at a time, until edges are just set and bottoms are golden brown, 8 to 10 minutes. Let cool on pans for 3 minutes. Remove from pans, and let cool completely on wire racks.

Note: *If sliced almonds and sanding or sparkling sugar aren't sticking as well, lightly dampen hands with water before rolling and coating dough balls.*

FRANGIPANE FILLING
Makes about ½ cup

⅔ cup (64 grams) super-fine blanched almond flour
2 tablespoons (24 grams) granulated sugar
2 tablespoons (28 grams) unsalted butter, cubed and softened
1 large egg yolk (19 grams), room temperature
½ teaspoon (2 grams) almond extract

1. In a small bowl, stir together flour and sugar until well combined. Add butter, egg yolk, and almond extract; stir until well combined, kneading together by hand if needed.

CANDIED PECAN AND DARK CHOCOLATE CHIP COOKIES

Makes about 20 cookies

Recipe by Erin Clarkson

These massive bakery-style cookies are a delicious twist on my classic chocolate chip cookies. They are loaded up with dark chocolate and have a delicious crunch and flavour from candied toasted pecans.

1   cup (227 grams) unsalted butter, softened
¾   cup plus 2 tablespoons plus 1 teaspoon (198 grams) firmly packed dark brown sugar
½   cup plus 2 tablespoons (124 grams) granulated sugar
1   large egg (50 grams), room temperature
1   teaspoon (6 grams) vanilla bean paste
2⅓   cups plus 1 tablespoon (300 grams) all-purpose flour
1   teaspoon (3 grams) kosher salt
½   teaspoon (2.5 grams) baking powder
½   teaspoon (2.5 grams) baking soda
10.5 ounces (300 grams) 70% cacao dark chocolate, roughly chopped
1   cup (150 grams) Candied Pecans (recipe follows)*, chopped
Flaked sea salt (optional)

1. In the bowl of a stand mixer fitted with the paddle attachment, beat butter and sugars at medium speed until light and fluffy, 3 to 4 minutes, stopping to scrape sides of bowl. Add egg and vanilla bean paste, beating until combined.
2. In a medium bowl, sift together flour, kosher salt, baking powder, and baking soda. Add flour mixture to butter mixture, and beat at low speed just until combined and a few streaks of flour remain. Add chocolate and Candied Pecans, and beat at low speed until combined.
3. Line a baking sheet with parchment paper.
4. Using a ¼-cup spring-loaded scoop, scoop dough (about 60 grams each), and roll into balls. Place on prepared pan. Lightly cover with plastic wrap, and refrigerate for 1 hour.
5. Preheat oven to 350°F (180°C). Line 3 to 4 baking sheets with parchment paper.
6. On a prepared pan, arrange 6 dough balls. (Keep remaining dough balls refrigerated.)
7. Bake until golden brown and edges are set, 14 to 15 minutes. (If cookies have lost their round shape in oven, use a round cookie cutter slightly larger than cookie to nudge back into a circular shape.) Sprinkle with sea salt (if using). Let cool on pan for 15 minutes. Remove from pan, and let cool completely on a wire rack. Repeat procedure with remaining dough, baking one batch at a time. Store in an airtight container for up to 3 days.

*Store-bought candied pecans can be substituted.

Notes: The dough for these cookies can be made ahead and baked straight from the freezer. To freeze, scoop the dough, and place on a parchment paper-lined baking sheet; freeze until solid, and transfer to an airtight container. Add 1 to 2 minutes to the bake time if baking from frozen.

To get big chocolate puddles on the tops of your cookies, chop up about 100 grams dark chocolate. Once you have scooped the dough into balls, flatten each ball and press a little of the extra chocolate onto the top and sides and then squish back into a ball. This gives you even distribution of the chocolate to create perfect puddles.

For best results, make this recipe by weight. The final texture of cookies can vary greatly depending on the amount of sugar and flour in the recipe, so it is important to ensure that the quantities are accurate.

CANDIED PECANS
Makes 1½ cups

¼   cup (50 grams) granulated sugar
1   tablespoon (14 grams) unsalted butter, room temperature
½   teaspoon (1.5 grams) kosher salt
1   cup (142 grams) pecan halves, toasted

1. Line a small baking sheet with a silicone baking mat or parchment paper.
2. In a medium saucepan, combine sugar, butter, and salt over medium heat. Add pecans, and cook, stirring frequently, until sugar is melted and nuts are evenly coated with sugar mixture, adjusting heat as needed. Pour mixture onto prepared pan; using a spatula, spread nuts out so they aren't clumped together. Let cool completely; break up any lumps. Store in an airtight container for up to 1 month.

Photo by Erin Clarkson

BROWNED BUTTER, WHITE CHOCOLATE, AND MACADAMIA COOKIES

Makes about 24 cookies

Recipe by Erin Clarkson

White chocolate and macadamia is a winning combination—smooth white chocolate pairs perfectly with crunchy macadamia nuts. Use nuts that have already been roasted and salted, which adds a depth of flavor to the cookie.

1 cup (227 grams) unsalted butter, room temperature
¾ cup (165 grams) firmly packed muscovado sugar*
½ cup (100 grams) granulated sugar
2 large eggs (100 grams), room temperature
1 teaspoon (6 grams) vanilla bean paste
2½ cups plus 2 tablespoons (330 grams) all-purpose flour
1 teaspoon (3 grams) kosher salt
¾ teaspoon (3.75 grams) baking powder
½ teaspoon (2.5 grams) baking soda
7 ounces (198 grams) white chocolate, roughly chopped
1⅓ cups (150 grams) roughly chopped roasted salted macadamia nuts
Flaked sea salt (optional)

1. Preheat oven to 350°F (180°C). Line 4 baking sheets with parchment paper.
2. In a medium saucepan, melt butter over medium heat. Cook, swirling pan frequently, until butter turns a medium-brown color and has a nutty aroma, 3 to 4 minutes. Remove from heat, and transfer to the bowl of a stand mixer; let cool slightly.
3. Add sugars to browned butter. Using the paddle attachment, beat at medium speed until combined, 1 to 2 minutes, stopping to scrape sides of bowl. With mixer on low speed, add eggs, one at a time, beating until combined after each addition. Beat in vanilla bean paste. Increase mixer speed to high, and beat until lightened in color and thickened, 2 to 3 minutes.
4. In a medium bowl, sift together flour, kosher salt, baking powder, and baking soda. Add flour mixture to butter mixture, and beat at low speed just until combined and a few streaks of flour remain. Beat in white chocolate and nuts until combined, about 10 seconds. Using a 2-tablespoon spring-loaded scoop, scoop dough (about 45 grams each) six times; roll into balls, and place 3 inches apart on a prepared pan. Cover remaining dough with plastic wrap.
5. Bake until centers are puffed and edges are set, 11 to 12 minutes. (If cookies have lost their round shape in oven, use a round cookie cutter slightly larger than cookie to nudge back into a circular shape.) Sprinkle with sea salt (if using). Let cool on pan for 10 minutes. Remove from pan, and let cool completely on a wire rack. Repeat procedure with remaining dough, baking one batch at a time. Store in an airtight container for up to 3 days.

If you don't have muscovado sugar, the same amount of dark brown sugar can be used instead.

Photo by Erin Clarkson

GINGER-MOLASSES SUGAR COOKIE SANDWICHES WITH SPICED CREAM CHEESE BUTTERCREAM

Makes 11 sandwich cookies

Recipe by Erin Clarkson

With a depth of flavor from the molasses, these rich sandwich cookies are rolled in ginger sugar to give them a sparkly, gingery finish.

1 cup (227 grams) unsalted butter, softened
1¼ cups (250 grams) granulated sugar, divided
⅔ cup (147 grams) firmly packed dark brown sugar
2 tablespoons (42 grams) molasses
1 large egg (50 grams), room temperature
1 teaspoon (6 grams) vanilla bean paste
2¼ cups (281 grams) all-purpose flour, sifted
5 teaspoons (10 grams) ground ginger, divided
1 teaspoon (3 grams) kosher salt
1 teaspoon (2 grams) ground cinnamon
½ teaspoon (2.5 grams) baking soda
½ teaspoon (1 gram) ground cardamom
Spiced Cream Cheese Buttercream (recipe follows)

1. Preheat oven to 350°F (180°C). Line 4 baking sheets with parchment paper.
2. In the bowl of a stand mixer fitted with the paddle attachment, beat butter, ¾ cup (150 grams) granulated sugar, brown sugar, and molasses at high speed until light and fluffy, 3 to 4 minutes, stopping to scrape sides of bowl. Add egg and vanilla bean paste, and beat at low speed until combined. Add flour, 4 teaspoons (8 grams) ginger, salt, cinnamon, baking soda, and cardamom, and beat at low speed just until combined, stopping to scrape sides and bottom of bowl.
3. In a small bowl, stir together remaining ½ cup (100 grams) granulated sugar and remaining 1 teaspoon (2 grams) ginger.
4. Using a 2-tablespoon spring-loaded scoop, scoop dough (about 40 grams each) six times. (Dough will be soft.) Roll each scoop into a ball; roll balls in ginger sugar, and place 3 inches apart on a prepared pan.

(Keep remaining dough in bowl.)
5. Bake until centers are puffed and edges are set, 9 to 11 minutes. Let cool completely on pan. Repeat procedure with remaining dough, baking one batch at a time.
6. Place Spiced Cream Cheese Buttercream in a pastry bag fitted with a ½-inch French star piping tip (Ateco #865). Pipe buttercream onto flat side of half of cookies. Place remaining cookies, flat side down, on top of buttercream. Refrigerate filled cookies in an airtight container for up to 2 days. Store unfilled cookies in an airtight container for up to 4 days.

SPICED CREAM CHEESE BUTTERCREAM
Makes 1¾ cups

⅓ cup plus 1 tablespoon (90 grams) unsalted butter, softened
¾ cup (169 grams) cold cream cheese
2¾ cups (330 grams) confectioners' sugar, sifted
1 teaspoon (2 grams) ground ginger
1 teaspoon (2 grams) ground cinnamon
1 teaspoon (6 grams) vanilla bean paste
½ teaspoon (1.5 grams) kosher salt
½ teaspoon (1 gram) ground cardamom

1. In the bowl of a stand mixer fitted with the paddle attachment, beat butter and cold cream cheese at high speed until pale and creamy, 3 to 4 minutes. Add confectioners' sugar, and beat at low speed until combined. Add ginger, cinnamon, vanilla bean paste, salt, and cardamom, and beat at low speed just until combined. Increase mixer speed to high, and beat until light and fluffy, 3 to 4 minutes. Use immediately.

Photo by Erin Clarkson

> **PRO TIP**
> If you are making these ahead of time, store the cookies and the frosting separately and assemble them on the day you are planning to serve.

HUNDREDS AND THOUSANDS BISCUITS

Makes about 32 cookies

Recipe by Erin Clarkson

These cookies are a combination of Erin Clarkson's two favorite childhood biscuits (what they call cookies in New Zealand)—her great-grandmother's shortbread recipe and hundreds and thousands biscuits, which are vanilla cookies with pink icing and sprinkles.

¾ cup plus 3 tablespoons (212 grams) unsalted butter, softened
⅔ cup (80 grams) confectioners' sugar, sifted
1 teaspoon (6 grams) vanilla bean paste
½ teaspoon (1.5 grams) kosher salt
2½ cups plus 1 tablespoon (321 grams) all-purpose flour
Royal Icing (recipe follows)
Nonpareils

1. In the bowl of a stand mixer fitted with the paddle attachment, beat butter, confectioners' sugar, vanilla bean paste, and salt at low speed; gradually increase mixer speed to high, beating until light and fluffy, 3 to 4 minutes, and stopping to scrape sides of bowl. Add flour, and beat at low speed just until combined.
2. Turn out dough onto a piece of plastic wrap, and press out into a rough rectangle. Wrap tightly in plastic wrap, and refrigerate for at least 2 hours or overnight.
3. Let dough stand at room temperature for 10 to 15 minutes.
4. Cut 4 (18x13-inch) sheets of parchment paper.
5. Divide dough in half, and place each half between 2 prepared parchment sheets. Using a rolling pin, gently flatten dough. Roll each half into an 18x13-inch rectangle, about ¼-inch thickness. (Remove top parchment and smooth down again if you are getting wrinkles.) Transfer dough rectangles, still between parchment, to baking sheets, and freeze for 15 to 20 minutes.
6. Preheat oven to 325°F (170°C). Line 3 to 4 baking sheets with parchment paper.
7. Using a 2½-inch fluted round cutter, cut dough, and place 1 inch apart on prepared

pans. Reroll scraps, and freeze for 5 to 10 minutes; cut dough. (If dough starts to soften, freeze for about 5 minutes to firm up.) Freeze for 10 minutes.
8. Bake, one batch at a time, until set and starting to turn golden, 12 to 13 minutes. Let cool on pans for 15 minutes. Remove from pans, and let cool completely on wire racks. Store in an airtight container until ready to ice.
9. Dip each cookie in Royal Icing. Let stand for 2 minutes; sprinkle with nonpareils. Let stand until icing is set, at least 1 hour. Store in an airtight container for up to 2 days.

Notes: *Store dough you are not working with in the freezer until ready.*

You will have a little Royal Icing left over—you need enough to be able to comfortably dip the cookies in it to get a good coating. Cover Royal Icing with a piece of plastic wrap, pressing wrap directly onto surface of icing, and refrigerate in an airtight container.

The sprinkles will start to bleed after 1 day, so just keep this in mind when you are preparing cookies.

ROYAL ICING

Makes 1⅓ cups

2 teaspoons (10 grams) water
Pink gel food coloring (optional)
3⅓ cups (400 grams) confectioners' sugar, sifted
2 large pasteurized egg whites* (60 grams), room temperature

1. In a medium bowl, whisk together 2 teaspoons (10 grams) water and food coloring (if using). Add confectioners' sugar and egg whites, and stir until well combined. Use immediately, or cover with a piece of plastic wrap, pressing wrap directly onto surface of icing, and refrigerate until ready to use.

*Pasteurized egg whites have been gently heated to kill harmful bacteria without cooking the actual egg, reducing the risk of salmonella.

Note: *Dissolving the food coloring in the water before you mix in the other ingredients helps the color disperse evenly.*

Photo by Erin Clarkson

CHOCOLATE AND CHERRY LINZER COOKIES

Makes about 20 sandwich cookies

Recipe by Erin Clarkson

Super chocolaty cookies get paired with a sweet cherry preserves filling for a classic chocolate-cherry flavor combination.

- 1 cup plus 1½ tablespoons (250 grams) unsalted butter, softened
- ¾ cup plus 1 tablespoon plus 1 teaspoon (100 grams) confectioners' sugar, sifted
- ½ teaspoon (2 grams) vanilla extract
- ¼ teaspoon kosher salt
- 2 cups plus 2½ tablespoons (270 grams) all-purpose flour
- ⅔ cup plus 1 tablespoon (55 grams) Dutch process cocoa powder
- ½ cup (160 grams) cherry preserves
- Garnish: confectioners' sugar

1. In the bowl of a stand mixer fitted with the paddle attachment, beat butter, confectioners' sugar, vanilla, and salt at low speed; gradually increase mixer speed to high, beating until light and fluffy, 3 to 4 minutes, and stopping to scrape sides of bowl.

2. In a medium bowl, whisk together flour and cocoa. Add flour mixture to butter mixture, and beat at low speed until just combined.

3. Cut 2 (18x13-inch) sheets of parchment paper. Turn out dough onto a parchment sheet; flatten into a rough rectangle, and top with second parchment sheet, smoothing out any wrinkles. Roll out dough between parchment into an 18x13-inch rectangle, about ⅛-inch thickness. (Remove top parchment and smooth down again if you are getting wrinkles.) Transfer dough, still between parchment, to a baking sheet, and freeze until completely solid, 20 to 30 minutes.

4. Preheat oven to 350°F (180°C). Line 2 baking sheets with parchment paper.

5. Remove top sheet of parchment from dough. Using a 2½-inch fluted round cutter, cut dough, and carefully place 1 inch apart on prepared pans. Using a ¾-inch star-shaped cutter, cut centers from half of cookies. Reroll scraps, freeze, and cut dough. Repeat procedure until all dough is used. (If dough becomes difficult to work with or too soft, freeze for about 5 minutes to firm up.) Freeze until ready to bake.

6. Bake, one batch at a time, until set, 16 to 17 minutes. Let cool on pans for 15 minutes. Remove from pans, and let cool completely on wire racks. Store in an airtight container until ready to use.

7. Spread or pipe 1 teaspoon (7 grams) preserves onto flat side of all solid cookies. Garnish cookies with cutouts with confectioners' sugar, if desired. Place cookies with cutouts, flat side down, on top of preserves. Store in an airtight container for up to 2 days.

Notes: *The chocolate cookie isn't super sweet, so feel free to increase the amount of sugar a little if you like.*

These cookies can be made ahead and stored in an airtight container for up to 3 days. Fill cookies just before serving.

Photo by Erin Clarkson

SNICKERDOODLE BISCOTTI

Makes 24 to 28 biscotti

Recipe by Laura Kasavan

Golden cinnamon-sugar biscotti dipped in white chocolate make for a delicious spin on classic snickerdoodle cookies! These twice-baked cookies bake up lightly golden and make a scrumptious treat with a cozy latte.

1	cup (200 grams) granulated sugar, divided
½	cup (113 grams) unsalted butter, melted and slightly cooled
¼	cup (52 grams) brandy
3	large eggs (150 grams), room temperature
3	cups (375 grams) all-purpose flour
1½	teaspoons (7.5 grams) baking powder
½	teaspoon (1.5 grams) kosher salt
2	teaspoons (4 grams) ground cinnamon
10	ounces (283 grams) white chocolate, chopped

1. In a large bowl, whisk together ¾ cup (150 grams) sugar, melted butter, and brandy. Add eggs, one at a time, whisking until smooth after each addition. Stir in flour, baking powder, and salt until combined and no streaks of flour remain. Cover with plastic wrap, and refrigerate for 30 minutes.

2. Preheat oven to 350°F (180°C). Line 2 baking sheets with parchment paper.

3. Divide dough in half. Using moistened hands, shape each half into a 10x4-inch rectangle, and place on prepared pans. (Dough will be sticky; shaping with wet hands will help.)

4. In a small bowl, stir together cinnamon and remaining ¼ cup (50 grams) sugar. Sprinkle loaves generously with cinnamon sugar, gently pressing into dough.

5. Bake until pale golden, 24 to 25 minutes. Using parchment as handles, carefully remove from pans, and let cool on wire racks for 15 minutes. Leave oven on.

6. Using a serrated knife, cut loaves crosswise into about ¾-inch slices. Place slices, cut side down, on prepared pans.

7. Bake for 10 minutes. Turn slices, and bake until golden and edges are dry, about 10 minutes more. Let cool completely on pans.

8. In the top of a double boiler, melt white chocolate over simmering water until smooth and glossy. Dip bottom of cooled biscotti in melted white chocolate. Return dipped biscotti to pans. Refrigerate until chocolate is set, about 20 minutes. Store in an airtight container for up to 5 days.

Photo by Laura Kasavan

CRANBERRY CHEESECAKE COOKIES

Makes 24 cookies

Recipe by Laura Kasavan

Cheesecake lovers will fall for these soft-batch graham cookies topped with Cream Cheese Buttercream and dollops of jeweled Cranberry Sauce.

½   cup (113 grams) unsalted butter, room temperature
4   ounces (113 grams) cream cheese, room temperature
¾   cup (150 grams) granulated sugar, plus more for rolling
¼   cup (55 grams) firmly packed light brown sugar
1   large egg (50 grams), room temperature
2   teaspoons (8 grams) vanilla extract
2¼   cups (281 grams) all-purpose flour
1   teaspoon (3 grams) cornstarch
1   teaspoon (5 grams) baking soda
½   teaspoon (1.5 grams) kosher salt
Graham cracker crumbs, for rolling
Cream Cheese Buttercream (recipe follows)
Cranberry Sauce (recipe follows)

1. In the bowl of a stand mixer fitted with the paddle attachment, beat butter and cream cheese at medium speed until smooth. Add sugars, and beat until fluffy, 3 to 4 minutes, stopping to scrape sides of bowl. Beat in egg and vanilla until combined.
2. In a medium bowl, whisk together flour, cornstarch, baking soda, and salt. With mixer on low speed, gradually add flour mixture to butter mixture, beating until combined. Cover and refrigerate for 3 hours or overnight.
3. Preheat oven to 350°F (180°C). Line 2 baking sheets with parchment paper.
4. Using a 1½-tablespoon spring-loaded scoop, scoop dough, and roll in granulated sugar to coat; roll in graham cracker crumbs to coat. Place 2 inches apart on prepared pans.
5. Bake until golden and tops and edges are set, 12 to 14 minutes, rotating pans halfway through baking. Let cool on pans for 10 minutes. Remove from pans, and let cool completely on wire racks.
6. Place Cream Cheese Buttercream in a pastry bag fitted with a 1-inch closed star piping tip (Wilton No. 2D). Pipe a ring of buttercream around edges of each cookie. Pipe or spoon Cranberry Sauce in center of buttercream ring. Serve immediately.

CREAM CHEESE BUTTERCREAM
Makes about 2 cups

½   cup (113 grams) unsalted butter, room temperature
4   ounces (113 grams) cream cheese, room temperature
¼   teaspoon kosher salt
2   teaspoons (8 grams) vanilla extract
3   cups (360 grams) confectioners' sugar, sifted

1. In the bowl of a stand mixer fitted with the paddle attachment, beat butter, cream cheese, and salt at medium speed until smooth, 2 to 3 minutes. Beat in vanilla. With mixer on low speed, gradually add confectioners' sugar, beating until combined. Increase mixer speed to medium-high, and beat until light and airy, 1 to 2 minutes. Use immediately.

CRANBERRY SAUCE
Makes about 1½ cups

3   cups (330 grams) fresh or frozen* cranberries
¾   cup (150 grams) granulated sugar
⅛   teaspoon kosher salt
2   tablespoons (30 grams) water
½   teaspoon (2 grams) almond extract

1. In a medium heavy-bottomed saucepan, cook cranberries, sugar, and salt over medium-high heat, stirring constantly, until cranberries begin to burst and mixture is boiling. Reduce heat to low; stir in 2 tablespoons (30 grams) water and almond extract, and simmer, stirring occasionally, for 5 minutes. Transfer to a glass bowl, and let cool completely.

If using frozen cranberries, there's no need to thaw—simply cook as directed.

Photo by Laura Kasavan

PEPPERMINT-CHOCOLATE SANDWICH COOKIES

Makes 12 sandwich cookies

Recipe by Laura Kasavan

Dark chocolate crinkle cookies sandwiched with peppermint buttercream are the ultimate cookie for chocolate-and-peppermint lovers! For an extra-festive touch, garnish the cookies with crushed peppermint candies.

4 ounces (113 grams) unsweetened chocolate, chopped
¼ cup (57 grams) unsalted butter, cubed
1¼ cups (156 grams) all-purpose flour
½ cup (43 grams) unsweetened cocoa powder
1 teaspoon (5 grams) baking powder
½ teaspoon (1.5 grams) kosher salt
¼ teaspoon (1.25 grams) baking soda
¾ cup (150 grams) granulated sugar, plus more for rolling
¾ cup (165 grams) firmly packed light brown sugar
2 large eggs (100 grams), room temperature
Confectioners' sugar, for rolling
Peppermint Frosting (recipe follows)
Garnish: roughly crushed round peppermint candies

1. Preheat oven to 325°F (170°C). Line 2 baking sheets with parchment paper.
2. In a medium microwave-safe bowl, combine chocolate and butter. Heat on high for 30 seconds; stir. Heat on high in 15-second intervals, stirring between each, until melted and smooth. Let cool slightly.
3. In a medium bowl, whisk together flour, cocoa, baking powder, salt, and baking soda.

4. In a large bowl, whisk together granulated sugar, brown sugar, and eggs until combined. Add cooled chocolate mixture, and whisk until smooth. Fold in flour mixture just until combined. (Mixture will resemble brownie batter.) Let dough stand at room temperature for 10 minutes.
5. Using a 1½-tablespoon spring-loaded scoop, scoop dough. Roll in granulated sugar to coat; roll in confectioners' sugar to coat. Place 2 inches apart on prepared pans.
6. Bake until puffed and cracked and edges are set, 16 to 18 minutes. Tap pans on a kitchen towel-lined counter to slightly flatten cookies. Let cool on pans for 15 minutes. Remove from pans, and let cool completely on wire racks.
7. Pipe or spread Peppermint Frosting onto flat side of half of cooled cookies. Place remaining cookies, flat side down, on top of frosting. Garnish with candies, if desired. Refrigerate in an airtight container for up to 1 week.

PEPPERMINT FROSTING
Makes about 2 cups

¾ cup (170 grams) unsalted butter, softened
⅛ teaspoon kosher salt
1 teaspoon (4 grams) vanilla extract
½ teaspoon (2 grams) peppermint extract
2 cups (240 grams) confectioners' sugar
1 tablespoon (15 grams) heavy whipping cream

1. In the bowl of a stand mixer fitted with the paddle attachment, beat butter and salt at medium speed until smooth, 2 to 3 minutes. Beat in extracts. With mixer on low speed, gradually add confectioners' sugar, beating until combined. Add cream; increase mixer speed to medium-high, and beat until light and airy, 1 to 2 minutes. Use immediately.

Photo by Laura Kasavan

FROSTED CITRUS COOKIES

Makes 24 cookies

Recipe by Laura Kasavan

Soft-batch citrus cookies topped with creamy swirls of Citrus Frosting make a zesty and bright addition to the holiday cookie table! Use any mix of citrus you love in these cookies.

¾   cup (170 grams) unsalted butter, softened
2   tablespoons (6 grams) citrus zest*
¾   cup (150 grams) granulated sugar
¼   cup (55 grams) firmly packed light brown sugar
1   large egg (50 grams)
1   teaspoon (4 grams) vanilla extract
2⅓   cups (292 grams) all-purpose flour
1   teaspoon (3 grams) cornstarch
1   teaspoon (5 grams) baking soda
½   teaspoon (1.5 grams) kosher salt
Citrus Frosting (recipe follows)
Garnish: candied citrus peel

1. In the bowl of a stand mixer fitted with the paddle attachment, beat butter and citrus zest at medium speed until smooth. Add sugars, and beat until fluffy, about 3 minutes, stopping to scrape sides of bowl. Beat in egg and vanilla until combined.
2. In a medium bowl, whisk together flour, cornstarch, baking soda, and salt. With mixer on low speed, gradually add flour mixture to butter mixture, beating until combined. Cover and refrigerate for 3 hours or overnight.
3. Preheat oven to 350°F (180°C). Line 2 baking sheets with parchment paper.
4. Using a 1½-tablespoon spring-loaded scoop, scoop dough, and place 2 inches apart on prepared pans.
5. Bake until golden and tops and edges are set, 12 to 14 minutes, rotating pans halfway through baking. Let cool on pans for 10 minutes. Remove from pans, and let cool completely on wire racks.
6. Using an offset spatula, spread Citrus Frosting onto cooled cookies. Garnish with candied citrus peel, if desired. Refrigerate in an airtight container for up to 2 days.

*I used a blend of orange, lemon, and lime zests.

CITRUS FROSTING
Makes about 2 cups

¾   cup (170 grams) unsalted butter, softened
¼   teaspoon kosher salt
1   tablespoon (3 grams) citrus zest
1   teaspoon (4 grams) vanilla extract
3   cups (360 grams) confectioners' sugar
1   tablespoon (15 grams) heavy whipping cream

1. In the bowl of a stand mixer fitted with the paddle attachment, beat butter and salt at medium speed until smooth, 2 to 3 minutes. Beat in citrus zest and vanilla. With mixer on low speed, gradually add confectioners' sugar, beating until combined. Add cream; increase mixer speed to medium-high, and beat until light and airy, 1 to 2 minutes. Use immediately.

Photo by Laura Kasavan

CHOCOLATE TOFFEE SHORTBREAD

Makes 12 cookies

Recipe by Laura Kasavan

Golden toffee shortbread cookies drizzled with dark chocolate are rich, buttery, and simply irresistible! Baked in a tart pan and sliced into wedges, these cookies are the perfect pairing of chocolate and toffee.

¾ cup (170 grams) unsalted butter, softened
¾ cup (150 grams) plus 1 tablespoon (12 grams) granulated sugar, divided
1 teaspoon (4 grams) vanilla extract
¼ teaspoon kosher salt
1¾ cups (219 grams) all-purpose flour
⅔ cup (100 grams) plus 3 tablespoons (28 grams) toffee bits, divided
2 ounces (57 grams) 63% cacao dark chocolate chips
Garnish: flaked sea salt

1. Spray a 9-inch fluted round removable-bottom tart pan with cooking spray.

2. In the bowl of a stand mixer fitted with the paddle attachment, beat butter and ¾ cup (150 grams) sugar at medium speed until creamy, 2 to 3 minutes, stopping to scrape sides of bowl. With mixer on medium-low speed, add vanilla and kosher salt, beating until combined. Add flour, and beat at low speed until combined and dough starts to come together. Beat in ⅔ cup (100 grams) toffee bits just until combined. Transfer dough to prepared pan, pressing into bottom and up sides. Cover and refrigerate until firm, about 1 hour.

3. Preheat oven to 350°F (180°C).

4. Using a sharp knife, score dough into 12 wedges, and prick all over with a wooden skewer. Sprinkle with remaining 1 tablespoon (12 grams) sugar. Place pan on a rimmed baking sheet.

5. Bake until top is light golden and center is set, 28 to 32 minutes. Let cool for 20 minutes. Using a sharp knife, cut into wedges. Let cool completely in pan.

6. Line a rimmed baking sheet with parchment paper. Place shortbread wedges in a single layer on prepared pan.

7. In a microwave-safe bowl, heat chocolate chips on high in 30-second intervals, stirring between each, until melted and smooth. Drizzle melted chocolate onto shortbread. Top with remaining 3 tablespoons (28 grams) toffee bits, and garnish with sea salt, if desired. Refrigerate until chocolate is set, about 20 minutes. Store in an airtight container for up to 3 days.

Photo by Laura Kasavan

MAKE AHEAD

Shortbread dough can be made up to 1 month in advance. After refrigerating dough for 1 hour, score dough into wedges, and prick all over with a wooden skewer. Wrap tart pan in foil, and place in a large resealable plastic bag to freeze. When you're ready to bake, you can bake the shortbread directly from the freezer, adding 2 to 3 minutes to the bake time.

PEPPERMINT MOCHA COOKIES

Makes about 45 cookies

Recipe by Laura Kasavan

Chocolate cookies with a dash of espresso powder are dipped in chocolate and sprinkled with crushed peppermint to offer the richness of a warm peppermint mocha. These cookies balance the flavors of chocolate and coffee with refreshing peppermint. Enjoy these festive cookies by the fire!

1 cup (227 grams) unsalted butter, softened
1 cup (200 grams) granulated sugar
1 large egg (50 grams), room temperature
1 teaspoon (2 grams) instant espresso powder
1 teaspoon (4 grams) vanilla extract
1 teaspoon (4 grams) peppermint extract, divided
2¾ cups (344 grams) all-purpose flour
½ cup (43 grams) unsweetened cocoa powder
¾ teaspoon (3.75 grams) baking powder
½ teaspoon (1.5 grams) kosher salt

16 ounces (454 grams) 60% cacao semisweet chocolate, chopped
6 ounces (180 grams) roughly crushed peppermint candies (about 30 candies)

1. In the bowl of a stand mixer fitted with the paddle attachment, beat butter and sugar at medium speed until creamy, 3 to 4 minutes, stopping to scrape sides of bowl. Add egg, espresso powder, vanilla, and ½ teaspoon (2 grams) peppermint extract, beating until combined.
2. In a medium bowl, whisk together flour, cocoa, baking powder, and salt. With mixer on low speed, gradually add flour mixture to butter mixture, beating until combined and dough starts to come together in large pieces.
3. Divide dough in half, and place each half on a piece of plastic wrap. Shape each half into a disk, and wrap tightly in plastic wrap. Refrigerate for 30 minutes.
4. Line 2 baking sheets with parchment paper.
5. On a lightly floured cutting board, roll half of dough to ¼-inch thickness. (Keep remaining dough in refrigerator.) Using a

2-inch round cutter lightly dipped in flour, cut dough, rerolling scraps once, and place on a prepared pan. Repeat procedure with remaining dough. Refrigerate for 30 minutes.
6. Preheat oven to 350°F (180°C).
7. Bake until tops and edges are set, 9 to 10 minutes, rotating pans halfway through baking. Let cool on pans for 10 minutes. Remove from pans, and let cool completely on wire racks.
8. In the top of a double boiler, melt chocolate over simmering water until smooth and glossy. Stir in remaining ½ teaspoon (2 grams) peppermint extract.
9. Dip tops of cooled cookies in melted chocolate. Place dipped cookies on parchment paper-lined pans, and sprinkle with candies. Refrigerate until chocolate is set, about 20 minutes. Refrigerate in a single layer in airtight containers for up to 5 days.

Photo by Laura Kasavan

BROWNED BUTTER CHOCOLATE PISTACHIO COOKIES

Makes 24 cookies

Recipe by Laura Kasavan

Slice-and-bake browned butter pistachio shortbread cookies dipped in chocolate make the ideal cookie for shortbread lovers! Roasted salted pistachios add incredible flavor to these buttery cookies.

¾   cup (170 grams) unsalted butter, cubed
¾   cup (150 grams) granulated sugar
1½   teaspoons (6 grams) vanilla extract
¼   teaspoon kosher salt
1¾   cups (219 grams) all-purpose flour
½   cup (57 grams) plus 3 tablespoons (21 grams) finely chopped roasted salted pistachios, divided
2   cups (340 grams) 46% cacao semisweet chocolate chips

1. In a medium saucepan, melt butter over medium heat. Cook, swirling pan occasionally, until butter turns a medium-brown color and has a nutty aroma, about 5 minutes. Pour browned butter into a shallow glass bowl, and freeze until solidified and the texture of softened butter, 45 minutes to 1 hour.

2. In the bowl of a stand mixer fitted with the paddle attachment, beat browned butter and sugar at medium speed until creamy, 2 to 3 minutes, stopping to scrape sides of bowl. With mixer on medium-low speed, add vanilla and salt, beating until combined. Add flour, and beat at low speed until combined and dough starts to come together. Add ½ cup (57 grams) pistachios, beating just until combined.

3. Divide dough in half, and place each half on a piece of plastic wrap. (Dough will be crumbly but will come together as you press it together with your hands). Roll each half into a 6½-inch log, using plastic wrap to help shape soft dough. Wrap logs tightly in plastic wrap, and refrigerate for 1 hour.

4. Preheat oven to 350°F (180°C). Line 2 baking sheets with parchment paper.

5. Using a sharp knife, cut logs crosswise into ½-inch-thick rounds, and place 2 inches apart on prepared pans. Using the bottom of a measuring cup, gently press rounds to make them perfectly level. (If dough rounds crack when flattening, simply press and smooth back together.) Refrigerate for 20 minutes.

6. Bake until golden, 16 to 20 minutes, rotating pans halfway through baking. Let cool on pans for 10 minutes. Remove from pans, and let cool completely on wire racks.

7. Line 2 rimmed baking sheets with parchment paper. Transfer cooled cookies to prepared pans, and freeze for 20 minutes.

8. In a medium microwave-safe bowl, heat chocolate chips on high in 30-second intervals, stirring between each, until melted and smooth.

9. Dip half of each cookie in melted chocolate, and return to pan. Using a spoon, drizzle melted chocolate onto dipped half of each cookie. Top cookies with remaining 3 tablespoons (21 grams) pistachios. Refrigerate until chocolate is set, about 20 minutes. Store in an airtight container for up to 3 days.

Photo by Laura Kasavan

PRO TIP
For uniformly round slice-and-bake cookies, split 2 empty paper towel rolls lengthwise down the middle. Refrigerate dough logs inside center of each cardboard roll until firm.

CHOCOLATE-PEPPERMINT PAN-BANGING COOKIES

Makes 12 cookies

Recipe by Sarah Kieffer

Chocolate and peppermint is a classic holiday combination, bringing to mind so many good memories: peppermint hot chocolate, peppermint mochas, cakes, and ice cream.

1 cup (227 grams) unsalted butter, softened
1½ cups (300 grams) granulated sugar
¼ cup (55 grams) firmly packed light brown sugar
1 large egg (50 grams), room temperature
2 tablespoons (30 grams) water
1 teaspoon (4 grams) vanilla extract
1 teaspoon (4 grams) peppermint extract
2 cups (250 grams) all-purpose flour
⅓ cup plus 1 tablespoon plus 1 teaspoon (32 grams) Dutch process cocoa powder
¾ teaspoon (2.25 grams) kosher salt
½ teaspoon (2.5 grams) baking soda
4 ounces (113 grams) 60% cacao bittersweet chocolate, roughly chopped
2 ounces (57 grams) 60% cacao bittersweet chocolate, melted
10 peppermint candies (60 grams), crushed

1. Position oven rack in center of oven. Preheat oven to 350°F (180°C). Line 3 baking sheets with foil, dull side up.

2. In the bowl of a stand mixer fitted with the paddle attachment, beat butter at medium speed until creamy, about 1 minute. Add sugars, and beat at medium speed until light and fluffy, 2 to 3 minutes. Add egg, 2 tablespoons (30 grams) water, and extracts, and beat at low speed until combined.

3. In a medium bowl, whisk together flour, cocoa, salt, and baking soda. Add flour mixture to butter mixture, and beat at low speed until combined. Beat in chopped chocolate. Using a ¼-cup spring-loaded scoop, scoop dough (85 grams each), and roll into balls. Place 4 dough balls on each prepared pan.

4. Bake, one batch at a time, until dough balls have spread flat but centers are puffed slightly, about 9 minutes; lift one side of pan about 4 inches, and gently let it drop against oven rack so edges of cookies set and centers fall back down. Bake until centers are puffed, about 2 minutes more; lift one side of pan about 4 inches, and gently let it drop against oven rack. Bake for 2 minutes more, and repeat lifting and dropping of pan to create ridges around edges of cookies. Bake until cookies have spread out and edges are set and rippled but centers are still soft, 2 to 3 minutes more. Let cool on pans on wire racks for 10 minutes. Remove from pans, and let cool completely on wire racks.

5. Drizzle melted chocolate onto cookies; sprinkle candies onto melted chocolate. Let stand until chocolate is set, about 30 minutes. Store in an airtight container for up to 2 days, or refrigerate in an airtight container for up to 3 days.

Photo by Sarah Kieffer

CHOCOLATE ORANGE SABLÉS

Makes about 36 cookies

Recipe by Sarah Kieffer

Sablés are rich and buttery on their own and are easily adapted to any flavor whim one may have. Chocolate and orange pair beautifully here: candied orange peel is delicious and elegant, and mini chocolate chips add just enough chocolate without overwhelming the orange.

1   cup (227 grams) unsalted butter, softened
1   cup (200 grams) granulated sugar
1   tablespoon (3 grams) orange zest
½   teaspoon (1.5 grams) kosher salt
1   large egg yolk (19 grams), room temperature
1   teaspoon (4 grams) vanilla extract
2¼   cups (281 grams) all-purpose flour
¼   cup (32 grams) finely chopped candied orange peel*
¼   cup (43 grams) 46% cacao semisweet mini chocolate chips
1   cup (200 grams) turbinado sugar or sanding sugar

1. In the bowl of a stand mixer fitted with the paddle attachment, beat butter at medium speed until creamy, about 1 minute. Add granulated sugar, orange zest, and salt, and beat until light and fluffy, 2 to 3 minutes, stopping to scrapes sides of bowl. With mixer on low speed, beat in egg yolk and vanilla until combined. Add flour, and beat at low speed just until combined. Beat in candied orange peel and chocolate chips until combined.
2. Turn out dough onto a clean surface, and shape into a 12-inch log. Place on a piece of plastic wrap a few inches longer than dough log. Sprinkle turbinado sugar or sparkling sugar on log, covering outside of dough. Gently press sugar into dough with your hands. Wrap log in plastic wrap, and refrigerate until firm, about 2 hours.
3. Position oven rack in center of oven. Preheat oven to 350°F (180°C). Line 3 baking sheets with parchment paper.
4. Using a serrated knife, slice dough log into ⅓-inch-thick rounds, and place about 2 inches apart on prepared pans.

5. Bake, one batch at a time, until edges are very light golden brown and centers are still pale, 14 to 16 minutes, rotating pan halfway through baking. Let cool completely on pans on wire racks. Store in an airtight container for up to 3 days.

Candied orange peel can be purchased online at amazon.com.

Photo by Sarah Kieffer

GINGER SUGAR COOKIES

Makes about 20 cookies

Recipe by Sarah Kieffer

Sugar cookies are a holiday tradition, and this version includes ginger in fresh, ground, and crystallized form. These cookies are crisp on the outside and chewy in the center, making for a perfect bite.

1   cup (227 grams) unsalted butter, softened
2¼ cups (450 grams) granulated sugar, divided
1   teaspoon grated fresh ginger
1   large egg (50 grams), room temperature
1   large egg yolk (19 grams), room temperature
1   teaspoon (4 grams) vanilla extract
2⅔ cups plus ¼ cup (364 grams) all-purpose flour
¾   teaspoon (3.25 grams) baking soda
¾   teaspoon (2.25 grams) kosher salt
¼   teaspoon (1.25 grams) cream of tartar
¼   cup (43 grams) finely diced crystallized ginger
1   teaspoon (2 grams) ground ginger

1. Position oven rack in center of oven. Preheat oven to 350°F (180°C). Line 3 baking sheets with parchment paper.
2. In the bowl of a stand mixer fitted with the paddle attachment, beat butter at medium speed until creamy, about 1 minute. Add 1¾ cups (350 grams) sugar and grated ginger, and beat at medium speed until light and fluffy, 2 to 3 minutes. Beat in egg, egg yolk, and vanilla until combined.
3. In a medium bowl, stir together flour, baking soda, salt, and cream of tartar. Add flour mixture to butter mixture, and beat at low speed just until combined. Beat in crystallized ginger just until combined.

4. In another medium bowl, whisk together ground ginger and remaining ½ cup (100 grams) sugar.
5. Using a 2-tablespoon spring-loaded scoop, scoop dough (about 45 grams each), and roll into balls. Roll each dough ball in ginger sugar, and place 3 inches apart on prepared pans.
6. Bake, one batch at a time, until edges are set and bottoms are light golden brown, 12 to 14 minutes, rotating pan halfway through baking. Let cool on pan on a wire rack for 5 to 10 minutes. Remove from pan, and let cool completely on wire racks. Store in an airtight container for up to 3 days.

Photo by Sarah Kieffer

MERINGUES WITH CACAO NIBS AND CARAMEL SWIRL

Makes 24 meringues

Recipe by Sarah Kieffer

Meringues always look so impressive, with their swoops and swirls and crisp white exterior. These feature cacao nibs for crunch and homemade Caramel for extra extravagance.

2 cups (400 grams) granulated sugar
1 cup (240 grams) egg whites (from about 8 large eggs), room temperature
¼ teaspoon kosher salt
⅛ teaspoon cream of tartar
¼ cup (40 grams) cacao nibs, finely chopped
2 teaspoons (8 grams) vanilla extract
½ cup (180 grams) Caramel (recipe follows)

1. Position oven racks in upper- and lower-middle positions of oven. Preheat oven to 200°F (93°C). Line 2 baking sheets with parchment paper.
2. In the heatproof bowl of a stand mixer, using a rubber spatula, gently stir together sugar, egg whites, salt, and cream of tartar until combined. Place bowl over a saucepan of simmering water. Cook, stirring constantly with rubber spatula and scraping sides of bowl, until sugar is melted and an instant-read thermometer registers 160°F (71°C), 4 to 5 minutes.
3. Return bowl to stand mixer. Using the whisk attachment, beat at low speed for 1 minute; slowly increase mixer speed to medium-high, and beat until glossy stiff peaks form and bowl is cool to the touch, 8 to 10 minutes. Add cacao nibs and vanilla, and beat at medium-low speed until combined.

4. Using a spoon, scoop mixture, and place 12 mounds on each prepared pan. Using the back of a wet spoon, smooth top of each mound. Place 1 teaspoon (7.5 grams) Caramel on top of each mound; using the tip of a butter knife, swirl Caramel into top of mounds.
5. Bake for 1 hour. Turn oven off, and leave meringues in oven with door closed for 30 minutes. Let cool completely on pans on wire racks. Store in an airtight container for up to 2 days.

CARAMEL
Makes 1½ cups

1¼ cups (250 grams) granulated sugar
¼ cup (60 grams) water
½ teaspoon (1.5 grams) kosher salt
½ cup (120 grams) heavy whipping cream
5 tablespoons (76 grams) unsalted butter, cut into 8 pieces
1 tablespoon (13 grams) vanilla extract

1. In a large heavy-bottomed saucepan, very gently stir together sugar, ¼ cup (60 grams) water, and salt. Cover with lid, and bring to a boil over medium-high heat; cook until sugar is melted and mixture is clear, 3 to 5 minutes. Uncover and cook until sugar is pale golden brown and a candy thermometer registers 300°F (150°C). Reduce heat, and cook until deep golden brown and a candy thermometer registers 325°F (170°C). Remove from heat, and add cream. (Mixture will bubble up vigorously, so be careful.) Add butter; add vanilla, and stir to combine. Let cool to room temperature. Refrigerate in an airtight container for up to 2 weeks.

Reprinted from *100 Cookies* by Sarah Kieffer with permission from Chronicle Books, 2020.

MIMOSA CUTOUT COOKIES

Makes 35 cookies

I paired orange zest-packed dough with bright Sparkling Wine Royal Icing to create a mimosa-flavored holiday cookie. This elegant showstopper is surprisingly simple to make thanks to an easy icing method. These cookies are dipped in royal icing, rather than piped and flooded, before getting finished off with a mix of white sprinkles for an easy yet sophisticated look.

1   cup (227 grams) unsalted butter, softened
2   cups (240 grams) confectioners' sugar
1   tablespoon (8 grams) tightly packed orange zest
1   large egg (50 grams), room temperature
1   teaspoon (6 grams) vanilla bean paste
3¼ cups (406 grams) all-purpose flour
2   teaspoons (10 grams) baking powder
1   teaspoon (3 grams) kosher salt
Sparkling Wine Royal Icing (recipe follows)
Garnish: assorted white sprinkles

1. Preheat oven to 350°F (180°C). Line 3 baking sheets with parchment paper.
2. In the bowl of a stand mixer fitted with the paddle attachment, beat butter, confectioners' sugar, and orange zest at low speed just until combined. Increase mixer speed to medium-low, and beat until fluffy, 2 to 3 minutes, stopping to scrape sides of bowl. Add egg and vanilla bean paste, beating until combined.
3. In a medium bowl, whisk together flour, baking powder, and salt. With mixer on low speed, gradually add flour mixture to butter mixture, beating until a dough forms. Divide dough in half; shape each half into a 7-inch disk. Wrap each disk in plastic wrap, and refrigerate for 30 minutes.
4. On a lightly floured surface, roll half of dough to ¼-inch thickness. Using desired cutters dipped in flour, cut dough; using a large offset spatula dipped in flour, place cut dough ¾ to 1 inch apart on prepared pans. Reroll and cut scraps as needed. Repeat with remaining dough. (See Note.)
5. Bake, one batch at a time, until edges are lightly golden, 8 to 10 minutes. Let cool on pan for 1 minute. Remove from pan, and let cool completely on wire racks.

6. Dip tops of cooled cookies in Sparkling Wine Royal Icing; pull straight out, and lightly shake back and forth, letting excess drip off as much as possible. Quickly turn cookies icing side up; using a wooden pick, spread icing into an even layer, popping and filling any air bubbles, if necessary. Garnish with sprinkles, if desired. Let stand until dry, at least 4 hours.

Note: *If dough is refrigerated for a longer period of time, let stand at room temperature until slightly softened, 10 to 20 minutes.*

SPARKLING WINE ROYAL ICING
Makes 2½ cups

1   (1-pound) package (454 grams) confectioners' sugar
6   tablespoons (90 grams) warm water (90°F/32°C to 110°F/43°C)
2½ tablespoons (25.5 grams) meringue powder
2½ to 3½ tablespoons (37.5 to 52.5 grams) sparkling wine, room temperature (70°F/21°C)

1. In the bowl of a stand mixer fitted with the paddle attachment, beat confectioners' sugar, 6 tablespoons (90 grams) warm water, and meringue powder at low speed until well combined, stopping to scrape sides of bowl. Increase mixer speed to medium; beat until mixture is the consistency of toothpaste, 3 to 5 minutes. Add sparkling wine, ½ to 1 teaspoon (2.5 to 5 grams) at a time, until icing reaches "10-second" consistency. (A ribbon of icing drizzled on surface should take 10 seconds to sink back into icing.)
2. Transfer icing to a large shallow bowl; cover with a damp paper towel, and let stand for 20 minutes. Using a wooden pick, pop and fill as many air bubbles that rise to the surface as possible before using.

PRO TIPS
Feel free to flavor your royal icing with your favorite extract to taste. Thin to 10-second consistency using room temperature water (70°F/21°C).

For a little stronger sparkling wine flavor, place 1½ cups (360 grams) sparkling wine in a small saucepan. Bring to a boil over medium-high heat; cook until reduced to ¼ cup (60 grams). Transfer mixture to a small bowl, and let cool to room temperature (70°F/21°C). Use reduced sparkling wine as directed to thin royal icing to 10-second consistency.

CLASSIC SUGAR COOKIES

Makes about 24 cookies (depending on size of cutters used and thickness of dough)

Recipe by Emily Hutchinson

You can't have the holidays without a delicious, soft sugar cookie. Perfected over years and years of baking, Emily Hutchinson considers this recipe to be the best sugar cookie recipe! Remember to read the recipe directions, Notes, and PRO TIPS before starting.

1	cup (227 grams) unsalted butter, softened
¾	cup (150 grams) granulated sugar
½	cup (60 grams) confectioners' sugar
¾	teaspoon (2.25 grams) kosher salt
1	large egg (50 grams)
1½	teaspoons (6 grams) vanilla extract
3	cups (375 grams) all-purpose flour
1½	teaspoons (7.5 grams) baking powder
	American Crusting Buttercream (recipe on page 342)

1. In the bowl of a stand mixer fitted with the paddle attachment, beat butter at medium speed for 30 seconds. Add sugars and salt, and beat at medium speed for 1 minute. With mixer on low speed, add egg and vanilla; beat for about 30 seconds.

2. In a medium bowl, whisk together flour and baking powder. Add flour mixture to butter mixture, and beat at low speed until dough comes together and starts to pull away from sides of bowl, 1 to 2 minutes. (Mixture may seem dry at first, but it will come together.)

3. Turn out dough onto a sheet of plastic wrap, and shape into a disk. Wrap in plastic wrap, and refrigerate for at least 1 hour.

4. Preheat oven to 375°F (190°C). Line baking sheets with parchment paper.

5. On a lightly floured surface, roll one-third of dough to ⅓- to ¼-inch thickness. (Keep remaining dough in refrigerator until ready to roll.) Using desired holiday cutters, cut dough, and place 2 inches apart on prepared pans. (See Notes.) Using a pastry brush, brush off any excess flour. Reroll and cut scraps as needed, refrigerating dough if it becomes too soft.

6. Bake until puffed and center is matte, 6 to 8 minutes. Using a small offset spatula, quickly press edges of cookies back into shape, if necessary. Let cool on pans for 1 minute. Remove from pans, and let cool completely on wire racks.

7. Pipe or spread American Crusting Buttercream onto cooled cookies as desired. (Alternatively, freeze cooled cookies in an airtight container for 2 hours or overnight; let thaw at room temperature for 1 hour, and pipe or spread American Crusting Buttercream onto cookies as desired. [See Notes.])

Notes: *To help the flour stick to your work surface, gently press your dough on the clean surface before dusting the surface with flour.*
To roll your dough to an even thickness, roll slowly up and down and then to the sides. If you run your hand across the top of your rolled dough, you can feel any bumps or slightly raised areas.

The dough can be refrigerated for 10 minutes after the cookies are cut out and placed on a baking sheet.

This recipe is meant to be frosted with American Crusting Buttercream (recipe on page 342). If you are looking for a sweeter cookie that you can just add sprinkles to, add extra vanilla or almond extract to sweeten the dough.

I prefer to freeze the baked cookies overnight. It gives them added moisture to keep them soft.

PRO TIPS

Adding the salt in with the sugars helps the salt dissolve through the dough better in this recipe. Regular table salt can be used, but make sure to reduce it to ½ teaspoon (3 grams). If you can find salted sweet cream butter, I recommend using that and omitting salt completely because salted sweet cream butter has the perfect amount of salt for these cookies.

I like to add ¼ teaspoon (1 gram) almond extract to my Classic Sugar Cookies recipe sometimes to give the cookies a holiday flavor.

Nice and thick cookies balance out the sweetness of the buttercream, so don't roll out the dough thinner than ¼ inch.

Aluminum-free baking powder should be double-acting, which means it's activated in mixing stage and baking stage. Best to keep aluminum out if we can, so I get aluminum-free.

Frosted cookies can be frozen for up to 2 weeks. To freeze them, be gentle and treat them like frosted cupcakes until they crust over. When you pull them out of the freezer, be sure to allow the buttercream to crust back over.

If you cream your butter and sugars together too much, it can lead to slight cracks in the baked cookie; cream as instructed.

GINGERBREAD CUTOUT COOKIES

Makes about 24 cookies (depending on size of cutters used and thickness of dough)

Recipe by Emily Hutchinson

Is there anything better than the smell of gingerbread baking in the oven? It brings me right back to my childhood, baking in the kitchen with my grandma. These cookies are nice and thick and keep their shape very well. They are perfectly chewy, spiced and brown sugared to holiday deliciousness. The buttercream frosting adds a creamy sweetness you won't want to leave off, but if you're in a pinch, simply add cinnamon hard candies or sprinkles before baking.

1	cup (227 grams) unsalted butter, softened
¾	cup (165 grams) firmly packed dark brown sugar
¼	cup (50 grams) granulated sugar
¾	teaspoon (2.25 grams) kosher salt
1	large egg (50 grams)
1½	teaspoons (6 grams) vanilla extract
¼	cup (85 grams) unsulphured molasses
3	cups (375 grams) all-purpose flour
2	teaspoons (4 grams) ground cinnamon
1½	teaspoons (7.5 grams) baking powder
1	teaspoon (2 grams) ground ginger
¼	teaspoon ground nutmeg
⅛	teaspoon ground cloves

American Crusting Buttercream (recipe on page 344)

1. In the bowl of a stand mixer fitted with the paddle attachment, beat butter at medium speed for 30 seconds. Add sugars and salt, and beat at medium speed for 1 minute. With mixer on low speed, add egg and vanilla; beat for about 30 seconds. Beat in molasses just until combined.

2. In a medium bowl, whisk together flour, cinnamon, baking powder, ginger, nutmeg, and cloves. Add flour mixture to butter mixture, and beat at low speed until combined. (Dough will be slightly sticky.)

3. Turn out dough onto a sheet of plastic wrap, and shape into a disk. Wrap in plastic wrap, and refrigerate for at least 1 hour.

4. Preheat oven to 375°F (190°C). Line baking sheets with parchment paper.

5. On a lightly floured surface, roll one-third of dough to ⅓- to ¼-inch thickness. (Keep remaining dough refrigerated until ready to roll.) Using desired holiday cutters, cut dough, and place 2 inches apart on prepared pans. (See Notes.) Using a pastry brush, brush off any excess flour. Reroll and cut scraps as needed, refrigerating dough if it becomes too soft.

6. Bake until puffed and center is matte, 6 to 8 minutes. Using a small offset spatula, quickly press edges of cookies back into shape, if necessary.

Let cool on pans for 1 minute. Remove from pans, and let cool completely on wire racks.

7. Pipe or spread American Crusting Buttercream onto cooled cookies as desired. (Alternatively, freeze cooled cookies in an airtight container for 2 hours or overnight; let thaw at room temperature for 1 hour, and pipe or spread American Crusting Buttercream onto cookies as desired. [See Notes.])

Notes: *To help the flour stick to your work surface, gently press your dough on the clean surface before dusting the surface with flour.*
To roll your dough to an even thickness, roll slowly up and down and then to the sides. If you run your hand across the top of your rolled dough, you can feel any bumps or slightly raised areas.

Alternatively, this dough can be rolled out between sheets of parchment paper.

I prefer to freeze the baked cookies overnight. It gives them added moisture to keep them soft.

AMERICAN CRUSTING BUTTERCREAM

Makes about 5 cups

Recipe by Emily Hutchinson

You can frost cookies with delicious, beautiful buttercream, and it won't get completely smashed when stacking—it's true! For this recipe, I cut the butter with vegetable shortening to form a crust. (They can still be smashed if a lot of pressure is applied.) The shortening helps give it a smoother texture, which is great for piping cookies. If you hate the idea of shortening in the buttercream, omit and double the amount of butter. They won't crust over quite as much—just enough to gently stack. It is a little sweet, but the confectioners' sugar makes a strong crust, which pairs nicely with not-too-sweet cookies. It's a perfect balance. Typically, for a buttercream recipe, you would mix until light and fluffy, but not with this recipe. You want the buttercream to be nice and smooth, so just mix for a minute or two.

1 cup (227 grams) unsalted butter, softened
1 cup (184 grams) vegetable shortening, softened
1 teaspoon (3 grams) kosher salt
2 teaspoons (8 grams) vanilla extract
9 cups (1,080 grams) confectioners' sugar, sifted
5 to 6 tablespoons (75 to 90 grams) 2% reduced-fat milk or heavy whipping cream

1. In the bowl of a stand mixer fitted with the paddle attachment, beat butter, shortening, and salt at medium speed until well combined. Add vanilla, and beat at medium speed for 1 minute. Add confectioners' sugar, and place a kitchen towel over mixer, (bowl of stand mixer will be full); beat at at low speed, and gradually increase speed to medium speed, beating until thick and combined. (Do not overmix.) Add 5 tablespoons (75 grams) milk or cream, and beat at medium-high speed until smooth, about 1 minute; add up to remaining 1 tablespoon (15 grams) milk or cream, 1 teaspoon (5 grams) at a time, if too thick. (Do not overmix.) Refrigerate in an airtight container for up to 1 week, or freeze in an airtight container for up to 3 months.

BUTTERCREAM PRO TIPS

Overmixing causes the buttercream to become a bit grainy, with tiny air bubbles. You want a nice and smooth consistency. If you see any air bubbles, beat them out with a rubber spatula by smacking it back and forth against the side of your mixer bowl.

You can still add your food colorings after mixing; it will not ruin the buttercream. I like to add food coloring in small batches, so I mix 1 to 2 cups at a time. Find what works best for you.

You can use all butter instead of half butter/half shortening and it will still form a crust, but the shortening gives it a smoother texture. If you use a vegetable shortening, I recommend Crisco. Make sure it's fresh and hasn't been sitting in the back of your cupboard; it gets rancid over time and develops a greasy, yucky taste. Fresh is best.

The weather is a huge factor. When it's hot out, you might need a tablespoon less of milk or cream; when it's cold, you may need an extra tablespoon. The temperature of your house and the humidity where you live will determine how much milk or cream to add. Start out with the minimum and slowly add to find out what works best for you. If you find it's too soft, add in ¼ cup (30 grams) confectioners' sugar to thicken it up. Be careful, though—it will begin to taste like straight confectioners' sugar if you add too much. After you make this once, you will find how much milk or cream works with your climate.

After piping your buttercream, let cookies stand for 8 to 12 hours to dry the crust before stacking; 24 hours makes the crust stronger. It won't be like royal icing—it can still get smashed.

Store frosted cookies in an airtight container at room temperature. You can freeze frosted cookies for up to 2 weeks, but I don't recommend more freezing time than that because it will change the texture of the buttercream.

Refrigerate unused buttercream in an airtight container. Let buttercream come to room temperature before using. It will be solid. I don't recommend freezing the buttercream itself—make a day or two before you need to frost the cookies—but if you have extra, you can freeze it in an airtight container for up to 3 months.

One batch of buttercream will frost 24 cookies for the completed set.

COLORING BUTTERCREAM

I mix my colors 1 cup at a time. The colors listed in each set of instructions will go together throughout the cookie set. The measurements of how much buttercream you will need are only if you are making 12 of the same cookie. The couplers and tips will also go through the whole set. You'll only need to follow what's listed if you're making a lot of that one cookie. If you are making the complete cookie set, the white will be used throughout and so will the gray, brown, red, and so on. The tips and couplers as well.

For red, use Wilton Red No-Taste Icing Color with Wilton Color Right Performance Food Coloring in Crimson/C. You may need ½ to 1 teaspoon Red No-Taste and 10 to 15 drops of the Color Right in Crimson/C per 1 cup buttercream. If you cover the bowl of red buttercream with plastic wrap and let stand overnight, the color will deepen. **For white,** use 1 teaspoon Wilton White-White Icing Color per 1 cup buttercream. **For dark green,** use ¼ to ½ teaspoon Wilton Gel Food Coloring in Kelly Green and 3 to 4 drops of AmeriColor Soft Gel Paste

Food Color in Forest Green per 1 cup buttercream. **For light green,** use a very small amount of Wilton Gel Food Coloring in Kelly Green, 1 drop per 1 cup buttercream. **For gray,** I use 1 drop of black gel food coloring (any brand) per 1 cup buttercream. **For brown,** use ½ teaspoon brown gel food coloring (any brand) per 1 cup buttercream.

TWO-TONED BUTTERCREAM

Red-and-white poinsettia petals are beyond gorgeous. You can stick to beautiful deep red, or you can really impress people and use this technique. I love two-toned buttercream for my flowers. It gives them a unique and realistic look. One of the things I love about this method is that the extra layer of plastic wrap keeps the buttercream from warming up in your hand so quickly. The large tips don't require couplers.

YOU WILL NEED:

Red American Crusting Buttercream
    (recipe on opposite page)
White American Crusting Buttercream
3 pastry bags, divided
2 couplers
Clear plastic wrap
Wilton No. 366 piping tip

STEP 1: Place red American Crusting Buttercream and white American Crusting Buttercream in separate pastry bags fitted with couplers.

STEP 2: Place an 18-inch-long sheet of plastic wrap horizontally, and without attaching a piping tip to the coupler, pipe several 6-inch-long lines of red American Crusting Buttercream. Continue to layer lines, piping lines on top of each other, so you create about a 2-inch-high mound in the middle. (It will be thick; we are using about 1 cup buttercream total.)

STEP 3: Pipe a 6-inch-long strip (½ inch thick and ⅓ inch high) of white buttercream in the middle of the red buttercream mound.

TWO-TONED BUTTERCREAM PRO TIPS

As you are piping, you will see where the color is going. You can adjust the tip to make it flow from the center or the sides. I always give the buttercream a big squeeze before I start in order to make sure my color is flowing right. You will want the thin white strip to come through the center of the tip, where the point of the "beak" is.

Don't overfill your pastry bag with buttercream. It warms up quickly in your hand and the flowers can get droopy. It's easier to pipe and guide your hand with less in your bag. Keep refilling for the best results. Fill the bag with ¾ to 1 cup buttercream.

I find it helpful to mix the different colors of buttercream in small batches at a time. Mix 1 cup buttercream to desired shade. Use gel food coloring because its more vibrant.

STEP 4: Grab the bottom edge of the plastic wrap, and fold up and over horizontally to the top edge of the plastic wrap. Twist the ends of the plastic wrap. Coil one end so the buttercream doesn't come out of the top when squeezing. Cut the other end about 2 inches from the buttercream.

STEP 5: Place the plastic wrap-encased buttercream, cut end down, in a pastry bag fitted with a Wilton No. 366 piping tip. The piping tip should be perfectly centered over the white icing.

STEP 6: Start squeezing from the top to see where the white will come out. You can gently move the tip to manipulate where the white will come through in the petals. Begin to pipe. Move tip accordingly if needed without removing the plastic wrap-encased buttercream from the pastry bag.

POINSETTIA COOKIES

Recipe by Emily Hutchinson

This cookie is one of Emily's most popular and original designs. You can add this to a cake or cupcakes as well. They are so beautiful and simpler than you'd think. Follow the instructions in Two-Toned Buttercream (page 343) on how to fill the pastry bag. The petals of the poinsettia aren't even the petals. The red, white, and pink/white petals are actually leaves; the flower is the center clusters.

YOU WILL NEED:
Two-Toned Buttercream (instructions on page 343)
6 to 8 (2½- to 3-inch) round cookies
Gold sugar pearls
½ cup green American Crusting Buttercream (recipe on
    page 342)
Pastry bag
1 coupler
Wilton No. 352 piping tip
Wilton No. 366 piping tip

STEP 1: Follow instructions for Two-Toned Buttercream on page 345.

STEP 2: Have the beak (pointed end) of your piping tip facing down. Holding your pastry bag of Two-Toned Buttercream at a 45-degree angle in the center of a cookie, gently squeeze the pastry bag (you will see the buttercream billow out the sides), and slowly move toward the outer edge—but not all the way to the edge, because you want to be able to turn the cookie without accidentally touching the buttercream. Stop squeezing, and pull away to form the petal. (The pressure will get lighter as the petals come to a point.)

STEP 3: Repeat procedure all the way around the cookie, creating a base of 6 petals and leaving a little room for the center petals.

STEP 4: Using the same technique as in step 2, pipe a smaller petal on top of the base petals, making sure not to pipe a small petal directly on top of a base petal.

STEP 5: Repeat procedure all the way around the center, creating 5 center petals.

STEP 6: Place the gold sugar pearls in the center of the petals.

STEP 7: Place green American Crusting Buttercream in a pastry bag fitted with a coupler and Wilton No. 352 piping tip. Using the same technique as in step 2, pipe leaves between base petals.

STEP 8: Turn your cookie as you go. That's why we don't want the petals to be longer than the cookie—they would get smudged.

STEP 9: Repeat procedure all the way around the cookie, creating 6 leaves.

STEP 10: Repeat procedure with remaining cookies.

SNOW GLOBE COOKIES

Recipe by Emily Hutchinson

What's more fun than shaking up a snow globe? Eating a snow globe cookie! Emily has brought that same magic and sparkle to these beautifully decorated cookies. It does require some extra steps and technique, but with practice, you will be very happy with how they turn out.

YOU WILL NEED:

1 cup white American Crusting Buttercream (recipe on page 342)
¼ cup brown American Crusting Buttercream
¼ cup gray American Crusting Buttercream
¼ cup red American Crusting Buttercream
¼ cup green American Crusting Buttercream
5 pastry bags
5 couplers
Parchment paper
Small offset spatula
1 (3-inch-wide) snow globe cookie cutter
4 (3-inch-wide) snow globe-shaped cookies
Baking sheet
Wilton No. 5 piping tip
Wilton No. 2 piping tip
Wilton No. 10 piping tip
Wilton No. 363 piping tip
Clear sugar crystals
White nonpareils

STEP 1: Place white, brown, gray, red, and green American Crusting Buttercream in separate pastry bags fitted with couplers.

STEP 2: Cut small pieces of parchment paper about 2 inches bigger than the snow globe cookies. Using a small offset spatula, spread white American Crusting Buttercream evenly on the parchment in a circle that's slightly bigger than the globe circle on the cookie. Make sure to get it nice and smooth. Place on a baking sheet, and freeze for at least 20 minutes. Using the snow globe cookie cutter, cut the circle for the globe. (Work very quickly so the buttercream doesn't thaw.)

STEP 3: Immediately place the cut circle of buttercream on the globe part of a cookie.

STEP 4: Using the offset spatula, gently smooth out any imperfections.

STEP 5: Fit the white buttercream pastry bag with a Wilton No. 5 piping tip, and pipe a border around the edge of the globe.

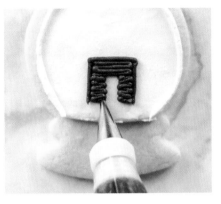

STEP 6: Fit the brown buttercream pastry bag with a Wilton No. 2 piping tip, and pipe the fireplace border (top section and sides); pipe back and forth within the border, leaving center open, to complete the fireplace.

STEP 7: Fit the gray buttercream pastry bag with a Wilton No. 10 piping tip, and pipe straight down the center of the fireplace to fill.

STEP 8: Fit the red buttercream pastry bag with a Wilton No. 5 piping tip, and pipe little stockings at the top of the fireplace, leaving a small space above each stocking.

STEP 9: Fit the white buttercream pastry bag with a Wilton No. 5 piping tip, and pipe a straight line across the top of each stocking for the fur lining of the stockings.

STEP 10: Turn the cookie so the globe is on the bottom. Fit the brown buttercream pastry bag with a Wilton No. 2 piping tip, and pipe a small line for a tree stump on both sides of the fireplace. Fit the green buttercream pastry bag with a Wilton No. 2 piping tip, and pipe horizontally back and forth to create an upside-down triangle for the tree shape.

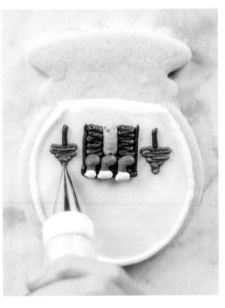

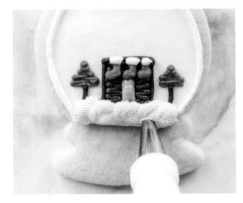

STEP 11: Turn the cookie right side up. Fit the white buttercream pastry bag with a Wilton No. 363 piping tip, and pipe the snow on the bottom of the globe in an up-and-down, playful motion to resemble fluffy snow.

STEP 12: Fit the gray buttercream pastry bag with a Wilton No. 10 piping tip. Slightly angle the bag toward you, with the tip about ¼ inch above the cookie. Starting just beneath the "snow," pipe horizontally back and forth all the way down the base, leaving a small border around edges.

STEP 13: To sparkle up the globe, add sugar crystals and nonpareils to the snow and the base. Repeat procedure with remaining cookies.

PRO TIPS

Change the design inside the snow globe to only trees or add a snowman.

Dip the offset spatula in very hot water for 1 minute, quickly dry with a towel, and then smooth the buttercream base of the globe; repeat until desired smoothness is achieved.

HOLIDAY STOCKING COOKIES

Recipe by Emily Hutchinson

One of the great holiday traditions is hanging stockings over the fireplace. These darling cookies match the stockings hanging in the snow globes in this cookie set. You can switch up the colors to make them your own. It looks lovely in any color.

YOU WILL NEED:

1 cup red American Crusting Buttercream (recipe on page 342)
1 cup white American Crusting Buttercream
2 pastry bags
2 couplers
Wilton No. 5 piping tip
Wilton No. 363 piping tip
6 to 8 (3-inch-wide) holiday stocking-shaped cookies
White confetti sprinkles, white nonpareils, and holly sprinkles (optional)

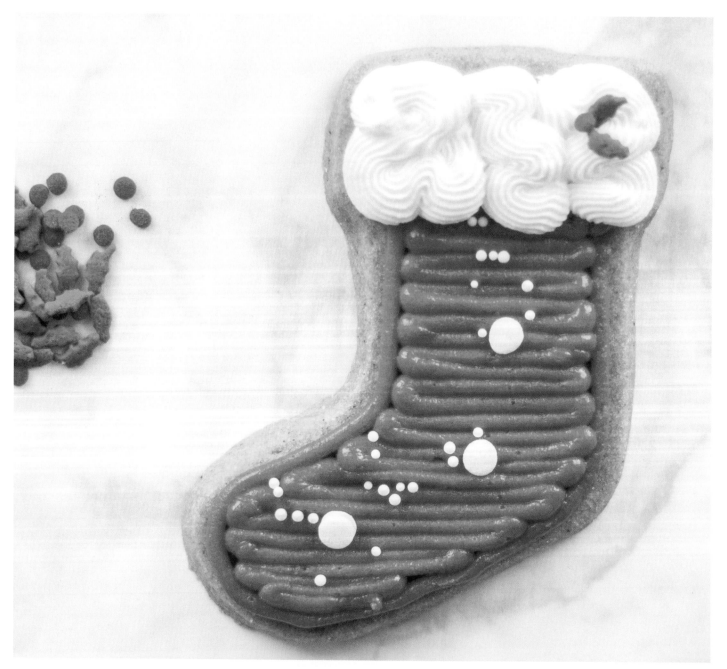

STEP 1: Place red and white American Crusting Buttercream in separate pastry bags fitted with couplers.

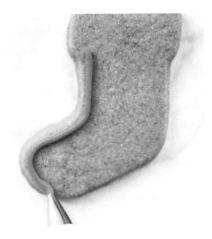

STEP 2: Fit the red buttercream pastry bag with a Wilton No. 5 piping tip, and pipe a border on the outside of the bottom of a cookie, leaving a small border around edges. (Don't pipe where the "fur" will go.)

STEP 3: Pipe just under the "fur" to close outline.

STEP 4: Holding the pastry bag at a slight angle, pipe back and forth horizontally, applying even pressure.

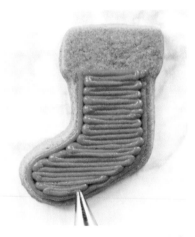

STEP 5: Pipe until you reach the end of the stocking.

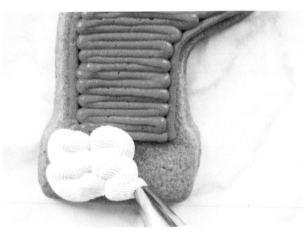

STEP 6: Turn the cookie so the bare portion is closest to you. Fit the white buttercream pastry bag with a Wilton No. 363 piping tip. Holding the bag at a 45-degree angle, pipe up and down and around, squeezing the bag so the buttercream billows out and the fur looks fluffy.

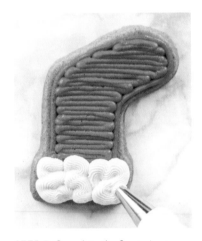

STEP 7: Complete the fur, trying to make it look fluffy by going up, down, and around. The stronger the flow, the fluffier it will be.

STEP 8: Place 3 white confetti sprinkles randomly on the stocking. (I like to use odd numbers when I decorate with sprinkles if I'm specifically placing them.)

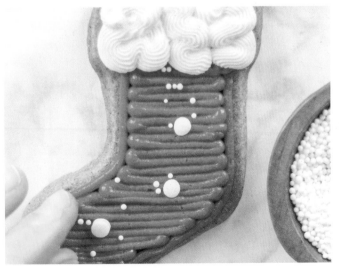

STEP 9: Randomly sprinkle nonpareils on the stocking to make it special.

STEP 10: If you have any cute holiday sprinkles, add them to the white fur. I love how the holly sprinkles look. Repeat procedure with remaining cookies.

WINTER TREE COOKIES

Recipe by Emily Hutchinson

For the trees in this cookie collection, Emily decided to pipe them shell (or teardrop) style because it adds some fun, elegance, and whimsy to the decorated trees. Having a white Christmas is completely magical. Let's bring that to life through this cookie.

YOU WILL NEED:
1¼ cups green American Crusting Buttercream (recipe on page 342)
¼ cup brown American Crusting Buttercream
¼ cup white American Crusting Buttercream
3 pastry bags
3 couplers
6 (3½-inch-long) tree-shaped cookies
Wilton No. 21 piping tip
Wilton No. 5 piping tip
Wilton No. 2 piping tip
White nonpareils (optional)

STEP 1: Place green, brown, and white American Crusting Buttercream in separate pastry bags fitted with couplers.

STEP 2: Turn a cookie so the top of the tree points toward you. Fit the green buttercream pastry bag with a Wilton No. 21 piping tip. Holding the bag at a 45-degree angle, with the piping tip about ¼ inch above the cookie, start squeezing the bag hard to allow the buttercream to billow or fan out so it forces the tip up; lower pressure as you pull toward you to create the first shell.

STEP 3: Pipe the sides of the cookie first and work your way in.

STEP 4: The fifth shell will be in the center of the first layer of branches.

STEP 5: Repeat steps 3 and 4 for the second layer of branches but slightly overlap to create dimension in the tree.

STEP 6: This layer will be a little tighter, but there will still be 5 shells.

STEP 7: For the third and final layer of shell branches, pipe sides and make them smaller.

STEP 8: The third shell will be the middle; elongate it to reach the second layer.

STEP 9: Turn the cookie right side up. Fit the brown buttercream pastry bag with a Wilton No. 2 piping tip, and pipe back and forth horizontally at the base to create the trunk.

STEP 10: Fit the white buttercream pastry bag with a Wilton No. 5 piping tip, and pipe up and down just under the top layer of branches to create snow in the center of the tree.

STEP 11: Pipe white buttercream up and down on the tip of the tree.

STEP 12: Pipe white buttercream up and down just under the middle layer of branches.

STEP 13:
Add sugar crystals or white nonpareils (if using) to fancy up the tree. Repeat procedure with remaining cookies.

TWINKLING TREE COOKIES

Recipe by Emily Hutchinson

Emily created this tree for a beautiful pink vintage cookie set and fell in love with this style. The sprinkles really draw your eyes in, making you fall in love with this cookie. The shell piping technique is fairly simple and so versatile.

YOU WILL NEED:
1¼ cups light green American Crusting Buttercream (recipe on page 342)
¼ cup brown American Crusting Buttercream
2 pastry bags
2 couplers
6 (3½-inch-long) tree-shaped cookies
Wilton No. 199 piping tip
Wilton No. 2 piping tip
White confetti sprinkles, colored sugar pearls, and white nonpareils

PRO TIP
Add just a drop of green gel food coloring to make the light green. You can make the trees any color to fit a different theme.

STEP 1: Place light green and brown American Crusting Buttercream in separate pastry bags fitted with couplers.

STEP 2: Turn a cookie so the top of the tree points toward you. Fit the light green buttercream pastry bag with a Wilton No. 199 piping tip. Holding the bag at a 45-degree angle, with the piping tip about ¼ inch above the cookie, start squeezing the bag hard to allow the buttercream to billow out so it forces the tip up; lower pressure as you pull toward you to create the first shell.

STEP 3: Pipe the very ends and work your way in.

STEP 4: The fifth branch will complete the first layer of branches.

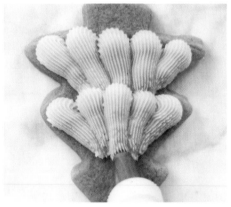

STEP 5: Repeat steps 3 and 4 for the second layer of branches but slightly overlap so no bare cookie shows in between branch layers.

STEP 6: The last layer will be smaller and tight, with 3 shells.

STEP 7: Turn the cookie right side up. Fit the brown buttercream pastry bag with a Wilton No. 2 piping tip. Holding the bag at a slight angle, pipe back and forth horizontally, applying steady pressure.

STEP 8: Place white confetti sprinkles and colored sugar pearls, one at a time, on buttercream. Make sure to place them all around the cookie.

STEP 9: Sprinkle white nonpareils all over cookie.

STEP 10: Repeat procedure with remaining cookies. Change the sugar pearls to fit any theme you're working with.

BARS

One pan is all you need to fulfill the most snack-worthy of cravings. Chocolate pairs with dulce de leche to create caramel magic, and vibrant Meyer lemons become your main squeeze in revamped lemon bars with a buttery macadamia nut base.

CHOCOLATE-DULCE DE LECHE BARS

Makes 24 bars

Based on the classic caramelitas, these buttery, nutty oat bars have a rich chocolate filling punctuated by dulce de leche. With a firm streusel-like base and topping protecting the gooey middle, these bars travel exceptionally well and will be equally well-received by loved ones near and far.

1¼ cups (156 grams) plus 1 tablespoon (8 grams) all-purpose flour, divided
1 cup (90 grams) quick-cooking oats
¾ cup (165 grams) firmly packed light brown sugar
¾ cup (170 grams) unsalted butter, melted and cooled for 5 minutes
1½ teaspoons (6 grams) tightly packed orange zest
½ teaspoon (2.5 grams) baking soda
½ teaspoon (1.5 grams) kosher salt
½ teaspoon (1 gram) ground cinnamon
¼ teaspoon ground cloves
⅔ cup (75 grams) chopped toasted pecans
¾ cup (128 grams) roughly chopped 66% cacao dark chocolate*, divided
¾ cup (128 grams) roughly chopped milk chocolate*, divided
¾ cup (224 grams) dulce de leche
Garnish: flaked sea salt

1. Preheat oven to 350°F (180°C). Spray a 9-inch square baking pan with cooking spray. Line pan with parchment paper, letting excess extend over sides of pan.
2. In a large bowl, stir together 1¼ cups (156 grams) flour, oats, brown sugar, melted butter, orange zest, baking soda, kosher salt, cinnamon, and cloves until well combined. Press half of dough (about 293 grams) into bottom of prepared pan.
3. Bake until lightly golden around edges, about 10 minutes. Let cool in pan on a wire rack for 20 minutes. Leave oven on.
4. Sprinkle pecans, ½ cup (85 grams) dark chocolate, and ½ cup (85 grams) milk chocolate onto prepared crust.
5. In a small microwave-safe bowl, stir together dulce de leche and remaining 1 tablespoon (8 grams) flour. Heat on high in 10-second intervals, stirring between each, until mixture can be drizzled from a spoon.

Drizzle mixture onto pecans and chocolate in pan, leaving a ½-inch border around edges of pan. Crumble remaining dough evenly over dulce de leche layer. (It's OK if some peeks through.) Top evenly with remaining ¼ cup (43 grams) dark chocolate and remaining ¼ cup (43 grams) milk chocolate.
6. Bake until chocolate is melted and crumble layer starts to turn golden brown, 15 to 20 minutes. Let cool completely in pan on a wire rack.
7. Using excess parchment as handles, remove from pan. Using a serrated knife, cut into bars. Garnish with sea salt, if desired. Store in an airtight container for up to 1 week.

We used Valrhona Caraïbe 66% Cacao Dark Chocolate Baking Fèves and Callebaut Milk Chocolate Baking Blocks.

APPLE SHORTCAKE

Makes 9 bars

A famed New Zealand favorite, apple shortcake is a nostalgic baked good from Down Under. Kiwi baking blogger Erin Clarkson claims that almost every grandmother in the country has a recipe for it tucked in their recipe book. Encased in a cakey pastry crust are sugared and cinnamon-spiced apple slices, creating something like a pie-cake hybrid you won't soon forget.

4   cups (500 grams) all-purpose flour
1   cup (200 grams) plus 3 tablespoons (36 grams) granulated sugar, divided, plus more for sprinkling
1¾   teaspoons (8.75 grams) baking powder
1¼   teaspoons (3.75 grams) plus ⅛ teaspoon kosher salt, divided
1   cup (227 grams) cold unsalted butter, cubed
3   large eggs (150 grams), divided and lightly beaten
¾   teaspoon (3 grams) almond extract
½   teaspoon (2 grams) vanilla extract
2   teaspoons (6 grams) cornstarch
1   teaspoon (2 grams) ground cinnamon
3   cups (330 grams) ¼-inch-thick wedges peeled Golden Delicious apples
2   cups (220 grams) ¼-inch-thick slices peeled Granny Smith apples
2   teaspoons (10 grams) fresh lemon juice
Garnish: confectioners' sugar

1. In the work bowl of a food processor, place flour, 1 cup (200 grams) sugar, baking powder, and 1¼ teaspoons (3.75 grams) salt; pulse until combined. Add cold butter, and pulse until mixture resembles coarse crumbs. Add 2 eggs (100 grams) and extracts; pulse just until dough comes together, stopping to scrape sides of bowl. (Mixture should be moist but not sticky and hold together when pinched.) Turn out dough, and divide in half; shape each portion into a 6-inch square. Wrap in plastic wrap, and refrigerate for at least 25 minutes.

2. Preheat oven to 350°F (180°C). Spray a 9-inch square baking pan with cooking spray. Line pan with parchment paper, letting excess extend over sides of pan.

3. Let dough stand at room temperature until softened, 10 to 15 minutes. On a lightly floured surface, roll 1 portion into a 13-inch square; place prepared pan in center of dough square. Using pan as a guide, cut out a 9-inch square, and transfer to prepared pan, pressing across bottom. (It's OK if dough tears while transferring; gently move to pan, and press together). Cut remaining rolled dough into 4 pieces; gently transfer to prepared pan, pressing all the way up sides and using excess dough to seal any seams with bottom.

4. In a medium bowl, stir together cornstarch, cinnamon, remaining 3 tablespoons (36 grams) sugar, and remaining ⅛ teaspoon salt. Add apples and lemon juice; stir until well combined. Spread apple mixture evenly on dough in pan.

5. On a lightly floured surface, roll remaining dough portion into a 9½-inch square; carefully place dough on top of apple mixture, pressing overlapping dough edges to seal. Trim dough edges level with apples, smoothing and sealing edges as needed. Brush top with remaining 1 egg (50 grams). Using the tines of a fork, prick dough several times to vent; sprinkle with sugar.

6. Bake until crust is golden brown and firm and a wooden pick inserted in center easily pierces apple layer, 50 minutes to 1 hour, rotating pan halfway through baking and loosely covering with foil to prevent excess browning, if necessary. Let cool in pan for 10 minutes. Using excess parchment as handles, carefully remove from pan, and let cool completely on a wire rack. Garnish with confectioners' sugar, if desired.

PRO TIPS

Shortcake dough can be made 1 day ahead, wrapped, and refrigerated. When ready to use, let stand at room temperature until slightly softened, 15 to 20 minutes.

Add a bit of finishing sparkle by sprinkling white sparkling sugar or sanding sugar on egg-washed, docked dough.

EGGNOG NANAIMO BARS

Makes 24 bars

The classic Canadian dessert gets a bold, boozy revamp thanks to a touch of eggnog and bourbon. The nutmeg in the eggnog helps cut the richness with aromatic spice while crunchy walnuts and coconut impart extra chewiness.

⅔ cup (150 grams) unsalted butter
½ cup (43 grams) unsweetened cocoa powder
⅓ cup plus 2 tablespoons (91 grams) granulated sugar
1 teaspoon (3 grams) kosher salt
1 large egg (50 grams)
1 large egg yolk (19 grams)
2⅓ cups (295 grams) shortbread cookie crumbs*
1¼ cups (105 grams) sweetened flaked coconut
½ cup (57 grams) finely chopped toasted walnuts
1 teaspoon (4 grams) vanilla extract
Eggnog Custard Filling (recipe follows)
6 ounces (170 grams) 64% cacao semisweet chocolate baking bars, finely chopped
2 tablespoons (28 grams) vegetable oil

1. Spray a 9-inch square baking pan with cooking spray. Line pan with parchment paper, letting excess extend over sides of pan.
2. In the top of a double boiler, combine butter, cocoa, sugar, and salt. Cook over simmering water, stirring frequently, until butter is melted. Whisk in egg and egg yolk until well combined; cook, stirring occasionally, until thickened and an instant-read thermometer registers 160°F (71°C), about 10 minutes. Remove from heat; stir in cookie crumbs, coconut, walnuts, and vanilla. Press mixture into bottom of prepared pan; let cool in pan on a wire rack for 30 minutes.
3. Using a small offset spatula, spread Eggnog Custard Filling onto prepared crust in a smooth, even layer. Refrigerate for 30 minutes.

4. In the clean top of a double boiler, combine chocolate and oil. Cook over simmering water, stirring frequently, until chocolate is melted and mixture is smooth. Working quickly, pour chocolate mixture over chilled filling. Using a small offset spatula and tilting pan as needed, spread chocolate mixture into an even layer; tap pan on a kitchen towel-lined counter several times to smooth chocolate mixture and release any air bubbles. Refrigerate for at least 1 hour or up to overnight.
5. Using excess parchment as handles, remove from pan; using a warm, dry, serrated knife, cut into bars. Serve at room temperature.

*We used Walkers Pure Butter Shortbread Cookies.

EGGNOG CUSTARD FILLING
Makes about 2 cups

¾ cup (170 grams) unsalted butter, softened
2½ tablespoons (24 grams) custard powder*

1 tablespoon (15 grams) bourbon
1 teaspoon (4 grams) vanilla extract
½ teaspoon (1 gram) ground nutmeg
3 cups (360 grams) confectioners' sugar
3½ tablespoons (52.5 grams) prepared eggnog

1. In the bowl of a stand mixer fitted with the paddle attachment, beat butter and custard powder at medium-low speed until creamy, 2 to 3 minutes, stopping to scrape sides of bowl. Beat in bourbon, vanilla, and nutmeg. With mixer on low speed, gradually add confectioners' sugar alternately with eggnog, beating until well combined and stopping to scrape sides of bowl. Increase mixer speed to medium, and beat for 1 minute. Use immediately.

*We used Bird's Custard Powder, available at select grocery stores and amazon.com.

DARK CHOCOLATE POMEGRANATE SKILLET BLONDIES

Makes 6 to 8 blondies

Recipe by Rebecca Firth

This wonder combines your favorite blondie components—rich caramel flavor and lots of vanilla—but adds in the tart bite of pomegranate and dark chocolate earthiness. If you don't have a cast-iron skillet, you can also use an 11x8-inch baking dish.

1 cup (227 grams) unsalted butter
1¾ cups (385 grams) firmly packed dark brown sugar
2 large eggs (100 grams), room temperature
1 large egg yolk (19 grams), room temperature
1 tablespoon (13 grams) vanilla extract
1½ teaspoons (7.5 grams) baking powder
1½ teaspoons (4.5 grams) sea salt
2¾ cups (344 grams) all-purpose flour
¾ cup (128 grams) 56% cacao dark chocolate chips
⅔ cup (99 grams) pomegranate arils

1. Position oven rack in center of oven. Preheat oven to 325°F (170°C). Butter a 10-inch cast-iron skillet.
2. In a small saucepan, melt butter over medium heat. Increase heat to medium-high, and cook, stirring constantly, until butter turns a medium-brown color and has a nutty aroma, 3 to 5 minutes. Remove from heat, and pour into the bowl of a stand mixer. Set aside until cool to the touch.
3. Add brown sugar, eggs, and egg yolk to browned butter; using the paddle attachment, beat at medium speed until light and fluffy, about 4 minutes, stopping to scrape sides of bowl. Add vanilla, and beat for 1 minute.
4. In a medium bowl, whisk together flour, baking powder, and salt. With mixer on low speed, add flour mixture to butter mixture, beating just until combined and no streaks of flour remain. Press half of dough into prepared skillet; using the back of a spatula, smooth top. Sprinkle half of chocolate and half of pomegranate arils onto dough in skillet. Top with remaining dough, smoothing top, and sprinkle with remaining chocolate and remaining pomegranate arils.
5. Bake until edges are golden and set and center jiggles slightly, about 33 to 35 minutes. Let cool completely in skillet. Best served the same day they are made.

Photo by Rebecca Firth

GUR CAKE

A Dublin favorite, gur cake has a number of quirky names within Ireland, from chester cake to donkey's gudge. The gur cake name is believed to hail from the term "gurrier," a nickname for children skipping school, who would purchase this affordable treat at bakeries. An economical invention of the 1930s, it made use of old sponge cake and bread crumbs to make a sticky, sweet, fruity filling. Encased in a flaky crust, this well-spiced delight has endured through the ages.

4   cups (340 grams) crumbled day-old sponge cake (about 12 ounces; see Irish Sponge Cake with Strawberry Preserves and Cream recipe on page 43)
3   cups (690 grams) strong-brewed Irish breakfast tea, cooled
Shortcrust Pastry (recipe follows)
⅔   cup (83 grams) all-purpose flour
1   teaspoon (5 grams) baking powder
1   teaspoon (3 grams) kosher salt
1   cup (220 grams) firmly packed light brown sugar
¼   cup (57 grams) unsalted butter, softened
1   tablespoon (6 grams) ground cinnamon
1½   teaspoons (3 grams) ground ginger
1½   teaspoons (3 grams) ground nutmeg
½   teaspoon (1 gram) ground cloves
⅔   cup (160 grams) whole milk, room temperature
3   large eggs (150 grams), room temperature and divided
1   tablespoon (4 grams) packed lemon zest
⅔   cup (112 grams) lightly packed golden raisins
½   cup (108 grams) halved dried figs (quartered if large)
Garnish: confectioners' sugar

1. Preheat oven to 350°F (180°C). Lightly spray a 13x9-inch baking pan with cooking spray. Line pan with foil, letting excess extend over sides of pan; lightly spray foil.
2. In a large bowl, place cake crumbs; pour tea over crumbs, making sure they are well coated and slightly submerged. Set aside to soak.
3. Let Shortcrust Pastry stand at room temperature until softened, 10 to 15 minutes. On a lightly floured surface, roll half of dough into a 13x9-inch rectangle, lightly flouring dough and work surface as needed. Place in bottom of prepared pan, pressing into an even layer.
4. In a medium bowl, whisk together flour, baking powder, and salt. Stir in brown sugar; using your fingers, rub butter into flour mixture until well combined. (Mixture should resemble wet sand.) Stir in cinnamon, ginger, nutmeg, and cloves until well combined.
5. Strain cake crumbs through a fine-mesh sieve, gently pressing on crumbs to release as much liquid as possible. Transfer cake crumbs to a large bowl. Add milk, 2 eggs (100 grams), and lemon zest, whisking to combine. Stir in flour mixture, raisins, and figs until well combined. Pour into prepared pan; using a small offset spatula, spread into an even layer.
6. On a lightly floured surface, roll remaining Shortcrust Pastry into a 13x9-inch rectangle, lightly flouring dough and work surface as needed. Place on top of cake crumbs mixture; using a small sharp knife, trim any uneven edges, if desired, and cut a few diagonal slashes across top.
7. In a small bowl, whisk remaining 1 egg (50 grams); brush onto pastry.
8. Bake until pastry is golden brown and filling can be heard bubbling, 55 minutes to 1 hour. Let cool completely in pan on a wire rack. Using excess foil as handles, remove from pan.
9. Using a serrated knife, cut into bars. Before serving, garnish with confectioners' sugar, if desired.

SHORTCRUST PASTRY
Makes 2 (13x9-inch) crusts

3½   cups (438 grams) all-purpose flour
⅔   cup (133 grams) granulated sugar
1   teaspoon (3 grams) kosher salt
1   cup (227 grams) cold unsalted butter, cubed
2   large eggs (100 grams), lightly beaten

1. In the work bowl of a food processor, place flour, sugar, and salt; pulse until combined. Add cold butter, and pulse until mixture is crumbly. Add eggs, and pulse just until dough comes together, stopping to scrape sides of bowl. (Mixture should be moist but not sticky and hold together when pinched.) Turn out dough, and divide in half; shape each half into a 5½-inch square. Wrap in plastic wrap, and refrigerate for at least 25 minutes.

GINGERBREAD CUSTARD BARS

Makes 9 bars

Based on the Pinterest wonder called magic custard cake, this recipe harnesses the chemistry of custard to create a miraculous baked good. One batter becomes three distinct layers during baking: fudgy bottom, custard center, and fluffy cake top. Breaking it down scientifically, you're separating your eggs to create two distinct bases, whipped egg whites like for a sponge cake and beaten, thickened egg yolks like for a custard. They are then mixed and folded in with flour, confectioners' sugar, and plenty of milk. During baking, the dense custard sinks and forms a rich base and middle while the egg white-lightened batter rises to the top.

5   **large eggs (250 grams), separated and room temperature**
¼   **teaspoon cream of tartar**
1   **cup (200 grams) granulated sugar, divided**
10   **tablespoons (140 grams) unsalted butter, melted and cooled slightly**
3   **tablespoons (63 grams) unsulphured molasses**
1¼   **cups (156 grams) all-purpose flour**
2   **teaspoons (4 grams) ground ginger**
2   **teaspoons (4 grams) ground cinnamon**
½   **teaspoon (1.5 grams) kosher salt**
½   **teaspoon (1 gram) ground nutmeg**
½   **teaspoon (1 gram) ground allspice**
½   **teaspoon (1 gram) ground cloves**
2½   **cups (600 grams) lukewarm whole milk (80°F/27°C to 85°F/29°C)**
½   **teaspoon (2 grams) vanilla extract**
Garnish: confectioners' sugar

1. Preheat oven to 325°F (170°C). Spray a 9-inch square baking pan with cooking spray. Line pan with parchment paper, letting excess extend over sides of pan.
2. In the bowl of a stand mixer fitted with the whisk attachment, beat egg whites and cream of tartar at medium-high speed until foamy, about 30 seconds. With mixer on medium-high speed, add ¼ cup (50 grams) granulated sugar in a slow, steady steam; increase mixer speed to high, and beat until stiff peaks form, 1 to 2 minutes. Transfer to a medium bowl, and set aside.
3. Return bowl to stand mixer. Using the paddle attachment, beat egg yolks and remaining ¾ cup (150 grams) granulated sugar at medium-high speed until pale yellow and mixture falls off paddle in ribbons, 2 to 3 minutes; scrape sides of bowl. With mixer on medium-low speed, add melted butter in a slow, steady stream; add molasses in a slow, steady stream. Increase mixer speed to medium, and beat until well combined, about 1 minute.
4. In another medium bowl, whisk together flour, ginger, cinnamon, salt, nutmeg, allspice, and cloves. With mixer on low speed, gradually add flour mixture to egg yolk mixture, beating just until combined and stopping to scrape sides of bowl. With mixer on low speed, add lukewarm milk in a slow, steady stream, stopping to scrape sides of bowl several times to make sure its evenly combined. Beat in vanilla. Using a balloon whisk, fold in egg white mixture in three additions. Pour into prepared pan.
5. Bake until lightly golden, center is barely jiggly, and an instant-read thermometer inserted in center registers 170°F (77°C) to 175°F (79°C), 30 to 40 minutes. Let cool completely in pan on a wire rack.
6. Using excess parchment as handles, remove from pan. Garnish with confectioners' sugar, if desired. Refrigerate in an airtight container for up to 3 days. Serve room temperature or chilled.

SALTED CARAMEL SNICKERDOODLE BARS

Makes 16 bars

Recipe by Erin Clarkson

These snickerdoodle bars are soft and chewy and sprinkled with cinnamon sugar and Caramel Shards before baking.

1 cup (227 grams) unsalted butter, softened
1¼ cups (250 grams) plus 2 tablespoons (24 grams) granulated sugar, divided
1 large egg (50 grams), room temperature
1 teaspoon (6 grams) vanilla bean paste
2⅔ cups (333 grams) all-purpose flour
½ teaspoon (2.5 grams) baking soda
½ teaspoon (2.5 grams) cream of tartar
½ teaspoon (1.5 grams) kosher salt
1 teaspoon (2 grams) ground cinnamon
Caramel Shards (recipe follows)
Garnish: flaked sea salt

1. Preheat oven to 325°F (170°C). Spray a 9-inch square baking pan with cooking spray. Line pan with parchment paper, letting excess extend over sides of pan.
2. In the bowl of a stand mixer fitted with the paddle attachment, beat butter and 1¼ cups (250 grams) sugar at high speed until light and fluffy, 4 to 5 minutes, stopping to scrape sides of bowl. Add egg and vanilla bean paste, and beat at medium speed until combined.
3. In a medium bowl, sift together flour, baking soda, cream of tartar, and kosher salt. Add flour mixture to butter mixture, and beat at low speed just until combined. (Dough will be thick.) Press dough into prepared pan, smoothing with an offset spatula.
4. In a small bowl, stir together cinnamon and remaining 2 tablespoons (24 grams) sugar. Sprinkle on top of dough. Sprinkle Caramel Shards on top of dough.
5. Bake until edges are slightly puffed, 25 to 30 minutes. Let cool completely in pan. (Bars will set as they cool.)
6. Using excess parchment as handles, remove from pan, and cut into bars. Garnish with sea salt, if desired. Store in an airtight container for up to 3 days.

CARAMEL SHARDS
Makes about 1 cup

½ cup (100 grams) granulated sugar

1. Line an 18x13-inch rimmed baking sheet with a silicone baking mat.
2. In a medium saucepan, heat sugar over medium heat, whisking occasionally, until melted. (Sugar will clump as it heats, but keep whisking and it will soon smooth out.) Cook, without stirring, until amber in color and just beginning to smoke slightly. Immediately pour onto prepared pan; lift mat to carefully spread caramel across mat to get as thin a layer as possible. Let cool completely.
3. Peel caramel off mat. Using a knife, cut caramel into pieces. (Be careful—shards are sharp.) Use immediately.

Photo by Erin Clarkson

PRO TIPS
Make the Caramel Shards before you start making the bars so the caramel has time to cool and set and is ready to sprinkle on top by the time you are finished making the dough for the bars.

Have everything ready to go for the Caramel Shards. There are a few seconds between a toasty caramel and a burnt sugar, so you want to be able to pour out the caramel as soon as it is ready.

FIFTEENS

Makes 16 bars

In Ulster, Northern Ireland, the beloved Fifteens are all about the numbers: 15 of (almost) each ingredient, from fruit to chocolate to marshmallows, stud this traybake. In our rendition, 15 marshmallows, candied cherries, chocolate féves, and digestive biscuits are mixed with sweetened condensed milk and sandwiched between coconut layers to create a singularly delicious no-bake treat.

1½ cups (126 grams) unsweetened desiccated coconut (see Note), divided
15 digestive biscuits* (221 grams)
15 regular-size marshmallows (94 grams)
15 candied cherries, halved (60 grams)
15 (66% cacao) dark chocolate feves*, chopped (58 grams)
¼ teaspoon kosher salt
¾ cup (228 grams) sweetened condensed milk
1 teaspoon (4 grams) vanilla extract

1. Spray an 8-inch square baking pan with cooking spray. Line pan with parchment paper, letting excess extend over sides of pan; spray parchment. Sprinkle ¾ cup (63 grams) coconut evenly in bottom of prepared pan.

2. In the work bowl of a food processor, pulse biscuits until pieces are ¼ inch or smaller; transfer to a medium bowl.

3. Using kitchen scissors, cut each marshmallow into 4 to 8 pieces. Add marshmallows, cherries, chocolate, and salt to biscuit crumbs; stir until well combined, breaking up any clumps of marshmallows by hand, if necessary. Add sweetened condensed milk and vanilla; stir until well combined. (Mixture will be quite sticky and should slightly resemble drop cookie dough.) Spoon mixture onto coconut in pan. Using a sheet of plastic wrap placed directly on surface, press mixture into an even layer. Sprinkle remaining ¾ cup (63 grams) coconut on top, lightly pressing into biscuit mixture. Cover and refrigerate until firm, 4 to 6 hours.

4. Using excess parchment as handles, remove from pan; using a serrated knife, cut into bars.

Note: *Desiccated coconut is unsweetened, very finely ground coconut with most of the moisture removed. If your local grocery store doesn't carry it, check specialty food stores or online.*

*We used Burton's Digestive Sweetmeal Biscuits and Valrhona Caraïbe 66% Cacao Dark Chocolate Féves.

PEPPERMINT MOCHA BROWNIES

Makes 24 bars

Recipe by Mike Johnson

Peppermint Mocha Brownies are your favorite holiday drink in dessert form—as in brownies with a hint of coffee and peppermint flavors shining through each bite, all decked out with crushed bits of striped peppermint candies sprinkled on top. Because when it's the holidays, nothing screams "festive" quite like something sweet and totally, unapologetically over the top.

1   tablespoon (6 grams) espresso powder
1   tablespoon (15 grams) boiling water
1   cup (200 grams) granulated sugar
1   cup (220 grams) firmly packed dark brown sugar
1   cup (85 grams) unsweetened natural or Dutch process cocoa powder
1   cup (227 grams) unsalted butter, melted

4   large eggs (200 grams), room temperature
2   teaspoons (8 grams) vanilla extract
1   teaspoon (4 grams) peppermint extract
1¼   cups (156 grams) all-purpose flour
½   teaspoon (1.5 grams) kosher salt
Crushed peppermint candies (optional)

1. Preheat oven to 350°F (180°C). Spray a 13x9-inch baking pan with cooking spray. Line pan with parchment paper, letting excess extend over sides of pan; spray parchment.
2. In a small bowl, stir together espresso powder and 1 tablespoon (15 grams) boiling water until a thick liquid or paste forms; set aside.
3. In a large bowl, whisk together sugars and cocoa. Add espresso mixture and melted butter, and whisk until combined. Add eggs, one at a time, whisking until combined after each addition. Stir in extracts. Using a rubber spatula or wooden spoon, fold in flour and salt just until combined. Spread batter in prepared pan.

4. Bake for 15 minutes. Sprinkle with candies (if using), and bake until a wooden pick inserted in center comes out with a few moist crumbs, 10 to 15 minutes more. Let cool completely in pan on a wire rack.
5. Using excess parchment as handles, remove from pan, and cut into bars. Store in an airtight container for up to 4 days.

Photo by Mike Johnson
Adapted from Even Better Brownies *(Page Street Publishing, 2020)*

PRO TIP
To crush peppermint candies, place and seal candies in a resealable plastic bag. On a kitchen towel-lined counter, use a rolling pin to pound and crush candies inside of the bag until desired consistency is reached.

VANILLA PUMPKIN SPICE BARS

Makes 12 bars

The warm spices and comforting autumn flavors in these frosted cakey bars are made even more aromatic with spiced vanilla.

1   cup (220 grams) firmly packed light brown sugar
¾   cup (170 grams) unsalted butter, melted
⅓   cup (67 grams) granulated sugar
1½   cups (366 grams) canned pumpkin
3   large eggs (150 grams), room temperature
1½   teaspoons (6 grams) pumpkin spice vanilla extract*
1½   cups (188 grams) all-purpose flour
1   teaspoon (5 grams) baking powder
¾   teaspoon (3.75 grams) baking soda
¾   teaspoon (2.25 grams) kosher salt
¾   teaspoon (1.5 grams) ground cinnamon
½   teaspoon (1 gram) ground nutmeg
½   teaspoon (1 gram) ground ginger
¼   teaspoon ground cloves
¼   teaspoon ground allspice
Pumpkin Spice Cream Cheese Frosting (recipe follows)
Garnish: ground cinnamon, finely chopped toasted pecans

1. Preheat oven to 350°F (180°C). Line a 13x9-inch baking pan with parchment paper, letting excess extend over sides of pan.
2. In a large bowl, whisk together brown sugar, melted butter, and granulated sugar until well combined. Add pumpkin, eggs, and pumpkin spice vanilla extract, stirring until combined.

3. In a medium bowl, sift together flour, baking powder, baking soda, salt, cinnamon, nutmeg, ginger, cloves, and allspice. Gradually add flour mixture to sugar mixture, whisking just until combined. (Batter will be smooth.) Pour batter into prepared pan. Using a mini offset spatula, smooth batter into an even layer. Run the tip of a knife through batter to help release any large air bubbles. Tap pan on kitchen towel-lined counter 2 to 3 times to level batter.
4. Bake until a wooden pick inserted in center comes out clean, 25 to 30 minutes. Let cool completely in pan. Spread Pumpkin Spice Cream Cheese Frosting in an even layer on top of cooled bars. Cover and refrigerate until frosting is set, at least 30 minutes.
5. Using excess parchment as handles, remove from pan, and cut into bars. Garnish with cinnamon and pecans, if desired.

*We used Heilala Pumpkin Spice Vanilla Extract.

PUMPKIN SPICE CREAM CHEESE FROSTING

Makes about 3 cups

8   ounces (226 grams) cream cheese, softened
½   cup (113 grams) unsalted butter, softened
1   teaspoon (4 grams) pumpkin spice vanilla extract*
¼   teaspoon kosher salt
1   (1-pound) package (454 grams) confectioners' sugar

1. In the bowl of a stand mixer fitted with the paddle attachment, beat cream cheese and butter at medium-low speed until smooth and creamy, about 1 minute. Add pumpkin spice vanilla extract and salt, and beat until combined. Reduce mixer speed to low, and slowly add confectioners' sugar, beating until combined. Increase mixer speed to medium, and beat until fluffy, about 1 minute.

*We used Heilala Pumpkin Spice Vanilla Extract.

CHOCOLATE CHAI-SPICED CRUMBLE BARS

Makes 18 bars

Recipe by Mike Johnson

Nothing ushers in the holidays more than spiced bakes. The creamy fudge filling of these bars pairs perfectly with the buttery spiced crust and topping, making them a perfect no-fuss holiday dessert.

- 3 cups (375 grams) all-purpose flour
- 1 cup (220 grams) firmly packed dark brown sugar
- 1 teaspoon (5 grams) baking powder
- 1 teaspoon (5 grams) baking soda
- 1 teaspoon (2 grams) ground cinnamon
- ½ teaspoon (1.5 grams) kosher salt
- ½ teaspoon (1 gram) ground ginger
- ¼ teaspoon ground cardamom
- ¼ teaspoon ground allspice
- ⅛ teaspoon ground black pepper
- 1 cup (227 grams) unsalted butter, melted
- 1 (14-ounce) can (397 grams) sweetened condensed milk
- 12 ounces (340 grams) 70% cacao dark chocolate, chopped
- 1½ teaspoons (6 grams) vanilla extract

1. Preheat oven to 350°F (180°C). Spray a 13x9-inch baking pan with cooking spray. Line pan with parchment paper, letting excess extend over sides of pan; spray parchment.

2. In a large bowl, whisk together flour, brown sugar, baking powder, baking soda, cinnamon, salt, ginger, cardamom, allspice, and pepper until combined. Stir in melted butter until a crumbly dough forms. Reserve 1½ cups (300 grams) dough. Press remaining dough evenly into bottom of prepared pan.

3. Bake until crust is raised and puffy, 10 to 12 minutes. Leave oven on.

4. In a medium saucepan, heat sweetened condensed milk and chocolate over low heat, stirring constantly, until chocolate is melted and mixture is smooth. Stir in vanilla. (Mixture will be thick.) Pour mixture onto crust, spreading with an offset spatula; sprinkle with reserved dough.

5. Bake until topping is light golden brown, 25 to 30 minutes. Let cool completely in pan on a wire rack.

6. Using excess parchment as handles, remove from pan, and cut into bars. Store in an airtight container for up to 1 week, or freeze in an airtight container for up to 3 months.

Photo by Mike Johnson

CHEESECAKE BARS WITH CHOCOLATE AND CARAMEL

Makes about 24 bars

Recipe by Sarah Kieffer

Cheesecake bars are a holiday favorite—they contain all the glory of cheesecake but are less fussy to make. This version swirls chocolate and caramel into the batter and is then topped with ganache.

1¼ cups (163 grams) graham cracker crumbs
1½ cups (300 grams) plus 3 tablespoons (36 grams) granulated sugar, divided
5 tablespoons (70 grams) unsalted butter, melted and divided
3 (8-ounce) packages (680 grams) cream cheese, room temperature
¾ cup (180 grams) sour cream, room temperature
1 tablespoon (13 grams) vanilla extract
¼ teaspoon kosher salt
3 large eggs (150 grams), room temperature
4 ounces (113 grams) 60% cacao bittersweet chocolate, melted and cooled
⅓ cup (100 grams) caramel sauce
6 ounces (175 grams) 60% cacao bittersweet chocolate, chopped
¾ cup (180 grams) heavy whipping cream

1. Position oven rack in center of oven. Preheat oven to 325°F (170°C). Line a 13x9-inch baking pan with parchment paper, letting excess extend over sides of pan.
2. In a medium bowl, whisk together graham cracker crumbs and 3 tablespoons (36 grams) sugar. Using a silicone spatula, stir in 4 tablespoons (56 grams) melted butter until combined. Press crumb mixture into bottom of prepared pan.
3. Bake for 10 minutes. Let cool completely. Wrap outside of pan in a double layer of foil, shiny side out. Leave oven on.
4. In the bowl of a stand mixer fitted with the paddle attachment, beat cream cheese at medium speed until light and completely smooth, 4 to 6 minutes, stopping to scrape sides of bowl. Add remaining 1½ cups (300 grams) sugar, and beat at medium speed until well combined, 2 to 3 minutes, stopping to scrape sides of bowl. Add sour cream, vanilla, and salt, and beat at medium speed for 2 to 3 minutes. With mixer on low speed, add eggs, one at a time, beating just until combined after each addition. Using a

silicone spatula, scrape sides and bottom of bowl, folding to ensure everything is combined.
5. Transfer ½ cup (about 120 grams) batter to a small bowl, and stir in melted chocolate. Pour remaining batter onto cooled crust, smoothing top with a small offset spatula. Alternately dollop chocolate batter and caramel sauce on top of plain batter. Drag tip of a butter knife through batter, creating swirls. Tap pan on a kitchen towel-lined counter a few times to release any air bubbles.
6. Bake until edges are puffed and set, center is jiggly, and an instant-read thermometer inserted in center registers 150°F (65°C), 30 to 35 minutes. Turn oven off, and leave cheesecake in oven with door ajar for 30 minutes. Let cool completely on a wire rack. Cover with a piece of parchment paper, and refrigerate for at least 6 hours or overnight.
7. In a small heatproof bowl, place chopped chocolate.
8. In a small saucepan, heat cream over medium-low heat just until bubbles form around edges of pan. (Do not boil.) Pour warm cream and remaining 1 tablespoon (14 grams) melted butter over chocolate; cover bowl with plastic wrap, and let stand for 5 minutes. Using a butter knife, stir until chocolate is melted and mixture is smooth. Let cool to almost room temperature, about 20 minutes.
9. Stir cooled ganache a few times. Pour ganache in center of cold cheesecake. Using an offset spatula, spread ganache over cheesecake, carefully smoothing it out as you spread it to edges. Refrigerate until ganache is set, about 30 minutes.
10. Using excess parchment as handles, remove from pan, and cut into bars. Refrigerate in an airtight container for up to 2 days.

Photo by Sarah Kieffer

MIXED BERRIES & CREAM BARS

Makes about 12 bars

An elegant spin on a familiar formula, the coolest dessert of summer has arrived. We paired a slightly salty pretzel cake base with a cream filling and topped it off with a scattering of fresh berries.

½ cup (113 grams) unsalted butter, softened

2 cups (400 grams) granulated sugar, divided

2 large eggs (100 grams)

2 teaspoons (8 grams) vanilla extract, divided

1 cup (125 grams) all-purpose flour

¾ cup (75 grams) finely ground pretzels (see Note)

1½ teaspoons (7.5 grams) baking powder

½ teaspoon (1.5 grams) kosher salt

½ cup (120 grams) whole milk

16 ounces (454 grams) cream cheese, softened

2 cups (480 grams) cold heavy whipping cream

6 ounces (170 grams) fresh raspberries

6 ounces (170 grams) fresh blueberries

6 ounces (170 grams) fresh blackberries

1. Preheat oven to 350°F (180°C). Place a 13x4-inch strip of foil in bottom and up sides of a 13x9-inch baking pan. (This strip will help you remove your bars from pan after freezing; the parchment paper tends to rip.) Line pan with parchment paper, letting excess extend over sides of pan.

2. In the bowl of a stand mixer fitted with the paddle attachment, beat butter and 1 cup (200 grams) sugar at medium speed until fluffy, 3 to 4 minutes, stopping to scrape sides of bowl. Add eggs, one at a time, beating well after each addition. Beat in 1 teaspoon (4 grams) vanilla.

3. In a medium bowl, whisk together flour, pretzels, baking powder, and salt. Gradually add flour mixture to butter mixture alternately with milk, beginning and ending with flour mixture, beating just until combined after each addition. Spoon batter into prepared pan, smoothing top.

4. Bake until a wooden pick inserted in center comes out clean, 15 to 20 minutes. Let cool completely in pan.

5. Clean bowl of stand mixer and paddle attachment. Using the paddle attachment, beat cream cheese at medium speed until smooth, about 1 minute. Add remaining 1 cup (200 grams) sugar, and beat at medium speed until smooth. Beat in remaining 1 teaspoon (4 grams) vanilla. Transfer to a large bowl, and set aside.

6. Clean bowl of stand mixer. Using the whisk attachment, beat cold cream at medium speed until thickened. Slowly increase mixer speed to medium-high, and beat until stiff peaks form. Using a whisk, fold about one-third of whipped cream

into cream cheese mixture until combined. Fold in remaining whipped cream just until combined. Spread onto cake layer, smoothing flat with an offset spatula. Lightly press berries into cream cheese mixture, leaving a ¼-inch border on all sides. Cover with plastic wrap, and freeze until set, at least 4 hours or overnight.

7. Let bars stand at room temperature for 20 minutes. Using excess parchment and foil as handles, remove from pan. Using a hot, dry knife, trim ¼ inch off each side, and cut into bars. Refrigerate until ready to serve.

Note: *To finely grind pretzels, place in the work bowl of a food processor, and pulse until finely ground, about 10 times. Alternatively, place pretzels in a resealable plastic bag, and crush with a rolling pin.*

PEPPERMINT PATTY BROWNIES

Makes 16 brownies

Recipe by Mike Johnson

This Peppermint Patty Brownies recipe is perfect for the chocolate-peppermint lovers in your life. These brownies should be refrigerated but can be enjoyed chilled or at room temperature.

1 cup (200 grams) granulated sugar
½ cup (63 grams) all-purpose flour
⅓ cup (25 grams) unsweetened natural or Dutch process cocoa powder
¼ teaspoon (1.25 grams) baking powder
¼ teaspoon kosher salt
½ cup (113 grams) unsalted butter, melted
2 large eggs (100 grams)
1 teaspoon (4 grams) vanilla extract
Peppermint Filling (recipe follows)
Chocolate Topping (recipe follows)

1. Preheat oven to 350°F (180°C). Spray an 8-inch square baking pan with cooking spray. Line pan with parchment paper, letting excess extend over sides of pan.
2. In a large bowl, whisk together sugar, flour, cocoa, baking powder, and salt.
3. In a medium bowl, whisk together melted butter, eggs, and vanilla until well combined. Add butter mixture to sugar mixture, stirring just until combined. Pour batter into prepared pan, spreading into an even layer.
4. Bake until a wooden pick inserted in center comes out with a few moist crumbs, 30 to 33 minutes. Let cool completely in pan.
5. Top cooled brownie layer with Peppermint Filling; using a damp offset spatula, smooth Peppermint Filling into an even layer. Refrigerate until set, about 30 minutes.
6. Top Peppermint Filling with Chocolate Topping. Slam pan on a kitchen towel-

lined counter to release any air bubbles. Refrigerate until topping is set, about 2 hours.
7. Using excess parchment as handles, remove from pan, and cut into bars. Serve chilled or at room temperature. Refrigerate in an airtight container for up to 3 days.

PEPPERMINT FILLING
Makes about 1 cup

2½ cups (300 grams) confectioners' sugar, sifted
1 tablespoon (14 grams) unsalted butter, softened
½ teaspoon (2 grams) peppermint extract
¼ teaspoon (1.5 grams) vanilla bean paste
2 to 4 tablespoons (30 to 60 grams) boiling water

1. In a medium bowl, place confectioners' sugar, butter, peppermint extract, and vanilla bean paste. Add 2 tablespoons (30 grams) boiling water, and stir until combined. (It should resemble a thick paste.) Add up to remaining 2 tablespoons (30 grams) boiling water, 1 teaspoon (5 grams) at a time, if needed. Use immediately.

CHOCOLATE TOPPING
Makes about ¾ cup

3.5 ounces (100 grams) 70% cacao dark chocolate, chopped
¼ cup (57 grams) unsalted butter

1. In the top of a double boiler, combine chocolate and butter. Cook over simmering water, stirring frequently, until melted and smooth. Use immediately.

Photo by Mike Johnson

STRAWBERRY SWIRL CHEESECAKE BARS

Makes 24 bars

For a simplified, strawberry-rich version of our classic cheesecake, look no further than these streamlined cheesecake bars. One bite into one of these bars reveals a surprising chocolate crumb crust, packing a cocoa note to accompany the sweet-tart strawberry jam-swirled top.

2   cups (220 grams) chocolate graham cracker crumbs (14 to 15 sheets)
¼   cup (57 grams) unsalted butter, melted
1⅓ cups (267 grams) plus 2 tablespoons (24 grams) granulated sugar, divided
½   teaspoon kosher salt, divided
2   cups (340 grams) finely chopped fresh strawberries
4   teaspoons (12 grams) cornstarch
3   (8-ounce) packages (680 grams) cream cheese, cubed and softened
3   tablespoons (24 grams) all-purpose flour
1   tablespoon (13 grams) vanilla extract
4   large eggs (200 grams), room temperature
1   cup (240 grams) sour cream, room temperature

1. Preheat oven to 350°F (180°C). Spray a 13x9-inch baking pan with baking spray with flour. Line pan with parchment paper, letting excess extend over sides of pan.

2. In a large bowl, stir together graham cracker crumbs, melted butter, 2 tablespoons (24 grams) sugar, and ¼ teaspoon salt until well combined; using a small straight-sided measuring cup, press into bottom of prepared pan.

3. Bake until set and fragrant, 8 to 10 minutes. Let cool on a wire rack for 30 minutes. Wrap bottom and sides of pan in a double layer of heavy-duty foil. Reduce oven temperature to 325°F (170°C).

4. In the container of a blender, combine strawberries and ⅓ cup (67 grams) sugar; purée until smooth. Strain strawberry mixture through an extra-fine-mesh sieve into a medium saucepan; whisk in cornstarch until well combined. Bring to a boil over medium heat; cook, whisking constantly, until mixture is thickened and no longer tastes like cornstarch, about 4 minutes. Remove from heat; let cool for 30 minutes. (Strawberry mixture will continue to thicken as it cools.)

5. In the bowl of a stand mixer fitted with the paddle attachment, beat cream cheese at medium speed until smooth and creamy, 1 to 2 minutes, stopping to scrape sides of bowl. Add flour, vanilla, remaining 1 cup (200 grams) sugar, and remaining ¼ teaspoon salt; beat at low speed just until combined. Increase mixer speed to medium, and beat until well combined, 1 to 2 minutes, stopping to scrape sides of bowl. Add eggs, one at a time, beating just until combined after each addition. Add sour cream; beat at medium-low speed until combined, 1 to 2 minutes, stopping to scrape sides of bowl. Pour mixture onto prepared crust, spreading into an even layer with a small offset spatula.

6. Working quickly, drop small dollops of cooled strawberry mixture on top of cream cheese mixture; using a wooden pick, swirl as desired. Place baking pan in a large roasting pan. Position oven rack so top of roasting pan is 6 to 6½ inches from top heating element; place roasting pan in oven, and add hot water to come 1 inch up sides of baking pan.

7. Bake until edges are set, top looks dry, center is almost set, and an instant-read thermometer inserted in center registers 150°F (66°C) to 155°F (68°C), 35 to 50 minutes, loosely covering with foil to prevent excess browning, if necessary. Let cool in pan on a wire rack for 1½ to 2 hours.

8. Refrigerate in pan on a wire rack overnight, loosely covering with foil only when completely cool to prevent condensation from forming on top of cheesecake.

9. Using excess parchment as handles, carefully remove from pan, and transfer to a cutting board. Using a warm dry knife, cut into bars.

CARROT CAKE CHEESECAKE BARS

Makes 24 bars

Who needs cream cheese frosting when you've got a layer of cheesecake filling? These bars combine two of our favorite cakes in one: crumbly chunks of carrot cake baked into a velvety layer of cheesecake. Fair warning: you may not be able to have one without the other ever again.

- 1½ cups (340 grams) unsalted butter, softened
- 1½ cups (330 grams) firmly packed light brown sugar
- 1¼ cups (250 grams) granulated sugar
- 2 large eggs (100 grams)
- 4 cups (500 grams) all-purpose flour
- 2 teaspoons (4 grams) ground cinnamon
- 2 teaspoons (4 grams) ground ginger
- 1½ teaspoons (4.5 grams) kosher salt
- 1 teaspoon (5 grams) baking powder
- 1 teaspoon (5 grams) baking soda
- ¼ teaspoon ground nutmeg
- ¼ teaspoon ground allspice
- 1½ cups (161 grams) lightly packed grated carrot
- Cheesecake Layer (recipe follows)

1. Preheat oven to 350°F (180°C). Line a 13x9-inch baking pan with parchment paper, letting excess extend over sides of pan.
2. In the bowl of a stand mixer fitted with the paddle attachment, beat butter and sugars at medium speed until fluffy, 3 to 4 minutes, stopping to scrape sides of bowl. Add eggs, one at a time, beating well after each addition.
3. In a large bowl, whisk together flour, cinnamon, ginger, salt, baking powder, baking soda, nutmeg, and allspice. With mixer on low speed, gradually add flour mixture to butter mixture, beating just until combined. Beat in carrot.
4. Evenly spread 4 cups (about 1,120 grams) dough in prepared pan. Top with Cheesecake Layer. Crumble remaining dough (about 2 cups [about 560 grams]) on top.
5. Bake until edges are set, center jiggles just slightly, and an instant-read thermometer inserted in Cheesecake Layer registers 175°F (79°C) to 180°F (82°C), 50 to 55 minutes. Let cool completely in pan on a wire rack. Cover and refrigerate for at least 4 hours or overnight.

6. Using excess parchment as handles, remove from pan, trim edges, if desired, and cut into bars.

CHEESECAKE LAYER
Makes 3⅓ cups

- 16 ounces (454 grams) cream cheese, softened
- 1 cup (200 grams) granulated sugar
- 1 tablespoon (8 grams) all-purpose flour
- 2 large eggs (100 grams)
- 1 tablespoon (13 grams) vanilla extract

1. In the bowl of a stand mixer fitted with the paddle attachment, beat cream cheese until smooth. Add sugar and flour, and beat until combined, stopping to scrapes sides of bowl. Add eggs, one at a time, beating until well combined after each addition. Beat in vanilla. Use immediately.

CRANBERRY STREUSEL BARS

Makes about 24 bars

Recipe by Sarah Kieffer

Cranberry desserts are often tart, but in this recipe, the fruit is tamed by sweetened condensed milk, making for a rich, creamy, crumbly bar. Make sure to use canned whole berry cranberry sauce and not gelled cranberry sauce. Cranberry liqueur will help bump the cranberry flavor, but it isn't essential to making them shine. Sarah used red food coloring to make the filling a brighter shade of cranberry-pink. Even without it, the creamy filling has lovely pops of rosy cranberry color.

2   (14-ounce) cans (792 grams) sweetened condensed milk
1   cup (320 grams) canned whole berry cranberry sauce*
2   tablespoons (30 grams) heavy whipping cream
2   tablespoons (30 grams) cranberry liqueur* (optional)
1   teaspoon (4 grams) vanilla extract
1   teaspoon (5 grams) fresh lemon juice
¾   teaspoon (1.5 grams) kosher salt, divided
Red food coloring (optional)
2¼ cups (281 grams) all-purpose flour
1½ cups (144 grams) almond flour
½   cup (110 grams) firmly packed light brown sugar
¼   cup (50 grams) granulated sugar
½   teaspoon (2.5 grams) baking soda
1   cup (227 grams) unsalted butter, softened
2⅓ cups (256 grams) fresh or thawed frozen* cranberries

1. Position oven rack in center of oven. Preheat oven to 350°F (180°C). Spray a 13x9-inch baking pan with cooking spray. Line pan with parchment paper, letting excess extend over sides of pan.
2. In a large bowl, whisk together sweetened condensed milk, cranberry sauce, cream, liqueur (if using), vanilla, lemon juice, ¼ teaspoon salt, and food coloring (if using) until combined.
3. In the bowl of a stand mixer fitted with the paddle attachment, beat flours, sugars, baking soda, and remaining ½ teaspoon (1.5 grams) salt at low speed until combined. Add butter, and beat at medium speed until mixture is crumbly. Press half of flour mixture into bottom of prepared pan.
4. Bake for 10 minutes. Leave oven on.
5. Carefully spread condensed milk mixture onto prepared crust. Scatter fresh cranberries on top; sprinkle remaining flour mixture on top.
6. Bake until filling is set and does not jiggle and topping is light golden brown, 18 to 22 minutes. Let cool completely in pan on a wire rack. Cover and refrigerate for 4 to 6 hours.
7. Using excess parchment as handles, remove from pan, and cut into bars. Serve cold or at room temperature. Refrigerate in an airtight container for up to 3 days.

We used Ocean Spray Whole Berry Cranberry Sauce. I like Tattersall Cranberry Liqueur, but cranberry schnapps is also an option. If using thawed frozen cranberries, pat dry.

Photo by Sarah Kieffer

GUINNESS BROWNIES

Makes 12 to 16 brownies

Raise a pint to your new favorite brownies. A double hit of extra stout beer in the batter and the frosting brings a tangy, hop-filled punch you never knew you needed.

2   cups (480 grams) Guinness Extra Stout
12 ounces (340 grams) 70% cacao bittersweet chocolate baking bars, finely chopped (about 2 cups)
2   teaspoons (4 grams) instant espresso powder
1½ cups (300 grams) granulated sugar
1   cup (227 grams) unsalted butter, melted
¼   cup (55 grams) firmly packed light brown sugar
4   large eggs (200 grams), room temperature
1   large egg yolk (19 grams), room temperature
2   teaspoons (8 grams) vanilla extract
1½ cups (188 grams) all-purpose flour
1   teaspoon (3 grams) kosher salt
Malted Frosting (recipe follows)
Garnish: bittersweet chocolate shavings

1. In a small saucepan, bring Guinness to a boil over medium-high heat. Reduce heat to medium-low, and simmer, stirring occasionally, until reduced to 1 cup (213 grams), about 35 minutes. Remove from heat, and let cool for 30 minutes.
2. Preheat oven to 350°F (180°C). Spray a 13x9-inch baking pan with cooking spray. Line pan with parchment paper, letting excess extend over sides of pan.
3. In the top of a double boiler, combine chocolate and espresso powder. Cook over simmering water, stirring occasionally, until chocolate is melted and mixture is smooth.
4. In a large bowl, whisk together granulated sugar, melted butter, brown sugar, eggs, egg yolk, and vanilla until well combined. Add chocolate mixture and ¾ cup (160 grams) reduced Guinness, whisking until well combined. (Reserve remaining reduced Guinness for Malted Frosting.)
5. In a medium bowl, whisk together flour and salt. Gradually add flour mixture to sugar mixture, whisking until well combined. Spoon batter into prepared pan; using a small offset spatula, smooth into an even layer.
6. Bake until a wooden pick inserted in center comes out with a few moist crumbs, about 35 minutes. Let cool completely in pan on a wire rack.
7. Using excess parchment as handles, remove from pan. Spoon and spread Malted Frosting onto cooled brownies as desired. Garnish with chocolate shavings, if desired, and cut into bars.

MALTED FROSTING
Makes about 3⅓ cups

⅔   cup (150 grams) unsalted butter, softened
½   teaspoon (1.5 grams) kosher salt
3¾ cups (450 grams) confectioners' sugar
½   cup (64 grams) malted milk powder
1½ teaspoons (3 grams) instant espresso powder
3 to 3½ tablespoons (37 to 43 grams) reduced Guinness Extra Stout reserved from Guinness Brownies (recipe precedes)
1   teaspoon (4 grams) vanilla extract

1. In the bowl of a stand mixer fitted with the paddle attachment, beat butter and salt at medium speed until smooth and creamy, 1 to 2 minutes, stopping to scrape sides of bowl. With mixer on low speed, gradually add confectioners' sugar, milk powder, and espresso powder, beating just until combined. Beat in reduced Guinness and vanilla; scrape sides of bowl. Increase mixer speed to medium, and beat until fluffy, about 2 minutes, stopping to scrape sides of bowl. Use immediately.

PRO TIP
Any leftover reduced Guinness can be gently brushed over brownies before spreading on the frosting.

PUMPKIN BLONDIES

Makes about 24 bars

Recipe by Sarah Kieffer

Blondies are a classic treat, but these take it up a notch with a swirl of both pumpkin and cream cheese.

¾ cup (183 grams) pumpkin purée
1⅓ cups (293 grams) firmly packed light brown sugar, divided
¾ teaspoon (1.5 grams) ground cinnamon
½ teaspoon (1 gram) ground ginger
¼ teaspoon ground nutmeg
1⅛ teaspoons (3 grams) kosher salt, divided
4 ounces (113 grams) cream cheese, room temperature
1¼ cups (250 grams) granulated sugar, divided
1 tablespoon (13 grams) plus 1 teaspoon (4 grams) vanilla extract, divided
2 cups (250 grams) all-purpose flour
1½ teaspoons (7.5 grams) baking powder
14 tablespoons (196 grams) unsalted butter
2 large eggs (100 grams), room temperature

1. In a small saucepan, stir together pumpkin, ⅓ cup (73 grams) brown sugar, cinnamon, ginger, nutmeg, and ⅛ teaspoon salt. Cook over medium heat until combined and some moisture from pumpkin has evaporated, about 10 minutes. Let cool completely.

2. In a small bowl, stir together cream cheese, ¼ cup (50 grams) granulated sugar, and 1 teaspoon (4 grams) vanilla until smooth.

3. Position oven rack in center of oven. Preheat oven to 350°F (180°C). Butter a 13x9-inch baking pan. Line pan with parchment paper, letting excess extend over sides of pan.

4. In a medium bowl, whisk together flour and baking powder.

5. In a medium saucepan, melt butter, remaining 1 cup (200 grams) granulated sugar, remaining 1 cup (220 grams) brown sugar, and remaining 1 teaspoon (3 grams) salt over medium heat. Remove from heat, and stir in remaining 1 tablespoon (13 grams) vanilla. Transfer to a large bowl, and let cool for about 15 minutes.

6. Add eggs to butter mixture, and whisk until combined. Stir in flour mixture just until combined. Pour batter into prepared pan, spread into an even layer. Alternately dollop pumpkin mixture and cream cheese mixture on top of batter. Drag the tip of a butter knife through batter, creating swirls.

7. Bake until a wooden pick inserted in center comes out with a few moist crumbs, 30 to 38 minutes, covering with foil halfway through baking to prevent excess browning. Let cool completely in pan on a wire rack.

8. Using excess parchment as handles, remove from pan, and cut into bars. Store in an airtight container for up to 2 days.

Photo by Sarah Kieffer

PRO TIP
Leave a small space in the center of the batter unswirled. This is the spot you want to insert your wooden pick into to check when the bars are done, as the cream cheese and pumpkin swirls will remain wet throughout baking.

MEYER LEMON BARS

Makes 8 to 10 bars

We've given tried-and-true lemon bars an epic Meyer lemon makeover. A macadamia-studded crumb crust makes the perfect buttery base for our tart Meyer lemon custard filling, and piped meringue dresses these bars up with a photo-worthy finish. We baked this recipe in a rectangular tart pan for a modern look, but a 9-inch fluted round removable-bottom tart pan will also yield beautiful results.

1   cup (125 grams) all-purpose flour
½   cup (113 grams) cold unsalted butter, cubed
½   cup (68 grams) finely chopped roasted salted macadamia nuts
⅓   cup (40 grams) confectioners' sugar
2   tablespoons (9 grams) plus 1 teaspoon (2 grams) packed Meyer lemon zest, divided
½   teaspoon kosher salt, divided
1¼ cups (250 grams) granulated sugar
3   large eggs (150 grams), room temperature
¼   cup (60 grams) Meyer lemon juice
¼   cup (57 grams) unsalted butter, melted
Meringue Topping (recipe follows)

1. Preheat oven to 350°F (180°C). Lightly spray a 13¾x4½-inch fluted removable-bottom tart pan with cooking spray.
2. In the work bowl of a food processor, combine flour, cold butter, nuts, confectioners' sugar, 1 teaspoon (2 grams) lemon zest, and ¼ teaspoon salt; pulse until dough forms large clumps and holds together when pressed between fingers. Press dough into bottom and up sides of prepared pan. Place pan on a rimmed baking sheet.

3. In a medium bowl, whisk together granulated sugar, eggs, lemon juice, melted butter, remaining 2 tablespoons (9 grams) lemon zest, and remaining ¼ teaspoon salt until smooth and well combined. Pour egg mixture into prepared crust.
4. Bake until filling is mostly set (it may jiggle just slightly) and crust is golden brown, about 30 minutes. Let cool completely on a wire rack. Gently remove from pan, and place on a serving platter.
5. Spoon Meringue Topping into a pastry bag fitted with a small open star piping tip (Wilton No. 32); pipe as desired. Using a kitchen torch, lightly toast meringue. Serve immediately.

MERINGUE TOPPING
Makes about 1½ cups

⅔   cup (133 grams) granulated sugar
¼   cup (60 grams) water
2   large egg whites (60 grams)
¼   teaspoon cream of tartar

1. In a small saucepan, bring sugar and ¼ cup (60 grams) water to a boil over high heat. Reduce heat to medium-high; cook until a candy thermometer registers 248°F (120°C).
2. Meanwhile, in the bowl of a stand mixer fitted with the whisk attachment, beat egg whites and cream of tartar at medium-high speed until stiff peaks form.
3. With mixer at medium speed, pour hot sugar mixture into egg white mixture in a slow, steady stream, avoiding the whisk; beat at medium-high speed until mixture cools to room temperature and is a spreadable consistency, about 10 minutes. Use immediately.

PRO TIP
No time to make meringue? These lemon bars are also lovely with a simple dusting of confectioners' sugar.

CREAMY WHITE RUSSIAN BARS

Makes 32 bars

The elegant White Russian cocktail is the delectable inspiration for these cheesecake bars loaded with coffee liqueur and cream. We added velvety black cocoa to the mix to create the tuxedo of dessert bars: always classy, never out of style.

Black Cocoa Shortcrust (recipe follows)
3   (8-ounce) packages (680 grams) cream cheese, room temperature and divided
¼   cup (60 grams) coffee liqueur*
2½ teaspoons (5 grams) dark-roast instant coffee granules
1   cup (200 grams) granulated sugar, divided
2   tablespoons (16 grams) all-purpose flour
3   teaspoons (12 grams) vanilla extract, divided
¼   teaspoon kosher salt
2   large eggs (100 grams), room temperature
¼   cup (60 grams) heavy whipping cream
1   teaspoon (2 grams) black cocoa powder

1. Preheat oven to 350°F (180°C). Spray a 13x9-inch baking pan with cooking spray. Line pan with parchment paper, letting excess extend almost to top of pan.
2. Let Black Cocoa Shortcrust stand at room temperature until slightly softened, 10 to 15 minutes, if necessary. Transfer dough to prepared pan, pressing to cover bottom of pan. Top with a piece of parchment paper, letting excess extend over edges of pan. Add pie weights.
3. Bake until edges are set and crust is fragrant, 15 to 20 minutes. Carefully remove parchment and weights. Let cool in pan on a wire rack for 25 minutes. Leave oven on.
4. In the bowl of a stand mixer fitted with the paddle attachment, beat 2 packages (454 grams) cream cheese at medium speed until smooth and creamy, 1 to 2 minutes, stopping to scrape sides of bowl.
5. In a small bowl, stir together liqueur and instant coffee until granules dissolve. Add liqueur mixture, ¾ cup (150 grams) sugar, flour, ¾ teaspoon (3 grams) vanilla, and salt to cream cheese; beat until well combined, 1 to 2 minutes, stopping to scrape sides of bowl. Add eggs, one at a time, beating just until combined after each addition. Pour cream cheese mixture onto prepared crust, spreading into an even layer with a small offset spatula. Gently tap sides of pan several times to release any air bubbles, popping any that rise to the surface with a wooden pick.
6. Bake until edges are set, top has a dulled finish, center is almost set, and an instant-read thermometer inserted in center registers 150°F (66°C) to 155°F (68°C), about 20 minutes. Immediately run a knife around pan to loosen bars from parchment; let cool in pan on a wire rack for 1½ to 2 hours.
7. Clean bowl of stand mixer and paddle attachment. Using the paddle attachment, beat remaining 1 package (226 grams) cream cheese at medium speed until smooth and creamy, 1 to 2 minutes, stopping to scrape sides of bowl. Add cream, remaining ¼ cup

(50 grams) sugar, and remaining 2¼ teaspoons (9 grams) vanilla; beat until smooth and well combined. Transfer ¼ cup (about 54 grams) cream cheese mixture to a small bowl; stir in black cocoa.
8. Spoon and spread remaining cream cheese mixture onto cooled cheesecake layer in pan. Drop small dollops of black cocoa mixture on top of cream cheese mixture; using a wooden pick, swirl as desired, being careful not to hit cheesecake layer underneath. Refrigerate for at least 1 hour or up to overnight, loosely covering with foil only when completely cool to prevent condensation from forming on top.
9. Using excess parchment as handles, remove from pan. Using a warm, dry knife, cut into bars.

*We used Kahlúa.

BLACK COCOA SHORTCRUST
Makes 1 (13x9-inch) crust

3   cups plus 2 tablespoons (391 grams) all-purpose flour
⅔   cup (133 grams) granulated sugar
½   cup (43 grams) black cocoa powder
1   teaspoon (3 grams) kosher salt
1   cup (227 grams) cold unsalted butter, cubed
2   large eggs (100 grams)

1. In the work bowl of a food processor, place flour, sugar, black cocoa, and salt; pulse until combined. Add cold butter, and pulse until butter pieces are no larger than ⅛ to ¼ inch. Add eggs; pulse just until dough comes together.
2. Turn out dough, and shape into a disk. Wrap in plastic wrap, and refrigerate for at least 25 minutes before using.

CRANBERRY SHORTCAKE BARS

Makes 16 bars

Recipe by Erin Clarkson

In New Zealand, "shortcake" refers to a "slice" (what Americans call a bar) that is made with two pieces of rolled-out sweet pastry and a fruit filling. Every grandmother in New Zealand has their own version. This simplified recipe uses half of the sweet pastry as the base and the other half crumbled on top. It is traditionally made with apple but is amazing with almost any fruit. Instead of apples, this version has a tangy whole cranberry filling, which works great with fresh or frozen fruit.

1   cup (227 grams) unsalted butter, softened
1¾   cups plus 2 tablespoons (374 grams) granulated sugar, divided
2   large eggs (100 grams), room temperature
1½   teaspoons (9 grams) vanilla bean paste, divided
3½   cups plus 2 tablespoons (454 grams) all-purpose flour
1¾   teaspoons (8.75 grams) baking powder
1   teaspoon (3 grams) kosher salt, divided
16   ounces (454 grams) fresh or frozen* cranberries
1   tablespoon plus 2 teaspoons (14 grams) tapioca starch
1   tablespoon plus 1 teaspoon (20 grams) water or fresh orange juice
Confectioners' sugar, for dusting

1. Preheat oven to 350°F (180°C). Spray a 9-inch square baking pan with cooking spray. Line pan with parchment paper, letting excess extend over sides of pan.
2. In the bowl of a stand mixer fitted with the paddle attachment, beat butter and ¾ cup (150 grams) granulated sugar at medium speed until light and fluffy, 3 to 4 minutes, stopping to scrape sides of bowl. Add eggs and 1 teaspoon (6 grams) vanilla bean paste, beating until combined.
3. In a medium bowl, sift together flour, baking powder, and ½ teaspoon (1.5 grams) salt. Add flour mixture to butter mixture, and beat at low speed until combined. Transfer 2 cups (475 grams) dough to

prepared pan, and press evenly into bottom of pan, smoothing surface with an offset spatula. Set remaining dough aside.
4. In a medium bowl, stir together cranberries, tapioca starch, 1 tablespoon plus 1 teaspoon (20 grams) water or orange juice, remaining 1 cup plus 2 tablespoons (224 grams) granulated sugar, remaining ½ teaspoon (1.5 grams) salt, and remaining ½ teaspoon (3 grams) vanilla bean paste with a spatula until well combined. Spoon cranberry mixture evenly onto dough in pan. (Do not press down too hard.) Crumble remaining dough in an even layer on top of cranberries.
5. Bake until topping is golden brown and filling is bubbly, 40 to 45 minutes. Let cool completely in pan.
6. Using excess parchment as handles, remove from pan, and cut into bars. Dust with confectioners' sugar. Store, loosely covered with a paper towel, at room temperature for up to 3 days.

*If using frozen cranberries, do not thaw them.

Photo by Erin Clarkson

PEPPERMINT BARK COOKIE BARS

Makes 12 bars

Recipe by Rebecca Firth

These are ridiculously delicious and are just oozing with holiday cheer. The cookie base sinks a bit after baking, but don't fret. It makes the perfect valley to hold all of the peppermint and ganache goodness.

½ cup (113 grams) unsalted butter, softened
¾ cup (150 grams) granulated sugar
1 large egg (50 grams), room temperature
1 large egg yolk (19 grams), room temperature
2 teaspoons (8 grams) vanilla extract
1 cup (125 grams) all-purpose flour
⅔ cup (85 grams) bread flour
2 teaspoons (6 grams) cream of tartar
1 teaspoon (5 grams) baking soda
½ teaspoon (1.5 grams) sea salt

1 cup (170 grams) finely chopped 56% cacao dark chocolate
¾ cup (180 grams) plus 2 tablespoons (30 grams) heavy whipping cream, divided
¼ cup (43 grams) finely chopped white chocolate
4 to 5 drops AmeriColor Bright White Soft Gel Paste (optional) (see Notes)
¾ cup (113 grams) crushed peppermint candies (about 22 candies)

1. Position oven rack in center of oven. Preheat oven to 325°F (170°C). Butter an 8-inch square baking dish. Line pan with parchment paper, letting excess extend over sides of pan.
2. In the bowl of a stand mixer fitted with the paddle attachment, beat butter and sugar at medium speed until light and fluffy, 4 to 5 minutes, stopping to scrape sides of bowl. With mixer on low speed, add egg and egg yolk, one at a time, beating until

combined after each addition. Add vanilla, and beat for 1 minute.
3. In a medium bowl, whisk together flours, cream of tartar, baking soda, and salt. Add flour mixture to butter mixture, and beat at low speed just until combined. Gently press dough into bottom of prepared pan. (See Notes.)
4. Bake until a wooden pick inserted in center comes out clean, 30 to 33 minutes. Let cool completely in pan on a wire rack.
5. In the top of a double boiler, combine dark chocolate and ¾ cup (180 grams) cream. Cook over simmering water, stirring frequently, until chocolate is melted and mixture is smooth. Remove from heat, and let cool, stirring occasionally.
6. In the top of a double boiler, combine white chocolate and remaining 2 tablespoons (30 grams) cream. Cook over simmering water, stirring frequently, until chocolate is melted and mixture is smooth. Remove from heat, and let stand until cool to the touch, stirring occasionally. As it cools, stir in soft gel paste (if using).
7. Sprinkle candies on top of cooled cookie base. Pour cooled dark chocolate ganache over candies; drizzle white chocolate ganache on top. Using the tip of a wooden pick, draw several figure eights through ganache layer. Refrigerate until ganache layer is set, 2 to 3 hours.
8. Using excess parchment as handles, remove from pan, and cut into bars. Store in an airtight container for up to 3 days.

Notes: *White chocolate often has a yellowish hue to it. You can add AmeriColor Soft Gel Paste in Bright White to brighten it up a bit.*

The cookie dough is difficult to press into the pan. Use an offset spatula or damp hands to evenly press it in.

Photo by Rebecca Firth

MISCELLANEOUS

IRISH COFFEE SODA BREAD PUDDING

Makes 6 servings

Recipe by Kayla Howey

Soda bread and rich custard are baked into a sweet bread pudding, flavored with coffee, topped with softly whipped cream, and drizzled with Irish Whiskey Caramel.

4   large eggs (200 grams)
¾   cup (165 grams) firmly packed light brown sugar
1   tablespoon (6 grams) instant espresso powder
1   tablespoon (15 grams) hot water (160°F/71°C to 180°F/82°C)
2   cups (480 grams) whole milk
½   cup (120 grams) brewed coffee, chilled
1   teaspoon (4 grams) vanilla extract
½   teaspoon (1.5 grams) kosher salt
Irish Soda Bread (recipe follows), cut into 1-inch cubes
2   tablespoons (24 grams) turbinado sugar
Irish Whiskey Caramel (recipe follows)
Whipped Cream (recipe follows)
Garnish: confectioners' sugar

1. Preheat oven to 350°F (180°C). Butter a 2-quart baking dish.
2. In a large bowl, whisk eggs. Add brown sugar, and whisk until smooth.
3. In a small bowl, whisk together espresso powder and 1 tablespoon (15 grams) hot water until dissolved. Add espresso mixture to egg mixture, whisking to combine. Add milk, coffee, vanilla, and salt, whisking until well combined. Add cubed Irish Soda Bread, and toss well. Pour into prepared pan, spreading evenly. Submerge bread, and let stand for 1 hour. Cover with foil.
4. Bake for 30 minutes. Uncover and sprinkle with turbinado sugar. Bake until an instant-read thermometer inserted in center registers at least 165°F (74°C), about 15 minutes more. Let cool for 10 minutes before serving. Serve warm with Irish Whiskey Caramel and Whipped Cream. Garnish with confectioners' sugar, if desired.

IRISH SODA BREAD
Makes 1 (7½-inch) loaf

Recipe courtesy of Darina Allen

16   ounces (454 grams) all-purpose flour
1   teaspoon (3 grams) kosher salt
½   teaspoon (2.5 grams) baking soda
1¾   cups (420 grams) whole buttermilk

1. Preheat oven to 450°F (230°C).

2. In a large bowl, whisk together flour, salt, and baking soda until well combined. Make a well in center, and add buttermilk. Using one hand like a claw, mix buttermilk into dry ingredients until dough forms a ball. (Dough should be sticky and slightly clumpy.)
3. Turn out dough onto a lightly floured surface, and gently shape into a ball. Transfer to a lightly floured baking sheet. Pat dough into a 1½-inch-thick disk. Using a knife, cut an "X" across top of dough. Using tip of knife, prick a hole into each of the four sections of dough.
4. Bake for 15 minutes. Reduce oven temperature to 400°F (200°C). Bake for 15 minutes more. Turn bread, and bake for 5 minutes more. Transfer to a cutting board, and let cool enough to handle, about 30 minutes.

IRISH WHISKEY CARAMEL
Makes 1⅓ cups

1   cup (200 grams) granulated sugar
¼   cup (60 grams) water
4   tablespoons (56 grams) unsalted butter, room temperature
½   cup (120 grams) heavy whipping cream, room temperature
¼   cup (60 grams) Irish whiskey
¼   teaspoon kosher salt

1. In a 2-quart heavy-bottomed saucepan, whisk together sugar and ¼ cup (60 grams) water until smooth. Cook over medium heat, without stirring, until melted and a golden-amber color. Remove from heat. Add butter, 1 tablespoon (14 grams) at a time, whisking until combined after each addition. Add cream and whiskey, and stir to combine. Return mixture to medium heat, and cook, stirring frequently, for 3 to 4 minutes. Stir in salt, and remove from heat. Let cool slightly before serving. If caramel cools completely, it will thicken. Simply reheat it to loosen, if needed.

WHIPPED CREAM
Makes 2 cups

1   cup (240 grams) cold heavy whipping cream
2   tablespoons (24 grams) granulated sugar

1. In the bowl of a stand mixer fitted with the whisk attachment, beat cold cream until foamy. Add sugar, and beat until soft peaks form. Refrigerate until ready to use.

Photo by Kayla Howey

YEAST DOUGHNUTS WITH VANILLA BEAN ICING

Makes about 14 doughnuts

This streamlined doughnut formula has you creating a lighter-than-air yeasted dough ideally fit for the fryer. Whether dipped in Vanilla Bean Icing or rolled in cinnamon sugar (see PRO TIP), the final product offers simple perfection in iconic style.

½ cup (120 grams) warm water (105°F/41°C to 110°F/43°C)
4 tablespoons (48 grams) granulated sugar, divided
2¼ teaspoons (7 grams) active dry yeast
4 to 4¼ cups (500 to 531 grams) unbleached all-purpose flour, divided
¾ cup (180 grams) whole milk, room temperature
½ cup (113 grams) unsalted butter, melted and cooled for 10 minutes
2 large eggs (100 grams), room temperature
¼ cup (32 grams) bread flour
1½ teaspoons (4.5 grams) kosher salt
½ vanilla bean, split lengthwise, seeds scraped and reserved
Vegetable oil, for frying
Vanilla Bean Icing (recipe follows)

1. In the bowl of a stand mixer, stir together ½ cup (120 grams) warm water, 1 tablespoon (12 grams) sugar, and yeast. Let stand until foamy, about 10 minutes.
2. Add 2 cups (250 grams) all-purpose flour, milk, melted butter, eggs, bread flour, salt, reserved vanilla bean seeds, and remaining 3 tablespoons (36 grams) sugar to yeast mixture; using the paddle attachment beat at low speed just until combined. Increase mixer speed to medium; beat until well combined,

about 1 minute. Add 2 cups (250 grams) all-purpose flour; beat at low speed just until combined. Increase mixer speed to medium; beat until well combined, about 1 minute.
3. Switch to the dough hook attachment; beat at medium speed just until dough starts to pull away from sides of bowl, 3 to 4 minutes; add up to remaining ¼ cup (31 grams) all-purpose flour, 1 tablespoon (8 grams) at a time, if needed. (Dough will still be quite soft and slightly sticky but should not seem excessively wet.)
4. Spray a large bowl with cooking spray. Place dough in bowl, turning to grease top. Cover and let rise in a warm, draft-free place (75°F/24°C) until doubled in size, 40 minutes to 1 hour. (Alternatively, cover and let rise in refrigerator overnight. When ready to use, proceed as directed.)
5. Spray 3 large baking sheets with cooking spray. Cut out 14 (6-inch) squares of parchment paper, and place on prepared pans. Spray parchment with cooking spray. Spray 3 large sheets of plastic wrap with cooking spray.
6. Punch down dough; turn out onto a heavily floured surface, and roll or pat to ½-inch thickness. Using a 3½-inch doughnut cutter dipped in flour, cut dough. Gently transfer doughnuts to prepared parchment squares, spacing at least 2 to 2½ inches apart. Reroll scraps, and let stand for 5 to 10 minutes; cut scraps. Cover doughnuts with prepared plastic wrap, spray side down, and let rise in a warm, draft-free place (75°F/24°C) until puffed, 40 minutes to 1 hour.
7. In a large heavy-bottomed saucepan, pour oil to a depth of 2 inches, and heat over medium heat until a deep-fry thermometer registers 365°F (185°C).

8. Line 2 large rimmed baking sheets with paper towels.
9. Working in batches, use parchment paper to gently pick up doughnuts and add to oil (do not place parchment paper in oil). Fry until golden brown, about 1 minute per side. Using a spider strainer, transfer doughnuts to prepared pans. Let cool completely.
10. Line 2 large rimmed baking sheets with parchment paper; place wire racks on prepared pans.
11. Holding 1 doughnut horizontally, dip doughnut halfway into Vanilla Bean Icing; lift straight out, and swirl in a circular motion, letting excess drip off. Quickly turn doughnut, and place, icing side up, on a prepared rack. Repeat with remaining doughnuts. Serve immediately, or let stand until icing is set, 20 to 30 minutes.

VANILLA BEAN ICING
Makes about 3⅓ cups

7⅓ cups (880 grams) confectioners' sugar, sifted
½ cup plus 1 tablespoon (135 grams) whole milk
6 tablespoons (126 grams) light corn syrup
¼ cup (57 grams) unsalted butter, melted
½ vanilla bean, split lengthwise, seeds scraped and reserved
½ teaspoon (1.5 grams) kosher salt

1. In a large bowl, stir together all ingredients until smooth and well combined. Use immediately.

1. To tell if you properly mixed your dough, study the consistency. This dough will be softer than others, and you won't be conducting a windowpane test to check gluten development. Instead, make sure it isn't excessively wet, only slightly sticky.
2. When punching out your doughnuts, don't twist the cutter, and keep it well-floured between each cut so it doesn't catch on the sticky dough. After you've rerolled the scraps for a second cutting, let the dough rest for 5 to 10 minutes to allow it to relax and make it easier to work with.
3. When gently poked, properly proofed doughnuts will hold the indentation without collapsing. If the dough just bounces back, the doughnuts are still underproofed and need more time. Wait another 5 to 10 minutes and then perform another poke test.

PRO TIP
For a cinnamon-sugar variation, let doughnuts cool for 10 to 15 minutes. In a medium bowl, stir together 1 cup (200 grams) granulated sugar and 4 teaspoons (8 grams) ground cinnamon. Working in batches, toss warm doughnuts in cinnamon-sugar mixture. Serve immediately.

A Feel for Frying

Much of the intimidation factor attached to making your own doughnuts is the frying. With our tutorial, you'll be able to face your fear of frying with confidence.

1. Before you fry, you need to have your oil prepped and ready. That means having it poured to a depth of 2 inches in your pot and at the temperature called for in the recipe (365°F/185°C in the case of our yeast doughnuts).

2. Placing the raw doughnut into the hot oil can be a bit hairy, but with our greased parchment paper acting as a sling, you should be able to gently slide the doughnut into the oil without a splash. Bubbles should immediately begin forming around the dough—if not, check the temperature of the oil to make sure it's hot enough.

3. While frying, it's important not to overcrowd the pot or it'll reduce the temperature of the oil, so cook 2 at a time. Because doughnuts have a hole in the center, they have extra surface area and, thus, cook faster than other doughs. In 1 minute's time, you'll turn them to reveal a golden underside.

4. Once both doughnuts have been turned and fried until golden, you'll want to immediately transfer them to prepared pans to cool. If icing, let cool completely. If using cinnamon sugar (see PRO TIP), let the doughnuts cool for only 10 to 15 minutes.

CHOCOLATE-GLAZED BAKED CAKE DOUGHNUTS

Makes 6 doughnuts

Tender-crumbed and coated in Chocolate Glaze, our baked cake doughnuts are all the fun of our other doughnuts minus the frying fuss. Be warned: this chocolate wonder is destined for dunking.

⅓ cup (67 grams) granulated sugar
⅓ cup (73 grams) firmly packed light brown sugar
1 large egg (50 grams), room temperature
¼ cup (57 grams) unsalted butter, melted and cooled for 5 minutes
¼ cup (56 grams) canola oil
2 teaspoons (8 grams) vanilla extract
1 cup (125 grams) unbleached all-purpose flour
¼ cup (31 grams) unbleached cake flour
1 teaspoon (5 grams) baking powder
½ teaspoon (1.5 grams) kosher salt
½ teaspoon (1 gram) ground nutmeg
¼ teaspoon ground cinnamon
½ cup (120 grams) whole milk, room temperature
Chocolate Glaze (recipe follows)
Garnish: chocolate sprinkles

1. Preheat oven to 400°F (200°C).
2. In the bowl of a stand mixer fitted with the paddle attachment, beat sugars and egg at medium speed until lightened in color and well combined, 1 to 2 minutes, stopping to scrape sides of bowl. Add melted butter, oil, and vanilla; beat at medium speed until well combined, 1 to 2 minutes.
3. In a small bowl, whisk together flours, baking powder, salt, nutmeg, and cinnamon. With mixer on medium-low speed, add flour mixture to sugar mixture alternately with milk, beginning and ending with flour mixture, beating just until smooth and combined after each addition, stopping to scrape sides of bowl.
4. Spray a 6-well Nordic Ware Classic Donut Pan with baking spray with flour.

5. Spoon batter into 2 large pastry bags; cut a ½-inch opening in each tip. Pipe batter into prepared wells. Firmly tap pan on kitchen towel-lined counter several times to spread batter and release any air bubbles.
6. Bake until a wooden pick inserted near center comes out clean, 12 to 15 minutes. Let cool in pan for 5 minutes; invert doughnuts onto a wire rack, and let cool completely.
7. Line a large rimmed baking sheet with parchment paper; place a wire rack on prepared pan, and spray with cooking spray.
8. Working quickly, place a doughnut in Chocolate Glaze; use a spoon or a small silicone spatula to coat completely. Using 2 forks placed on opposite sides under doughnut, gently lift out of glaze, letting excess drip off; transfer to prepared rack. Use the point of a wooden pick to pop any air bubbles in glaze. Garnish with sprinkles, if desired. Repeat with remaining doughnuts. Let stand until glaze is set, about 30 minutes.

CHOCOLATE GLAZE
Makes about 1½ cups

3 cups (360 grams) confectioners' sugar
⅓ cup (25 grams) Dutch process cocoa powder
1 tablespoon (3 grams) instant espresso powder
6 tablespoons (90 grams) whole milk
1½ tablespoons (31.5 grams) light corn syrup
1½ teaspoons (6 grams) vanilla extract
½ teaspoon (1.5 grams) kosher salt

1. In a large bowl, sift together confectioners' sugar, cocoa, and espresso powder. Add milk, corn syrup, vanilla, and salt; stir until smooth and well combined. Use immediately.

1. To keep things clean and easy, neatly pipe the batter into the pan to further spread the batter. Tap pan on a kitchen towel-lined counter several times to release any air bubbles.
2. For perfectly glazed doughnuts, submerge your doughnut completely in the Chocolate Glaze, using a spoon to drizzle glaze over any naked spots. You'll need to work quickly, or the glaze will begin to set in a clumpy manner.
3. Using 2 forks placed on opposite sides under doughnut, gently lift out of glaze, letting excess drip off—too heavy of a glaze will lead to an uneven coating. Once placed on a wire rack, use a wooden pick to pop any air bubbles in glaze.

FRENCH CRULLERS WITH CITRUS GLAZE

Makes 9 to 10 crullers

Crullers are one of the many delicious offshoots of pâte à choux, the versatile French pastry dough that you cook twice, once on the stove and once in the oven. In this form, choux pastry is piped with a star tip into ridged rounds, which then get fried and dipped in a bright Citrus Glaze.

1   **cup plus 2 tablespoons (141 grams) all-purpose flour**
½   **teaspoon (1 gram) ground cardamom**
¼   **teaspoon ground ginger**
1   **cup (240 grams) water**
6   **tablespoons (84 grams) unsalted butter, cubed and softened**
1   **tablespoon (12 grams) granulated sugar**
½   **teaspoon (1.5 grams) kosher salt**
½   **teaspoon (2 grams) vanilla extract**
3   **large eggs (150 grams), room temperature**
1   **large egg white (30 grams), room temperature**
Vegetable oil, for frying
Citrus Glaze (recipe follows)

1. Spray a large rimmed baking sheet with cooking spray. Cut 10 (3¼-inch) squares of parchment paper; place on prepared pan. Spray parchment with cooking spray.
2. In a small bowl, whisk together flour, cardamom, and ginger. Set aside.
3. In a medium saucepan, combine 1 cup (240 grams) water, butter, sugar, salt, and vanilla; bring to a boil over medium-high heat. Remove from heat; add flour mixture all at once, stirring with a wooden spoon until combined. Return mixture to medium-high heat; cook, stirring constantly, until smooth and a skin forms on bottom of pan, about 2 minutes.
4. Transfer mixture to the bowl of a stand mixer fitted with the paddle attachment, and beat at medium-low speed for 2 minutes. Add eggs, one at a time, beating until combined after each addition and stopping to scrape sides of bowl. (Batter will appear broken but will come back together as eggs are incorporated.) Add egg white; beat until a smooth, glossy dough forms. (Dough should pass the "V" test [see Notes] and will hold a slight peak when pinched between fingers.) Cover and refrigerate for 30 minutes.
5. In a large heavy-bottomed saucepan, pour oil to a depth of 2 inches, and heat over medium heat until a deep-fry thermometer registers 370°F (188°C).
6. Place dough in a large pastry bag fitted with a ½-inch open star piping tip (Ateco #827). Applying even pressure, pipe a large circle within each prepared parchment square. To join ends, gently press piping tip into starting point of circle; release pressure and then pull up while continuing to trace around circle. (Dough will pinch off.) Wet your finger with water; gently smooth and seal overlapping ends. Let stand at room temperature for 20 minutes.
7. Line a baking sheet with parchment paper; place a wire rack on prepared pan.
8. Working in batches, carefully add piped dough to oil, parchment side up. Cook until puffed and golden brown, about 3 minutes per side, discarding parchment halfway through frying. (It's OK if some crullers burst slightly in spots.) Using a spider strainer, remove crullers, and let drain on prepared rack. Let cool for about 15 minutes.
9. Line a baking sheet with parchment paper; place a wire rack on prepared pan, and spray with cooking spray.
10. Place a cruller in Citrus Glaze; coat on all sides. Using 2 forks placed on opposite sides under cruller, gently lift out of glaze, letting excess drip off, and place on prepared rack. Let stand until glaze is set, about 15 minutes.

Notes: *When the pâte à choux base for these crullers has reached the right consistency, it will fall off the paddle attachment and the excess dough left in its wake will be in a "V" shape.*

If crullers deflate soon after removing from oil, they were not cooked for long enough. Increase frying time slightly for next batch.

CITRUS GLAZE
Makes about 1⅓ cups

3   **cups (360 grams) confectioners' sugar, sifted**
5   **tablespoons (75 grams) whole milk**
2½   **tablespoons (52.5 grams) light corn syrup**
2   **teaspoons (4 grams) packed lemon zest**
1   **teaspoon (5 grams) tightly packed orange zest**
½   **teaspoon (2 grams) vanilla extract**
½   **teaspoon (1.5 grams) kosher salt**

1. In a large bowl, stir together all ingredients until smooth. Use immediately.

1. Applying even pressure, pipe a large circle within each prepared parchment square. To join ends, gently press piping tip into starting point of circle; release pressure and then pull up while continuing to trace around circle. Dough will naturally pinch off, so don't panic.
2. Wet your finger with water; gently smooth and seal overlapping ends. Don't fuss over making it look perfect. When you fry your crullers, slight cracks and some burst bubbles are bound to happen, so don't sweat the small stuff.

Whoops! This is a deflated cruller that has been fried for too short of a time. If you take it out too quickly, the choux will deflate rapidly once out of the oil. So, keep an eye on the temperature and the timer when frying these!

GINGERBREAD DUTCH BABY PANCAKE

Makes 4 servings

Classic Dutch baby pancakes are like the decadent hybrid of a popover and a pancake. The batter comes together in a blender—no stand mixer required—and then gets baked in a piping-hot buttered skillet. Rich enough to be served for a holiday breakfast or festive weeknight dessert, our gingerbread version is warmly spiced and packs a hint of molasses. We finished it all off with a dollop of lemony whipped cream, maple syrup, and a scattering of ruby red pomegranate arils.

¾ cup (180 grams) whole milk, room temperature
½ cup (63 grams) all-purpose flour
3   large eggs (150 grams), room temperature
2   tablespoons (28 grams) firmly packed light brown sugar
1¾ teaspoons (3.5 grams) ground ginger
1   teaspoon (1 gram) instant espresso powder*
1   teaspoon (7 grams) molasses (not blackstrap)
¾ teaspoon (1.5 grams) ground cinnamon
½ teaspoon (1 gram) ground cloves
½ teaspoon (1 gram) ground allspice
¼ teaspoon kosher salt
3   tablespoons (42 grams) unsalted butter, softened
1   cup (240 grams) cold heavy whipping cream
2   tablespoons (14 grams) confectioners' sugar
1   tablespoon (4 grams) packed lemon zest
Garnish: confectioners' sugar, pomegranate arils

1. Place a 10-inch cast-iron skillet in oven. Preheat oven to 425°F (220°C).

2. In the container of a blender (see Note), combine milk, flour, eggs, brown sugar, ginger, espresso powder, molasses, cinnamon, cloves, allspice, and salt; process until smooth and well combined, stopping to scrape sides of container as needed. (Batter will be thin.)

3. Remove hot skillet from oven. Add butter, and let melt, brushing all over bottom and up sides of skillet. Carefully pour batter into hot skillet.

4. Bake until golden brown and puffed, about 20 minutes. Reduce oven temperature to 300°F (150°C), and bake for 5 minutes more.

5. Meanwhile, in a large bowl, combine cold cream, confectioners' sugar, and lemon zest; whisk until stiff peaks form.

6. Serve Dutch baby immediately with whipped cream. Garnish with confectioners' sugar and pomegranate arils, if desired.

*We used Williams Sonoma Espresso Powder.

Note: *A food processor can also be used. If you don't have either at your disposal, you can also whisk the batter together by hand until smooth and well combined.*

SHAPE & STEAM YOUR BUNS

1. Create your makeshift steamer basket by poking 20 evenly spaced holes in the bottoms of 2 (9-inch) round foil cake pans. Place 1 cake pan, upside down, in a large Dutch oven, and pour water to a depth of ½ inch in pot. Carefully flatten remaining cake pan to use as a steamer rack.

2. Divide dough into 12 portions (about 59 grams each). Shape 1 portion into a ball, and press into a 3-inch disk. (Keep remaining dough covered to prevent it from drying out.) Using a small rolling pin, roll edges of disks to ¼-inch thickness, creating a 4½-inch circle, keeping the center thicker than the edges. (The thinner edges will help your pleats have better definition.) Repeat with remaining dough.

3. Place a circle of dough in the palm of your hand. Place 1 rounded tablespoon prok mixture (about 24 grams) in center. Using the thumb and forefinger of your other hand, pleat and pinch dough edges to enclose filling, rotating dough in your palm as you go.

4. Tightly pinch together the top to seal, pulling dough up to a point and pinching off excess dough. (For best shape, place shaped bun on a work surface and gently cup with both hands to round it out.) Repeat with remaining dough circles and remaining pork mixture.

BARBECUE PORK BUNS

Makes 12 buns

These buns represent dim sum heaven at home. We created our own makeshift steamer basket out of disposable aluminum foil cake pans (see Shape & Steam Your Buns on opposite page), but feel free to use a steamer basket if you have one.

3	tablespoons (42 grams) canola oil, divided
2	cloves garlic (10 grams), minced
1½	teaspoons (8 grams) minced fresh ginger
8	ounces (226 grams) cooked pork*, chopped into ¼-inch pieces
1½	tablespoons (27 grams) hoisin sauce
1	tablespoon (14 grams) oyster sauce
1½	teaspoons (7.5 grams) rice vinegar
1½	teaspoons (7.5 grams) low-sodium soy sauce
4	tablespoons (48 grams) plus 1 teaspoon (4 grams) granulated sugar, divided
2	tablespoons (4 grams) finely chopped fresh chives
½	cup (120 grams) warm water (105°F/41°C to 110°F/43°C)
2¼	teaspoons (7 grams) active dry yeast
3	cups (375 grams) all-purpose flour
¼	cup (32 grams) cornstarch
½	cup (120 grams) whole milk, room temperature
½	teaspoon (1.5 grams) kosher salt

Garnish: chopped fresh chives

1. In a large skillet, heat 1 tablespoon (14 grams) oil over medium heat. Add garlic and ginger; cook, stirring frequently, until softened, 1 to 2 minutes. Add pork, hoisin sauce, oyster sauce, vinegar, soy sauce, and 1 teaspoon (4 grams) sugar. Cook, stirring occasionally, until heated through, 2 to 3 minutes. Remove from heat; stir in chives. Let cool completely.

2. In the bowl of a stand mixer, stir together ½ cup (120 grams) warm water, 1 tablespoon (12 grams) sugar, and yeast by hand until combined. Let stand until foamy, about 10 minutes.

3. In a medium bowl, sift together flour and cornstarch. Add flour mixture, milk, salt, remaining 3 tablespoons (36 grams) sugar, and remaining 2 tablespoons (28 grams) oil to yeast mixture. Using the dough hook attachment, beat at medium-low speed just until combined, stopping to scrape sides of bowl. Increase mixer speed to medium, and beat until a smooth, elastic dough forms, 8 to 10 minutes. Check dough for proper gluten development using the windowpane test. (See Note.) Cover and let rise in a warm, draft-free place (75°F/24°C) until doubled in size, about 30 minutes.

4. Poke 20 evenly spaced holes in bottoms of 2 (9-inch) round foil cake pans. Place 1 cake pan, upside down, in a large Dutch oven*, and pour water to a depth of ½ inch in pot. Carefully flatten remaining cake pan to use as a steamer rack. Cut out 12 (4-inch) squares of parchment paper.

5. Punch down dough, and turn out onto a lightly floured surface. Gently knead a few times to release air bubbles. Divide dough into 12 portions (about 59 grams each). Shape 1 portion into a ball, and press into a 3-inch disk. (Keep remaining dough covered to prevent it from drying out.) Using a small rolling pin, such as a fondant rolling pin, roll edges of disk to ¼-inch thickness, creating a 4½-inch circle, keeping center thicker than edges. (Thinner edges will help your pleats have better definition.) Repeat with remaining dough.

6. Place a circle of dough in the palm of your hand. Place 1 rounded tablespoon pork mixture (about 24 grams) in center. Using the thumb and forefinger of your other hand, pleat and pinch dough edges to enclose filling, rotating dough in your palm as you go. Tightly pinch together the top to seal, pulling dough up to a point and pinching off excess dough. (For best shape, place shaped bun on a work surface and gently cup with both hands to round it out.)

7. Place each bun on a parchment square, and arrange on a rimmed baking sheet. (It's best to begin steaming buns about 30 minutes after shaping. If you need more time to shape your buns, loosely cover buns with plastic wrap, and place in the refrigerator to keep them from overproofing.) Repeat with remaining dough circles and remaining pork mixture.

8. Place 3 buns, still on parchment squares, on prepared steamer rack; place over inverted cake pan in prepared pot, and cover with lid. Bring water to a boil over high heat; immediately reduce heat to medium-high, and steam buns for 15 minutes. Immediately turn off heat, and let buns stand in the unopened pot for 2 minutes.

9. Using two pairs of tongs, carefully remove buns by lifting steamer rack from pot. Remove buns from rack. Repeat with remaining buns, adding additional water to pot as needed. Garnish with chives, if desired.

We used Trader Joe's Fully Cooked Pork Belly. Instead of a Dutch oven, a deep skillet or wok can also be used.

Note: *Test the dough for proper gluten development using the windowpane test. Pinch off (don't tear) a small piece of dough. Slowly pull the dough out from the center. If the dough is ready, you will be able to stretch it until it's thin and translucent like a windowpane. If the dough tears, it's not quite ready. Beat for 1 minute, and test again.*

RECIPE INDEX

index

CREDITS

Editorial
Editor-in-Chief Brian Hart Hoffman
VP/Culinary & Custom Content
Brooke Michael Bell
Group Creative Director
Deanna Rippy Gardner
Managing Editor Kyle Grace Mills
Assistant Editor Sandi Shriver
Editorial Assistant Alex Kolar
Copy Editor Meg Lundberg

Cover
Photography by Stephanie Welbourne
Steele
Food Styling by Megan Lankford
Styling by Sidney Bragiel

Bake from Scratch Photographers
Jim Bathie, William Dickey,
Mac Jamieson, Stephanie Welbourne
Steele

Test Kitchen Director
Irene Yeh

Bake from Scratch Food Stylists/
Recipe Developers
Laura Crandall, Kathleen Kanen,
J.R. Jacobson, Megan Lankford,
Tricia Manzanero, Vanessa Rocchio,
Taylor Franklin Wann

Bake from Scratch Stylists
Courtni Bodiford, Sidney Bragiel,
Lucy Finney, Mary Beth Jones,
Lily Simpson, Melissa Sturdivant
Smith, Dorothy Walton

Contributing Photographers
Johannah Chadwick, Chris Court,
Ben Dearnley, Nicole du Bois,
Eliesa Johnson, Bree McCool, Geni
Mermoud, Alison Miksch, Daniel
Muller, Joann Pai, Hector Sanchez,
Marcy Black Simpson, Reese Talbot,
Mark Weinberg

Contributing Food Stylists/Recipe
Developers
Majed Ali, Darina Allen, Justin Burke-
Samson, Erin Clarkson, Margaret
Dickey, Zoë François, Angela Garbacz,
Emily Hutchinson, Tracey Jeffrey,
Kellie Gerber Kelley, Erin Jeanne
McDowell, Clodagh McKenna, Erin
Merhar, Maria Provenzano, Shane
Smith, Gemma Stafford

Contributing Food Stylists/Recipe
Developers & Photographers:
Johannah Chadwick, Alice Choi,
Erin Clarkson, Rebecca Firth, Zoë
François, Kayla Howey, Mike Johnson,
Laura Kasavan, Sarah Kieffer, Kylie
Mazon-Chambers,
Bree McCool, Joann Pai, Allie
Roomberg, Hector Sanchez,
Reese Talbot, Mark Weinberg

Contributing Stylists:
Caroline Blum, Steve Pierce

Resources
Page 4-5
Photograpy by Erin Clarkson
Page 6-7
Photograpy by Hector Sanchez